Financial Capability and Asset Development

Financial Capability and Asset Development

Research, Education, Policy, and Practice

EDITED BY
JULIE BIRKENMAIER
MARGARET SHERRADEN
JAMI CURLEY

UNIVERSITY PRESS

Oxford University Press is a department of the University of Oxford.
It furthers the University's objective of excellence in research, scholarship,
and education by publishing worldwide.

Oxford   New York
Auckland   Cape Town   Dar es Salaam   Hong Kong   Karachi
Kuala Lumpur   Madrid   Melbourne   Mexico City   Nairobi
New Delhi   Shanghai   Taipei   Toronto

With offices in
Argentina   Austria   Brazil   Chile   Czech Republic   France   Greece
Guatemala   Hungary   Italy   Japan   Poland   Portugal   Singapore
South Korea   Switzerland   Thailand   Turkey   Ukraine   Vietnam

Oxford is a registered trademark of Oxford University Press in the UK
and certain other countries.

Published in the United States of America by
Oxford University Press
198 Madison Avenue, New York, NY 10016

© Oxford University Press 2013

All rights reserved. No part of this publication may be reproduced, stored in a
retrieval system, or transmitted, in any form or by any means, without the prior
permission in writing of Oxford University Press, or as expressly permitted by law,
by license, or under terms agreed with the appropriate reproduction rights organization.
Inquiries concerning reproduction outside the scope of the above should be sent to the
Rights Department, Oxford University Press, at the address above.

You must not circulate this work in any other form
and you must impose this same condition on any acquirer.

Library of Congress Cataloging-in-Publication Data
Financial capability and asset development : research, education, policy, and practice / edited by Julie
Birkenmaier, Margaret Sherraden, Jami Curley.
  p. cm.
  ISBN 978-0-19-975595-0 (hardback : alk. paper)
  1. Finance, Personal—Study and teaching.   2. Poor families.   I. Birkenmaier, Julie.
II. Sherraden, Margaret S.   III. Curley, Jami.
HG179.F4615 2013
332.024—dc23
2012029015

9 8 7 6 5 4 3 2 1
Printed in the United States of America
on acid-free paper

CONTENTS

Acknowledgments vii
Contributors ix
Introduction xi
Margaret Sherraden

PART ONE Theory and Background 01

1. Building Blocks of Financial Capability 03
   Margaret Sherraden

2. Social Workers and Financial Capability in the Profession's First Half-Century 44
   Paul H. Stuart

3. Paradigms of Anti-poverty Policy 62
   David Stoesz

PART TWO Innovations in Financial Capability 83

4. Financial Capability among Survivors of Domestic Violence 85
   Cynthia K. Sanders

5. Low-Income Parents of Preschool Children: Financial Knowledge, Attitudes, Behaviors, and Ownership 108
   Deborah D. Adams and Sondra G. Beverly

6. Financial Issues and an Aging Population: Responding to an Increased Potential for Financial Abuse and Exploitation 129
   Phillip McCallion, Lisa A. Ferretti and Jihyun Park

7. Improving Financial Capacity among Low-Income Immigrants: Effects of a Financial Education Program 156
   Min Zhan, Steven G. Anderson and Jeff Scott

8. Developing Financial Capability through IDA Saving Clubs 174
   Jonas Parker

9. Income Tax Time as a Time to Build Financial Capability 192
   Jennifer L. Romich, Nicole Keenan, Jody Miesel and Crystal C. Hall

10. Building Financial Capability of Native American Households: The Role of the EITC 207
    Kristen Wagner

11. Financial and Asset-Building Capabilities of Southwest Border Working Families: An Action Research Approach to Culturally Responsive Economic Resiliency Behaviors 228
    Bárbara J. Robles

PART THREE Social Work Education, Practice, and Curriculum Development 249

12. Financial Capabilities of Service Providers in the Asset-Building Field 251
    Vernon Loke, Julie L. Watts and Sally A. Kakoti

13. The Role of Social Work in Financial Capability: Shaping Curricular Approaches 278
    Julie Birkenmaier, Teri Kennedy, James Kunz, Rebecca Sander and Shelley Horwitz

14. Building the Capacity of Social Workers to Enhance Financial Capability and Asset Development 302
    J. Michael Collins and Julie Birkenmaier

15. Conclusion: Building Financial Capability and Assets of Financially Vulnerable Families 323
    Margaret S. Sherraden

Index 333

ACKNOWLEDGMENTS

This book is the result of the work of many scholars, policy advocates, historians, and others, as well as of organizations. Countless people assisted us in providing ideas, suggestions, and feedback. First and foremost, we are indebted to the talented and dedicated scholars who contributed chapters.

We thank many people for reading parts of this book and generously offering their suggestions: Steven Anderson, Beth Baca, Mahasweta Banerjee, Marla Berg-Weger, Edward Berkowitz, Sandy Beverly, Janet Boguslaw, Richard Caputo, John Caskey, Rosemary Chapin, Gina Chowa, Ram Cnaan, Mat Despard, Julie Drolet, Jodi Jacobson, Teri Kennedy, Jim Kunz, Leslie Leighninger, Younghee Lim, Caezilia Loibl, Vernon Loke, Nancy Morrow-Howell, Yolanda Padilla, Carolina Reid, Kameri Christy-McMullin, Lewis Mandell, Elaine Maag, James Patterson, Salome Raheim, Rebecca Sander, Michael Sherraden, David Stoesz, Paul Stuart, Kate Wilber, Beadsie Woo, and Michael Vaughn.

We are indebted to many others who have taught us and influenced our thinking about financial capability and asset development, including Ray Boshara, Li-chen Cheng, Gina Chowa, Reid Cramer, William Elliott, Bill Emmons, Steve Fazzari, Tahira Hira, Jean Hogarth, Lissa Johnson, Howard Karger, Cassandra Kaufman, Elaine Kempson, David Lander, Sharon Laux, Annamaria Lusardi, Emily McGinnis, Lew Mandell, Anya Mayans, Sudha Nair, Melvin Oliver, Will Paxton, Rajiv Prabhakar, Karen Rowlingson and the CHASM team, Juan Saavedra, Ed Scanlon, Meg Schnabel, Mark Schreiner, Trina Williams Shanks, Tom Shapiro, Michael Sherraden, Fred Ssewamala, Carolina Trivelli, Paul Webley, and Viviana Zelizer.

We are grateful for financial support for various parts of this volume from The Ford Foundation, the Charles Stewart Mott Foundation, and Wells Fargo Advisors. We could not have completed this volume without ongoing support of the Center for Social Development at Washington University in St. Louis, Missouri; Saint Louis University; and the University of Missouri, St. Louis.

We are deeply grateful to dedicated undergraduate and graduate students Katie Terrell, Hannah Shanks, Erin Moriarty, and Natalie Alcorn, who worked tirelessly alongside us to produce this volume. We greatly appreciate the skillful work of Julia Stevens at the Center for Social Development who edited the entire manuscript. Thanks to Maura Roessner, Dana Bliss, and Nicholas Liu at Oxford University Press for their unwavering support and logistical assistance for this book.

Julie dedicates this book to Phil, Corina, and Ben, but especially to Phil for his willingness to be a sounding board for new ideas, and for his steadfast support and encouragement.

Margaret dedicates this book to Michael, Catherine, and Sam, and to her students, whose lives inspired her interest in financial capability.

Jami dedicates this book to her family David, Cori, Zachary, Proscovia, Elijah, and Bailee.

JB
MSS
JC

CONTRIBUTORS

Deborah D. Adams, Ph.D., Associate Professor, University of Kansas

Steven Anderson, Ph.D., Director of School of Social Work, Arizona State University

Julie Birkenmaier, Ph.D., Associate Professor, Saint Louis University

Sondra G. Beverly, Ph.D., Senior Scholar, Center for Social Development, Washington University in St. Louis

Jami Curley, Ph.D., Associate Professor, Saint Louis University

J. Michael Collins, Ph.D., Assistant Professor, University of Wisconsin, Madison

Lisa A. Ferretti, L.M.S.W., Research Assistant Professor and Codirector, Center for Excellence in Aging and Community Wellness, University at Albany-SUNY

Crystal C. Hall, Ph.D., Assistant Professor, University of Washington

Shelley Horwitz, MSW, Program Director, Post-Master's Program in Advanced Clinical Social Work, Hunter College, The City University of New York

Sally A. Kakoti, M.S.W., Research Assistant, Eastern Washington University

Nicole Keenan, Ph.D. Research Assistant, University of Washington

Teri Kennedy, Ph.D., B.S.W. Program Coordinator, Arizona State University

James Kunz, Ph.D., Associate Professor and Program Director, McDaniel College

Vernon Loke, Ph.D., Assistant Professor, Eastern Washington University

Phillip McCallion, Ph.D., Professor and co-Director, Center for Excellence in Aging and Community Wellness, University at Albany-SUNY

Jody Miesel, Ph.D., Candidate, University of Washington

Jihyun Park, Ph.D., Research Assistant, Center for Excellence in Aging and Community Wellness, University at Albany-SUNY

Jonas Parker, Ph.D., Manager of Operations and Special Projects, Doorways to Dreams (D2D) Fund

Bárbara J. Robles, Ph.D., Division of Consumer and Community Affairs, The Board of Governors of the Federal Reserve System

Jennifer L. Romich, Ph.D., Associate Professor, University of Washington

Rebecca Sander, Ph.D., Director of Research for the Social Work Community Outreach Service, University of Maryland

Cynthia K. Sanders, Ph.D., Associate Professor, Boise State University

Jeff Scott, Ph.D. candidate, Adjunct Lecturer, University of Illinois at Urbana-Champaign

Margaret Sherraden, Ph.D., Professor, University of Missouri, St. Louis and Research Professor, Washington University in St Louis

David Stoesz, Ph.D., Professor, Virginia Commonwealth University

Paul H. Stuart, Ph.D., Professor, Florida International University

Kristen Wagner, Ph.D., Assistant Professor, University of Missouri, St. Louis

Julie L. Watts, M.S.W., Lecturer, University of Washington, and Burst for Prosperity

Min Zhan, Ph.D., Associate Professor, University of Illinois at Urbana-Champaign

INTRODUCTION
MARGARET SHERRADEN

Contemporary families face increasingly complex financial calculations and decisions, which are exacerbated in an era of economic downturn. The financial lives of low-income families are especially challenging. Coping with declining incomes and wealth, families have to figure out how to make ends meet, where to cut back, and how to obtain extra income. They need to understand and know how to obtain available workplace and public benefits. They have to know how to file taxes and in each cycle decide how best to use their annual lump sum tax credit or refund. Meanwhile, they have to pay keen attention to their credit score; their ability to obtain a job, rent an apartment, or purchase a piece of furniture could depend on it. They have to figure out the types of insurance they must or should have. They have to find small surpluses to set aside in case of emergencies and, when possible, set savings aside for future security. Those with problem debt confront decisions about which part to pay, which can wait, and, if the debt is insurmountable, how to pursue bankruptcy. Families underwater on their mortgages have to understand what this means and what to do, including possibly planning for a future spell of homelessness. Often, these and other financial decisions are more complex because they involve extended family members or friends who are part of a network of people who back each other up during tight economic times or crises.

Financial decisions in this context require financial knowledge and skills, as well as emotional resilience. Worried, anxious, and stressed about economic survival, low-income and financially vulnerable families often cope with disappointment and the likelihood that hopes and dreams have to be set aside. Perhaps most difficult, they face a society that attributes financial troubles to their behavior, including poor management, lack of thrift, or moral failure. These societal attitudes play out in demeaning interactions at the public benefits office, in the insistent calls from creditors and debt collectors, and in well-meaning but often misguided attempts by educators and counselors to change financial behavior without also making optimal decisions realistic.

Individual shortcomings and miscalculations surely contribute to economic difficulties, and it is important to help people optimize their decision making. However, the sheer volume nationwide of household debt, foreclosures, and poverty, along with declining net worth, are not the result of individual behaviors alone. These trends point to differential access to structures of opportunity which has been severely aggravated by the current economic downturn. Fundamental changes in policy and services are required to give low-income families a fighting chance for financial survival and a more hopeful future. In this context, it makes sense to focus on building financial capability in low-income and financially vulnerable families—including both their ability and opportunity to act in their best financial interest.

This volume explores the concepts of financial capability and asset building. It analyzes some of the nation's groundbreaking approaches to building financial capability and assets in ordinary households. The goal is to highlight the state of knowledge, achievements, and challenges in financial capability around the nation, and promote professional social work and human services education and training in financial capability and asset building.

GROWING FINANCIAL VULNERABILITY OF US HOUSEHOLDS

Financial vulnerability is on the rise in US households. At this writing, official unemployment is over 8%, a figure that conceals much higher rates among some groups including a nearly 14% rate among African Americans and 36.5% among African American youth (Bureau of Labor Statistics, 2012). Official unemployment does not include an almost equal number of people who have given up looking or are marginally employed and prefer to work more. The recession contributed to decreases in median family income, from $49,600 in 2007 to $45,800 in 2010, and the percentage of families who saved (Bricker, Kennickell, Moore, & Sabelhaus, 2012). Poverty rates are rising. Over 46 million (15.1%) Americans lived in poverty in 2010 compared to 43.6 million (14.3%) the year before—the largest annual increase in the 52 years that the Census has tracked poverty (US Census, 2011). This number includes 39% of African American children, 35% of Hispanic children, and 12.4% of White children (Tavernise, 2011).

Income inequality has increased over several decades. In the past three decades, the share of income of the top 1% increased by 276%, while the share of the bottom fifth increased less than 20%, the middle three-fifths by 40%, and the top fifth by 65%, although the trend moderated by 2010 (Bee, 2012; Brick et al., 2002; Congressional Budget Office, 2011). The share of pretax income to the top 1% of Americans increased from 8.9% in 1976 to 20.9% in 2008 (Atkinson, Piketty & Saez, 2011). Income inequality has hit minority groups especially hard. From 2007 to 2009, median income in African American households fell over 7%, compared to 4% among Whites (Nutting, 2011).

Wealth inequality has increased as well, revealing deep and growing disparities between rich and poor, young and old, and non-White and White. Median net worth declined nearly 40% between 2007 and 2010, including a 100% decline in the lowest quartile from $1,300 to zero (Bricker el al., 2012). Although wealth levels fell across the board during the economic downturn, African Americans and Hispanics were affected more than Whites. In 2009, the ratio of median net worth in White households ($92,000) compared to African American households

($4,900) was 19:1, while the ratio of White to Hispanic households ($6,325) was 15:1 (Taylor, Fry, & Kochhar, 2011). The Center for Responsible Lending estimates that 20% of African American and Hispanic homeowners will lose their homes during the current housing crisis (Bocian, Li, & Ernst, 2011). More than one-third of young households (headed by someone under 35) have a net worth of zero or less, nearly double the share in 1984, compared to households headed by someone 65 and older, whose net worth is 47 times greater than the young (Fry, Cohn, Livingston, & Taylor, 2011). Half of families with children are "asset poor," meaning their total financial net worth (excluding their home equity) is below 25% of the federal poverty level (Aratani & Chau, 2010). Finally, with respect to gender, women own only 36 cents for every dollar of wealth owned by men, even though women earn 78 cents for every dollar earned by men, and the situation is worse for single women (Chang, 2010).

HOW FAMILIES COPE

Given these dismal data, it is not surprising that one-quarter of Americans report it is unlikely they could access $2,000 within 30 days in the event of an emergency and that nearly half are "financially fragile" (Lusardi, Schneider, & Tufano, 2011). These facts about financial vulnerability do not imply that families lack financial survival skills. On the contrary, low-income households adopt economic survival strategies and engage in financial decision making, which they often do with perseverance and skill (Davis, 1992; Edin & Lein, 1997; Ehrenreich, 2001; Muske & Winter, 1999). People in poverty track and evaluate financial decisions (Rainwater, Coleman, & Handel, 1959; Zelizer, 1989). They strive to balance income streams and expenses. They draw on support networks, including families, peers, communities, and social assistance systems (Edin & Lein, 1997; Lusardi, Schneider & Tufano, 2011; Stack, 1974). Financially vulnerable households weigh the benefits of mainstream and alternative financial products and services, often choosing products from both sectors to manage their finances (Barr, 2004; Caskey, 1994; Venkatesh, 2006). Evidence is growing that even the poorest households in the world set aside small savings for emergencies, life cycle needs, and future opportunities (Collins, Morduch, Rutherford, & Ruthven, 2009; Rutherford, 2000).

Notwithstanding efforts to cope with financial strain, many people suffer short-term and long-term ill effects. Ample evidence links financial strain with social, psychological, and physical ills. Lack of income and assets has clear and direct implications for a family's ability to provide tangible necessities for a healthy life, and to shape future opportunities for themselves and their children. Dealing with the informal economy and alternative financial products can heap more costs and stress on otherwise difficult lives (Squires & Kubrin, 2006; Venkatesh, 2006). Financial problems can lead to a downward spiral of economic instability. Problem debt leads to further financial strain and, in some cases, to further loss of income and assets (Pleasance, Buck, Balmer, & Williams, 2007). For example, a family might lose their house to foreclosure, leading to a period of homelessness, loss of employment, and uprooting children from their neighborhood and school, leading to further instability, loss of resources, strain on family relationships, and social problems.

In this way, financial problems shape not only a household's balance sheet, but also affects social, emotional, and physical well-being. Financial troubles, perhaps especially those that lead to problem debt—debt that families cannot meet in the near or foreseeable future (Lea, 1999)—contribute to psychological and health distress, and may diminish people's ability to engage in productive problem solving (Arashiro, 2011; Brunner & Marmot, 1999; Deaton, 2011; Lea, Webley, & Walker, 1995; Melhuish, Belsky, & Malin, 2008; O'Neill, Sorhaindo, Xiao, & Garman, 2005). Debt may be particularly damaging (Cooke, Barkham, Audin, & Bradley, 2004; Drentea & Lavrakas, 2000; Jenkins et al., 2008; Jenkins, Fitch, Hurlston, & Walker, 2009; Kim, Garman, & Sorhaindo, 2003; Taylor, Pevalin, & Todd, 2007). Psychological ill effects include low life satisfaction, malaise, depression, and low self-esteem and self-efficacy. For example, financial problems are associated with "higher mental stress, lower reported life satisfaction, and health problems associated with anxiety or depression" in a panel study in the United Kingdom (Taylor, Jenkins, & Sacker, 2009, p. 91). Debt also has a negative impact on people's relationships with spouses, children, and friends (Pleasance et al., 2007). Money troubles, specifically credit card debt, may contribute to poor health behavior (Drentea & Lavrakas, 2000; O'Neill et al., 2005). Negative health effects may be particularly potent when economic inequality is higher (Adler & Snibbe, 2003; Emerson, 2009; Sapolsky, 2005), and when financial hardship is persistent over a long period of time (Kahn & Pearlin, 2006; Pleasance et al., 2007)

The associations are strong, but causation is complex and often goes in both directions. In other words, financial problems contribute to ill health and interpersonal strain, but ill health also contributes to financial problems (Adams, Hurd, McFadden, Merrill, & Ribeiro, 2003; Jenkins, Fitch, Hurlston, & Walker, 2009; Smith, 1999). For example, people with chronic health problems, especially those who lack adequate health insurance coverage, will pay large amounts of money to get health care (Himmelstein, Warren, Thorne, & Woolhandler, 2005). Addictions to gambling, smoking, alcohol, drugs, or spending, can amplify people's financial difficulties and lead to further psychological and physical health problems. People with mental health problems or cognitive impairments and other disabilities may become increasingly unable to make sound financial decisions, placing their financial well-being at risk (Fitch, Simpson, Collard, & Teasdale, 2007; Kolata, 2010; Triebel et al., 2009).

BUILDING FINANCIAL CAPABILITY AND ASSETS

These trends require a thoughtful and vigorous response (Ehrenreich, 2001; Hacker & Piersen, 2010). Families require knowledge and skills to deal with an increasingly complex and challenging array of economic decisions. They should understand their financial goals and have knowledge and skills for financial management, especially in a world of diminishing resources. They need to understand how to interact with financial providers, and how to discern good options from bad ones. They must be able to plan effectively in ways that build financial stability and create future opportunities for their family members. They should know how and where to get help and guidance.

But individual knowledge and skills are not enough. Families also require access to income and asset-building opportunities and financial services that enable them to participate fully in social and economic life. Financial vulnerability is not the result of individual action alone but is embedded in social, political, and economic conditions (Sabates-Wheeler & Devereaux, 2008). Tackling financial vulnerability will require action at the institutional level. In other words, families need stable sources of income and opportunities to build wealth over their lifetimes (M. Sherraden, 1991). They need appropriate financial products and services that optimize their ability to manage money effectively. They also need access to the right kind of information, counseling, and guidance at the appropriate time.

This book focuses on the importance of both aspects of financial capability: increasing financial knowledge and skills on one hand and improving access to assets and financial services and products on the other.

In chapter 1, Margaret Sherraden examines the concept of financial capability. In keeping with the capability approach (Sen, 1999) and the basic tenet of the individual in environment perspective, she suggests that financial capability is simultaneously an individual and structural idea. Financial capability is a combination of people's ability to act along with their opportunity to act in their best interests (Johnson & Sherraden, 2007). In other words, financially capable people are financially literate, but also have access to beneficial financial products and services that contribute to financial functioning, financial well-being, and life chances. Financial capability practice, therefore, requires working to improve a household's ability to make proper financial decisions, but also addressing problems of unemployment, low-wage jobs, a deficient safety net, and lack of access to beneficial financial products and services and asset-building mechanisms. Moreover, in keeping with the principle of self-determination, financial capability practice brings the voices of low-income and financially vulnerable people into the policy discussion.

Social work brings a unique historical commitment to vulnerable populations, especially those who lack financial resources. Paul Stuart, in chapter 2, focuses on the early years of the social work profession, exploring the work of charity organization and settlement house movements in helping clients improve financial capability through productive activity, bill paying, saving for the future, and participating as independent members of economic society. If much of this agenda sounds tailored to a capitalist agenda, it was, according to Stuart. Social workers tried to help clients adjust to the society in which they lived. Changes in the client's environment generally assumed a continuation of the current social order as it existed. However, social workers were creative and imaginative advocates. Case workers as well as community workers engaged in financial education, financial counseling, and interventions designed to increase the financial well-being of groups of poor people. The efforts of academic social workers were facilitated by early affiliations with the developing discipline of home economics, which focused on home finance as well as the more familiar cooking, design, and textile areas. Stuart's chapter describes the efforts of social workers to help clients improve their financial capability from the Progressive Era to the New Deal, and prospects for financial capability as a focus for social workers in the 21st century.

In chapter 3, David Stoesz situates financial capability in the US policy context. For many years Stoesz has explored the political landscape, looking for creative ways to refocus policy on the financial well-being of ordinary families. He focuses on three paradigms of antipoverty policy that evolved during the 20th century: the welfare entitlement paradigm, the tax credit paradigm, and the asset-building paradigm. He describes the philosophical bases, policy components, and relationship with other antipoverty paradigms and considers the implications of the burgeoning fringe economy and the Great Recession. The chapter concludes by proposing a capability paradigm that integrates previous antipoverty efforts and maximizes the aspirations of citizens.

As Stuart and Stoesz emphasize, social work practitioners and scholars have played an important historical role in financial capability and its resurgence in the 21st century. Since the New Deal, social workers have been instrumental in development of income security policy and programs. More recently, social workers were the first to focus attention on the importance of assets in low-income households (M. Sherraden, 1991), and later to test innovations such as matched savings accounts, including IDAs and Children's Development Accounts (Curley, Ssewamala, & Sherraden, 2009; McKernan & Sherraden, 2007; Schreiner & Sherraden, 2007; M. S. Sherraden & McBride, 2010). Several chapters that follow analyze key innovations.

INNOVATIONS IN FINANCIAL CAPABILITY POLICY AND PRACTICE

The next group of chapters presents recent research by scholars on the role of financial capability in generating economic well-being in diverse populations in the United States. Each chapter addresses a different approach to building financial capability, including varying levels and types of financial education and financial services and those targeted to different population groups. Each chapter contributes to understanding the financial situation of, and the approach to improving financial capability within, particular groups and develops an agenda for future research, policy, practice, and education.

Families across the spectrum of society share many of the same financial capability challenges but often face unique issues. In chapter 4, Cynthia K. Sanders analyzes a pioneering effort to build financial capability among women survivors of domestic violence. Sanders highlights the fact that survivors of domestic violence often lack financial resources and knowledge and that many women remain with or return to an abusive partner because they are economically dependent (Sanders, Weaver, & Schnabel, 2007). Understanding and addressing financial dimensions of abuse is essential to helping women successfully deal with domestic violence. This chapter describes an innovative community collaborative that uses financial advocacy to build financial capability among low-income survivors of domestic violence. The chapter documents successes and challenges in bringing women into the banking system, providing a platform for teaching about household financial management, and using Individual Development Accounts (IDAs) to build assets.

In chapter 5, Deborah Adams and Sondra Beverly focus on the youngest members of society. They report findings from a large experimental study of child development accounts (CDAs) on financial knowledge, attitudes, practices, and ownership among Head Start children's low-income parents. Surveys with parents of students attending fourteen Head Start centers administered by a community-based organization in an economically distressed county in the North Central region of the United States show that there is a need for financial education in addition to access to quality financial products.

At the other end of the life cycle, older adults, whose numbers are increasing rapidly, face financial challenges of a different nature. In chapter 6, Phillip McCallion, Lisa A. Ferretti, and Jihyun Park discuss the importance of preserving income and assets, including housing, through the retirement years. They point out that the financial well-being of older adults is affected by many factors but that financial exploitation plays a key role. They review the effectiveness of financial education aimed at older adults and identify gaps. The chapter addresses the role of social work and adult protective services in prevention and management of financial concerns including in legal remedies and treatment of psychosocial consequences.

Turning to low-income immigrants, Min Zhan, Steven Anderson, and Jeff Scott in chapter 7 examine the effects of a financial management training program on financial knowledge and practices. They document low levels of financial capability among immigrants. The program was effective in improving the financial knowledge and related financial behaviors of immigrant participants, and immigrants gained more in financial knowledge from the training than other participants. Implications are discussed for developing programs to improve the financial capacity of low-income immigrants.

Jonas Parker's chapter 8 focuses on savings clubs as a method for working with very low-income African American women in developing financial capability. Saving clubs are among the oldest and most prevalent financial institutions in the world, offering their members social support to commit to and achieve financial goals. Parker's chapter analyzes how women organized into saving clubs and used IDAs to promote financial capability through a sustained, experiential learning environment. Participants in the savings clubs engaged in critical reflection on their own financial behaviors and attitudes.

Moving from savings to taxes, three chapters discuss how tax credits and tax preparation sites contribute to financial capability among financially vulnerable populations. After filing a federal income tax return, many low-to-moderate-income working families receive lump sum refunds equal to one, two, or more months of earnings. Chapter 9 by Jennifer L. Romich, Nicole Keenan, Jody Miesel, and Crystal C. Hall presents research about tax-filers' experiences with the Earned Income

Tax Credit (EITC). Based on interviews with 38 clients of a community-based volunteer tax preparation service, they find that respondents have generally accurate ideas about the likelihood and size of refunds, and that their understanding is based on a broad-stroke understanding of tax rules, as well as ideas of citizenship and deservedness. The authors conclude that practitioners should be aware of the importance of income tax refunds, and should help families avoid common pitfalls. Further, they call on practitioners to contribute to public policies that support financial capability at tax time.

Kristen Wagner in chapter 10 also investigates the tax system as a tool for building financial capability, but focuses specifically on Volunteer Income Tax Assistance (VITA) sites as a gateway to connecting rural American Indian communities to financial information, services, and products. She analyzes empirical data on financial issues and behaviors of low-income Native American families and the critical role of VITA sites in bridging the gap between financial needs and opportunities. Through improved access to the EITC and financial services, providers can build financial capability in rural Native American households.

The Southwest border region of the United States presents challenges similar to those of rural American Indian communities, including poverty, poor infrastructure, and lack of economic opportunity. Bárbara Robles, in chapter 11, presents data that documents financial management strategies of Southwest border working families over a 5-year period. Her research with people at community-based organizations offering free tax-preparation services in Texas, New Mexico, Arizona, and California finds that border families' financial behaviors provide provocative empirical evidence of culturally defined economic resilience and financial capability.

PROFESSIONAL ROLES IN BUILDING FINANCIAL CAPABILITY

Many professional groups are engaged in financial capability work. These include social workers, family and consumer specialists, financial counselors, credit counselors, financial planners, accountants, lawyers, and bankers, as well as economists, policy makers, policy advocates, and researchers. Some provide direct services to families, and others are engaged in policy research and reform efforts (Abt Associates, 2006; Rupured, Most, & Sherraden, 2000; Tufano, 2009).

As a practical matter, social workers are the professional group most likely to be working directly with low-income and financially vulnerable families, and therefore, should be a central focus of solutions. Financial vulnerability frequently accompanies—or is at the heart of—issues that social workers confront in their daily work. Social workers help families stabilize household finances and build a sound financial future. They assist families whose financial troubles compound problems associated with ill health, mental illness, substance abuse, domestic violence, child abuse and neglect, homelessness, immigration, and marital dissolution.

Social work education has not kept pace with these policy, practice, and research developments, although this is beginning to change (Birkenmaier, Kennedy, Kunz,

Sander, & Horwitz, chapter 13, this volume). Social workers generally are knowledgeable about public assistance benefits, but they report lack of understanding, skills, and confidence in working with families on a range of financial issues (Despard & Chowa, 2010; M.S. Sherraden, Laux, & Kaufman, 2007; Jacobson, Svoboda, & Elkinson, 2012). Few schools of social work include courses or content on household financial management, consumer finance, behavioral economics, financial products and services, consumer law, asset building, and financial education (Loke, Watts, & Kakoti, chapter 12, this volume; Rupured et al., 2000). In other words, social work students are unlikely to learn about household budgeting and planning, managing bank accounts, funding postsecondary education, home-buying, building a credit record, paying debt, filing for bankruptcy, selecting insurance, sorting through tax options, or choosing a retirement plan for low-income and vulnerable families. Yet social workers report they need these skills (Despard & Chowa, 2010). Without basic financial management principles, terminology, tools, and information on where to refer clients for specialized assistance, they are limited in their ability to help and advocate for low-income and other financially vulnerable people.

As Vernon Loke, Julie Watts, and Sally Kakoti point out in chapter 12, service providers regularly work with individuals and families who are economically distressed or disadvantaged, and they are uniquely positioned to help increase the financial capabilities of these populations, specifically in the area of asset building. Little, however, is known about the financial capabilities of the service providers themselves, or about how prepared they feel to work with clients on asset building. Results of a survey of service providers indicate that they have very positive self-assessments of their financial capabilities, and the overwhelming majority report high levels of functioning across various financial practice domains. However, the level of financial literacy among the providers is no better than that among the general population, suggesting that there is a need to improve their financial capabilities.

In chapter 13, turning to what universities are doing to prepare social workers for financial capability practice, Julie Birkenmaier, Teri Kennedy, James Kunz, Rebecca Sander, and Shelley Horwitz underscore the lack of training most social workers receive but point to some promising initiatives. They describe educational innovations in New York, Maryland, and Arizona that aim to increase financial literacy and capability among social work students and practitioners. Courses represent a range of approaches including a social issues approach to economics, sustainable family asset and community capacity building, and financial literacy for social workers. The analysis focuses on elements of partnerships, program interests and resources, flexible development, and measurement of outcomes in each program. The chapter concludes with implications for social work education.

J. Michael Collins and Julie Birkenmaier, in chapter 14, highlight a growing array of financial capability resources that are available to practitioners, many of which are designed specifically for service providers who are working directly with financially vulnerable populations. This chapter develops a framework for practitioners seeking to improve their financial capability skills and reviews resources, education, and certifications for practitioners who are seeking appropriate education and training opportunities.

CONCLUSION

Building financial capability in US households has gained new urgency in the face of a sustained economic downturn, rising inequality, and increasing financialization of daily affairs. Families are coping simultaneously with shrinking household resources and increasingly complex financial decisions. This situation challenges social workers and other professionals to focus their work on building household financial capability, especially in low-income and financially vulnerable households. At the same time, policy and program reforms are required that can make it possible for ordinary families to make positive financial choices. The chapters that follow offer numerous examples and evidence, along with suggestions for constructive strategies. These studies together are a substantial step toward informing professional practice that aims to build financial capability and assets for US families.

REFERENCES

Abt Associates (2006). *Evaluation of first accounts demonstration: Providing financial services to unbanked individuals.* Retrieved September 30, 2011, from http://www.abtassociates.com/page.cfm?PageID=1800&FamilyID=1800&PBL=1

Adams, P., Hurd, M. D., McFadden, D., Merrill, A., & Ribeiro, T. (2003). Healthy, wealthy, and wise? Tests for direct causal paths between health and socioeconomic status. *Journal of Econometrics, 112,* 3–56.

Adler, N. E., & Snibbe, A. C. (2003). The role of psychosocial processes in explaining the gradient between socioeconomic status and health. *Current Directions in Psychological Science, 12*(4), 119–123.

Arashiro, Z. (2011). *Money matters in times of change: Financial vulnerability through the life course.* Brotherhood of St Laurence, Australia. Retrieved from http://www.bsl.org.au/pdfs/Arashiro_Money_matters_times_of_change__2011.pdf

Aratani, Y., & Chau, M. (2010). *Asset poverty and debt among families with children.* Retrieved from http://www.nccp.org/publications/pdf/text_918.pdf

Atkinson, A. B., Piketty, T., & Saez, E. (2011). Top income in the long run of history. *Journal of Economic Literature, 49*(1), 3–71.

Barr, M. (2004). Banking the poor. *Yale Journal on Regulation, 21,* 121.

Bee, A. (2012). *Household income inequality within U.S. counties: 2006–2010 American Community Survey Briefs.* US Department of Commerce, Economics and Statistics Administration. Retrieved from http://www.census.gov/prod/2012pubs/acsbr10-18.pdf.

Bocian, D. G., Li, W., Reid, C., & Quercia, R. G. (2011). *Lost ground, 2011: Disparities in mortgage lending and foreclosures.* Durham, NC: Center for Responsible Lending. Retrieved from http://www.responsiblelending.org/mortgage-lending/research-analysis/Lost-Ground-2011.pdf

Bricker, J., Kennickell, A. B., Moore, K. B., & Sabelhaus, J. (2012). Changes in U.S. family finances from 2007 to 2010: Evidence from the Survey of Consumer Finances.

Federal Reserve Bulletin, 98(2), 1–80. Retrieved from http://www.federalreserve.gov/pubs/bulletin/2012/pdf/scf12.pdf

Brunner, E., & Marmot, M. (1999). Social organisation, stress and health. In M. Marmot & R. G. Wilkinson (Eds.), *Social determinants of health* (pp. 17–43). Oxford: Oxford University Press.

Bureau of Labor Statistics. (2012). *Table A-2. Employment status of the civilian population by race, sex, and age*. Retrieved from http://www.bls.gov/news.release/empsit.t02.htm

Caskey, J. P. (1994). *Fringe banking: Check-cashing outlets, pawnshops, and the poor.* New York: Russell Sage Foundation.

Chang, M. (2010). *Shortchanged: Why women have less wealth and what can be done about it*. Oxford: Oxford University Press.

Collins, D., Morduch, J., Rutherford, S., & Ruthven, O. (2009). *Portfolios of the poor: How the world's poor live on $2 a day*. Princeton and Oxford: Princeton University Press. Retrieved from www.financialdiaries.com/index.htm

Congressional Budget Office. (2011, October). *Trends in the distribution of household income between 1979 and 2007* (CBO Summary). Retrieved from http://www.cbo.gov/ftpdocs/124xx/doc12485/WebSummary.pdf

Cooke, R., Barkham, M., Audin, K., & Bradley, M. (2004). Student debt and its relation to student mental health. *Journal of Further and Higher Education, 28*(1), 53–66.

Curley, J., Ssewamala, F., & Sherraden, M. (2009). Institutions and saving in low income households. *Journal of Sociology and Social Welfare, 36*(3), 9–32

Davis, E. P. (1992). Financial management practices among households with differing resource constraints. *Journal of Consumer Education, 10*, 27–31.

Deaton, A. S. (2011). *The financial crisis and the well-being of Americans* (NBER Working Paper 17128). Retrieved from http://www.nber.org/papers/w17128

Despard, M. R., & Chowa, G. A. N. (2010). Social workers' interest in building individuals' financial capabilities. *Journal of Financial Therapy, 1*(1), 23–41.

Drentea, P., & Lavrakas, P. J. (2000). Over the limit: The association among health status, race and debt. *Social Science and Medicine, 50*, 517–529.

Edin, K., & Lein, L. (1997). *Making ends meet: How single mothers survive welfare and low-wage work*. New York: Russell Sage Foundation.

Ehrenreich, B. (2001). *Nickel and dimed: On not getting by in America*. New York: Holt.

Emerson, E. (2009). Relative child poverty, income inequality, wealth, and health. *Journal of the American Medical Association, 301*(4), 425–426.

Fitch, C., Simpson, A., Collard, S., & Teasdale, M. (2007). Mental health and debt: challenges for knowledge practice and identity. *Journal of Psychiatric and Mental Health Nursing, 14*, 128–133.

Fry, R., Cohn, D., Livingston, G., & Taylor, P. (2011, November). *The rising age gap in economic well-being: The old prosper relative to the young*. Retrieved from http://www.pewsocialtrends.org/files/2011/11/WealthReportFINAL.pdf

Hacker, J. S., & Pierson, P. (2010). *Winner-take-all politics: How Washington made the rich richer—and turned its back on the middle class*. New York: Simon & Schuster.

Himmelstein, D. U., Warren, E., Thorne, D., & Woolhandler, S. (2005). Illness and injury as contributors to bankruptcy. *Health Affairs, 24*(1). Retrieved from http://content.healthaffairs.org/cgi/content/full/hlthaff.w5.63/DC1.

Jacobson, J., Svoboda, D., & Elkinson, A. (2012). *Strengthening social workers' capacity to improve clients' financial capability and economic well-being: An evaluation*. Poster presented at the Society for Social Work Research, Washington, DC, January 11–15.

Retrieved from http://www.ssw.umaryland.edu/fsw/events/powerpoints/Jacobson_sswr_poster_2012.pdf

Jenkins, R., Bhugra, D., Bebbington, P., Brugha, T., Farrell, M., Coid, J.,... Meltzer, H. (2008). Debt, income and mental disorder in the general population. *Psychological Medicine, 10*, 1–9.

Jenkins, R., Fitch, C., Hurlston, M., & Walker, F. (2009). Recession, debt and mental health: Challenges and solutions. *Mental Health in Family Medicine, 6*, 85–90.

Johnson, E., & Sherraden, M. S. (2007). From financial literacy to financial capability among youth. *Journal of Sociology and Social Welfare, 34*(3), 119–145.

Kahn, J. R., & Pearlin L. I. (2006). Financial strain over the life course and health among older adults. *Journal of Health and Social Behavior, 47*, 17–31.

Kim, J., Garman, E. T., & Sorhaindo, B. (2003). Relationships among credit counseling, clients' financial well-being, financial behaviors, financial stressor events, and health. *Financial Counseling and Planning, 14*(2), 75–87.

Kolata, G. (2010, October 30). Money woes can be early clue to Alzheimer's. *New York Times*, A1, A4.

Lea, S. E. G. (1999). Credit, debt, and problem debt. In P. E. Earl & S. Kemp (Eds.), *The Elgar companion to consumer research and economic psychology* (pp. 139–144). Cheltenham, UK: Edward Elgar.

Lea, S. E. G., Webley, P., & Walker, C. M. (1995). Psychological factors in consumer debt: Money management, economic socialization and credit use. *Journal of Economic Psychology, 16*, 111–134.

Lusardi, A M., Schneider, D. J., & Tufano, P. (2011). *Financially fragile households: Evidence and implications* (National Bureau of Economic Research, Working Paper 17072). Retrieved from http://www.nber.org/papers/w17072

McKernan, S. M., & Sherraden, M. (Eds.). (2007). *Asset building and low-income families*. Washington, DC: Urban Institute Press.

Melhuish, E., Belsky, J., & Malin, A. (2008). *An investigation of the relationship between financial capability and psychological well-being in mothers of young children in poor areas in England*. London: Institute for the Study of Children, Families and Social Issues, Birkbeck College, University of London. Retrieved from http://www.fsa.gov.uk/pubs/occpapers/op30.pdf

Muske, G., & Winter, M. (1999). Cash flow management: A framework of daily family activities. *Financial Counseling and Planning, 19*(1), 1–12.

Nutting, R. (2011, February 9). Wealth of Black families has disappeared. *Market Watch*. Retrieved from http://www.marketwatch.com/story/wealth-of-black-families-has-disappeared-2011-02-09

O'Neill, B., Sorhaindo, B., Xiao, J. J., & Garman, E. T. (2005). Health, financial well-being, and financial practices of financially distressed consumers. *Consumer Interests Annual, 51*, 80–82.

Pleasance, P., Buck, A., Balmer, N. J., & Williams, K. (2007). *A helping hand: The impact of debt advice on people's lives*. London: Legal Services Research Centre. Retrieved from http://www.lsrc.org.uk/publications/Impact.pdf

Rainwater, L., Coleman, R. P., & Handel, G. (1959). *Workingman's wife*. New York: Oceana Publications.

Rupured, M., Most, B., & Sherraden, M. (2000). Improving family financial security: A family economics-social work dialogue. *Financial Counseling and Planning, 11*(2), 1–7. Retrieved from http://www.nefe.org/pages/whitepaperfamilyecon.html

Rutherford, S. (2000). *The poor and their money*. New Delhi and New York: Oxford University Press.

Sabates-Wheeler, R., & Devereaux, S. (2008). Transformative social protection: The currency of social justice. In A. Barrietos & D. Hulme (Eds.), *Social protection for the poor and poorest: Concepts, policies and politics* (pp. 64–84). London: Palgrave Macmillan.

Sanders, C. K., Weaver, T. L., & Schnabel, M. (2007). Economic education for battered women: An evaluation of outcomes. *Affilia: Journal of Women and Social Work, 22*(3), 240–254.

Sapolsky, R. (2005, December). Sick of poverty. *Scientific American*, 93–99.

Schreiner, M., & Sherraden, M. (2007). *Can the poor save? Saving and asset building in individual development accounts*. New Brunswick, NJ: Transaction.

Sen, A. (1999). *Development as freedom*. New York: Anchor Books.

Sherraden, M. (1991). *Assets and the poor: A new American welfare policy*. Armonk, NY: M. E. Sharpe.

Sherraden, M. S., Laux, S., & Kaufman, C. (2007). Financial education for social workers. *Journal of Community Practice, 15*(3), 9–36.

Sherraden, M. S., & McBride, A. M., with Beverly S. G. (2010). *Striving to save: Creating policies for financial security of low-income families*. Ann Arbor: University of Michigan Press.

Smith, J. (1999). Healthy bodies and thick wallets: The dual relation between health and economic status. *Journal of Economic Perspectives, 13*(2), 145–166.

Squires G. D., & Kubrin, C. E. (2006). *Privileged places: Race, residence, and the structure of opportunity*. Boulder, CO: Lynne Rienner.

Stack, C. B. (1974). *All our kin: Strategies for survival in a Black community*. New York: Harper and Row.

Tavernise, S. (2011, September 29). Hispanic children in poverty exceed Whites, study finds. *New York Times*, A16.

Taylor, M., Jenkins, S., & Sacker, A. (2009). *Financial capability and wellbeing: Evidence from the BHPS* (Occasional Paper Series 34). London: The Financial Services Authority.

Taylor, M. P., Pevalin, D. J., & Todd, J. (2007). The psychological costs of unsustainable housing commitments. *Psychological Medicine, 37*, 1027–1036.

Taylor, P., Fry, R. & Kochhar, R. (2011, July 26). *Wealth gaps rise to record highs between Whites, Blacks, Hispanics: Twenty to one*. Retrieved from http://www.pewsocialtrends.org/files/2011/07/SDT-Wealth-Report_7-26-11_FINAL.pdf

Triebel, K. L., Martin, R., Griffith, H. R., Marceaux, J., Okonkwo, O. C., Harrell, L.,… Marson, D. C. (2009). Declining financial capacity in mild cognitive impairment: A 1-year longitudinal study. *Neurology, 73*(12), 928–934. Retrieved from http://www.ncbi.nlm.nih.gov/pmc/articles/PMC2754335/?tool=pubmed

Tufano, P. (2009). Consumer finance. *Annual Review of Financial Economics, 1*, 227–247.

US Census. (2011). *Poverty 2009 and 2010* (American Community Survey Briefs). Retrieved from http://www.census.gov/prod/2011pubs/acsbr10-01.pdf

Venkatesh, S. A. (2006). *Off the books: The underground economy of the urban poor*. Cambridge, MA, and London: Harvard University Press.

Zelizer, V. A. (1989). The social meaning of money: Special monies. *American Journal of Sociology, 95*, 342–377.

Financial Capability and Asset Development

PART ONE

Theory and Background

1

Building Blocks of Financial Capability

MARGARET SHERRADEN

In an era of rising financial instability and growing inequality, many families face two major challenges. They lack financial knowledge and skills to make optimal financial decisions in an increasingly complex financial landscape. Simultaneously, they lack access to appropriate and beneficial financial services that create conditions for financial stability, well-being, and confidence in the future. People need both—financial knowledge and financial inclusion—to build financially secure and hopeful lives. When individuals have both, they become financially capable. This chapter explores the idea of financial capability and calls for greater attention to research and professional training in building financial capability, especially in low-income and financially vulnerable households.[1]

The concept of financial capability bridges the disciplines of economics, psychology, and sociology, taking into account how individual action and behavior, human psychology, and social structure influence household financial management and decision making.[2] Although economists, psychologists, and sociologists view human behavior through different lenses, together they offer a promising way forward for improving financial functioning and well-being.

FINANCIAL CAPABILITY

Financial capability is both an individual and a structural idea. It combines a person's *ability to act* with their *opportunity to act*. In this way, people are able to "understand, assess, and act in their best financial interest" (Johnson & Sherraden, 2007, p. 124). The key distinction between financial literacy and financial capability, according to this definition, is that to be financially capable, people must be more than financially literate; they must also have access to financial products and services that allow them to act in their best financial interest. Together, ability and opportunity contribute to a person's financial functioning in ways that lead to improved financial well-being and life chances.

Capability has a particular meaning, derived from the seminal work of philosophers Amartya Sen and Martha Nussbaum. As Sen writes, "Capabilities ... are notions of freedom in the positive sense: what *real opportunities* you have regarding the life you may lead" (Sen, 1987, p. 36, emphasis added). According to Nussbaum, who applies capability theory to human development and welfare, the idea of capability takes into account not only people's *internal capabilities* (e.g., ability, knowledge, skills) but also the *external conditions* and array of opportunities available (e.g., access to products, services, and institutions), which together make up their *combined capabilities* (2000, p. 85). Nussbaum suggests that policies, laws, regulations, and practices should provide opportunities for all individuals to develop the full range of capabilities that lead to well-being.

While people must possess internal capabilities, certain external conditions also must exist in order for people to be capable.[3] As Nussbaum notes, internal capabilities may exist even when external conditions do not: "a society might do quite well at producing internal capabilities but might cut off the avenues through which people actually have the opportunity to function in accordance with those capabilities" (2011, p. 21). Similarly, internal capabilities may be lacking; a society could do "well in creating contexts for choice in many areas" (combined capabilities) but not "educate its citizens or nourish the development of their powers of mind" (internal capabilities) (2011, p. 22). Both are needed in order for people to function. The key point is that they are interactive; internal capabilities are "developed, in most cases, in interaction with the social, economic, familial, and political environment" (Nussbaum, 2011, p. 21).

It is important to point out that this understanding of financial capability is different from that commonly used today. More typically, "financial capability" often is used synonymously with "financial literacy" or more broadly to refer to a set of individual qualities—including knowledge and skills, attitude, habit, motivation, confidence, self-efficacy, and behavior—that lie within the individual (Atkinson, McKay, Kempson, & Collard, 2006; Dixon, 2006; Lusardi, 2010; Transact, 2009).[4] Although attitudes, motivation, confidence, and behavior suggest contextual variables (i.e., they are qualities that are not considered entirely innate), context is not integrated into most current conceptualizations of financial capability. Definitions sometimes include context, but looking closer, changing external conditions is rarely operationalized.[5]

By contrast, we suggest that financial capability does not reside solely within the individual. Instead, it captures a relationship between individuals and their social reality; financial capability depends on what is possible for people living in a particular society. In other words, people make financial decisions based on innate ability, knowledge, and skills, but also on what is within their "realm of possibility." For example, when researchers hear financially vulnerable people say that mainstream financial products and services are not meant for them (Kempson & Finney, 2009), it suggests a chasm between the financial worlds of rich and poor. In this way, a feeling of confidence may not be so much an expression of individual ability and skill in making financial decisions, but an expression of the individual's economic and social position and influence in relation to mainstream financial and economic institutions. Real options and opportunities in people's environment shape their assumptions and understanding about *what is possible*. It is this link between individual and structure that influences attitudes, motivation, confidence, self-efficacy, and behavior. In this way, the social, economic, and political context is internalized in people's perceptions and expectations and is likely to influence behavior (Reynolds & Pemberton, 2001).[6]

Institutions play an important role in capability theory because they are the principal conduits for social, economic, and political realities in an individual's life. Institutions give shape and meaning to human behavior; they do not "just constrain options: they establish the very criteria by which people discover their preferences" (Powell & DiMaggio, 1991, p. 11). Expanding financial capability, especially in populations that are underserved, requires more than offering better-designed products and services (although these can make a difference). It also requires changing the ways that financial institutions include (or exclude) low-income and financially vulnerable populations. For example, we know that institutional change, including public policy reform, is required to address deep and persistent inequalities in wealth by gender and race (Conley, 1999; Conley & Ryvicker, 2005; Gittleman & Wolff, 2004; Keister, 2000; Oliver & Shapiro, 1995; Schneider, 2011).

Despite the challenges of making significant change, institutional theory provides ways to think about how to increase access to opportunity for financially vulnerable households. For example, in their work on saving and asset building in low-income households, Michael Sherraden and colleagues identify a bundle of institutional constructs that shape saving in households (Beverly et al., 2008; M. Sherraden, 1991; M. Sherraden & Barr, 2005; M. Sherraden, Schreiner, & Beverly, 2003). These include access, information, incentives, facilitation, expectations, restrictions, and security. These constructs may also provide a way to examine and measure how well policy and financial institutions serve financially vulnerable households more generally.

Another strand of research that informs the way we can think about financial opportunity (and address constructs identified in institutional theory) comes from behavioral economics. Behavioral economics provides key insights into how people actually behave when confronted with financial decisions, pointing out that human psychology leads individuals to make nonrational and sometimes suboptimal (yet understandable) decisions, even when they are relatively well informed (Maital, 1982; Tversky & Kahneman, 1986; Wärneryd, 1999). At the same time, this body of work demonstrates that financial products and services can be designed in ways that make good financial choices more likely (Thaler & Sunstein, 2008). As Richard Thaler and Cass Sunstein suggest in their book *Nudge*, "choice architecture" can channel financial behaviors toward positive results (2008). Some financial products take into account these very human ways that people behave, for example, in providing simple choices and automatic features.

A final theoretical point about capability has implications for voice and influence in institutional change. Sen points out in *Development as Freedom* that public policies can enhance people's lives through expanded opportunity and that people can influence the direction of public policy "by the effective use of participatory capabilities by the public" (1999, p. 18). In fact, Sen writes, "*The two-way relationship* is central" (1999, p. 18, emphasis in original). In societies that enhance capabilities, people are engaged in defining capabilities and may be more likely to challenge injustices through individual and collective action. For example, using extensive empirical evidence that famines are less likely to occur in democracies, Sen (1981) demonstrates that ordinary people must have the ability to be heard and influence policy decisions. In this way, capability theory includes the idea that ordinary people gain "voice" (Hirschman, 1970). In financial capability, we would expect that ordinary people would have greater voice, and play a greater role, in shaping their financial world and economic well-being.

In sum, improving financial functioning in financially vulnerable families is not simply a matter of changing individual behavior, but also a matter of changing institutions. But how can it be accomplished? The remainder of the chapter examines what we know about the building blocks of financial capability. The first part defines and discusses how people develop knowledge and skills for managing their financial lives. The second part focuses on financial inclusion of financially vulnerable groups in the United States, components of inclusion, and innovations in expanding participation. The third part brings these discussions together in an examination of how combining the two leads to financial capability. The concluding section addresses the role of social work and other applied scholarship in research and practice in building financial capability in low-income and financially vulnerable households.

THE FIRST BUILDING BLOCK: FINANCIAL LITERACY

A financially literate person has the knowledge, ability, skills, and confidence to make good financial decisions (Huston, 2010). As the current chair of the board of governors of the Federal Reserve System, Ben Bernanke, explained in 2006 testimony before the US Senate Committee on Banking, Housing, and Urban Affairs, financial literacy improves financial decisions and economic outcomes:

> Clearly, to choose wisely from the variety of products and providers available, consumers must have the financial knowledge to navigate today's increasingly complex financial services marketplace. Consumers with the necessary skills to make informed financial decisions about purchasing a home, financing an education or their retirement, or starting a business will almost certainly be economically better off than those lacking those vital skills.

Today, in the face of growing evidence that many Americans lack sufficient financial knowledge and skills, a vocal chorus has joined Bernanke in calling for financial education. The US government has developed a National Strategy for Financial Literacy with four goals: (1) to increase awareness of and access to effective financial education; (2) to determine and integrate core financial competencies;[7] (3) to improve financial education infrastructure; and (4) to identify, enhance, and share effective practices (US Department of Treasury, 2011b).

Overall, studies suggest that people have low levels of financial literacy (Bernheim, 1998; Hilgert, Hogarth, & Beverly, 2003; Lusardi, Mitchell, & Curto,

2010; NCEE, 2005; OECD, 2005). A recent national study with a sample of 1,500 US adults, found that people think they know more than they really do as measured by simple questions about interest, inflation, and risk/diversification. For instance, among those who gave themselves the highest score in math, 52% were unable to do two simple calculations involving interest rates and inflation (FINRA, 2009b). Further, 64% of respondents with credit cards and checking accounts who agreed with the statement "I am good at dealing with day-to-day financial matters," engage in behaviors that generated fees or high costs (FINRA, 2009b, p. 35). Five waves of financial literacy assessments with high school students (1997 to 2006) by the Jump$tart Coalition for Personal Financial Literacy suggest low levels of financial knowledge (Mandell, 2008). Half of adults over 40 in a national survey lack knowledge of their pensions, health coverage, and other key financial facts (Nelson, 2007). Two-thirds of adults could not answer a range of personal finance questions correctly in a nationally representative study, falling short especially on credit management and investment questions (Hilgert, Hogarth, & Beverly, 2003). Similarly, a national study finds levels of understanding about debt are also low (Lusardi & Tufano, 2009).

Young people, minorities, and those with less income and education perform at lower levels in surveys and tests (Anderson, Zhan, & Scott, 2004; Applied Research and Consulting, 2009; Mandell, 2008). Although these tests may not address many financial survival skills of low-income families "that are relevant to [their] personal and economic circumstances" (Kempson & Atkinson, 2009, p. 16), low levels of financial knowledge and skills can take a financial toll on any household. This may be especially true in low-income households where the margin for error is small and poor financial choices can have profound consequences. When a low-income family does not grasp the full meaning of credit card interest rates and debit card fees, for example, the results can be more damaging than in a wealthier household where there is a financial cushion. To illustrate, a woman we interviewed as part of a study on savings in low-income households reported that she used her credit card to pay for everything. Assuming she had to pay only the monthly minimum payment, she did not realize that interest was accumulating.[8] "I didn't know that it worked like that," she explained, "I didn't read the fine print on some of them. So we wound up ruining the credit that we had" (M. S. Sherraden & McBride, 2010, p. 109). Since credit ratings determine the likelihood and cost of future borrowing, as well as influence other important aspects of people's lives, lack of understanding about credit cards placed her in a difficult financial situation. It took her years to pay off the credit card balance and rebuild a decent credit rating. Affluent households also misuse credit cards, but, in contrast to poor households, they are more likely to have a financial cushion, so even when they fail to pay in full each month, they may be less likely to default, and thus avoid severe damage to their credit rating.

Financial knowledge and skills are a key building block of financial capability. How do people learn about financial matters and what is known about how to generate higher levels of capability especially in financially vulnerable households?[9] First, *financial socialization* provides a foundation of attitudes, knowledge, and skills as children observe and learn from their families and others as they grow up, a process that continues into adulthood. Second, *financial education* also contributes to people's knowledge and skills. Finally, people seek *financial information and guidance* from counselors and others, especially when faced with difficult financial decisions.

Financial Socialization across the Life Course

Cognitive, behavioral, and environmental influences shape people's financial socialization, or the "values, attitudes, standards, norms, knowledge, and behaviors" that guide financial understanding and approaches to financial decisions (Schuchardt et al., 2009, p. 86; see also Ward, 1974). Understanding the economic world and one's place in it begins in early childhood and continues through life (Furnham, 1999; John, 1999).[10] Some people are better financial decision makers than others because they are able to delay gratification to benefit their overall financial well-being. For example, self-control learned in childhood can affect financial well-being later in life (Moffitt et al., 2011).

People absorb from their environment what they have the opportunity to observe and experience, beginning with parents who model financial behavior, including use of products and services (Hira, 1997; Mandell, 2008; Marshall & Magruder, 1960).[11] Parents are "an important channel" through which young adults acquire financial knowledge (Clarke, Heaton, Israelsen, & Eggett, 2005; Lusardi, Mitchell, & Curto, 2010, p. 374). Parenting style, in particular, may have important financial socialization effects (Otto, forthcoming). People are more likely to invest in stocks if their family does, even among minorities (Chitegi & Stafford, 1999). Likewise, low-income children who receive encouragement and hands-on support by parents are more likely to save (Kempson, Atkinson, & Collard, 2006). People who had a savings account as adolescents are more likely to have accounts as adults (Friedline, Elliott, & Nam, 2011). Another study shows a small but significant relationship between parent financial behavior and orientation and their children's financial behavior in childhood and adulthood (Webley & Nyhus, 2006).

Opportunities for social learning vary, as do exposure and access to financial opportunities, depending on a person's place in society and opportunity to learn and practice, and these have important implications for how people think about, and behave regarding, financial matters (Gutter, Garrison, & Copur, 2010). Some studies suggest that many parents do not share important financial teaching with their children (Bowman, 2011; Zelizer, 1994). Some children grow up learning about financial markets around the dinner table, while others do not. Wealthier families, for example, are likely to have information and experience with mainstream financial services and are better prepared to guide their children (Stacey, 1987). The financial lessons that low-income parents can share with their children often are not cheerful ones; they try to shield young ones from financial distress (M. S. Sherraden & McBride, 2010).

Family is also only the first of many agents of socialization that also include peers and media (Beutler & Dickson, 2008; Furnham & Argyle, 1998; John, 1999; McNeal, 1987; Moschis, 1985). People continue to absorb financial lessons, attitudes, and values through life. The individual's stage of development, as well as the social, cultural, political, and economic context in which they live, shapes socialization across the life course (Elder & Giele, 2009). In studies of financial socialization, relatively few focus on adults, especially studies that examine cohort differences across historical periods, such as financial socialization among those who grew up during the Great Depression compared to those who grew up in the more affluent 1960s.

Financial Education

The limits of what people learn from financial socialization, combined with growing financial complexity of people's lives and financial products and services, have prompted many to call for more financial education (US Department of Treasury, 2006). Policymakers, practitioners, and financial institutions have responded with a proliferation of financial education programs. In 2009, 36 states required personal finance content standards and 13 required courses or parts of courses dedicated to personal finance (Council for Economic Education, 2011). Some financial education programs aim to reach broad and diverse audiences, such as students or the public at large, while others target special groups. Some have a wide focus, covering topics such as basic numeracy, spending, planning, budgeting, earning, credit, debt, bill paying, saving, managing financial risk, investing, or taxes (Godsted & McCormick, 2007; Hogarth, 2006). Other financial education programs concentrate on specialized knowledge and skills for particular financial moments in time, such as buying a car or a home, or taking out a student loan. Methods for teaching also differ widely, ranging from public service announcements to curricular approaches to intensive experiential education.

Overall, the impact of financial education is positive, although somewhat mixed.[12] One study, for example, finds that adults who grew up in states that mandated a personal finance course in high school had higher savings rates than those who grew up in states that lacked such a mandate (Bernheim, Garrett, & Maki, 2001), although another study finds that mandates for financial education have no significant effect (Cole & Shastry, 2009). A pre-post assessment of a nationwide high school personal finance curriculum showed that students retained financial knowledge over a three-month period and reported increased confidence in financial management (Danes, 2004). A study with very low-income families in subsidized housing who participated in mandatory financial education showed improvements in self-reported financial knowledge, financial behavior, savings, and credit scores compared to a control group (Collins, 2010). A large quasi-experimental study finds positive impact of financial education on financial knowledge among high school students in the period after instruction, although it is unknown if they retain knowledge over time (Walstad, Rebeck, & MacDonald, 2010). In contrast, Mandell, who followed Jump$tart Coalition surveys of high school students for over a decade, concluded that there is no apparent relationship between financial education in school and financial literacy scores (2008). However, others note, the Jump$tart test does not control for what was taught, the quality or amount of instruction, or baseline knowledge (Walstad, Rebeck, & MacDonald, 2010).

The lack of consistent results is due in part to the wide range of objectives, audiences, activities, and timing and design of studies of financial education (Braunstein & Welch, 2002; Hathaway & Khatiwada, 2007; Hogarth, 2006). Some have suggested that financial education helps people make better decisions when they focus on "specialized knowledge about financial issues, markets, and products" (Altman, 2011, p. 38). For example, a study of "Get Checking"—a program that provides financial education about account management after the individual has been reported to ChexSystems for bank account abuse or mismanagement—finds that participants began recording transactions and communicating more with financial institutions (Haynes-Bordas, Kiss, & Yilmazer, 2008). Meta-analyses may be helpful in consolidating findings across multiple studies. In the meantime, several questions remain unclear, including the optimal age to initiate financial education, necessary content, the best teaching methods, and how these factors might vary across target groups (Burhouse, Gambrell, & Harris, 2004). More research is required on the effects of financial education on low-income and minority households and other financially vulnerable households (Hathaway & Khatiwada, 2007; Lutheran Immigration and Refugee Services, 2008; Lyons, Chang, & Scherpf, 2006; Schuchardt et al., 2009). Finally, impact studies using experimental and quasi-experimental methods will help ascertain the contributions of financial education to financial functioning and well-being (Holden, Kalish, Scheinholtz, Dietrich, & Novak, 2009; Lyons, Palmer, Jayaratne, & Scherpf, 2006; Martin, 2007; McCormick, 2008).

Financial Advice and Guidance

Sometimes people need financial advice (Murray, 2011). They may need guidance in assessing advantages and disadvantages of different financial products and services. They may need help dealing with financial problems brought on or exacerbated by job loss, divorce, health and mental health problems, home foreclosure, problem debt, severe poverty, and disability. Interventions vary by substantive focus, method and intensity, and type of provider. The substantive focus of financial advice and guidance may include a range of issues, such as obtaining public benefits, credit, debt modification, foreclosure prevention services, bankruptcy, insurance—or planning for saving, education, home buying, taxes, investment, or retirement.

Like financial education, advice and guidance differ by goal, method, and length and intensity. Goals may focus on near- or long-term financial decisions, planning, or problem solving. Interventions may be in person, by telephone, or online, and individual- or group-based. Guidance comes in several forms, including planning and advice, counseling, coaching, and mentoring. In practice, however, definitions remain unclear and often overlap, perhaps reflecting professional boundaries more than real differences in approach.[13] *Financial planning and advice* dispensed by professional financial planners is largely fee-based and aimed at the nonpoor. Growing numbers of colleges and universities, human service organizations, and online services offer free or low-fee planning and advice services. The growing field of *financial counseling* (and *financial therapy*) is problem- or crisis-focused and therapeutic in nature but maintains a focus on financial issues (Collins & Murrell, 2010). *Financial coaching* is different from financial counseling because it helps clients identify and achieve financial goals through a client-directed process aimed at behavior change (Collins & Murrell, 2007; Mangan, 2010). Financial coaches may be trained and certified or volunteers (Collins & Murrell, 2007).[14] *Financial mentoring* provides ongoing role models for positive financial behavior for children and adults. Mentors are more likely to be peers or volunteers rather than professionals.

Today, despite the great need for help, people in financial trouble face a confusing and uneven patchwork of public, private, and nonprofit financial counseling agencies. People worry that advice they receive might cost money or that the IRS may learn about their finances. Online advice is easy to find if an individual has computer access, but it is often difficult to apply or to know if the advice is appropriate and legitimate. Advisors, planners, counselors, coaches, and mentors represent a variety of disciplines, including peer counselors, consumer and family economists, housing counselors, credit counselors, financial planners, lawyers, and social workers. For people in financial difficulty, it is hard to know where to get quality advice and guidance. In response, a number of organizations have or are developing professional certification that makes it easier for consumers to identify qualified sources of guidance, although even these are often unregulated (Collins & Birkenmaier, chapter 14, this volume).[15]

Studies that examine effectiveness of financial advisors and counselors suggest positive results, but as yet there are relatively few studies and outcomes are challenging to compare because of the diversity of programs and approaches and the lack of quality data (Caskey, 2006; Hornburg, 2004). Impact research with appropriate research designs can generate testable propositions, better measures, and valid and reliable results (Collins, Baker, & Gorey, 2007; Collins & O'Rourke, 2009; Hornburg, 2004; Mallach, 2001).

In her blog *Financial Literacy and Ignorance*, Annamaria Lusardi, director of the Financial Literacy Center,[16] contends that financial illiteracy "concentrated among particular population subgroups—those with low-income and low education, minorities, and women ... is often the result of personal choice, of parents' education, and of an individual's access and exposure to financial education" (2007). While financial socialization, financial education, and financial advice and guidance are undoubtedly important, it is doubtful that *by themselves* they will make people financially capable. People also need access to quality financial products and services. The next section addresses the extent to which low-income and financially vulnerable groups have access to these resources to become financially capable. It also highlights features of quality products and services and offers examples of promising financial services innovations.

THE SECOND BUILDING BLOCK: FINANCIAL INCLUSION

Even the most educated have difficulty keeping pace with the growing complexity of modern financial life. As Lauren Willis observes, "The gulf between the literacy levels of most Americans and that required to assess the plethora of credit, insurance, and investment products sold today—and the new products as they are invented tomorrow—cannot realistically be bridged" (2008, p. 3). Willis and others argue that a focus on financial education blames the victim and "provides a convenient excuse for society to refrain from assisting consumers who are experiencing poor financial outcomes" (2008, p. 45; see also Gross, 2005; Williams, 2007).

For low-income individuals and families, financial inclusion means, at a minimum, having access to a safe place to deposit money, a place to store precautionary savings, a means to generate savings and investment, reasonably priced small dollar credit, and simple insurance products (Caskey, 1994, 2005; Kempson, Whyley, Caskey, & Collard, 2000; E. Seidman, 2008; M. Sherraden, 1991).

Underserved Households

Unfortunately, this array of basic and beneficial financial products and services is out of reach for many households (Barr, 2004; Bucks, Kennickell, Mach, & Moore, 2009; Carr & Schuetz, 2001; Hogarth, Anguelov, & Lee, 2005). According to the Survey of Consumer Finances, 1 in 12 households are unbanked, that is, they "lack any kind of deposit account at an insured depository institution" (FDIC, 2012, p. 4). Nearly 1 in 4 low-income households are estimated to be unbanked (Bucks et al., 2009).[17] Minority groups, unmarried heads of household, the young,[18] and people with less formal education, lower income, and fewer financial assets are overrepresented among the unbanked (Abt Associates, 2006; Caskey, 2005; FDIC, 2009; FINRA, 2009b; Stegman, Lobenhofer, & Quinterno, 2003). There are many reasons why people are unbanked, such as poor credit history, past account management problems, cultural and language barriers, geographic location, and lack of knowledge and familiarity. For example, branch bank closings in the wake of the economic crisis have disproportionately affected poorer communities (Schwartz, 2011). Job status and payment method also influences whether people have a financial account (Pew Health Group, 2010). Among those who are unbanked, 72% say they do not have enough money to warrant an account, 35% do not want to share personal information, 35% do not like dealing with banks, 23% say hours or location are inconvenient, and 22% say the banks would not open an account, according to another nationally representative study (FINRA, 2009b). Other studies find that managing and worrying about overdrafts, bouncing checks, fees, and generally keeping up with the account weigh on people's minds (Barr, Dokko, & Feit, 2011).

When people lack access to appropriate banking products and services, they turn to other financial products and services, which often increase costs over time (Caplovitz, 1967).[19] For example, a nationally representative study finds that 71% of the unbanked sometimes used money orders to pay bills, and 47% used check cashing stores to cash checks (FINRA, 2009b). Alternative, or "fringe," financial services include financial services operating outside of federally insured banks and thrifts (Barr, 2004; Berry, 2005; Caskey, 1994; FDIC, 2009; Karger, 2005). These include check cashing outlets, pawnshops, payday loans, rent-to-own, tax refund lenders, car title loans, pyramid schemes, and loan sharks (FDIC, 2009). Alternatives also include informal savings instruments such as rotating savings and credit associations (ROSCAs), and savings clubs. While some may offer convenient and appropriate alternatives, such as low-cost check cashing and prepaid cards, many are predatory and engage in unfair, deceptive, or fraudulent practices (Squires & Kubrin, 2006).

The line between the mainstream and alternatives is increasingly blurred; both sectors provide check cashing, mobile banking, and online person-to-person lending (FDIC, 2009). Unbanked immigrants may avoid bank accounts, using remittances as a money management tool (Pew Health Group, 2010). Moreover, as the recent subprime lending crisis revealed, products and services that exploit vulnerable and unsophisticated consumers are found in both alternative and mainstream financial services sectors. Further, many people use mainstream and alternative financial services simultaneously. These so-called underbanked are unable to meet their financial services needs within the mainstream financial services sector (Pew Health Group, 2010).[20]

Although alternatives often provide greater access, they lack consumer protections, can be expensive and time consuming, and may lead to problem debt (C. Choi, 2010; Fellowes & Mabanta, 2008). Costs associated with check cashing, tax refund anticipation loans, and payday loans illustrate the high cost of using these services. According to one estimate, a family earning $18,000 a year can spend up to $500 on basic payment products at check cashing facilities (Caskey, 2005, p. 153; see also Fellowes, 2006). In addition to these high costs, homeowners with subprime mortgages pay substantially more than those with prime mortgages (AECF, 2005). The First Nations Development Institute reports that refund anticipation loans (RALs), which offer quick access to tax refunds, charge between 50% and 500% annual interest in Native communities in the United States, among the poorest communities in the country (First Nations Development Institute, 2008). Overall, working poor families who receive the earned income tax credit (EITC) spent an estimated $600 million on RAL fees in 2006 (Wu & Fox, 2008). Another alternative product, payday loans, helps people make ends meet, but in the process, may lead to problem debt and an array of other negative outcomes (Fox, 2009).

Ultimately, however, neither mainstream nor alternative financial products are meeting the needs of low-income households. As Michael Barr, former Assistant Secretary for Financial Institutions in the US Treasury, writes,

> The financial services mismatch between the needs of [low- and moderate-income] households and the products and services offered to them largely forces these households to choose among the high-fee, ill-structured products offered by both banking and [alternative financial services] institutions. (2009, p. 67)

As a result, many households rely instead on cash transactions and cash saved at home, a risky approach to cash management (FDIC, 2009; Pew Health Group, 2010). In a recent study on savings in low-income households, one respondent stored emergency money in "little stashes here and little stashes there." Unfortunately, she reported that the money tended to disappear quickly. "Something always come up, though, and I ended up spending it. And then I'd get started back over again and then something always come up and I ended up spending it" (M. S. Sherraden & McBride, 2010, p. 143). Regrettably, keeping large amounts of cash on hand is unsafe not only because of the threat of spending it but also because it cannot accrue interest and is at risk for theft (Beverly, McBride, & Schreiner, 2003; Mullainathan & Shafir, 2009).

Key Features of Inclusive Financial Products and Services

Emerging evidence in fields of behavioral economics, and economic psychology, anthropology, sociology, and social work suggests features that may extend the reach of financial products and services into financially vulnerable households. Appropriate financial products and services that are accessible, affordable, financially attractive, easy to use, flexible, secure, and reliable will enable them to participate fully in social and economic life (Collins et al., 2009; M. Sherraden, Schreiner, & Beverly, 2003; Thaler & Sunstein, 2008).[21] These features are discussed below and illustrated in the next section with innovations aimed at building financial capability.[22]

APPROPRIATE

Financial services are appropriate when they meet the diverse needs of vulnerable populations. Determining the most appropriate financial services involves taking into account age, gender, education, cultural background, and financial situation on forms and types of financial services. To illustrate, financial services that take into account increasing rates of physical, cognitive, and social network limitations in older years may be appropriate (Wells, 2011). Likewise, immigrants and refugees may prefer cross-national access that allows them and their relatives in the country of origin to access accounts and facilitate sending remittances across international borders (Vexler, Rocchio, Salem, & Vélez, 2008).

ACCESSIBLE

This refers to the ability and right to approach, enter, use, and communicate with a financial institution (Beverly et al., 2008). Factors, small and large, pose access barriers to low-income households. Barriers are not limited to location (Fellowes & Mabanta, 2008).[23] They also include psychological discomfort, language barriers, and inconvenient hours (Berry, 2005; Caskey, 1994, 2005; FDIC, 2009). Particular groups, such as immigrants who do not speak English or are unfamiliar with US banking, may feel out of place in mainstream financial institutions (Lutheran Immigration and Refugee Services, 2008; Osili & Paulson, 2006).

Low-income households are often ineligible for checking accounts because of poor credit records and prior problems with managing an account.[24] Some bank products, such as direct deposit, do not accommodate irregular income streams.

In recognition of the importance of accessibility, some small banks have transformed the way they reach out to lower-income customers. For example, Union Bank in California created "Cash & Save" outlets, seeking to draw clientele away from check cashing outlets, after they learned customers "didn't want marble lobbies, comfy chairs, free coffee, and regular business hours." "For them, Formica countertops were perfectly fine, so long as they could access their money when and where they needed it" (Beaudin, 2006, p. 69; Stegman, 2001).

Affordable

Financial products and services must be affordable. However, the underserved report that financial products are too expensive given the small scale of their financial transactions (Bucks et al., 2009; Caskey, 2005; FDIC, 2009).[25] Among the top five reasons cited by the *previously banked* for why they are *now unbanked*, 34% said they do not have enough money to warrant an account, 26% do not want or see the value in an account, and 12% said service charges are too high (FDIC, 2009). A survey of unbanked households finds that a top concern about bank accounts is high fees (29%), followed by confusing fees and high minimum balances (14%) (Barr, 2009, p. 76). For example, a young mother with three children reported paying $240 in bank fees—$20 for each of 12 bounced checks—because her husband's paycheck arrived late at the bank: "I was just devastated.... We paid hundreds of dollars in check charges that just killed me. And I thought, 'No more!'" They closed their checking account and joined the ranks of the unbanked (M. S. Sherraden & McBride, 2010, p. 98). For these reasons, programs are developing simple "plain vanilla" accounts that have low threshold requirements (i.e., are relatively easy for low-income people to qualify for and maintain).

Financially Attractive

At the same time, financial services can be financially attractive by offering high returns, low fees, matches, bonuses, prizes, and other benefits. These features are available to bank customers who make large deposits or maintain high account balances. Unfortunately, they are largely out of reach of the poor.[26] In fact, low-income people often are subject to high costs for falling below minimum balance requirements (Berry, 2005; Caskey, 1994). Innovations in savings products are providing evidence on how to offer financial benefits, such as savings matches and benchmarks, to households with low incomes (see e.g., NYC Department of Consumer Affairs, 2009; Pender, 2012). Numerous studies suggest that savings matches and bonuses, in particular, attract people to open accounts and encourage saving, although for some segments, the rate of return may also be an effective incentive (M. Sherraden, 1991; Kempson & Finney, 2009; Schreiner & Sherraden, 2007; M. S. Sherraden & McBride, 2010).

Easy to Use (with Automatic Features)

The wide array of available financial products and services is confusing, and products are often difficult to use. Especially for those with little experience, low numeracy skills, and lack of financial knowledge, choosing and using financial products and services can be daunting (Berry, 2005; Lusardi & Mitchell, 2007). This suggests that products should be simple and transparent, and information should be clear and readily understandable to all, including non-English speakers, and people with low literacy or disabilities (Kempson & Finney, 2009).

But these features are not enough. Behavioral economics, a field that analyzes how psychology affects economic decisions, provides insights about why. Since it is human nature to avoid making difficult or unpleasant financial decisions, people tend to procrastinate and take the "path of least resistance," (J. J. Choi, Laibson, Madrian, & Metrick, 2002). To illustrate, people are more likely to save for retirement (important, but unpleasant because it is more enjoyable to spend money now than to save it for the future) when they are part of an "opt-out" savings plan that automatically transfers money to a retirement account. There are several reasons for this. An "opt out" plan yields more participants than an "opt in" plan because most people stay with the default (path of least resistance). Most people save for retirement by precommitting to transfer some wages to a retirement account. In this way, a "saver" does not have to decide to save each month; it happens automatically. Further, it keeps cash out of pockets and checking accounts where it is far easier to spend. Moreover, people tend to think about or "frame" their retirement account differently, further inhibiting its use (e.g., "it's for my retirement—not for spending") (Tversky & Kahneman, 1986). In other words, direct deposit into a retirement account (or other savings account) reduces the willpower required to save, making it easier because it happens *automatically*.

Thus, the design of financial products and services can pad "the path of least resistance," and "nudge" people toward better financial choices (Thaler & Sunstein, 2008, p. 83). Unfortunately, features that make financial products easier and more effective are often unavailable and unfamiliar to people with low incomes. Their employers often do not offer direct deposit into checking accounts, and typically do not offer or contribute to employee retirement accounts. Reaching low-income households with easy-to-use financial products and services, including asset-building opportunities, requires special designs.

Many savings innovations build on behavioral economics principles, usually by making saving easier through automatic features, providing social support, or making saving more financially attractive through the use of incentives (M. Sherraden, 1991; Tufano & Schneider, 2010). Among the best known is Save More Tomorrow™, which increases retirement saving through default enrollment and incentives (Thaler & Benartzi, 2004). Other examples include "Keep the Change," a bank-led program that rounds up debit card withdrawals to the nearest dollar and transfers the difference to a savings account (McGeer, 2007). The bank matches these small savings 1:1 for three months and 5% after that, up to an annual maximum of $250. In a year and a half, 4.3 million customers saved $400 million ($93 on average).[27] "Keep the Change" is a simple, customer recruiting and loyalty program that encourages bank customers to use a debit card and simultaneously build small savings (Mierzwa, 2007; Tufano, 2009; Tufano & Schneider, 2009).

Some studies suggest that introducing an element of excitement or thrill through savings account prizes or lotteries might attract interest (Kempson & Finney, 2009; Tufano & Schneider, 2010). In "Save to Win," which uses "thrill" as a savings incentive (Tufano & Schneider, 2009), credit unions entered everyone who made a $25 deposit into their savings accounts into a lottery to win $100,000 and small monthly prizes. More than 11,000 people saved $8.6 million in 2009, including a large proportion of people with low incomes who had not saved regularly in the past (Stuhldreher, 2010). "Save to Win" capitalizes on the excitement of lotteries as well as the common belief that winning the lottery is the most likely method for obtaining a large sum of money (Tufano & Schneider, 2009, 2010).[28] However, approaches such as "Save to Win" may encourage people to think that lotteries (even gambling) are a good bet.

Flexible

Flexibility also is a necessary feature of financial services for low-income families (Collins, Morduch, Rutherford, & Ruthven, 2009; Kempson & Finney, 2009). Income streams are often irregular and unpredictable (M. S. Sherraden & McBride, 2010). Expenses are similarly irregular, some predictable (such as school supplies or a wedding) and some unpredictable (such as a health emergency). At the same time, the margin for error is slim; large or small unexpected expenses, such as a car repair, a theft, or school field trip money, can strain or cause havoc. Lacking emergency savings, low-income families may have to borrow in a hurry, sometimes incurring high fees (Lusardi, Mitchell, & Curto, 2010).

Although not all low-income families need and want the same financial products, some flexible features may be welcome. This might include accounts that allow people to "transact in any sum, no matter how small, at any time" (Collins et al., 2009, pp. 181–182). In savings and insurance, deposits might be more adaptable, permitting small and intermittent payments (perhaps lapsing altogether during hard times) and allowing flexibility to use savings for unexpected events (Kempson & Finney, 2009). Similarly, there is evidence of demand for savings products that allow withdrawals, as well as commitment products that discourage withdrawals (Kempson & Finney, 2009; M. S. Sherraden & McBride, 2010). Similarly, loan payments might take into account financial instability, permitting borrowers to pay larger sums when money is more plentiful and smaller sums when it is scarce.

Secure and Reliable

Finally, financial products and services should be secure and reliable. A legacy of exploitation and discrimination, including the recent wave of subprime lending that led to the economic crisis, has further fueled widespread skepticism of financial institutions in low-income and minority communities (Carr & Schuetz, 2001). A study of unbanked households in Detroit, for example, suggests that account security is a key barrier for customers who otherwise would want an account (Barr, 2009), and a national survey finds that 7% of the previously banked report they "do not trust banks" (FDIC, 2009).

Regulation can help. Although the Federal Deposit Insurance Corporation (FDIC) protects accumulations up to $250,000 in bank accounts,[29] the recent financial crisis has made clear that more consumer protections and regulations are needed to shelter low-income consumers from unsafe products and services (Barr, 2004; Campbell, Jackson, Madrian, & Tufano, 2011; Tufano, 2009; Warren & Bar-Gill, 2008). Regulation has not caught up with new financial products, such as prepaid cards and mobile banking, which raise significant reliability and security risks (Barr, 2009). Recent legislation may begin to protect consumers from excesses that brought on the Great Recession of 2008 (Boshara et al., 2010). The Credit Card Accountability Responsibility and Disclosure Act of 2009 expands credit card protections,[30] and the Dodd-Frank Wall Street Reform and Consumer Protection Act of 2010 increases federal banking and securities regulation on financial enterprises.[31] The latter also created the Bureau of Consumer Financial Protection, which may increase transparency and reduce fragmentation and inefficiencies in regulation (Tennyson, 2009).[32]

However, regulation is not enough. Financial institutions have a legacy of discrimination to overcome if they hope to attract impoverished and minority communities as future customers. This requires products and services that meet other criteria, such as affordability and accessibility.

Financial Inclusion Innovations

For illustrative purposes, this section highlights two types of innovations that use these principles to expand financial inclusion in the United States.[33] "Bank On," begun by a coalition of banks, credit unions, nonprofits, and local government to reach the unbanked and underbanked in San Francisco, offers low-threshold products to low-income clients. The initiative aims to reduce an estimated $40 million a year spent at check cashers and payday lenders.[34] Within 5 years, an estimated 71,000 starter bank accounts were open and active (Phillips & Stuhldreher, 2011, p. 1).[35] The "Bank On" model is being piloted or planned in about 70 cities and 6 states, with mixed results (Phillips & Stuhldreher, 2011). Cities for Financial Empowerment builds on Bank On and the New York City financial empowerment model (NYC Department of Consumer Affairs, 2011) aimed to build financial stability in lower income households across the nation.[36]

The fastest growing, and perhaps most promising alternative to traditional banking, is so-called branchless banking (Boyd, Jacob, & Tescher, 2007; Busette & Gencer, 2010; Center for Financial Inclusion, 2008). Many see a very different future for banking services in low-income communities because of the high cost of offering low-balance accounts (Caskey, 2005; Barr, 2004). Especially with increased regulation, branchless banking offers a low-cost alternative.

Branchless banking uses cards or codes to access financial services through ATMs, direct deposit, mobile phones, prepaid cards, debit cards, online banking, and electronic check conversion.[37] Mobile banking is revolutionizing banking, especially in developing countries, as it leverages mobile technology to allow budgeting, payments, depositing, and withdrawals through the use of cell phones (Mas & Mayer, 2011). As Maria Otero (2011), a pioneer in microfinance and currently in the US State Department recently observed: "After spending most of my career in pursuit of financial inclusion, I can't tell you how delighted I am that the answer is finally at our fingertips. And not just our fingertips … but in the hands of poor, non-banked individuals around the world."

Branchless banking can link benefits and social assistance that are already delivered electronically to savings and other financial instruments (Barr, 2007; Stegman, 1999; Stegman, Lobenhofer, & Quinterno, 2003).[38] Furthermore, unbanked individuals report they would use low-cost, low-risk options such as debit cards, prepaid debit cards, and payroll cards that allow them to withdraw funds through an ATM (Barr, Bachelder, & Dokko, 2006; Fellowes & Mabanta, 2008; Hogarth, Anguelov, & Lee, 2005; Romich, Gordon, & Waithaka, 2009).[39]

Payment cards, the fastest growing segment of branchless banking in the United States, include debit, prepaid debit, and payroll cards (not gift cards) that permit users to receive income, make purchases, pay bills, and withdraw cash electronically (Barr et al., 2011).[40] Depending on the type, payment cards may be loaded by an individual, government-benefit program, employer, reward program, or health benefit program (CFSI, 2010). Payment cards, for example, permit saving through a linked bank account that is separate from the account for the card (Barr et al., 2011). Generally, payment cards are safer than carrying cash, protected against fraud and theft, less expensive than cashing checks at a check casher or using money orders, and promising as a large-scale alternative to mainstream banking.

Challenges to Building Financial Capability through Financial Inclusion

Notwithstanding the growth of promising innovations for financial inclusion, several major challenges remain. First, the types of innovations discussed above still cover only a small proportion of low-income households in the United States. Compared to many other countries, the United States lags in offering branchless banking through mobile phones, while online banking has limited applicability in many low-income households due to lack of secure Internet access. Innovations should inform policy development that can reach millions of low-income families with appropriate financial services (M. Sherraden, 2011). Related to this, we still have a great deal to learn about needs for financial products and services in poor communities.[41]

Second, many innovative products raise questions for how to safeguard the financial lives of low-income families (Barr, 2009, p. 69; Block, 2011; Busette & Gencer, 2010). For example, while branchless banking holds promise, questions remain about security and privacy, regulatory issues, pricing, and accessibility (Boyd, Jacob, & Tescher, 2007).[42] Neither a public nor a private payment card program "offers a broadly available payment card product that is affordable, transparent, and reflects the preferences" of low- and moderate-income households (Barr et al., 2011, pp. 4–5). Fees are often high and confusing, and users may not know if their card is federally insured or if it will help build their credit score (Barr et al., 2011; CFSI, 2010; C. Choi, 2010), especially in the fast growing area of branchless banking that lies outside of existing consumer protections.[43] Increasing fragmentation of financial services, along with their growing complexity, suggests a need for financial education, guidance, and alternative ways of linking financial products (Stone & Sledge, 2011).

Despite the challenges, these and other innovations suggest that it is possible to design beneficial products and services and extend financial inclusion to ordinary households. They illustrate how features—such as accessibility, affordability, financial attractiveness, ease of use, security, and reliability—can shape quality financial products and services and build long-term financial stability and opportunities for development.

But by themselves, financial services innovations cannot ensure financial capability. People also must know how to manage their household financial decisions and when and how to use financial services. Combining financial education and guidance and appropriate financial services will build financial capability.

FINANCIAL CAPABILITY: LINKING FINANCIAL LITERACY AND FINANCIAL INCLUSION

The argument for financial literacy is that people who are knowledgeable and skilled money managers will be able to make informed financial decisions and improve financial behavior (Figure 1.1). The argument for financial inclusion is that access to appropriate and quality financial services will increase financial opportunities (Figure 1.2).

Figure 1.3 brings these ideas together into a schematic depiction of financial capability. The combined influence of financial knowledge and skills with financial inclusion generates financial capability, which results in both the *ability to act* and the *opportunity to act*.[44] Financially capable people are able to behave and

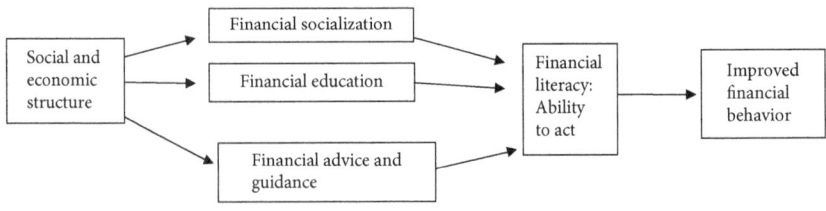

Figure 1.1 Financial Literacy

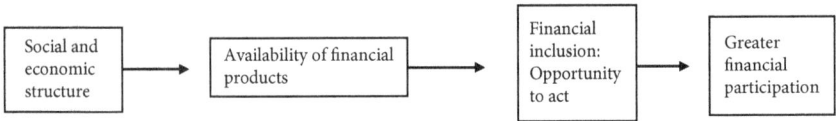

Figure 1.2 Financial Inclusion

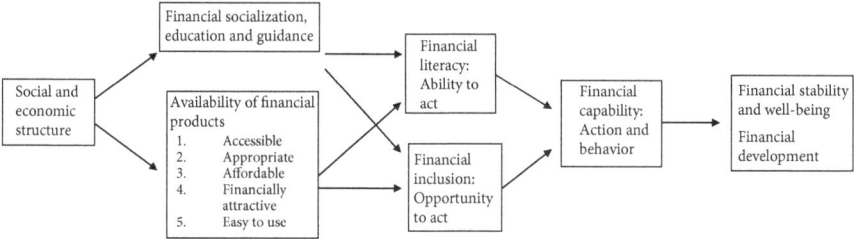

Figure 1.3 Financial Capability

act in their best financial interests. Individual behavior is not always required; some things happen (action) without individual behavior. For example, an employer-based retirement plan requires a signature when the employee signs up, but thereafter, accumulation of retirement savings requires no special behavior from the individual (other than going to work). Financial capability, in turn, contributes to greater financially stability, well-being, and opportunities for future development.

To illustrate, we turn to an example. Let's say that Jewell, a 16-year-old youth,[45] begins her first job at a fast food restaurant. Simultaneously, she enrolls in a high school financial education course, where she learns how to open and manage a secured checking account, and how to sign up for direct deposit of her paycheck. When she goes to the bank to open the checking account, she also learns about a special no-fee youth savings account that requires only a small initial deposit, and bonuses for reaching savings targets.[46] Because, eventually, Jewell wants to buy a house, she opens the savings account and arranges to send $20 a month automatically from checking to her savings account. In school, she also learns about higher yield savings vehicles. When she finishes high school and enters community college, she moves into a slightly better paying job. After several years, during which she participates in a free homebuyer course, she reaches her savings goal, transfers her money to a higher yield savings instrument and continues saving. Although she has to borrow occasionally from her savings, after 12 years of saving, when she is 28 years old, she has saved enough for a down payment on a house and some repairs, with a little left over for emergencies.

In this example, a young person actively engages in her financial life, learning and doing at the same time. This interaction between financial knowledge and skills and financial inclusion is central to the idea of financial capability. Using knowledge she gained from school, she developed an early and positive relationship with a financial institution, gained a sense of mastery in money management, and felt more secure because her money was safer and she was accumulating savings (financial well-being). She also avoided exploitative alternative financial services, ubiquitous in the community where she lived. Eventually she had enough money to invest in a house (financial development). Moreover, she felt more in control of her life, which may have helped build her personal resilience. We have little empirical evidence on financial control and well-being, although there is some evidence that desirable financial behavior contributes to overall well-being

(Kim, Garman, & Sorhaindo, 2003), and evidence of a correlation between debt and psychological ill-health, although causal direction is not clear.

Over time, feedback effects may generate even more learning (higher financial knowledge and skills) and lead to the use of more beneficial financial products and services (more financial inclusion), and greater financial capability. As Nussbaum writes, internal capabilities (in this case, financial ability, knowledge, and skills) and external conditions (access to beneficial financial products and services) are each important, but interact in ways that make the combination more potent than the sum of each of its parts (2000).

According to this schema, however, when financial education and access to quality financial products are not available simultaneously, the impact may be less effective—in some cases even harmful. Suppose that instead Jewell arranges with her employer to deposit $20 a month of her wages to a regular savings account,[47] but the bank does not offer a special youth savings account. She occasionally withdraws some savings using the bank ATM.[48] She has trouble tracking the withdrawals, and the bank begins to assess fees because of her low balance. When she realizes what is happening, she becomes scared and discouraged. She withdraws her remaining savings and closes the account. Saving seems futile and the bank unfair. Instead, she saves her money at home, where it is more likely to be spent, lent, or stolen. When she needs emergency money, she turns to a payday lender who charges such high rates of interest that she must take out another loan to pay the first. This leads to problem debt and a poor credit rating, which affects her ability to secure good interest rates and may even affect her ability to get a job or an apartment. What may be worse, these experiences leave Jewell with a negative view of financial institutions, leaving her with diminished capability to act in her best financial interests in the future.

Today, unfortunately, the second scenario is more likely than the first. Even when young people take a financial education class in high school, their employers are unlikely to offer direct deposit, and youth are unlikely to have access to an incentivized youth savings account. Parents, who often use alternative financial products, may not be in a position to help their children navigate mainstream financial products and services. Moreover, youth may not be thinking about long-term saving in part because their parents may have no experience in long-term financial investing.

The consequences of low financial capability can be even more serious. In recent years, easy credit, low incomes, and poor money management, among other factors, have contributed to severe financial problems among low- and moderate-income families (Introduction, this volume). For example, many low-income families, in pursuit of the American Dream of homeownership, purchased houses with subprime loans, and subsequently lost them to foreclosure, or are "under water" on their mortgages (AECF, 2005). Even financially literate borrowers eligible for prime loans utilized subprime loans because of heavy marketing and targeting in low-income communities. In one year alone (2009), almost three-quarters of a million subprime loans were in foreclosure (Mortgage Bankers Association, 2010).

These examples suggest that failing to connect internal capability (financial knowledge and skills) and external conditions (financial products and services) could produce what Amartya Sen calls an "unfreedom" that limits a person's capabilities (1999, p. 86). In practical terms, these examples represent the loss of hope and sense of a future, as well as widespread and tragic loss of household net worth. Financial instability and loss have associated negative psychological costs that have important implications for well-being (Taylor, Jenkins, & Sacker, 2009).

Fortunately, there have been advances in promoting financial capability in low-income households. First, innovations in savings combine a financial product with financial education to build financial capability in families who have been largely excluded from asset-building policies in the past (Howard 1999; L. S. Seidman, 2001; M. Sherraden, 1991; Woo, Rademacher, & Meier, 2010). Individual Development Accounts (IDAs) and Children's Development Accounts (CDAs) use incentives (often a 1:1 or 2:1 match) to attract savings and help people build assets for investment purposes (M. Sherraden, 1991). Some form of financial education usually accompanies IDAs. Research finds that low-income people can and do save for longer-term goals, and they respond to incentives (Schreiner & Sherraden, 2007).

A second example is a promising approach from New York City, which integrates financial counseling into service delivery systems (Bloomberg & Mintz, 2011), and has generated a number of banking products and services including streamlined bank accounts, savings accounts, along with financial education and counseling in low-income neighborhoods. The bank account, SafeStart Bank Accounts, is a savings account with a starting balance of $25, an ATM card, and no overdraft or monthly fees (Fernholz, 2010; NYC Department of Consumer Affairs, 2009, 2010a). The savings account, SaveNYC (which has now expanded nationally and is called SaveUSA), is an incentivized matched savings program designed to encourage short-term savings among low- to middle-income tax filers (Bloomberg, 2012). Twenty-five financial empowerment centers reach nearly half of the unbanked households in New York (NYC Department of Consumer Affairs, 2010b; NYC Department of Consumer Affairs, 2011; Santos, 2011).

Empirical Evidence on Financial Capability

Empirical evidence on financial capability is promising but nascent (Baker & Dylla, 2007). Studies show an association between financial knowledge and positive financial practices, although causality is unclear (Courchane & Zorn, 2005; Hilgert, Hogarth, & Beverly, 2003; Monticone, 2010). In other words, most studies examine a "bundle" of services—such as an account, financial education, and support—without isolating their independent effects. However, there is some evidence on financial capability. In one study, for example, experience with financial products (bank account and investing) explains more variance in investment knowledge than a high school financial education course (Peng, Bartholomae, Fox, & Cravener, 2007). A comparison of financial education-only and financial education-plus-IDA finds that participants in the latter tested significantly higher on financial knowledge on average, although the two groups, both low-income, differed in important ways (Anderson, Zhan, & Scott, 2004). Two large randomized control trials in India and Indonesia find that people who received small subsidies for opening a bank account had much higher account opening rates and use of the account, than those who received only financial education (Cole, Sampson, & Zia, 2011). Another study finds some higher financial management skills among soldiers who owned a savings account in high school (Bell, Gorin, & Hogarth, 2009). In the Small Dollar Loan program piloted by FDIC, default rates appear to be lower in products accompanied by savings and financial education; however, limited sample size and program variation temper these results (Miller, Burhouse, Reynolds, & Sampson, 2010).

Leading with Financial Product

Some programs "lead" with offers of a financial product but also include financial education. The financial product draws interest, and the addition of education aims to improve understanding and product management. For example, Individual and Child Development Accounts, college savings plans, homebuyer programs, income tax preparation, public benefits, jobs, emergency aid, and saving clubs focus on product outreach but sometimes also offer financial education. There is some evidence that outcomes improve with the addition of financial education. For example, there is independent contribution of financial education (up to 10 hours) on opening an account and saving performance in IDAs (Schreiner & Sherraden, 2007). But another randomized study of IDAs in Canada called Learn$ave finds that the group that received 15 hours of financial management training and case management services did not save more than the group with the saving match only, although qualitative findings suggest the educational content may have been inadequate (Leckie, Shek-Wai Hui, Tattrie, Robson, & Voyer, 2010). Another study that encouraged low-income participants to open bank accounts finds that those who did not plan to open an account had good financial reasons, suggesting the importance of providing financial education and financial services at the same time (Lyons & Scherpf, 2004). A large-scale matched savings program in the UK, Saving Gateway, found a low take-up rate for financial training and advice (8% to 18% in different phases), and in qualitative interviews, participants expressed lack of enthusiasm (Kempson & Finney, 2009, p. 46).

Programs that lead with financial services find that offers of financial education are not an enticement to participate. After discovering that "getting a bank account is not an incentive to go to a [financial education] class" in Bank On San Francisco, the program decoupled financial education requirements from account opening (Phillips & Stuhldreher, 2011, p. 13). An evaluation of the federal government's First Accounts program, which aimed to bring low-income households into the financial mainstream, finds that few participants took up the free education services (Abt Associates, 2006). A study assessing the effects of offering online banking along with financial and computer literacy to low-income participants finds that participants were drawn by the technology, although implementation challenges diminished effectiveness overall (Servon & Kaestner, 2008).

LEADING WITH FINANCIAL EDUCATION

Other programs lead with financial education but also offer a financial product or service. This type of experiential education may increase motivation, attention, focus, and absorption of information (Johnson & M. S. Sherraden, 2007; O'Neill, 2006). Some research suggests that even an imagined product may make financial education more effective (McCormick, 2008; Russell, Brooks & Nair 2006). For example, financial education using a stock market game has better outcomes than didactic approaches (Mandell, 2008). Unbanked participants in a financial education program in Chicago were encouraged to open a bank account. When offered a bank account by a bank representative who attended the financial education workshop, the take-up rate (and use of other complementary bank products) was significantly higher than among unbanked participants who attended a workshop without a bank representative present (Bertrand, Mullainathan, & Shafir, 2006). A survey of financial education programs in San Francisco reported increased participation in financial education programs that also offered incentives with tangible benefits (L. Choi, 2009). For example, homebuyer education programs offering a tangible benefit (such as down payment assistance) may draw more low-income participants and incentivize participation in financial education or coaching.

Some studies question combining financial education and products. For example, Lewis Mandell's research finds that individual motivation, more than owning stocks or credit cards, leads to better performance on a financial literacy assessment (Mandell, 2004; Mandell & Klein, 2009). A qualitative study of a youth savings account and financial education program finds that participants attribute increased financial knowledge to financial education workshops but not to holding assets, but youth also express dislike for financial education sessions (Scanlon & Adams, 2009).

Future applied research should focus on understanding the discrete and summative contributions of financial education, guidance, and financial products and services. Research should also explore if effectiveness differs by approaches to financial education and across variations in financial products. Offering financial education and a savings account with automatic deposit features, for example, may have stronger effects on savings than offering financial education and a matched savings account. More work is needed to identify the key indicators of financial knowledge and skills and financial inclusion, as well as financial stability, well-being, and financial development. Research should also examine what works for diverse groups of financially vulnerable people (e.g., different stages of life, gender, cultural backgrounds, and perceptions of risk). What works for different population groups? Greater clarity across these questions will generate more effective policy and practice.

NEXT STEPS IN BUILDING FINANCIAL CAPABILITY

Financial capability leads to greater financial stability and a brighter financial future. Researchers and practitioners are beginning to understand how to build financial capability in low-income and financially vulnerable households. Families also need access to quality financial products and services appropriate to their circumstances. For many financial matters, getting the services right is just as important. For example, a person with a steady income, a retirement account (with an employer contribution), and access to free banking and safe and inexpensive insurance is a long way toward being financially capable. One such professional recently underscored the impact of the benefits he receives as part of his employment: "My [financial] illiteracy is undetected and irrelevant. It is my option-rich environment that—regardless of my personal financial literacy—provides me with financial services, accessibility, and inclusion." Nonetheless, theoretical and empirical evidence suggests that understanding financial basics and how to manage money and make optimal financial decisions is also essential, but impact will be limited if financial education and counseling is done in isolation from improving access to quality financial services.

NOTES

1. Recently, financial vulnerability has been operationalized by Lusardi, Schneider, and Tufano (2011) as the estimated one-half of Americans unable to access $2,000 in 30 days in the event of an emergency. However, we use the term along the lines of others, such as Chambers (1989), who suggests a broader definition: Financial vulnerability refers not only to having a low income but more generally to "defencelessness, insecurity, and exposure to risk, shocks, and stress," including loss of assets (p. 1).
2. For detailed discussion of these perspectives, especially as it concerns saving in low-income households, see Beverly and Sherraden (1999), Beverly et al. (2008), and M. S. Sherraden and McBride, 2010.
3. The principle of "person-in-environment" in social work bears some similarities (Kondrat, 2002).
4. As described by a 2009 financial capability survey: "financial capability encompasses multiple aspects of behavior relating to how individuals manage their resources and how they make financial decisions (including the factors they consider and the skill sets they use). It is a multi-dimensional concept that requires looking at individual behavior from various angles" (FINRA, 2009a, p. 4).
5. An exception is the President's Advisory Council on Financial Capability, which defines financial capability as financial education and financial access, although some of its work appears to equate financial capability with education, as is evident in this statement concerning youth: "Financial capability starts with financial education" (US Department of Treasury, 2011a, p. 1).
6. We distinguish between an individual's expectations (what an individual expects to actually occur given existing constraints) and aspirations (what an individual would like to occur given the best circumstances) and suggest that expectations are a stronger predictor of behavior.
7. The core competencies mentioned refer to the ability of consumers to make informed decisions about their personal finances and include: earning, spending, saving, borrowing, and financial protection (US Department of Treasury, 2010).
8. Fortunately, recent regulatory changes are already beginning to prevent this type of situation, although more protections are needed, according to the Consumer

9. Federation of America, The Center for Responsible Lending, and other consumer research and protection groups. (http://www.federalreserve.gov/consumerinfo/wyntk_creditcardrules.htm)
9. There are other streams of inquiry, reviewed in Xiao, Collins, Ford, and colleagues (2010).
10. There are cognitive developmental limits (Berti & Bombi, 1988).
11. Scholars note a high correlation between financial literacy and parent education and level of financial investment (Lusardi, Clark, Fox, Grable, & Taylor, 2010; Mandell, 2008).
12. The number of financial education and effectiveness studies is too numerous to cover in detail here. (Detailed reviews of the research include: Agarwal, Amromin, Ben-David, Chomsisengphet, & Evanoff, 2011; Atkinson, 2008; Braunstein & Welch, 2002; Buckland, 2011; Caskey, 2006; Courchane & Zorn, 2005; Fox, Bartholomae, & Lee, 2005; Hathaway & Khatiwada, 2007; Hogarth, 2006; Lusardi et al., 2010; Lyons, 2005; Lyons, Palmer, Jayaratne, & Scherpf, 2006; Martin, 2007; Schuchardt et al., 2009.)
13. Financial guidance also may include financial case management and financial tutoring, but these terms are ill-defined.
14. For example, the Community Services Society of New York City has organized a volunteer Financial Coaching Corps (http://www.cssny.org/programs/entry/financial-coaching-corps).
15. In the United Kingdom, which has made strides in designing a universally accessible system of financial advice, policy makers are examining a national accreditation system for personal advisors to ensure quality services (Ben-Galim & Lanning, 2010).
16. The Financial Literacy Center is a joint project of The Rand Corporation, Dartmouth College, and the Wharton School of Business at the University of Pennsylvania. (http://www.rand.org/labor/centers/financial-literacy.html)
17. The "unbanked," according to the FDIC, include all those who answer "no" to the question: "Do you or does anyone in your household currently have a checking or savings account?" (Bachelder et al., 2008).
18. Although the preretirement (ages 45–64) group, especially minority and low-income, has high rates of unbanked (16.5 million), suggesting challenges for saving for retirement (Jackson et al., 2010).
19. People also turn to credit. In New York City, residents are less likely than the national average to be unbanked, yet in nine of the ten poorest neighborhoods they are more likely to have a credit card than a bank account (NYC Department of Consumer Affairs, 2011).
20. According to the FDIC estimates that 21% are underbanked, defined as households that "hold a bank account, but also rely on alternative financial services providers" (Burhouse & Osaki, 2012, p. 4).
21. There are many definitions of financial inclusion and exclusion. This one draws from Stein, Randhawa, and Bilandzic (2010); and the Center for Financial Inclusion, which also calls for a "full suite of quality financial services" and "with dignity for the clients" as key features (http://www.centerforfinancialinclusion.org/Page.aspx?pid=1941).
22. There are other important areas for consideration, including other ways that people transfer funds, manage risk and credit, and invest. However, we limit the discussion to checking and savings accounts because they are basic for financial management.

23. Fellowes and Mabanta (2008) report that 56% of lower-income neighborhoods have bank and credit union branches, compared to nonbanks, which are located in 31% of such neighborhoods.
24. Insufficient funds in an account can lead to fees for overdrafts and bounced checks, refusal by banks to issue a checking account, and reports to the ChexSystem®, which, similar to a credit report, follows a patron and may prevent the individual from opening accounts in other banks for a period of up to five years.
25. For their part, banks also argue that offering low-balance accounts is expensive (Barr, 2004).
26. As David Caplovitz (1967) pointed out several decades ago, the poor "pay more," including for financial services (AECF, 2005; Fellowes, 2006).
27. The bank has benefited from the 1.8 million new savings accounts and 1.3 million new checking accounts over 19 months (Mierzwa, 2007).
28. In 2007, lottery revenues in the United States almost reached $24 billion (American Gaming Association, 2010), and sales are up during the economic crisis (Matheny, 2011).
29. http://www.fdic.gov/consumers/consumer/information/fdiciorn.html
30. S. 414, http://www.govtrack.us/congress/bill.xpd?bill=s111-414&tab=summary
31. http://frwebgate.access.gpo.gov/cgibin/getdoc.cgi?dbname=111_cong_bills&docid=f:h4173enr.txt.pdf
32. Officially, the law's (H. R. 4173—605) purpose is "to implement and, where applicable, enforce Federal consumer financial law consistently for the purpose of ensuring that all consumers have access to markets for consumer financial products and services and that markets for consumer financial products and services are fair, transparent, and competitive" (http://frwebgate.access.gpo.gov/cgi-bin/getdoc.cgi?dbname=111_cong_bills&docid=f:h4173enr.txt.pdf).
33. In an effort to reach scale, some innovations piggyback on other institutions. For example, the US Treasury is piloting a refund program in 2011 that has features of a checking account. In the planned pilot, 600,000 people will receive offers for a debit card for tax refunds that has free bill paying, free ATM withdrawals at select machines, and spending without added fees (Reddy, 2011). Evaluation will measure take-up, comparing different approaches in charges and messaging (Reddy, 2011). Other examples include an automatic savings option associated with the Earned Income Tax Credit (Wagner, chapter 10, this volume), bank-at-school initiatives (Cruce 2002; Rhine, Reeves, Castro, Wides, & Williams, 2009), and automatic savings deposits at birth (Clancy, Lassar, & Taake, 2010).
34. http://www.frbsf.org/community/issues/assets/bankonsf/index.html
35. http://bankonsf.org/index
36. http://www.cfecoalition.org/cfeAboutCFECoalition.aspx?ID=2
37. http://www.ftc.gov/bcp/edu/pubs/consumer/credit/cre14.pdf. Internationally, governments and financial institutions are linking branchless banking and government-to-people (G2P) programs that use electronic banking to transfer social assistance payments, pay wages, and send pension payments to households (Mas, 2008; Pickens, Porteous, & Rotman, 2009).
38. Electronic benefit transfer (EBT) is used widely by federal and state governments (see http://fms.treas.gov/eta/background.html).
39. Other innovations provide low-cost/small dollar credit alternatives to pawnshop, payday, and auto title loans (Sanders & Forman, 2010). These may include small

dollar loans or salary advances from banks and credit unions, salary advances by employers, creditor payment plans, emergency assistance programs, and military loans (Center for Responsible Lending, 2010). For example, FDIC guidelines allow banks to offer loans up to $2,500 (with no/low origination fees and a maximum 36% annual percentage rate, or APR), and credit unions offer loans to members at even lower rates (FDIC Small Dollar Loan Program, http://www.fdic.gov/smalldollarloans/; Miller, Burhouse, Reynolds, & Sampson, 2010).

40. See Barr et al. (2011) and Flores (2011) for description and analyses of prepaid cards. One type, reloadable prepaid cards, with an estimated value of $120 billion in 2009, can be used where the card brand is accepted (CFSI, 2010; Flores, 2011).
41. Studies underscore the difficulty in recruiting low-income and unbanked individuals into IDA programs, with implications for demand (Sherraden & McBride, 2010).
42. Interestingly, research in Kenya, for example, which has a high penetration of mobile banking among the poor, finds that people do not lose money at higher rates using this technology compared to traditional banking or savings groups, and furthermore, they resolved problems more quickly (Zollman & Collins, 2010).
43. People may not understand fees and may also be liable for losses. For example, losses may result if they do not report errors promptly, or if they lose their cards (http://www.fms.treas.gov/eft/regulations.html). Although the FTC advises card owners to notify their financial institution by certified letter with return receipt requested (keeping a copy for their own records), this advice is likely to go unheeded in many households. Moreover, there is little recourse after 60 days. http://www.ftc.gov/bcp/edu/pubs/consumer/credit/cre14.pdf
44. We intentionally use opportunity to "act" instead of "behave." Improvements to financial well-being may occur without individual behavior. For example, retirement savings plans often require only one "behavior" (sign-up for an employer-based retirement plan), but accumulations happen automatically without any further behavior (automatic transfers and employer matches).
45. Jewell is a composite sketch from qualitative interviews with low-income savers conducted by the author and colleagues (Sherraden, Johnson, Guo, & Elliott, 2010; Sherraden & McBride, 2010).
46. Some Children's Development Account (CDA) programs offer these kinds of incentives.
47. Even this service may not be available. Many low-wage employees have no access to direct deposit.
48. Some banks now offer ATM withdrawal protection so that customers cannot overwithdraw from their accounts; nonetheless, many charge fees for low balances.

REFERENCES

Abt Associates. (2006). *Evaluation of first accounts demonstration: Providing financial services to unbanked individuals*. Retrieved from http://www.abtassociates.com/page.cfm?PageID=1800&FamilyID=1800&OWID=2109767657&CSB=1

Agarwal, S., Amromin, G., Ben-David, I., Chomsisengphet, S., & Evanoff, D. (2012). Financial counseling, financial literacy, and household decision making. In O. Mitchell & A. Lusardi (Eds.), *Financial literacy: Implications for retirement security and the financial marketplace*. New York: Oxford University Press.

Altman, M. (2011). *Behavioural economics perspectives: Implications for policy and financial literacy*. Research paper prepared for the Task Force on Financial Literacy, Canada. Retrieved from http://www.financialliteracyincanada.com/documents/consultation-2/Altman-09-02-2011-eng.pdf

American Gaming Association. (2010). *Gaming revenue: Current-year data*. Retrieved from http://www.americangaming.org/Industry/factsheets/statistics_detail.cfv?id=7

Anderson, S. G., Zhan, M., & Scott, J. (2004). Targeting financial management training at low-income audiences. *Journal of Consumer Affairs, 38*(1), 167–177.

Annie E. Casey Foundation (AECF). (2005). *Building family and economic success: The high cost of being poor*. Retrieved from http://www.aecf.org/KnowledgeCenter/Publications.aspx?pubguid={20B3E620-1897-4DAE-B5C6-8E33D9A7AA8D}

Applied Research and Consulting LLC. (2009). *Financial capability in the United States: Initial report of research findings from the 2009 national survey*. New York: Author.

Atkinson, A. (2008). *Evidence of impact: Review of policy evaluation literature*. Bristol: University of Bristol, Personal Finance Research Centre. Retrieved from http://www.fsa.gov.uk/pubs/consumer-research/crpr68.pdf

Atkinson, A., McKay, S., Kempson, E., & Collard, S. (2006). *Levels of financial capability in the UK: Results of a baseline survey*. Bristol: University of Bristol. Retrieved from http://www.pfrc.bris.ac.uk/completed_research/fincap_baseline.html

Bachelder, E., Alexander, E. K., Yu, L., Bellows, C., Stanton, J., Rumble, J., & Barr, M. S. (2008). *Banks' efforts to serve the unbanked and underbanked for the Federal Deposit Insurance Corporation* (Final Report). Boston, MA: Dove Consulting.

Baker, C., & Dylla, D. (2007). *Analyzing the relationship between account ownership and financial education*. Washington, DC: New America Foundation. Retrieved from http://www.newamerica.net/files/Microsoft%20Word%20-%20Account%20Ownership%20and%20Financial%20Education-Elec.pdf

Barr, M. (2004). Banking the poor. *Yale Journal on Regulation, 21*, 121.

Barr, M. (2007). An inclusive, progressive national savings and financial services policy. *Harvard Law and Policy Review, 1*, 161–184.

Barr, M. (2009). Financial services, saving, and borrowing among low- and moderate-income households: Evidence from the Detroit Area Housing Financial Services Survey. In R. M. Blank & M. S. Barr (Eds.), *Insufficient funds: Savings, assets, credit, and banking among low-income households* (pp. 66–96). New York: Russell Sage Foundation.

Barr, M. S., Bachelder, E., & Dokko, J. (2006). Payments innovations in serving low- and moderate-income households: Policy, and evidence from a new survey. *Proceedings* (pp. 448–460). Chicago: Federal Reserve Bank of Chicago. Retrieved from http://econpapers.repec.org/article/fipfedhpr/y_3a2006_3ap_3a448-460.htm

Barr, M. S., Dokko, J. K., & Feit, E. M. (2011). *Preferences for banking and payment services among low- and moderate-income households* (Finance and Economics Discussion Series 2011-13). Washington, DC: Federal Reserve Board, Divisions of Research & Statistics and Monetary Affairs. Retrieved from http://www.federalreserve.gov/pubs/feds/2011/201113/201113pap.pdf

Beaudin, L. (2006). From marble to Formica: How the Union Bank of California attracts lower-income people to traditional banking. What Works. *Stanford Social Innovation Review*. Retrieved from http://faculty-gsb.stanford.edu/heath/documents/2007/2006FA_wworks_UnionBank.pdf

Bell, C., Gorin, D., & Hogarth, J. M. (2009, April). *Does financial education affect soldiers' financial behaviors?* Paper presented at the 2009 Federal Reserve System, Community Affairs Research Conference. Retrieved from http://www.kansascityfed.org/publicat/events/community/2009carc/Hogarth.pdf

Ben-Galim, D., & Lanning, T. (2010). *Strength against shocks: Low-income families and debt.* London: IPPR.

Bernanke, B. S. (2006, May 23). *Financial literacy.* Testimony before the Committee on Banking, Housing, and Urban Affairs of the United States Senate. Retrieved from http://www.federalreserve.gov/newsevents/testimony/bernanke20060523a.htm

Bernheim, B. D. (1998). Financial literacy, education, and retirement saving. In Mitchell, O. S., & Scheiber, S. J. (Eds.), *Living with defined contribution pensions: Remaking responsibility for retirement* (pp. 38–68). Philadelphia, PA: University of Pennsylvania.

Bernheim, B. D., Garrett, D. M., & Maki, D. M. (2001). Education and saving: The long-term effects of high school financial curriculum mandates. *Journal of Public Economics, 80*(3), 435–465.

Berry, C. (2005). To bank or not to bank? A survey of low-income households. In N. P. Retsinas & E. S. Belsky (Eds.), *Building assets, building credit: Creating wealth in low-income communities* (pp. 47–70). Cambridge, MA: Joint Center for Housing Studies, and Washington, DC: Brooking Institution Press.

Berti, A. E., & Bombi, A. S. (1988). *The child's construction of economics* (G. Duveen, Trans.). Cambridge: Cambridge University Press.

Bertrand, M., Mullainathan, S., & Shafir, E. (2006). A behavioral-economics view of poverty. *American Economic Review, 94*(2), 419–423.

Beutler, I., & Dickson, L. (2008). Consumer economic socialization. In J. J. Xiao (Ed.), *Handbook of consumer finance research* (pp. 83–102). New York: Springer.

Beverly, S. G., Moore McBride, A., & Schreiner, M. (2003). A framework of asset-accumulation stages and strategies. *Journal of Family and Economic Issues, 24*(2), 143–156.

Beverly, S. G., Sherraden, M., Cramer, R., Shanks, T. W., Nam, Y., & Zhan, M. (2008). Determinants of asset holdings. In S. M. McKernan & M. Sherraden (Eds.), *Asset building and low-income families* (pp. 89–152). Washington, DC: Urban Institute Press.

Beverly, S. G., & Sherraden, M. (1999). Institutional determinants of saving: Implications for low-income households and public policy. *Journal of Socio-Economics, 28*, 457–473.

Birkenmaier, J., Sherraden, M. S., & Curley, J. (Eds.). (forthcoming). *Financial capability and asset development: Research, education, policy, and practice.* New York and Oxford: Oxford University Press.

Block, S. (2011, January 18). Prepaid card fees can hurt; If you don't choose carefully, they can squeeze you dry. *USA Today*, p. 6A.

Bloomberg, M. (2012). *SaveUSA program implementation: Insights from the field.* The City of New York, Department of Consumer Affairs, Office of Economic Empowerment. Retrieved from http://www.nyc.gov/html/ofe/downloads/pdf/SaveUSA_Implementation_Brief.pdf

Bloomberg, M., & Mintz, J. (2011). *Municipal financial empowerment: A supervitamin for public programs.* The City of New York, Department of Consumer Affairs, Office of

Economic Empowerment. Retrieved from http://www.nyc.gov/html/dca/downloads/pdf/SupervitaminReport.pdf

Boshara, R., Gannon, J., Mandell, L., Phillips, J. W. R., & Sass S. (2010). *Consumer trends in the public, private, and nonprofit sector*. Paper presented at the 2010 National Endowment for Financial Education Colloquium, Denver, CO.

Bowman, S. W. (2011). Multigenerational interactions in Black middle class wealth and asset decision making. *Journal of Family and Economic Issues, 32*, 15–26.

Boyd, C., Jacob, K., & Tescher, J. (2007). *Mobile financial services and the underbanked: Opportunities and challenges for Mbanking and Mpayments*. Chicago: The Center for Financial Services Innovation. Retrieved from http://www.finextra.com/Finextra-downloads//featuredocs/mbanking%5B1%5D.pdf

Braunstein, S., & Welch, C. (2002). Financial literacy: An overview of practice, research, and policy. *Federal Reserve Bulletin, 88*, 445–457. Retrieved from http://www.federalreserve.gov/pubs/bulletin/2002/1102lead.pdf

Buckland, J. (2011). *Money management on a shoestring: A critical literature review of financial literacy and low-income people*. Canada: Task Force on Financial Literacy. Retrieved from http://www.financialliteracyincanada.com/documents/consultation-2/Buckland-09-02-2011-eng.pdf

Bucks, B. K., Kennickell, A. B., Mach, T. L., & Moore, K. B. (2009, February). Changes in U.S. family finances from 2004 to 2007: Evidence from the Survey of Consumer Finances. *Federal Reserve Bulletin,* A1–A56. Retrieved from http://www.federalreserve.gov/pubs/bulletin/2009/pdf/scf09.pdf

Burhouse, S., Gambrell, D., & Harris, A. (2004). Delivery systems for financial education in theory and practice. *FYI: An update on emerging issues in banking*. Retrieved from http://www.fdic.gov/bank/analytical/fyi/2004/092204fyi.html

Burhouse, S., & Osaki, Y. (2012). 2011 FDIC National Survey of Unbanked and Underbanked Households. Federal Deposit Insurance Corporation (FDIC), September. Retrieved from http://www.fdic.gov/householdsurvey/2012_unbankedreport.pdf

Busette, C. M., & Gencer, M. (2010). *Mobile financial services for the underbanked in the U.S.: Preliminary findings from EARN's mobile financial services research initiatives* (EARN Research Brief). San Francisco, CA: EARN.

Campbell, J. Y., Jackson, H. E., Madrian, B. C., & Tufano, P. (2011). Consumer financial protection. *Journal of Economic Perspectives, 25*(1), 91–114.

Caplovitz, D. (1967). *The poor pay more: The consumer practices of low-income families*. New York: The Free Press.

Carr, J. H., & Schuetz, J. (2001). *Financial services in distressed communities: Framing the issues, finding solutions*. Washington, DC: Fannie Mae Foundation. Retrieved October 26, 2011, from http://www.fanniemaefoundation.org/programs/financial.PDF

Caskey, J. P. (1994). *Fringe banking: Check-cashing outlets, pawnshops, and the poor*. New York: Russell Sage Foundation.

Caskey, J. P. (2005). Reaching out to the unbanked. In M. Sherraden (Ed.), *Inclusion in asset building: Assets, poverty, and public policy* (pp. 149–166). New York: Oxford University Press.

Caskey, J. P. (2006). *Can personal financial management education promote asset accumulation by the poor?* (Policy Brief). Terre Haute: Indiana State University, Networks Financial Institute. Retrieved from http://www.networksfinancialinstitute.org

Center for Financial Inclusion. (2008). *Financial inclusion glossary*. Retrieved from http://www.centerforfinancialinclusion.org/Page.aspx?pid=1941

Center for Financial Services Innovation. (2010). *The nonprofit's guide to prepaid cards*. Retrieved from http://cfsinnovation.com/sites/default/files/CFSI%20Nonprofit%20 Guide%20to%20Prepaid_0.pdf

Center for Responsible Lending. (2010). *Alternatives to payday loans*. Retrieved from http://www.responsiblelending.org/payday-lending/tools-resources/alternatives-to-payday-loans.html

Chambers, R. (1989). Editorial introduction: Vulnerability, coping and policy. *IDS Bulletin, 20*(2), 1–7.

Chitegi, N. S., & Stafford, F. P. (1999). Portfolio choices of parents and their children as young adults: Asset accumulation by African-American families. *American Economic Review, 89*(2), 377–380.

Choi, C. (2010, October 4). Living with a bank: Fees and confusing galore. *The Huffington Post*. Retrieved from http://www.huffingtonpost.com/huff-wires/20101004/us-going-bankless/

Choi, J. J., Laibson, D., Madrian, B. C., & Metrick, A. (2002). Defined contribution pensions: Plan rules, participant decisions, and the path of least resistance. In J. M. Poterba (Ed.), *Tax policy and the economy* (Vol. 16, pp. 67–113). Cambridge, MA: MIT Press.

Choi, L. (2009). *Financial education in San Francisco: A study of local practitioners, service gaps and promising practices* (Working Paper 2009-08). San Francisco, CA: Federal Reserve Bank of San Francisco. Retrieved from http://www.frbsf.org/community

Clancy, M., Lassar, T., & Taake, K. (2010). *Saving for college: A policy primer* (CSD Policy Brief 10-27). St. Louis, MO: Washington University, Center for Social Development.

Clarke, M. C., Heaton, M. B., Israelsen, C. L., & Eggett, D. L. (2005). The acquisition of family financial roles and responsibilities. *Family and Consumer Sciences Research Journal, 33*(4), 321–340.

Cole, S., & Shastry, G. K. (2009). *Smart money: The effect of education, cognitive ability, and financial literacy on financial market participation* (Harvard Business School Working Paper 09-071). Cambridge, MA: Harvard Business School. Retrieved from http://www.hbs.edu/research/pdf/09-071.pdf

Cole, S. A., Sampson, T., & Zia, B. (2011). Prices or knowledge? What drives demand for financial services in emerging markets? *Journal of Finance, 66*(6), 1933–1967. Retrieved from http://www.hbs.edu/research/pdf/09-117.pdf

Collins, D., Morduch, J., Rutherford, S., & Ruthven, O. (2009). *Portfolios of the poor: How the world's poor live on $2 a day*. Princeton, NJ, and Oxford: Princeton University Press.

Collins, J. M. (2010). Effects of mandatory financial education on low income clients. *Focus, 27*(1), 13–17.

Collins, J. M., & Murrell, K. (2010). Using a financial coaching approach to help low-income families achieve economic success: Challenges and opportunities for the field. Madison, WI: University of Wisconsin Cooperative Extension. Retrieved from http://fyi.uwex.edu/financialcoaching/files/2010/07/Using-a-Financial-Coaching-Approach.pdf

Collins, J. M., & O'Rourke, C. (2009). Financial education and counseling: Still holding promise. *Journal of Consumer Affairs, 44*(3), 483–498.

Conley, D. (1999). *Being Black, living in the Red: Race, wealth and social policy in America*. Berkeley: University of California Press.

Conley, D., & Ryvicker, M. (2005). The price of female headship: Gender, inheritance, and wealth accumulation in the United States. *Journal of Income Distribution, 13*(3), 41–56.

Council for Economic Education. (2011). *Survey of the states 2011:* The State of Economic and Personal Finance Education in our Nation's Schools. Retrieved from http://www.councilforeconed.org/wp/wp-content/uploads/2011/11/2011-Survey-of-the-States.pdf

Courchane, M., & Zorn, P. (2005). *Consumer literacy and credit worthiness*. Paper presented at the Federal Reserve System Conference. Retrieved from http://www.chicagofed.org/digital_assets/others/events/2005/promises_and_pitfalls/paper_literacy.pdf

Cruce, A. (2002). *School-based savings programs, 1930–2002* (CSD Working Paper 02-7). St. Louis, MO: Washington University, Center for Social Development.

Danes, S. (2004). *Evaluation of the NEFE high school financial planning program, 2003–2004*. Minneapolis, MN: University of Minnesota. Retrieved from http://hsfpp.nefe.org/loadFile.cfm?contentid=273

Dixon, M. (2006). *Rethinking financial capability: Lessons from economic psychology and behavioural finance*. London, UK: IPPR. Retrieved from https://www.ippr.org/publicationsandreports/publications.asp?id=471

Elder, G. H. Jr., & Giele, J. Z. (Eds.) (2009). *The craft of life course research*. New York & London: Guilford.

Federal Deposit Insurance Corporation (FDIC). (2009). Alternative financial services: A primer. *FDIC Quarterly, 3*(1), 39–47. Retrieved from http://www.fdic.gov/bank/analytical/quarterly/2009_vol3_1/FDIC140_QuarterlyVol3No1_AFS_FINAL.pdf

Fellowes, M. (2006). *From poverty, opportunity: Putting the market to work for lower income families*. Washington, DC: The Brookings Institution Metropolitan Policy Program. Retrieved from http://www.brookings.edu/~/media/Files/rc/reports/2006/07poverty_fellowes/20060718_PovOp.pdf

Fellowes, M., & Mabanta, M. (2008). *Banking on wealth: America's new retail banking infrastructure and its wealth-building potential*. Washington, DC: Brookings Institution, Metropolitan Policy Program.

Fernholz, T. (2010, June). Making bank. *The American Prospect, 21*(5), 21.

FINRA. (2009a). *Financial capability in the United States: National survey executive summary*. Retrieved from http://www.finrafoundation.org/web/groups/foundation/@foundation/documents/foundation/p120535.pdf

FINRA. (2009b). *Financial capability in the United States, Report on the National Survey Component of the National Financial Capability Study*. Retrieved from http://www.finrafoundation.org/web/groups/foundation/@foundation/documents/foundation/p120536.pdf

First Nations Development Institute and Center for Responsible Lending. (2008). *Borrowed time: Use of Refund Anticipation Loans among EITC filers in Native American communities*. Longmont, CO: First Nations Development Institute. Retrieved from http://www.responsiblelending.org/other-consumer-loans/refund-anticipation-loans/borrowed-time-rals-in-native-american-communities.pdf

Flores, G. M. (2011). *Analysis of reloadable prepaid cards in an environment of rising consumer banking fees*. Retrieved from http://bretton-woods.com/media/51f57d9869e66aa1ffff8159ffffd502.pdf

Fox, J. E. (2009). *Research findings illustrate the high risk of high-cost short-term loans for consumers*. Retrieved from http://www.paydayloaninfo.org/elements/www.paydayloaninfo.org/File/CFA_Fringe_Loan_Product_Harm_Research.pdf

Fox, J. J., Bartholomae, S., & Lee, J. (2005). Building the case for financial education. *Journal of Consumer Affairs, 39*, 195–214.

Friedline, T., Elliott, W., & Nam, I. (2011). Predicting savings in young adulthood: The role of adolescent savings. *Journal of the Society for Social Work and Research, 2*(1), 1–22.

Furnham, A. (1999). The saving and spending habits of young people. *Journal of Economic Psychology, 20*, 677–697.

Furnham, A., & Argyle, M. (1998). *The psychology of money*. London: Routledge.

Gittleman, M., & Wolff, E. N. (2004). Racial differences in patterns of wealth accumulation. *Journal of Human Resources, 39*(1), 193–227.

Godsted, D., & McCormick, M. H. (2007). *National K-12 financial literacy research overview* (Networks Financial Institute Report 2007-NFI-03). Retrieved from http://www.networksfinancialinstitute.org/Lists/Publication%20Library/Attachments/86/2007-NFI-03_Godsted-McCormick.pdf

Gross, K. (2005). Financial education: Panacea, palliative, or something worse?. *St. Louis University Public Law Review, 24*, 307–312.

Gutter, M. S., Garrison, S., & Copur, Z. (2010). Social learning opportunities and the financial behaviors of college students. *Family and Consumer Sciences Research Journal, 38*(4), 387–404.

Hathaway, I., & Khatiwada, S. (2007). *Do financial education programs work?* (Federal Reserve Bank of Cleveland Working Paper No. 08-03). Retrieved from http://www.clevelandfed.org/research/workpaper/2008/wp0803.pdf

Haynes-Bordas, R., Kiss, D. E., & Yilmazer, T. (2008) Effectiveness of financial education on financial management behavior and account usage: Evidence from a "Second Chance" program. *Journal of Family and Economic Issues, 29*(3), 362–390.

Hilgert, M. A., Hogarth, J. M., & Beverly, S. G. (2003). Household financial management: The connection between knowledge and behavior. *Federal Reserve Bulletin* (July), 309–322.

Hira, T. K. (1997). Financial attitudes, beliefs and behaviors. Differences by age. *Journal of Consumer Studies and Home Economics, 21*, 271–290.

Hirschman, A. O. (1970). *Exit, voice, and loyalty: Responses to decline in firms, organizations, and states*. Cambridge, MA: Harvard University Press.

Hogarth, J. (2006, November). *Financial education and economic development*. Paper presented at the G8 International Conference on Improving Financial Literacy, Moscow.

Hogarth, J. M., Anguelov, C. E., & Lee, J. (2005). Who has a bank account? Exploring changes over time, 1989–2001. *Journal of Family and Economic Issues, 26*(1), 7–30.

Holden, K., Kalish, C., Scheinholtz, L., Dietrich, D., & Novak, B. (2009). *Financial literacy programs targeted on pre-school children: Development and evaluation*. Retrieved from http://www.cunapfi.org/download/168_CUNA_Report_PHASE_ONE_FINAL_4-28-9.pdf

Hornburg, S. P. (2004). *Strengthening the case for homeownership counseling: Moving beyond "a little bit of knowledge."* Cambridge, MA: Harvard University, Joint Center for Housing Studies. Retrieved from http://www.jchs.harvard.edu/publications/homeownership/w04-12.pdf

Howard, C. (1999). *The hidden welfare state: Tax expenditures and social policy in the welfare state*. Princeton, NJ: Princeton University Press.

Huston, S. J. (2010). Measuring financial literacy. *Journal of Consumer Affairs*, *44*(2), 296–316.

Jackson, A. M., Ortega, D. V. S., Costle, E., Gaberlavage, G., Karp, N., Walters, N., & Vasallo V. (2010). *A portrait of older unbanked and underbanked consumers: Highlights of a national survey*. Washington, DC: AARP Public Policy Institute. Retrieved from http://assets.aarp.org/rgcenter/ppi/econ-sec/underbank-economic-full-092110.pdf

John, D. (1999). Consumer socialization of children: A retrospective look at twenty-five years of research. *Journal of Consumer Research*, *26*(3), 183–213.

Johnson, E., & Sherraden, M. S. (2007). From financial literacy to financial capability among youth. *Journal of Sociology and Social Welfare*, *34*(3), 119–145.

Jump$tart Coalition for Personal Financial Literacy. (2007). *National standards in K-12 personal finance education*. Washington, DC: Jump$tart Coalition. Retrieved from http://www.jumpstart.org/national-standards.html

Karger, H. (2005). *Shortchanged: Life and debt in the fringe economy*. San Francisco, CA: Berrett-Koehler.

Keister, L. A. (2000). Race and wealth inequality: The impact of racial differences in asset ownership on the distribution of household wealth. *Social Science Research*, *29*(4), 477–502.

Kempson, E., & Atkinson, A. (2009). *Measuring levels of financial literacy at an international level*. Mimeo. Paris: OECD.

Kempson, E., Atkinson, A., & Collard, S. (2006). *Saving for children: A baseline survey at the inception of the Child Trust Fund* (HM Revenue & Customs Research Report 18). London: HMRC.

Kempson, E., & Finney, A. (2009). *Saving in lower-income households: A review of the evidence*. Bristol: University of Bristol, Personal Finance Research Centre. Retrieved from http://www.bristol.ac.uk/geography/research/pfrc/themes/psa/lower-income-households.html

Kempson, E., Whyley, E., Caskey, J., & Collard, S. (2000). *In or out? Financial exclusion: A literature and research review*. London: UK Financial Services Authority. Retrieved from http://www.bris.ac.uk/geography/research/pfrc/themes/finexc/pfrc0002.pdf

Kim, J. Garman, E. T., & Sorhaindo, B. (2003). Relationships among credit counseling, clients' financial well-being, financial behaviors, financial stressor events, and health. *Financial Counseling and Planning*, *14*(2), 75–87.

Kondrat, M. E. (2002). Actor-centered social work re-visioning "person-in-environment" through a critical theory lens. *Social Work*, *47*(4), 435–448.

Leckie, N., Shek-Wai Hui, T., Tattrie, D., Robson, J., & Voyer, J. P. (2010). *Learning to save, saving to learn: LearnSave individual development accounts project*. Ottawa: Social Research and Demonstration Corporation. Retrieved from http://www.srdc.org/uploads/learnSave_final_EN.pdf

Lusardi, A. (2007, October 28). The importance of being financially literate. *Financial literacy and ignorance* [blog]. Retrieved from http://annalusardi.blogspot.com/2007/10/importance-of-being-financially.html

Lusardi, A. (2010, February 26). *Americans' financial capability*. Report prepared for the Financial Crisis Inquiry Commission. Retrieved from http://fcic-static.law.stanford.edu/cdn_media/fcic-testimony/2010-0226-Lusardi.pdf

Lusardi, A., Clark, R. L., Fox, J., Grable, J., & Taylor, E. (2010). *Promising learning strategies, interventions, and delivery methods in financial literacy education: What techniques, venues, tactics, mechanisms, etc., show the most promise to promote and achieve financial well-being?* Paper presented at the 2010 National Endowment for Financial Education Colloquium, Denver, CO.

Lusardi, A., & Mitchell, O.S. (2007). Baby boomer retirement security: The role of planning, financial literacy, and housing wealth. *Journal of Monetary Economics, 54*, 205–224.

Lusardi, A., Mitchell, O. S., & Curto, V. (2010). Financial literacy among the young: Evidence and implications for consumer policy. *Journal of Consumer Affairs, 44*(2), 358–380.

Lusardi, A., Schneider, D., & Tufano, P. (2011). *Financially fragile households: Evidence and implications* (NBER Working Paper 17072). Cambridge, MA: National Bureau of Economic Research.

Lusardi, A., & Tufano, P. (2009). *Debt literacy, financial experiences, and overindebtedness* (NBER Working Paper No. 14808). Cambridge, MA: National Bureau of Economic Research.

Lutheran Immigration and Refugee Services (LIRS). (2008). *Financial literacy for newcomers*. Retrieved from http://www.lirs.org

Lyons, A. C. (2005). Financial education and program evaluation: Challenges and potentials for financial professionals. *Journal of Personal Finance, 4*(4), 56–68.

Lyons, A. C., Chang, Y., & Scherpf, E. (2006). Translating financial education into behavior change for low-income populations. *Financial Counseling and Planning, 17*(2), 27–45.

Lyons, A. C., Palmer, L., Jayaratne, K. S. U., & Scherpf, E. (2006). Are we making the grade? A national overview of financial education and program evaluation. *Journal of Consumer Affairs, 40*(2), 208–235.

Lyons, A. C., & Scherpf, E. (2004). Moving from unbanked to banked: Evidence from the Money Smart Program. *Financial Services Review, 13*(3), 215–231.

Maital, S. (1982). *Minds, markets and money*. New York: Basic Books.

Mallach, A. (2001). *Home ownership education and counseling: Issues in research and definition*. Philadelphia: Federal Reserve Bank of Philadelphia. Retrieved from http://www.phil.frb.org/community-development/publications/discussion-papers/homeowner.pdf

Mandell, L. (2004). *Financial literacy: Are we improving? Results of the 2004 National Jump$tart Survey*. Washington, DC: Jumpstart Coalition.

Mandell, L. (2008). Financial literacy in high school. In Lusardi, A. (Ed.), *Overcoming the saving slump: How to increase the effectiveness of financial education and saving programs* (pp. 257–279). Chicago: University of Chicago Press.

Mandell, L., & Klein (2009). The impact of financial literacy education on subsequent financial behavior. *Journal of Financial Counseling and Planning, 20*(1), 15–24.

Mangan, B. (2010). *Advancing financial coaching for low-income populations: Midstream lessons from EARN* (EARN White Paper). San Francisco: EARN. Retrieved from http://www.earn.org/files/EARN_coaching_whitepaper_Mar_2010.pdf

Marshall, H. R., & Magruder, L. (1960). Relations between parent money education practices and children's knowledge and use of money. *Child Development, 31*(2), 253–284.

Martin, M. (2007). *A literature review on the effectiveness of financial education* (Working Paper 07-03). Richmond, VA: Federal Reserve of Richmond. Retrieved from http://www.richmondfed.org/publications/research/working_papers/2007/wp_07-3.cfm

Mas, I. (2008, October). Realizing the potential of branchless banking: Challenges ahead. *CGAP Focus Note*, Number 50.

Mas, I., & Mayer, C. (2011). *Savings as forward payments: Innovations on mobile money platforms* (Social Science Research Network Working Paper Series). Retrieved from http://ssrn.com/abstract=1825122

Matheny, K. (2011, September 1). Lottery ticket sales increase across country. *USA Today*. Retrieved from http://www.usatoday.com/money/economy/story/2011-09-01/Lottery-ticket-sales-increase-across-country/50222366/1

McCormick, M. H. (2008). *The effectiveness of youth financial education*. Washington, DC: New America Foundation. Retrieved from http://newamerica.net/publications/policy/effectiveness_youth_financial_Education_0

McGeer, B. (2007, May 31). Bankers hope a dollar saved is a customer earned. *American Banker*, p. 2A. Retrieved from http://www.brandkeys.com/news/press/053107.AB.Banks.pdf

McNeal, J. U. (1987). *Children as consumers: Insights and implications*. Lexington, MA: Lexington Books.

Mierzwa, E. (2007). Bank of America wants customers to keep their change. *Cascade*, 64. Retrieved from http://www.phil.frb.org/community-development/publications/cascade/64/08_bank-wants-customers-to-keep-their-change.cfm

Miller, R. A., Burhouse, S., Reynolds, L., & Sampson, A. G. (2010). A template for success: The FDIC's small-dollar loan pilot program. *FDIC Quarterly*, 4(2), 28–41. Retrieved from http://www.fdic.gov/bank/analytical/quarterly/2010_vol4_2/FDIC_Quarterly_Vol4No2_SmallDollar.pdf

Moffitt, T. E., Arseneault, L., Belsky, D., Dickson, N., Hancox, R. J., Harrington, H., … Caspi, A. (2011). A gradient of childhood self-control predicts health, wealth, and public safety. *Proceedings of the National Academy of Sciences*, 108(7), 2693–2698.

Monticone, C. (2010). How much does wealth matter in the acquisition of financial literacy? *Journal of Consumer Affairs*, 44(2), 403–422.

Mortgage Bankers Association. (2010). *National Delinquency Survey, 2009*. Washington, DC: Mortgage Bankers Association.

Moschis, G. P. (1985). The role of family communication in consumer socialization of children and adolescents. *Journal of Consumer Research*, 11, 898–913.

Mullainathan, S., & Shafir, E. (2009). Savings policy and decisionmaking in low-income households. In R. M. Blank & M. S. Barr (Eds.), *Insufficient funds: Savings, assets, credit, and banking among low-income households* (pp. 121–146). New York: Russell Sage Foundation.

Murray, T. S. (2011). *Financial literacy: A conceptual review*. Research paper prepared for the Task Force on Financial Literacy, Canada. Retrieved from http://www.financialliteracyincanada.com/documents/consultation-2/Murray-09-02-2011-eng.pdf

Nelson, D. V. (2007). *AARP bulletin poll on financial literacy*. Washington, DC: American Association of Retired Persons. Retrieved from http://www.aarp.org/money/budgeting-saving/info-2007/financial_literacy.html

NYC Department of Consumer Affairs. (2009, August). *The $aveNYC Account: Innovation in asset building* (Research Brief). Retrieved from http://www.nyc.gov/html/ofe/downloads/pdf/savenyc_research_brief2009.pdf

NYC Department of Consumer Affairs. (2010a). *Findings from the Citywide Financial Services Study*. Retrieved from http://www.nyc.gov/html/ofe/downloads/pdf/FinServicesStudy_022510.pdf

NYC Department of Consumer Affairs. (2010b). *FE Brief*. Retrieved from http://www.nyc.gov/html/ofe/downloads/pdf/fe_brief_june2010.pdf

NYC Department of Consumer Affairs. (2011, February). *Mayor Bloomberg and Consumer Affairs Commissioner Mintz celebrate the 10,000th Financial Empowerment Center client*. Retrieved from http://www.nyc.gov/html/ofe/html/news/news.shtml

Nussbaum, M. C. (2000). *Women and human development: The capabilities approach*. Cambridge: Cambridge University Press.

Nussbaum, M. C. (2011). *Creating capabilities: The human development approach*. Cambridge, MA: Belknap Press of Harvard University Press.

Oliver, M. L., & Shapiro, T. M. (1995). *Black wealth/White wealth: A new perspective on racial inequality*. New York: Routledge.

O'Neill, B. (2006). *IDA financial education: Quantitative and qualitative impacts*. Paper presented at the Eastern Family Economics and Resource Management Association. Retrieved from http://mrupured.myweb.uga.edu/conf/3.pdf

Organization for Economic Cooperation Development (OECD). (2005). *Improving financial literacy: Analysis of issues and policies*. Paris: Author.

Osili, U. O., & Paulson, A. (2006). *What can we learn about financial access from U.S. immigrants?* (WP 2006-25). Chicago: Federal Reserve Bank of Chicago. Retrieved from http://www.chicagofed.org/digital_assets/publications/working_papers/2006/wp2006_25.pdf

Otero, M. (2011, May 16). *Panel remarks on growth through innovation in Africa: Mobile financial services and financial inclusion*. Washington, DC: Brookings Institution. Retrieved from http://www.state.gov/g/163618.htm

Otto, A. (forthcoming). Saving in childhood and adolescence: Insights from developmental psychology. *Economics of Education Review*.

Pender, K. (2012, September 19). Funds match for kids' educational extras. San *Francisco Chronicle*. Retrieved from http://www.sfgate.com/business/networth/article/Funds-match-for-kids-educational-extras-3878706.php#page-1

Peng, T. M., Bartholomae, S., Fox, J. J., & Cravener, G., (2007). The impact of personal financial education delivered in high school and college courses. *Journal of Family and Economic Issues, 28*, 265–285.

Pew Health Group. (2010). *Unbanked by choice: A look at how low-income Los Angeles households manage the money they earn*. Washington, DC: Pew Health Group. Retrieved from www.pewtrust.org/safebanking

Phillips, L., & Stuhldreher, A. (2011). *Building better bank ons: Top 10 lessons from Bank on San Francisco*. Washington, DC: New America Foundation. Retrieved from http://newamerica.net/publications/policy/building_better_bank_ons

Pickens, P., Porteous, D., & Rotman, S. (2009). Banking the poor via G2P payments. *CGAP Focus Note, 58*. Washington, DC: CGAP & DFID.

Powell, W. W., & DiMaggio, P. J. (Eds.). (1991). *The new institutionalism in organizational analysis*. Chicago and London: University of Chicago Press.

Reddy, S. (2011, January 13). Tax refunds move to debit cards. *Wall Street Journal*.

Reynolds, J. R., & Pemberton, J. (2001). Rising college expectations among youth in the United States: A comparison of the 1979 and 1997 NLSY. *Journal of Human Resources, 36*(4), 703–726.

Rhine, S. L. W., Reeves, W., Castro, B., Wides, B., & Williams, J. L. (2009). School-based bank savings programs: Bringing financial education to students. *Community Development Insights*. Washington, DC: US Department of the Treasury, Comptroller of the Currency. Retrieved from http://www.occ.gov/static/community-affairs/insights/Insights-Schoolbasedbank.pdf

Romich, J., Gordon, S., & Waithaka, E. (2009). *A tool for getting by or getting ahead? Consumers' views on prepaid cards* (Policy Brief 9). Terre Haute: Indiana State University, Networks Financial Institute.

Russell, R., Brooks, R., & Nair, A. (2006). *Evaluation of the youth financial literacy trial program*. Melbourne, Australia: RMIT University.

Sanders, L., & Forman, B. (2010). *Going for growth: Promoting access to wealth building financial services in Massachusetts gateway cities* (Policy Brief). Retrieved from http://www.massinc.org/~/media/Files/Mass%20Inc/Research/Full%20Report%20PDF%20files/Going%20for%20Growth%20III.ashx

Santos, F. (2011, March 29). Giving money-management advice to those who need it most. *New York Times*, A16.

Scanlon, E., & Adams, D. (2009). Do assets affect well-being? Perceptions of youth in a matched savings program. *Journal of Social Service Research, 35,* 33–43.

Schneider, D. (2011). Wealth and the marital divide. *American Journal of Sociology, 117*(2), 627–667.

Schreiner, M., & Sherraden, M. (2007). *Can the poor save? Saving and asset building in Individual Development Accounts*. New Brunswick, NJ: Transaction.

Schuchardt, J., Hanna, S. D., Hira, T. K., Lyons, A. C., Palmer, L., & Xiao, J. J. (2009). Financial literacy and education research priorities. *Journal of Financial Counseling and Planning, 20*(1), 84–95.

Schwartz, N. D. (2011, February 23). Next teller, please (2.4 miles away). *New York Times*, B1, 4.

Seidman, E. (2008, February 13). *The Community Reinvestment Act: Thirty years of accomplishments, but challenges remain*. Testimony to the House Committee on Financial Services. Retrieved from http://archives.financialservices.house.gov/hearing110/ht021308.shtml

Seidman, L. S. (2001). Assets and the tax code. In T. M. Shapiro & E. N. Wolff (Eds.), *Assets for the poor: The benefits of spreading asset ownership* (pp. 324–356). New York: Russell Sage Foundation.

Sen, A. (1981). *Poverty and famines: An essay on entitlement and deprivation*. New York: Oxford University Press.

Sen, A. (1987). The standard of living: Lecture II, lives and capabilities. In G. Hawthorn (Ed.), *The standard of living* (pp. 20–38). Cambridge: Cambridge University Press.

Sen, A. (1999). *Development as freedom*. New York: Anchor Books.

Servon, L. J., & Kaestner, R. (2008). Consumer financial literacy and the impact of online banking on the financial behavior of lower-income bank customers. *Journal of Consumer Affairs, 42*(2), 271–305.

Sherraden, M. (1991). *Assets and the poor: A new American welfare policy*. Armonk, NY: M. E. Sharpe.

Sherraden, M. (2011). Asset-based social policy and financial services: Toward fairness and inclusion. In R. D. Plotnick et al. (Eds.), *Old assumptions, new realities: Economic security for working families in the 21st century* (pp. 125–149). New York: Russell Sage Foundation.

Sherraden, M., & Barr, M. S. (2005). Institutions and inclusion in saving policy. In N. Retsinas & E. Belsky (Eds.), *Building assets, building credit: Bridges and barriers to financial services in low-income communities* (pp. 286–315). Washington, DC: Brookings Institution Press.

Sherraden, M., Schreiner, M., & Beverly, S. (2003). Income, institutions, and saving performance in individual development accounts. *Economic Development Quarterly*, *17*(1), 95–112.

Sherraden, M. S., Johnson, L., Guo, B., & Elliott, W. (2010). Financial capability in children: Effects of participation in a school-based financial education and savings program. *Journal of Family and Economic Issues*, *32*, 1577–1584.

Sherraden, M. S., & McBride, A. M., with Beverly S. G. (2010). *Striving to save: Creating policies for financial security of low-income families*. Ann Arbor: University of Michigan Press.

Squires G. D., & Kubrin, C. E. (2006). *Privileged places: Race, residence, and the structure of opportunity*. Boulder, CO: Lynne Rienner.

Stacey, B. G. (1987). Economic socialization. In S. Long (Ed.), *Annual Review of Political Science*, *2*, 1–23.

Stegman, M. A. (1999). *Savings for the poor: The hidden benefits of electronic banking*. Washington, DC: Brookings Institution Press.

Stegman, M. A. (2001). Banking the unbanked: Untapped market opportunities for North Carolina's financial institutions. *Journal of the University of North Carolina School of Law and North Carolina Banking Institute*. Retrieved from http://ccc.unc.edu/documents/CC_BankingUnbankedNC.pdf

Stegman, M. A., Lobenhofer, J. S., & Quinterno, J. (2003). *The state of electronic benefit transfer (EBT)* (Working Paper). Chapel Hill: The University of North Carolina at Chapel Hill, Center for Community Capitalism. Retrieved from http://www.ccc.unc.edu/documents/cc_ebt2003.pdf

Stein, P., Randhawa, B., & Bilandzic, N. (2010). Toward universal access: Addressing the global challenge of financial inclusion. In S. Fardoust, Y. Kim, & C. Sepulveda (Eds.), *Postcrisis growth and development: A development agenda for the G-20* (pp. 439–502). Retrieved from http://siteresources.worldbank.org/DEC/Resources/PCGD_439-502.pdf

Stone, C., & Sledge, J. (2011). *Financial first encounters: An examination of the fractured financial landscape facing youth today*. Retrieved from http://cfsinnovation.com/publications/list/Research%20Papers

Stuhldreher, A. (2010, January 7). Credit unions launch a savings lottery, and everyone hits the jackpot. *Washington Post*.

Taylor, M., Jenkins, S., & Sacker, A. (2009). *Financial capability and wellbeing: Evidence from the BHPS* (Occasional Paper Series 34). London: The Financial Services Authority.

Tennyson, S. (2009). *Analyzing the role for a consumer financial protection agency* (Policy Brief 13). Terre Haute: Indiana State University, Networks Financial Institute.

Thaler, R. H., & Benartzi, S. (2004). Save More Tomorrow™: Using behavioral economics to increase employee saving. *Journal of Political Economy*, *112*(1), S164–187.

Thaler, R. H., & Sunstein, C. R. (2008). *Nudge: Improving decisions about health, wealth and happiness*. New Haven, CT, and London: Yale University Press.

Transact . (2009). Financial capability. *Transact: National forum for financial inclusion*. Retrieved from http://www.transact.org.uk/page.asp?section=248&sectionTitle=Financial+Capability

Tufano, P. (2009). Consumer finance. *Annual Review of Financial Economics*, *1*, 227–247.

Tufano, P., & Schneider, D. (2009). Using financial innovation to support savers: From coercion to excitement. In R. M. Blank & M. S. Barr (Eds.), *Insufficient funds: Savings, assets, credit, and banking among low-income households* (pp. 149–190). New York: Russell Sage Foundation.

Tufano, P., & Schneider, D. (2010). Supporting saving by low- and moderate-income families. *Focus*, *27*(10), 19–25.

Tversky, A., & Kahneman, D. (1986). Rational choice and the framing of decisions. In D. Kahneman & A. Tversky (Eds.), *Choices, values, and frames* (pp. 209–223). New York: Cambridge University Press and Russell Sage Foundation. (First published in 1986 in *Journal of Business*, *59*(4), 5251–5278.)

US Department of Treasury. (2006). *Taking ownership of the future: The national strategy for financial literacy*. Washington, DC: Financial Literacy and Education Commission.

US Department of Treasury. (2010, August 26). Financial education core competencies: Comment request. *Federal Register*, *75*, 165. Retrieved from http://www.scribd.com/doc/36534958/U-S-financial-Literacy-US-Dept-of-the-Treasury-FLEC-Core-Competencies-FRN

US Department of Treasury. (2011a, April). *Youth Subcommittee: Ideas for improving youth financial capability*. President's Advisory Council on Financial Capability. Retrieved from http://www.treasury.gov/resource-center/financial-education/Pages/April212011.aspx

US Department of Treasury. (2011b, November). *Why and how: Background report, Developing the 2011 National Strategy*. Retrieved from http://www.treasury.gov/resource-center/financial-education/Documents/National%20Startegy%20Background.pdf

Vexler, J., Rocchio, M., Salem, J., & Vélez, R. (2008). *Immigrant use of financial services and unmet needs: A survey of Mexican immigrants in Chicago*. Retrieved from http://www.appleseednetwork.org/Portals/0/Documents/Publications/Access%20to%20Financial%20Institutions%20and%20Use%20of%20Financial%20Services%20final.pdf

Walstad, W. B., Rebeck, K. M., & MacDonald, R. A. (2010). The effects of financial education on the financial knowledge of high school students. *Journal of Consumer Affairs*, *44*(2), 336–356.

Ward, S. (1974). Consumer socialization. *Journal of Consumer Research*, *1* (September), 1–14.

Wärneryd, K. E. (1999). *The psychology of saving: A study on economic psychology*. Cheltenham, UK: Elgar.

Warren, E., & Bar-Gill, O. (2008). Making credit safer. *University of Pennsylvania Law Review*, *1*, 1–101.

Webley, P., & Nyhus, E. K. (2006). Parents' influence on children's future orientation and saving. *Journal of Economic Psychology*, *27*, 140–164.

Wells, J. (2011). *An inclusive approach to financial products: Beyond financial inclusion: involving older people*. Retrieved from http://www.engagenetwork.co.uk/content/images/downloads/Beyond_Financial_Inclusion_report.pdf

Williams, T. (2007). Empowerment of whom and for what? Financial literacy education and the new regulation of consumer financial services. *Law and Policy*, *29*(2), 226–256.

Willis, L. (2008). Against financial literacy education. *Iowa Law Review*, *94*, 3–55. Retrieved from http://papers.ssrn.com/sol3/papers.cfm?abstract_id=1105384

Woo, B., Rademacher, I., & Meier, J. (2010). *Upside down: The $400 billion federal asset-building budget.* Washington, DC: Corporation for Enterprise Development & The Annie E. Casey Foundation. Retrieved from http://www.aecf.org/KnowledgeCenter/Publications.aspx?pubguid={6D62ACDE-6BAC-4000-A356-5185344AFC46}

Wu, C. C., & Fox, J. A., (2008). *Coming down: Fewer refund anticipating loans, lower prices from some providers, but quickie tax refund loans still burden the working poor.* Washington, DC: National Consumer Law Center and Consumer Federation of America. Retrieved from http://www.consumerfed.org/elements/www.consumerfed.org/file/finance/RAL_2008_Report_final.pdf

Xiao, J., Collins, M., Ford, M., Keller, P., Kim, J., & Robles, B. (2010). A review of financial behavior research: Implications for financial education. *Consortium on Implications of Research in Personal Finance*. Denver, CO: National Endowment for Financial Education, August.

Zelizer, V. A. (1994). *The social meaning of money: Pin money, paychecks, poor relief, and other currencies.* New York: Basic Books.

Zollman, J., & Collins, D. (2010). Financial capability and the poor: Are we missing the mark? *FSD Insights*. Nairobi, Kenya: FSD Kenya, CGAP, and Bankable Frontier Associates. Retrieved from http://www.fsdkenya.org/insights/11-01-12_FSD_Insights_Branchless_banking_issue_02.pdf

2

Social Workers and Financial Capability in the Profession's First Half-Century

PAUL H. STUART

During the post–World War II suburbanization of the United States, as families moved from the working class into the middle class, from cities to the suburbs, and from renting to owning homes, they incurred debt in a variety of new ways. These debts—incurred through home mortgages and time purchases of household appliances, furniture, and recreational goods and services—meant that the new middle-class lifestyle was "sustained by a heavy bet on the future—long-term mortgages for the home, the installment plan for the future" (Wilensky & Lebeaux, 1965, p. 113). For millions of families, middle-class incomes depended on two jobs and, often, overtime pay. In addition, the prosperity of the post–World War II era was unevenly distributed, and there were barriers to the social mobility that had at first appeared to be within the grasp of all.

As borrowers were encouraged to take on more debt than they could sustain, new problems and "new opportunities for service" arose, as detailed in *Industrial Society and Social Welfare* by Wilensky and Lebeaux (1965, p. 174). They cite an examination of the finances of 83 middle-income young suburban couples, who "prefer the high-interest installment plan to the free charge account[s]" often provided by stores. The couples "show colossal indifference to and ignorance of 12 and 18% interest rates of 'revolving credit plans' at the department store" (p. 175). In response to these trends, Wilensky and Lebeaux (1965) advocate that family service agencies should undertake "skilled, hard-headed advisement of clients in the purchase of homes and expensive commodities" for the "increasing numbers of people" experiencing "real problems."

Prescient as this observation seems today, the half-century following the publication of *Industrial Society and Social Welfare* saw only isolated attempts to incorporate building clients' financial capability into social work practice. In part, social work practice followed social policy. The New Frontier and Great Society programs of the 1960s focused on social services to prepare clients for the work force and political mobilization. After Richard Nixon's victory in the presidential election of 1968, job training programs and income supports became ascendant. Although social work practice theorists considered environmental modification a promising intervention, this has usually meant the social worker acting to modify the environment on behalf of the client rather than the social worker acting to help clients increase their financial capability.

In 1973, Richard M. Grinnell, Jr., called for a renewal of environmental modification by social caseworkers. His definition of environmental modification included "enriching the environment through provision of new stimuli, outlets, resources, and services" and "helping the individual make profitable use of these opportunities and inputs" (p. 219). While this definition would have been quite compatible with interventions designed to create institutions to promote increased financial capability, Grinnell did not include such interventions. Similarly, Kemp, Whittaker, and Tracy (1997) did not explicitly discuss building clients' financial capability in their otherwise excellent exposition of person-environment practice, an approach to social work practice.

Wilensky and Lebeaux (1965) presented the idea of social workers doing financial counseling as something new, a response to the unprecedented growth of the suburban middle class, fueled by industrial expansion. However, a glance at the history of social work practice suggests that social workers and their predecessors in state charities, private charity organizations, and settlement houses were heavily invested in building the financial capability of their clients in the Gilded Age and Progressive Era, through advice-giving, financial education, and the creation of new institutions for saving and borrowing. As Charlotte Towle observed in 1930, "In the long life of social work, one is aware of fluctuating emphases... Back and forth the pendulum swings [but] change does not necessarily imply growth; it may imply regression" (p. 341). This chapter will review social workers' concern with clients' financial capability in the profession's early history, explore the decline of professional concern for financial capability, and conclude with the importance of building client financial capability today.

SOCIAL WORK AND POVERTY

The interest of early social workers in financial capability originated from the mission of the emerging social work profession—the alleviation and prevention of poverty (Popple & Reid, 1999). Often expressing their goals in moralistic terms, early social workers attempted to build up the financial capability of families and neighborhoods in a society that was experiencing increasing disparities in wealth and income, even as the average wages of industrial workers were rising. Building financial capability, social workers believed, would secure the financial position of poor people, smoothing out the swings of good times and bad that seemed to characterize their clients' lives.

Social work as an occupation originated during a period of crisis in American society. Urbanization, immigration, and industrialization resulted in increasing and seemingly unbridgeable chasms between urban and rural people, between rich and poor, native-born and immigrants, and Protestants, Catholics, Christians, and Jews (Addams, 1893b). In a period of increasing crisis, social workers, like other progressives, attempted to heal the rifts in the society by providing practical advice (in Charity Organization Societies), by being good neighbors (in settlement houses), or by saving children (in nascent public and private child welfare agencies) (Stuart, 1999a). Unlike child welfare workers, charity organization and settlement workers regarded themselves as generalist practitioners—they engaged with clients or neighbors about a range of problems that the clients or neighbors were experiencing and attempted to resolve those problems. As was the case with child welfare workers, many of the problems encountered by charity organization and settlement workers resulted from poverty, so service to the poor, specifically finding ways to prevent poverty and bring the poor out of poverty, dominated professional discussions at the turn of the twentieth century.

Charity organization societies (COS) and settlement houses were established in most American cities between 1880 and 1910. Charity organization societies attempted to organize charitable giving, directing assistance to those found to be "truly needy" and studying the causes of poverty. Settlement house residents moved into immigrant neighborhoods, becoming neighbors of the poor; neighborliness would result, it was hoped, in bridging the gaps between social classes. As Jane Addams (1893a), put it, Hull House was started

> in the belief that the mere foothold of a house, easily accessible, ample in space, hospitable and tolerant in spirit, situated in the midst of the large foreign colonies which so easily isolate themselves in American cities, would be in itself a serviceable thing for Chicago. Hull House endeavors to make social intercourse express the growing sense of the economic unity of society (p. 27).

Both charity workers and settlement residents emphasized the development of financial capability. Settlement house residents helped organize the Women's Trade Union League in 1903 as a means to improve the working conditions and pay of women workers (Davis, 1964). Josephine Shaw Lowell, the secretary of the Charity Organization Society of the City of New York (NYCOS), argued that all workers needed a living wage, one that made it possible "to secure what they have learned to consider the necessaries of life" (Lowell, 1911b, p. 412). She enjoined friendly visitors

> to make special efforts to persuade the family to prepare for the future and to lay by for the idle time of the next year; [they] can then inculcate lessons in economy and in saving which may be the means of lifting the family permanently on to a higher level than they would ever have attained without [the visitors'] friendly encouragement (Lowell, 1911a, pp. 147–148).

Emphasizing thrift and savings, then, seemed a key to solving the problem of poverty. Poor people needed access to financial institutions.

Charity organizations promoted what we would call today the empowerment of the poor, as well as providing good advice and persuasion; Lowell argued that workers needed to organize labor unions to secure decent compensation. In 1890, she founded the New York Consumers' League, an organization that pressured employers to improve the wages and working conditions of women workers in New York City. Nine years later, Lowell and other members of the New York Consumers' League helped establish the National Consumers' League.

THRIFT AND SAVINGS

Thrift was a catchword of charity organizations; visitors were instructed to use their influence to guide families, and especially husbands, in the direction of savings and careful budgeting. Lowell (1884) outlined a variety of provident schemes that would "help people to help themselves" (p. 109). She pointed out that savings banks, by the 1880s "immense business enterprises," had been initiated in Europe during the eighteenth century as charitable enterprises, a way to help poor people manage their financial resources. In the United States, savings banks were established early in the nineteenth century, many of them by reformers. By the 1870s, savings banks held "between a quarter and a third of all the wealth in all the financial institutions in the country" (Wadhwani, 2006, pp. 126–127).

Mary Richmond, secretary of the Baltimore Charity Organization Society (COS), advised friendly visitors to develop habits of thrift among the poor. Thrift was not a "merely economic" virtue, but an indication of a person's optimism and self-commitment. Visitors could advocate thrift "for both economic and moral reasons" (Richmond, 1899, pp. 108, 110). In the 1880s and 1890s, charity organization societies created savings banks, small loan programs, and pawnshops for the poor as alternatives to commercial enterprises that often exploited or ignored the poor. Savings was a necessary aspect of thrift, according to Mary Willcox Brown (1899), who was to succeed Mary Richmond as secretary of the Baltimore COS. Savings institutions were essential; the savings bank was "educational because it shows an improvident class the need of foresight; a thriftless body the utility of being frugal. It is educational because it teaches men to be independent and trains children to recognize the power they have of accumulating a small capital" (p. 71).

Based on a successful experiment initiated by the Charity Organization Society of Newport, Rhode Island, in 1879, the Castleton Charity Organization Society, on New York's Staten Island, created a savings society for its clients in 1883. According to Anne Townsend Scribner (1887), of the Castleton COS, "The main objects gained… by the introduction of the Savings Society are two: first, the inculcation of thrift; and, second, the aid to friendly visitors which the society offers. To raise the needy above the need of relief is one of the first principles of the Charity Organization Societies. That the Savings Society is a wonderful aid in this work of helping the poor to help themselves has been proved beyond question by the society's work on Staten Island" (p. 144).

The savings plan was simple; volunteer collectors visited families weekly to collect a prearranged amount to be saved, providing a receipt for the deposit. Once deposited, the funds could be withdrawn at any time, as needed for emergencies or when the amount saved was enough for a major purchase. Like industrial life insurance policies that were marketed to the poor beginning in the 1870s, the savings plan provided a form of budgeting that enabled poor people to plan for the future (Stalson, 1942). The plan proved to be popular, even providing an *entrée* for friendly visitors to the homes of families "where entrance would be impossible on other than a business footing" (Scribner, 1887, p. 146). Soon other charity organizations on Staten Island joined in the project. The NYCOS established a "Penny Provident Fund," aimed largely at schoolchildren, in 1899. The fund provided savings stamps for persons who saved from one to fifty cents, and encouraged them to establish regular savings accounts when the savings amounted to $10 or more. Within a year, the fund had ten thousand depositors and deposits of over $3,600 (Cruce, 2001; "How to Save Pennies," 1890).

Reformers and self-help organizations continued to establish savings banks and other financial resources for the poor during the Progressive Era. The Independent Order of St. Luke, an African American self-help organization, established the Provident Savings Bank of Richmond, Virginia, in 1903. As a result, Maggie Lena Walker, the grand secretary-treasurer of the order, was the first woman to head a bank in the United States (Brown, 1989; Simmons, 1975).

Although they were criticized for their often amateurish approach to problems of urban poverty (Cummings, 1892), settlement houses, like charity organization societies, engaged in efforts to improve the financial capability of their neighbors. Settlement residents espoused a goal of "the protection and enhancement of working-class standards of living" (Woods & Kennedy, 1922, p. 200). In addition to their support for labor unions, settlement houses studied small loans taken by their neighbors and introduced savings plans and small loan enterprises (Report of the Social Settlement Committee, 1896). Some settlements also introduced cooperative ventures such as buying clubs to provide groceries, coal, and other necessities to neighbors at a reasonable cost. Residents of New York's Greenwich House were informed about the neighborhood's savings banks, postal savings offices, penny provident stamp stations, sources of loans, and laws regulating loans in New York State. "Trustworthy loan associations," residents were informed, were "unfortunately few in number" (Dinwiddie & Ferguson, 1913, p. 39). Many charged "all that the traffic will bear," in the words of Robert Treat Paine, a Boston philanthropist and treasurer of the Workingman's Loan Association (Paine, 1895, p. 15), even adding fees to excessive interest rates.

LOANS

Both COS workers and settlement house residents viewed themselves as generalists in social work; they encountered a variety of problems and developed solutions for them (Stuart, 1999a). The savings plans developed in the late nineteenth century were examples of responses to a perceived problem. When periods of unemployment increased the demand for credit, charity organization societies established remedial or provident loan associations, organizations that made "small loans at reasonable rates" (National Federation of Remedial Loan Associations, 1919, p. 33; for an example of a charity organization society that organized a remedial loan association, see Johnson, 1916). However, the extent of the financial problems encountered by clients suggested that more specialized action was necessary.

Most troubling was the increasing use of credit—both for immediate needs and for major purchases. In 1895, Joseph Lee reported that loan sharks, installment buying, and pawn shops were charging "from 36% to 100% per annum" interest on loans to poor people (p. 506). Chattel mortgages, loans on movable personal property such as household furniture, carried reported interest rates as high as 120% in Cambridge, Massachusetts (Birtwell, 1899). Improved regulation of small loans, particularly reducing interest rates and fees, seemed to be the solution, but most state laws delegated regulation of small loans to municipalities, complicating reform efforts. A survey of pawnshops in ten cities revealed effective annual interest rates of between 30% and 300% (Patterson, 1899).

In 1894, the NYCOS organized the Provident Loan Society of New York as a separate organization, with offices in the United Charities Building, headquarters for a number of charitable and philanthropic organizations, including the NYCOS. The purpose of the society was to "help people help themselves without loss of self-respect" by providing loans at reasonable interest rates to the neediest (Provident Loan Society, 1919, p. 21). The success of the Provident Loan Society resulted in the organization of similar "remedial loan" organizations in cities across the country and the organization of a national organization, the National Federation of Remedial Loan Associations (Ham, 1910).

Although the founding of the Provident Loan Society had "partially solved" the small loan problem in New York "for those who can borrow on the pledge of personal property," difficulties remained for people in need of small loans (Wassam, 1908, p. iv). The New York School of Philanthropy's Bureau of Social Research, which had been created as a result of a grant from the Russell Sage Foundation (RSF), conducted studies of salary lenders and the chattel loan business in 1908 and 1909. Clarence W. Wassam's *The Salary Loan Business in New York City* (1908) found that salary lending—loans secured by the borrower's future paycheck—was widespread, and lenders charged very high interest rates. Arthur H. Ham's *The Chattel Loan Business* (1909) described businesses in New York that loaned small amounts of money using personal property, such as household furniture, as collateral. Although a small number of loan associations started by philanthropic organizations were doing good work, Ham concluded that they did not provide effective competition; many chattel lenders continued to charge very high rates of interest, tacking on fees that made the effective interest rate even higher.

In 1909, RSF, the "center of intelligence of the charity organization movement" (Hammack, 1994), created a Remedial Loan Division to encourage the formation of remedial loan associations and to advocate for legislation to regulate small loan programs, with Ham as the director (Anderson, 2008). In addition to serving as the director of the RSF Remedial Loan Division, Ham served as a vice president of the New York Provident Loan Society. Ham and other reformers lobbied for legislation regulating small loan businesses that catered to the poor, and encouraged the formation of remedial loan associations in other cities. The foundation also supported the organization of a National Federation of Remedial Loan Associations, and Ham and representatives of local societies discussed the remedial loan movement at several National Conferences of Charities and Correction and at the New York Academy of Political Science in the 'teens. Ham was a member of a standing committee on remedial loans which planned several sessions at the 1910 National Conference (Organization of the Conference for 1910, 1909). By the 1920s, lobbying for regulatory legislation and monitoring the implementation of regulations were seen as professional responsibilities, in part because of the example of the remedial loan campaign (Bruno, 1923).

Over the next three decades, the Russell Sage Foundation was successful in setting up numerous remedial loan associations and credit unions and in securing regulatory legislation in 34 states, based on a model law, the Uniform Small Loan Law, drafted by Ham and his associates. Although the impetus for remedial loan associations and small loan regulation originated with the charity organization societies, social workers were not for the most part involved in the operation of the loan associations. The New York Provident Loan Society hired "a practical pawnbroker," a person with experience in the business, not a social worker, to manage its credit business when it was established in 1894 (Provident Loan Society, 1919). Although remedial loan societies were encouraged to cooperate with charity organization societies, specialization resulted in the separation of social workers from the activity.

The federal government reformed the national banking system with the enactment of the Federal Reserve Act of 1913 (38 Stat. 251), which established the Federal Reserve System. However, the Act regulated national banks and not small lenders, who usually operated on a local level (Mehrling, 2002). The Glass-Steagall Act of 1933 (48 Stat. 162) separated commercial banking and investment banking and created the Federal Deposit Insurance Corporation (FDIC), which insured bank deposits. As was the case with the Federal Reserve System, the FDIC did not regulate small lenders. Thus, reform efforts directed at small lenders focused on the state rather than the federal level (Kelso, 1948b).

THE FAMILY BUDGET

Much early research in social work focused on the cost of living and the budget necessary for a family to maintain an adequate standard of living. English studies, notably Charles Booth's *Life and Labour of the People of London* (1889–1903) and Seebohm Roundree's *Poverty: A Study of Town Life* (1901), inspired much of this work (Appelbaum, 1977; O'Connor, 2001). *Hull-House Maps and Papers* (Residents of Hull-House, 1895), which included data on the incomes and expenditures of people in Chicago's near West Side, provides an early example, as does W. E. B. DuBois's *The Philadelphia Negro* (1899). Margaret F. Byington's *Homestead: The Households of a Mill Town* (1910), a volume of the Pittsburgh Survey funded by the NYCOS, included data on workers' incomes and the cost of living. The first article published in the new social work research journal, the *Social Service Review*, was Leila Houghteling's "The Budget of the Unskilled Laborer" (1927a), a summary of her book-length study of Chicago workers, *The Income and Standard of Living of Unskilled Laborers in Chicago* (1927b). Houghteling, a former superintendent of the United Charities of Chicago's Haymarket district, earned one of the first doctorates awarded by the University of Chicago School of Social Service Administration and was a member of its faculty at the time of her death in 1927 ("Leila Houghteling," 1927).

In his review of estimates of the poverty line between 1904 and 1965, Gordon M. Fisher (1997) found that "much of the work on poverty lines and standard budgets during the first two decades of the twentieth century was done by social workers." As a result, studies of the poverty line were not mere "sociological investigation" but "constructive work" as Jane Addams put it: "using investigation as the basis of wide-ranging programs of community mobilization and action [and] using investigation as the basis of publicity" (O'Connor, 2001, p. 31).

Diana Karter Appelbaum (1977) analyzed studies of the poverty line completed from 1906 to the 1970s. She concluded that the theoretical family budgets on which the poverty line was based reflected arbitrary judgments as well as prevailing social values. Estimates of the poverty line "served the dual purposes of providing a definition of poverty... and of furnishing guidelines to social workers to help them decide how much aid a family needed to reach an adequate level" (p. 516).

Initially, social workers used family budgets to provide a guide to calculating the appropriate amount of assistance to be provided to a relief recipient (Goodyear, 1906). In time, budget studies came to have other uses as well. Data on the cost of living could provide guidance for reform efforts, as sociologist Robert C. Chapin (1910) told the National Conference of Charities and Correction. After comparing workers' wages in several industries to the cost of living, Chapin concluded that "it is difficult to believe that [these workers earn] a living wage, save for a single man" (p. 456).

In 1912, the National Conference's Committee on Standards of Living and Labor called for minimum wage commissions to be established in each large city to estimate the cost of living as the basis for a minimum wage. The committee's report would be endorsed by Progressive Party presidential candidate Theodore Roosevelt and would provide the domestic plank of the 1912 Progressive Party Platform (Stuart, 1999b). Committee member Florence Kelley (1912), general secretary of the National Consumers' League, which had been campaigning for minimum wage legislation since 1908, told the conference that

> insufficient wages underlie a vast proportion of the need for correctional and reformatory work. They entail upon the community child labor, tuberculosis, underfeeding, lack of refreshing sleep, and the consequent nervous breakdown. They underlie industrial employment of mothers, whose neglected children consequently fail in health and morals. The children in turn crowd the hospitals, dispensaries, juvenile courts, and custodial institutions

(p. 396). A minimum wage commission would study the cost of living in a city and recommend minimum wage rates based on their investigations (Lovejoy, 1912).

The Committee on Standards of Living and Labor had recommended minimum wage legislation affecting all workers, but the earliest minimum wage legislation in the United States provided for women workers only. In 1912, Massachusetts enacted the first minimum wage legislation, a weak bill that provided for a Commission that could make recommendations for minimum wages for women in particular industries (Berkowitz & McQuaid, 1988). However, Oregon first amended its constitution to permit minimum wage legislation for men and women, and then enacted minimum wage legislation that provided minimum wages for women. By 1913, seven states had enacted minimum wage laws and five additional states were studying the issue (Kelley, 1913).

The provision of mothers' pensions by both private and public agencies provided another use for the family budget. Caroline Goodyear (1906), a District Agent for the NYCOS, calculated a minimum budget for an "adequate standard of living" in New York City to guide decisions about the amount of pensions, ongoing as opposed to emergency relief, granted to families. This was to be the first of numerous studies of adequate family budgets. The New York Association for Improving the Condition of the Poor (AICP) calculated family budgets for recipients of its widow's pension program, usually in consultation with a dietitian and the mother (Matthews, 1914). A NYCOS report found that a family budget "helps family and social worker to plan ahead with reference to necessary expenditures rather than adjusting present expenditures simply to meet present needs" (Committee on Home Economics, 1919, p. 1).

As public mothers' pension programs were established, beginning in Illinois and Missouri in 1911, social workers in the new public entities administering the new public programs became engaged in estimating budget needs (Goodwin, 1997). Gertrude Vaile (1914), a graduate of the Chicago School of Civics and Philanthropy (now the University of Chicago School of Social Service Administration) and executive director of the Denver Board of Charities and Corrections, told the National Conference that

> the size of pension is another point needing careful consideration. We feel strongly that if a pension is to be granted at all it should be sufficient to exempt the family from the need of any other charitable relief and maintain a wholesome and dignified standard of living. Only on that basis can a family be expected to live as they should... The amount of the pension is determined by making a careful estimate of the necessary budget and subtracting from it what the family can provide from their own resources (p. 675).

As educational programs for the new profession of social work were established, budgeting and the social worker's role in using budgets with clients were topics for course work and for publications. For example, the Chicago School of

Civics and Philanthropy published *The Charity Visitor* (Sears, 1918). This "handbook for beginners" included advice for new social workers and a chapter on "Estimating a Family Budget" by Florence Nesbitt, a pioneer dietician and social worker. Nesbitt's chapter was also published separately by the Chicago Council of Social Agencies as *The Chicago Standard Budget* (Nesbitt, 1918a).

SOCIAL WORK AND HOME ECONOMICS

The association of social work with another nascent profession—home economics—supported the interest in family budgets. Although "the widest possible variation… will be found among the families that come under the social worker's care," Florence Nesbitt (1918b) observed,

> the need for certain educational work is practically universal. None of the mothers are familiar with the simple principles of nutrition which must be known by one who would make intelligent choice of foods. None possess such a knowledge of the comparative values of different foods, kinds of clothing, household materials and supplies, as will enable them to lay out their money to the best advantage. All need more or less instruction in dietetic standards and help in planning the family budget. (p. 26).

In a Children's Bureau study of mothers' pension administration in nine locations nationwide, Nesbitt (1923) found that the social workers "gave a great deal of instruction in diet, management of income, and care of health… they taught the mothers to keep expense accounts and to budget their incomes" (p. 34).

Nesbitt was "one of the best-known home economists in social service" ("Our Contributors," 1935, p. 690), and had a long career bridging the two professions. Beginning as a dietitian in the Cook County Mothers' Pension program, she spent most of her career in social work, becoming assistant general superintendent of the United Charities of Chicago by the 1930s. By the mid-1930s, the *Chicago Standard Budget*, revised several times since its appearance in 1918, was regarded as an authoritative source for estimating family needs (Douglas, 1935).

The American Home Economics Association had a Social Work Committee in the 1910s and early 1920s. The committee encouraged home economists to attend the National Conference of Social Work. At the 1917 National Conference, the committee sponsored a luncheon discussion of the relationship between home economics and social work (Winslow, 1917). The committee's chair, Emma Winslow, was on the faculty of Columbia University's Teachers College and a member of the NYCOS Committee on Home Economics. In 1919, the committee published Winslow's pamphlet, *Budget Planning in Social Case Work*.

In addition to Nesbitt and Winslow, Sophonisba Breckinridge, an instructor and head of the Research Department at the Chicago School of Civics and Philanthropy, taught in the Department of Household Administration at the University of Chicago and served as assistant dean of women from 1904 until 1920, when the Chicago School became the university's School of Social Service

Administration (SSA) and Breckinridge a full-time SSA faculty member. Marion Talbot, a pioneer in home economics, a mentor to Breckinridge, headed the Department of Household Administration and served as Dean of Women at the University of Chicago during those years.

Much of home economics was practiced in the public schools, through classes in cooking, textiles, and child care; however, many home economists realized "the large scope of the field and the fact that it could not all be reached through the school" (Mid-winter meeting, 1921, p. 10). Although Nesbitt and Winslow remained active in social work circles during the 1920s, and Breckinridge was an important figure in the social work profession during the 1920s and 1930s, interest in interprofessional collaboration faded during the decade. Social work entered a period of expansion, with the establishment of new professional schools, the expansion of state-supported social and health services for children, and an increasing professional self-consciousness.

Homemaker services were provided by some private social agencies in the 1920s and in state public assistance programs established by the Social Security Act of 1935, sometimes under the supervision of home economists. As in the Mothers' Pension and private family welfare programs of the 1920s, social workers provided social services to beneficiaries of the public assistance programs established by the Social Security Act. Although caseloads were often very large, many social workers in public assistance provided financial advice to their clients. In addition, the Works Progress Administration provided a Housekeeping Aides Program for unemployed women in the 1930s and early 1940s. Nonprofessionals who had been trained by home economists and social workers provided housekeeping services on a temporary basis to families in need of them, usually because of the mother's illness (Morlock, 1942). However, although the homemakers provided some instruction in household management, including budgeting, the focus of most homemaker programs was on providing substitute services when the mother was away from home (Brewster, 1965).

PROFESSION-BUILDING AND SOCIAL MOVEMENTS

In part, the decline of interest in home economics—and in building clients' financial capability generally—may have been an unintended consequence of increased specialization in social work, and the directions that specialization took (Stuart, 1999a). Even by 1910, it seemed that there were too many social movements, each focused exclusively on a particular goal. In that year, Mary E. Richmond, the chairperson of the National Conference's Committee on Families and Neighborhoods, convened a conference session on "The Inter-Relation of Social Movements." Richmond observed that "more social movements, national in scope, have been organized during the last ten years than the sum of all the movements organized before that date and still surviving" (Richmond, 1910, p. 212). The result of this proliferation had been confusion—although many of the national movements had been initiated by settlement houses or charity organization societies, the average worker felt estranged from the movement and had difficulty relating to it.

At the session, Howard S. Braucher, of the Playground Association of America; Owen R. Lovejoy, of the national anti-child-labor movement; Lawrence Veiller, of the National Housing Association; and Alexander M. Wilson, of the National Association for the Prevention of Tuberculosis outlined their organizations' campaigns and solicited social worker participation. Richmond (1910) addressed three pleas to the national organizations: (1) to relate the national movements to the work of the charity organization societies and the settlements, (2) to recognize the rehabilitation of families and neighborhoods as necessary and important, and (3) to link the specialized goals together, not only with neighborhood and family workers but also with each other. Richmond recommended that the specialized social movements recognize the work of charity organization societies and settlement houses—family and neighborhood rehabilitation—as important in itself and as a potential ally in their more specialized campaigns. To do so, the specialists would need to make their campaigns intelligible to generalists, in particular charity and settlement workers.

However, fragmentation characterized reform campaigns in the 1920s. As had happened with the provident loan movement, reform campaigns focused on achieving limited goals in a difficult policy environment. Both charity work and settlement work became more specialized during the decade. Settlement houses focused increasingly on recreation and adult education (Stuart, 1990). Charity work became family case work, ironically as a result of Richmond's prodding. She led an RSF effort to create a national organization of charity organization societies, which became the American Association for Organizing Family Social Work in 1919 and the Family Welfare Association of America in 1930. Family social workers became increasingly interested in psychological aspects of casework and in 1930, two years after Richmond's death, labor activist A. J. Muste complained that family agencies, the successors to the COS, "have gone psychiatric in a world which has gone industrial" (Stuart, 1999a, p. 51).

Some social workers continued to be concerned with financial capability. Robert W. Kelso, a leading social work administrator in the 1920s and 1930s, who became the first director of the University of Michigan's social work program in 1935, published a monograph on the small loan business in the United States in 1948. After tracing the history of remedial loans and efforts to regulate the small loan business, Kelso offered an optimistic assessment of the social responsibility of small loan businesses:

Today, under the protection of [regulatory] statutes, a legitimate business can set itself up as a genuine banker for the low-income family, making a decent profit, sufficient to encourage capital to remain in the business of selling credit. At the same time the necessitous borrower can seek a loan, however small, with full knowledge of what he has to pay back, and certainty that sharp practice will not force him to pay more for credit than a legally defined and predetermined amount (Kelso, 1948a, pp. 42–43).

Another social worker, Helen Hall, the headworker of Henry Street Settlement in New York, was engaged throughout her career in consumer affairs. She chaired the

National Federation of Settlements committee that commissioned a study of unemployment in 1928, on the eve of the Great Depression (Andrews, 1997). During the 1930s, she served as consumer representative on the New York State Milk Advisory Committee and was a founder of the Consumers' National Federation. She was a board member of Consumer's Union in the 1950s. With two other settlement houses, Henry Street Settlement sponsored a study of consumer and credit practices of low-income people, which became sociologist David Caplovitz's *The Poor Pay More* (1963). In contrast to Kelso's optimistic conclusions fifteen years earlier, Caplovitz found that the cost of credit for poor people was far higher than for the middle class. In an address to the National Conference of Social Work in 1966, Assistant Secretary of Labor Esther Peterson cited Caplovitz and called for new regulatory legislation "on this whole complex of consumer credit and contracts," echoing presentations at the conference a half-century earlier (Peterson, 1966, p. 50). However, when Caplovitz left academic research in the 1980s, he became a bankruptcy lawyer rather than a social worker (Reifner, 1992).

Gordon Fisher (1997) has observed that, while social work was the primary profession involved in the construction of family budgets during the Progressive Era and the 1920s, economists became dominant after World War II. In 1948, the Bureau of Labor Statistics (BLS) unveiled "the city worker's family budget," developed by economist Dorothy S. Brady of the BLS and an advisory committee chaired by economist Hazel Kyrk of the University of Chicago. The committee included "experts in the fields of consumption economics, standards of living, and labor economics" but not social work (Brady, 1948, p. 312). The city worker's family budget, which would be revised periodically by the BLS and which would inform estimates of the poverty line in the 1960s, would provide "a modest but adequate standard of living" (Kellogg & Brady, 1948, p. 133).

CONCLUSION

Social workers withdrew from improving the financial capability of clients as other, more expert, professions took up the task. Now, more than half a century after other professions and groups took responsibility, there is little or no professional assistance available to clients, providing an opportunity and a challenge to the profession. Interest in building clients' financial capability may be growing as larger numbers of people are affected by problems resulting from financial illiteracy and excessive interest rates. The winner of the 2009 Influencing State Policy contest for BSW students and her faculty mentor, for example, worked on a successful statewide campaign to regulate the interest rates charged by payday lenders in Ohio (Influencing State Policy, 2010).

The times seem right for a revival of interest in increasing the financial capability of social workers' clients. The "mortgage meltdown" of 2008 illustrated the problem of overextended borrowing. But this is only a part of the problem. Wilensky and Lebeaux's warning in 1958 that middle- and lower middle-class people were in danger of overborrowing seems prescient. Today, payday loans, credit card debt, and other forms of installment debt endanger consumers

(Longman & Boshara, 2009; Stegman, 2007). In the past, social work's genius was its willingness to confront the real problems encountered by people, their clients and neighbors. Today, social workers must again develop interventions that will increase the financial capability of the many people who are trapped by the ongoing economic crisis.

REFERENCES

Addams, J. (1893a). The objective value of a social settlement. In H. C. Adams (Ed.), *Philanthropy and social progress* (pp. 27–56). New York: Thomas Y. Cromwell.

Addams, J. (1893b). The subjective necessity for social settlements. In H. C. Adams (Ed.), *Philanthropy and social progress* (pp. 1–26). New York: Thomas Y. Cromwell.

Anderson, E. (2008). Experts, ideas, and policy change: The Russell Sage Foundation and small loan reform, 1909–1941. *Theory and Society, 37*, 271–310.

Andrews, J. (1997). Helen Hall and the Settlement House Movement's response to unemployment. *Journal of Community Practice, 4*(2), 65–75.

Appelbaum, D. K. (1977). The level of the poverty line: A historical survey. *Social Service Review, 51*, 514–523.

Berkowitz, E., & McQuaid, K. (1988). *Creating the welfare state: The political economy of twentieth-century reform* (2nd ed.). New York: Praeger.

Birtwell, M. L. (1899). Chattel mortgages. *Proceedings of the National Conference of Charities and Correction, 26*, 296–305.

Brady, D. S. (1948). The city worker's family budget. *Proceedings of the National Conference of Social Work, 75*, 310–316.

Braucher, H. S. (1910). The social worker and the Playground Association of America. *Proceedings of the National Conference of Charities and Correction, 37*, 219–222.

Brewster, B. M. (1965). Extending the range of child welfare services. *Children, 12*(4), 145–150.

Brown, E. B. (1989). Womanist consciousness: Maggie Lena Walker and the Independent Order of St. Luke. *Signs, 14*, 610–633.

Brown, M. W. (1899). *The development of thrift*. New York: Macmillan.

Bruno, F. J. (1923). The co-operation of social workers with public officials in the enforcement of law—from the point of view of social workers with private agencies. *Proceedings of the National Conference of Charities and Correction, 50*, 327–333.

Byington, M. (1910). *Homestead: The households of a mill town*. New York: Charities Publication Committee.

Caplovitz, D. (1963). *The poor pay more: Consumer practices of low-income families*. New York: Free Press.

Chapin, R. C. (1910). Present wages and the cost of living. *Proceedings of the National Conference of Charities and Correction, 37*, 449–457.

Committee on Home Economics, Charity Organization Society of the City of New York. (1919). *Budget planning in social case work* (COS Bulletin No. 3). New York: Charity Organization Society of the City of New York.

Cummings, E. (1892). University settlements. *Quarterly Journal of Economics, 6*(3), 257–279.

Cruce, A. (2001). *A history of progressive-era school savings banking 1870 to 1930* (CSD Working Paper 01-3). St. Louis, MO: Washington University, Center for Social Development.

Davis, A. F. (1964). The women's trade union league: Origins and organization. *Labor History, 5*(1), 3–17.

Dinwiddie, E. W., & Ferguson, M. (1913). *The social worker's handbook* (Greenwich House Publications, No. 5). New York: Greenwich House.

Douglas, P. H. (1935). Social-work policies and collective bargaining. *Proceedings of the National Conference of Social Work, 62*, 525–534.

DuBois, W. E. B. (1899). *The Philadelphia Negro: A social study.* New York: Oxford Univesity Press, 2007.

Fisher, G. M. (1997). *An overview of (unofficial) poverty lines in the United States from 1904 to 1965.* Retrieved September 30, 2011, from http://www.census.gov/hhes/povmeas/publications/povthres/fisher4.html.

Goodyear, C. (1906). A study of the minimum practicable cost of an adequate standard of living in New York City. *Proceedings of the New York State Conference of Charities and Correction, 7*, 40–53.

Goodwin, J. L. (1997). *Gender and the politics of welfare reform: Mothers' pensions in Chicago, 1911–1929.* Chicago: University of Chicago Press.

Grinnell, R. M., Jr. (1973). Environmental modification: Casework's concern or casework's neglect? *Social Service Review, 47*, 208–220.

Ham, A. E. (1909). *The chattel loan business.* A report prepared under the direction of the Bureau of Social Research, New York School of Philanthropy. New York: Charities Publication Committee.

Ham, A. E. (1910). A year's progress in remedial loan work. *Proceedings of the National Conference of Charities and Correction, 37*, 487–493.

Hammack, D. C. (1994). A center of intelligence for the charity organization movement: The foundation's early years. In D. C. Hammack & S. Wheeler, *Social Science in the Making: Essays on the Russell Sage Foundation, 1907–1972* (pp. 1–34). New York: Russell Sage Foundation.

Houghteling, L. (1927a). The budget of the unskilled laborer. *Social Service Review, 1*, 1–35.

Houghteling, L. (1927b). *The income and standard of living of unskilled laborers in Chicago.* Chicago: University of Chicago Press.

How to save pennies. (1890, March). *Current Literature, 4*(3), 231–233.

Influencing State Policy. (2010). *Winners in ISP contests.* Retrieved September 30, 2011, from http://www.statepolicy.org.

Johnson, F. R. (1916). The case worker's contact with unemployment. *Proceedings of the National Conference of Charities and Correction, 43*, 199–204.

Kelley, F. (1912). Minimum wage board. *Proceedings of the National Conference of Charities and Correction, 39*, 395–403.

Kelley, F. (1913). The present state of minimum wage legislation. *Proceedings of the National Conference of Charities and Correction, 40*, 229–234.

Kellogg, L. S., & Brady, D. S. (1948). The city worker's family budget. *Monthly Labor Review, 62*(2), 133–170.

Kelso, R. W. (1948a). *Social background of the small loan business in the United States.* Ann Arbor: University of Michigan Press.

Kelso, R. W. (1948b). Social implications of the small loan business in the United States. *Modern Law Review, 11*(2), 143–149.

Kemp, S. P., Whittaker, J. K., & Tracy, E. M. (1997). *Person-environment practice: The social ecology of interpersonal helping.* New York: Aldine de Gruyter.

Lee, J. (1895). Evils growing out of extortionate usury. *Proceedings of the National Conference of Charities and Correction, 22*, 506–508.

Leila Houghteling (1889–1927). (1927). *Social Service Review, 1*, 148.

Longman, P., & Boshara, R. (2009). *The next Progressive era: A blueprint for broad prosperity*. Sausalito, CA: Polipoint Press.

Lovejoy, O. R. (1910). The national child labor movement. *Proceedings of the National Conference of Charities and Correction, 37*, 232–236.

Lovejoy, O. R. (1912). Standards of living and labor: Report of the committee. *Proceedings of the National Conference of Charities and Correction, 39*, 376–394.

Lowell, J. S. (1884). *Public relief and private charity*. New York: G. P. Putnam's Sons. Available at http://www.archive.org/details/publicreliefpriv00loweuoft

Lowell, J. S. (1911a). Duties of friendly visitors. In W. R. Stewart, *The philanthropic work of Josephine Shaw Lowell* (pp. 142–150). New York: Macmillan. (Original work published in 1883.)

Lowell, J. S. (1911b). The living wage. In W. R. Stewart, *The philanthropic work of Josephine Shaw Lowell* (pp. 109–415). New York: Macmillan. (Original work published in 1898.)

Matthews, W. H. (1914, June 6). Widows' families, pensioned and otherwise. *The Survey, 32*, 270–275.

Mehrling, P. (2002). Economists and the Fed: Beginnings. *Journal of Economic Perspectives, 16*, 207–218.

Mid-winter meeting. (1921). *Bulletin of the American Home Economics Association, 7*(1), 3–20.

Morlock, M. (1942). Supervised homemaker service. *Journal of Home Economics, 34*, 77–80.

National Federation of Remedial Loan Associations. (1919). Constitution. In *Eleventh Annual Convention of the National Federation of Remedial Loan Associations* (p. 33). National Federation of Remedial Loan Associations.

Nesbitt, F. (1918a). *The Chicago standard budget*. Chicago: Chicago Council of Social Agencies.

Nesbitt, F. (1918b). *Household management*. Social Work Series. New York: Russell Sage Foundation.

Nesbitt, F. (1923). *Standards of public aid to children in their own homes* (Children's Bureau Publication No. 118). Washington, DC: US Government Printing Office.

O' Connor, A. (2001). *Poverty knowledge: Social science, social policy, and the poor in twentieth-century U. S. history*. Princeton, NJ: Princeton University Press.

Organization of the Conference for 1910. (1909). *Proceedings of the National Conference of Charities and Correction, 36*, 590.

Our contributors. (1935). *Journal of Home Economics, 27*, 690.

Paine, R. T. (1895). The empire of charity (President's address). *Proceedings of the National Conference of Charities and Correction, 22*, 1–15.

Patterson, W. R. (1899). Pawn-shops. *Proceedings of the National Conference of Charities and Correction, 26*, 305–311.

Peterson, E. (1966). Labor standards and consumer protection. *The Social Welfare Forum, 1966: Official Proceedings of the National Conference on Social Welfare, 93*, 40–51.

Popple, P., & Reid, P. N. (1999). A profession for the poor? A history of social work in the United States. In G. R. Lowe & P. Nelson Reid, (Eds.), *The professionalization *of poverty: Social work and the poor in the twentieth century* (pp. 9–28). New York: Aldine de Gruyter.

Provident Loan Society. (1919). *The Provident Loan Society of New York, Twenty-fifth anniversary, 1894–1919.* New York: Author.

Reifner, U. (1992). The difficulties of conducting social research with a moral commitment: In memory of David Caplovitz. *Journal of Consumer Policy, 15*(4), 463–467.

Report of the Social Settlement Committee. (1896). *Proceedings of the National Conference of Charities and Correction, 23*, 166–175.

Residents of Hull-House. (1895). *Hull-House Maps and Papers: A Presentation of Nationalities and Wages in a Congested District of Chicago.* New York: Thomas Y. Crowell & Company.

Richmond, M. E. (1899). *Friendly visiting among the poor: A handbook for charity workers.* New York: Macmillan.

Richmond, M. E. (1910). The inter-relation of social movements: Report of the Committee on Families and Neighborhoods. *Proceedings of the National Conference of Charities and Correction, 37*, 212–218.

Scribner, A. T. (1887). The savings society. *Proceedings of the National Conference of Charities and Correction, 14*, 143–149.

Sears, A. (1918). *The charity visitor: A handbook for beginners* (3rd ed.). Chicago: Chicago School of Civics and Philanthropy.

Simmons, C. W. (1975). Maggie Lena Walker and the Consolidated Bank and Trust Company. *Negro History Bulletin, 38*, 345–349.

Stalson, J. O. (1942). *Marketing life insurance: Its history in America.* Cambridge, MA: Harvard University Press.

Stegman, M. A. (2007). Payday lending. *Journal of Economic Perspectives, 21*, 169–190.

Stuart, P. H. (1990). Settlement houses: Changing sources of innovation in social work. In H. H. Weisman (Ed.), *Serious play: Creativity and innovation in social work* (pp. 198–208). Silver Spring, MD: National Association of Social Workers.

Stuart, P. H. (1999a). "In a world gone industrial": Specialization and the search for social work practice above the poverty line. In G. R. Lowe & P. Nelson Reid, (Eds.), *The professionalization of poverty: Social work and the poor in the twentieth century* (pp. 51–61). New York: Aldine de Gruyter.

Stuart, P. H. (1999b). Linking clients and policy: Social work's distinctive contribution. *Social Work, 44*(4), 335–347.

Towle, C. (1930). Changes in the philosophy of social work. *Mental Hygiene, 14*, 341–368.

Vaile, G. (1914, February 28). Administering mothers' pensions in Denver. *The Survey, 31*, 673–675.

Veiller, L. (1910). The National Housing Association. *Proceedings of the National Conference of Charities and Correction, 37*, 222–227.

Wadhwani, R. D. (2006). Protecting small savers: The political economy of economic security. *Journal of Policy History, 18*(1), 126–144.

Wassam, C. W. (1908). *The salary loan business in New York City.* A report prepared under the Direction of the Bureau of Social Research, New York School of Philanthropy. New York: Charities Publication Committee.

Wilensky, H. L., & Lebeaux, C. N. (1965). *Industrial society and social welfare: The impact of industrialization on the supply and organization of social welfare services in the*

United States (paperback ed., with new introduction by H. L. Wilensky). New York: Free Press. (Original work published in 1958.)

Wilson, A. M. (1910). The National Association for the Prevention of Tuberculosis. *Proceedings of the National Conference of Charities and Correction, 37*, 227–232.

Winslow, E. A. (1917). National Conference of Charities and Corrections. *Journal of Home Economics, 9*(9), 411–414.

Winslow, E. A. (1919). *Budget planning in social case work* (Bulletin No. 3). New York: Committee on Home Economics, Charity Organization Society.

Woods, R. A., & Kennedy, A. J. (1922). *The settlement horizon: A national estimate.* New York: Russell Sage Foundation.

3

Paradigms of Anti-poverty Policy

DAVID STOESZ

By the beginning of the 21st century, American public policy had evolved divergent streams of revenues for low-income households. These income sources have become organized into networks of assistance—anti-poverty paradigms (Hall, 1993; Kuhn, 1970)—designed to address the circumstances of families in poverty. Three anti-poverty paradigms are discernable, each representing different welfare philosophies, operating under distinct organizational auspices, and instituting separate eligibility criteria: the Welfare Entitlement Paradigm, the Tax Credit Paradigm, and the Asset-Building Paradigm. Under these paradigms, disparate anti-poverty programs have evolved at cross-purposes to one another and provided uneven benefits to significant numbers of low-income Americans. The lack of coordination between various anti-poverty paradigms has often subverted governmental efforts to aid poor households, whose circumstances worsened due to static family income during the latter decades of the 20th century and were further eroded by the Great Recession that began in late 2007. Efforts of low-income households to address increasing expenses with diminishing income fueled an enormous fringe economy that charged extraordinary fees and interest, effectively subverting public welfare. The capability philosophy of Amartya Sen (2009) and Martha Nussbaum (2000) provides a unifying framework for addressing poverty that requires an anti-poverty paradigm congruent with the 21st century.

This chapter reviews the anti-poverty paradigms that evolved during the 20th century: the Welfare Entitlement Paradigm, the Tax Credit Paradigm, and the Asset-Building Paradigm. Each is described with respect to philosophical base, policy components, and relationship with other anti-poverty efforts. The implications of the burgeoning fringe economy and the Great Recession, and their relationship to the anti-poverty paradigms, are considered. The chapter concludes by proposing a Capability Paradigm that integrates previous anti-poverty efforts.

THE WELFARE ENTITLEMENT PARADIGM: ASSISTING THE UNEMPLOYED AND THE POOR

The Welfare Entitlement Paradigm is predicated on the belief that structural flaws inherent in capitalism require that government intervention through the welfare state is necessary to assist the poor. The state thus assures income for citizens who have marginal employment or who do not work (Beland, 2010). Early governmental anti-poverty programs were established through the Social Security Act of 1935, which created a public system for income redistribution outside the market economy (Gilbert, 1995, p. 129). Redistributing resources generated by advanced capitalism according to principles of equality or equity, the welfare state promised to assure a measure of social and economic justice for the disenfranchised.

During the post–World War II era, unprecedented economic growth provided governments with the resources necessary to subsidize the growth of the European and US welfare states. At its zenith in the 1960s, the Welfare Entitlement Paradigm was endorsed by welfare philosophers on both sides of the Atlantic. Wilensky and Lebeaux (1965) wrote that "under continuing industrialization all institutions will be oriented toward and evaluated in terms of social welfare aims. The 'welfare state' will become a 'welfare society'" (p. 127). British philosopher Richard Titmuss (1968) asserted that the welfare state would morph into a "welfare world" (p. 127). Speaking internationally, James Midgley (1998) summed up the consensus: "Most scholars believe that the modern welfare state represents the culmination of an inevitable and desirable process of social evolution" (p. 441). Income security, as a right of citizenship, was guaranteed by the welfare state for the poor through public assistance benefits.

The Welfare Entitlement Paradigm was established through the Social Security Act of 1935, the culmination of New Deal efforts to address the economic dislocation caused by the Great Depression. Built on Progressive faith in professional expertise and the capacity of government to ameliorate the circumstances of the immigrant and urban poor, the Social Security Act consolidated disparate state assistance programs to destitute families into one coherent framework under federal auspices. Structurally, the Social Security Act instituted two types of programs: social insurance for those in the labor force (Social Security and Unemployment Compensation) and public assistance for those presumed not to be employable (Aid to the Blind [AB], Aid to the Disabled [AD], Old Age Assistance [OAA], and Aid to Dependent Children [ADC]). In the ensuing decades, social insurance programs were more effective than public assistance benefits at abating poverty, largely because they provided benefits to a broader spectrum of Americans.

Despite its standing as the crown jewel of the American Welfare State, the Social Security Act would prove problematic for future programming. Harry Hopkins, New Deal architect and director of the Works Progress Administration, set up a national network of state agencies, rather than nongovernmental agencies, to disburse assistance. To appease southern members of Congress, the Social Security Act excluded domestic and agricultural workers from a federal pension, a provision that would assure the South of two decades of cheap labor that was overwhelmingly African American (Quadagno, 1994). The more generous provisions of social insurance programs, Social Security and Unemployment Insurance, favored male workers, while the public assistance program, ADC, provided inferior benefits to female dependents (Gordon, 1994; Skocpol, 1992). Federalism, through which states established eligibility criteria and benefit levels for public assistance programs that the federal government then subsidized, complicated the administration of aid to poor families. These features would fester into structural problems within the American welfare state. The exclusion of voluntary agencies left the nonprofit sector a subsidiary player in anti-poverty efforts. The denial of benefits to African Americans would worsen their economic circumstances, which were only partially rectified by the 1960s Great Society. The gender discrepancy between social insurance and public assistance programs became untenable as increasing numbers of mothers entered the labor market, contributing to calls for welfare reform. Finally, federalism contributed to a "welfare bureaucracy" whose "red tape" became synonymous with inefficiency (Van Oorschot, Opielka, & Pfau-Effinger, 2008).

The severity of destitution made public welfare a welcome addition to social policy. The expansion of government social programs helped reduce the number of poor households from 65% in 1940 to about 15% at century's end (Farley, 1996). Initially, OAA, AD, AB, and ADC articulated the Welfare Entitlement Paradigm, depending on states for a large portion of benefits as well as program administration. With the mid-1960s War on Poverty, these public assistance programs were augmented by Food Stamps, Medicaid, Head Start, and other anti-poverty initiatives. During this period, most states opted to include a parent's needs under ADC, and the program became Aid to *Families* with Dependent Children (AFDC). Abetted by the Welfare Rights Movement, class action suits pursued by legal services expanded eligibility for welfare, driving caseloads into the stratosphere (Haskins, 2006).

The welfare state evolved as federal and state government programs were enacted to assist Americans who suffered from insecurity due to poverty, unemployment, illness, disability, and discrimination. Programs under this paradigm are sited primarily within the federal Department of Health and Human Services and parallel state agencies. Eligibility requirements often mandated low income and low assets to obtain benefits, with frequent recertification. Examples of programs within the Welfare Entitlement Paradigm include Temporary Assistance for Needy Families (TANF), the Supplemental Nutrition Assistance Program (SNAP, formerly Food Stamps), Supplemental Security Income (SSI), and Medicaid. By 2004, the Welfare Entitlement Paradigm had justified the creation of 80 public assistance programs at a federal cost of $534 billion (House Ways and Means Committee, 2008).

During the 1970s, a large crack emerged in the Welfare Entitlement Paradigm (Stoesz, 2000). Many southern states resisted the expansion of public welfare and failed to increase benefits with inflation. As a result, the true value of public assistance for AFDC fell 50% during the last quarter of the 20th century. Rather than providing income security, the welfare entitlement was assuring about half of eligible families substandard benefits that gradually deteriorated in value. The Welfare

Entitlement Paradigm lost further momentum with the ascendance of conservatism during the 1980s. The rapid increase in welfare caseloads provided the context for a crescendo of criticism about welfare voiced by the Right. Neoliberals bridled at the perceived consequences of welfare: increasing out-of-wedlock pregnancies, high school drop-out rates, and rates of juvenile delinquency, and an oppositional culture by the minority poor (Novak, 1987). In 1965, Daniel Patrick Moynihan, a Department of Labor analyst, had penned a confidential analysis on what he termed "the Negro family" in which he attributed minority poverty not only to discrimination but also to deteriorating family structure. The failure of Black marriages, he argued, cast children onto welfare so often that Black children were seven times more likely to be on AFDC than White children (Moynihan, 1965). Conservative critics of welfare extended the neoliberal critique, claiming that the welfare entitlement contributed to behavioral poverty, subsidizing outcomes that were antisocial (Mead, 1986; Murray, 1984). The election of Ronald Reagan as president in 1980 resulted in sharp cuts in social welfare caseloads in 1981, although the 1988 Family Support Act, which instructed AFDC mothers to engage in education and job training or enter the labor market, produced disappointing results for conservatives.

In a period of conservative dominance of social policy, the Clinton presidency proved a brief interregnum, but even liberal analysts documented a stubborn degree of dependency on the part of welfare recipients. While 48% of new AFDC recipients were off the program within two years, 49% remained eligible longer than five years; at any given time, more than half of AFDC recipients had been receiving benefits for more than eight years (House Ways and Means Committee, 1996). Once Republicans gained control of Congress in 1994, Clinton conceded to conservatives by signing the Personal Responsibility and Work Opportunity Reconciliation Act (PRWORA) in 1996. PRWORA terminated the cash entitlement and installed a rigorous work program with time limits, which reduced caseloads by 60%, and thus halted the momentum of the Welfare Entitlement Paradigm (Haskins, 2006). Liberals noted that poverty remained largely unchanged even for welfare mothers in the labor market (Meyer & Cancian, 1998). One study found that between 18% and 30% of welfare mothers had a significant disability (Loprest & Acs, 1995). Another found that 37% of those who left returned to the program within one year and 50% within two (Meyer & Cancian, 1998).

A suitable replacement for the Welfare Entitlement Paradigm has yet to emerge, largely because public welfare has focused on income maintenance, and has arguably impeded the capability of low-income households. The eligibility requirements for public assistance programs, such as TANF, limit family resources to a range from about $1,000 to $3,000: minimally prosperous families, such as those with a dependable automobile needed for work, are ineligible for benefits. TANF's "work-first" strategy, through which recipients must take the first available job, discourages recipients from searching for optimal employment, and the practice of many states to disallow job training and education consigns many poor households to dead-end jobs. The federal 5-year time limit and even shorter state-imposed time limits discontinue benefits for families transitioning from welfare to work, a poignant problem for those who need training and education to secure well-paying jobs and for the poorest families that require long-term support (Lawinski, 2010; Ridzi, 2009). A decade after its inception, welfare reform achieved disparate outcomes: many welfare recipients were employed, yet eligible for other public assistance programs, such as SNAP and Medicaid; concurrently, the percentage of TANF-eligible families actually receiving benefits ("take-up rate") dropped from 84% in 1994 to 42% in 2003 (Department of Health and Human Services, 2007, p. 18), and most of the eligible not receiving benefits were children (Epstein, 2010).

The Welfare Entitlement Paradigm enjoyed wide support from the 1930s until the 1980s when conservative critiques successfully advanced welfare reform. Meanwhile, a different approach to poverty, the Tax Credit Paradigm, evolved through the tax system to specifically benefit low-income working families. The Tax Credit Paradigm grew rapidly during the latter decades of the 20th century, appealing to liberals and conservatives because it was predicated on rewarding work.

THE TAX CREDIT PARADIGM: REWARDING THE WORKING POOR

The Tax Credit Paradigm utilizes tax policy to allocate benefits by exempting specific activities from taxation, thus benefiting certain groups. A few tax expenditures generate payments to low-income families. In competition with the Welfare Entitlement Paradigm, the Tax Credit Paradigm originated in the late 19th and early 20th centuries, as corporations, such as American Express in 1875 and Standard Oil in 1903, made pensions available to workers: by 1930, 420 private pension plans had been established by industry (Jackson, 1977). The exemption of private pension plans from the income tax was enacted in 1913, validating "welfare capitalism" as a benefit to industrial society (Howard, 1997, p. 62). "Throughout the 1920s, then, large corporations continued to dominate the welfare field" (Berkowitz & McQuaid, 1980, p. 56). When wage and price controls during World War II hampered corporate recruiting, business began augmenting salaries with health care and other benefits, subsidies that were also exempt from taxation, laying the foundation for employer-based health care in the United States (Jacobs & Skocpol, 2010).

Welfare capitalism was based on neoclassical economic philosophy, the belief that markets were the optimal method for distributing resources with individuals behaving rationally in relation to prices as determined by supply and demand. Tax expenditures were used to benefit low-income workers through public policy beginning in the 1970s with the Earned Income Tax Credit (EITC), the result of President Nixon's failed attempt to enact a guaranteed annual income through the Family Assistance Plan (FAP). As conceived by Moynihan, then an advisor to Nixon, all public assistance programs could be consolidated under FAP, a federal program, intended to achieve significant efficiencies and reduce welfare stigma. FAP faltered when Senator Russell Long, then-chair of the Senate Finance Committee, refused to assure an income floor for welfare mothers while working families remained exposed to the vagaries of the labor market. Subsequently, OAA, AB, and AD were merged into Supplemental Security Income (SSI) and placed under the management of the Social Security Administration (Bowler, 1974). While Nixon abandoned a guaranteed annual income for the poor, Senator Long persevered, and the EITC became law in 1975, providing a tax refund for low-income working families (Bowler, 1974).

As a tax credit, the EITC was added to a lengthy list of benefits by virtue of exclusion from taxation. By excluding corporate pensions, health insurance coverage, and the interest on mortgages from taxation, the Internal Revenue Service annually provided hundreds of billions of dollars of benefits to millions of middle-class Americans. Significantly, such tax credits enjoyed broad bipartisan support, allowing Republicans and Democrats to show their allegiance to middle-class voters. As a refundable tax credit, however, the EITC paid a rebate to families whose income fell below a certain level (Holt, 2006). By the end of the 20th century, tax credits, several of which were also refundable, had been crafted to address specific concerns: the Welfare to Work Tax Credit, the Work Opportunity Tax Credit, the Child Tax Credit, the Low-Income Housing Tax Credit, and the Adoption Tax Credit, among others (House Ways and Means Committee, 2004). By 2005, 15 states complemented the federal EITC with state refundable tax credits for low-income families (Holt, 2006).

Refundable tax credits had several advantages. Foremost, the volume of revenues was significant: for example, the EITC benefited 22 million low-income families $41.2 billion in 2006, and the Child Tax Credit was projected to benefit 35 million families $52 billion in 2010 (Urban Institute, 2008). Moreover, tax credits were open-ended. Unlike welfare after PRWORA, which was capped at $16.5 billion annually, the amount refunded by tax credits was contingent on the number of eligible tax filers. Tax credits also avoided the welfare assets test: refunds were apportioned according to earned income, regardless of the tax filer's wealth. In 1986 the EITC was indexed for inflation, thus the value of refunds increased automatically, a provision that had not been affixed to AFDC/TANF. Finally, tax credits avoided the stigma of welfare. Instead of repeated visits to an impersonal welfare department to complete lengthy applications for public assistance, tax credits were accessed by filing a W-1040 electronically or by mail. An important indicator of the value of the tax credit paradigm is the take-up rate, which approximated 75%, far above the 50% typical of public assistance programs. Thirty years after enactment of the EITC, $205 billion in tax expenditures have benefited low-income families (Cramer, Rourke, Cooper, & Luengo-Prado, 2009).

Despite its virtues, the Tax Credit Paradigm was not without shortcomings. Because receipt of benefits requires participation in the tax system, families that do not file taxes are ineligible. Since benefits favor families with children, childless families receive less. Due to the complexity of the tax code, many families resort to commercial tax preparers to file returns and in order to access benefits immediately agree to Refund Anticipation Loans (RALs), which consume 6% of the value of the EITC. Many low-income households spend their refund at once rather than save a portion, and miss an opportunity to establish savings that could buffer them against future expense shocks (Holt, 2006).

While the Tax Credit Paradigm addressed several problems of the Welfare Entitlement Paradigm, it has failed to fully amplify the capabilities of low-income families. About three-fourths of tax credits actually benefit families earning over $50,000 annually, leaving much less for the poor (Cramer et al., 2009). Tax credits are specifically targeted and not well integrated and thus do not provide a firm platform from which low-income households can attain upward mobility. Qualification for tax credits requires participation in the tax system, a problem for immigrant households who may fear deportation. The interception of tax refunds for child support owed dissuades many poor working fathers from filing federal taxes. Others, including the poorest households, may be better off operating in the informal economy and not reporting taxable income at all. Finally, the failure of welfare departments to provide tax preparation services means that clients and workers resort to RALs through commercial tax preparers, effectively losing a portion of the tax refund to the commercial sector. Thus, the Tax Credit Paradigm has been significantly more beneficial for affluent families and corporations than low-income households.

The Tax Credit Paradigm expanded exponentially during the last decades of the 20th century. Like the Welfare Entitlement Paradigm, the Tax Credit Paradigm focused on cash benefits intended to boost the consumption of low-income families. By century's end, proponents of both of the consumption-oriented anti-poverty paradigms were confronted with a problem: despite increased appropriations, poverty endured. With increasing economic disparities between rich and poor, support grew for an anti-poverty approach that endeavored to accelerate the upward mobility of low-income households by encouraging them to accrue assets.

THE ASSET-BUILDING PARADIGM: ENCOURAGING THE POOR TO ACCRUE WEALTH

In contrast to the anti-poverty paradigms that encourage consumption, the Asset-Building Paradigm provides incentives for low-income households to save in order to acquire assets, and encourages economic development in low-income neighborhoods. The philosophical basis of the Asset-Building Paradigm is derived from neoclassical economics, which assumes "that individuals and households are focused on expected future income and long-term consumption patterns" (M. Sherraden, 2001, p. 310), although this has been modified by behavioral economics, which recognizes that people often make decisions that subvert their economic well-being (M. Sherraden, 2009). Thus, the behavioral factor is essential to the Asset-Building Paradigm:[1]

> People think and behave differently when they are accumulating assets, and the world responds to them differently as well. More specifically, assets improve economic stability; connect people with a viable, hopeful future;

stimulate development of human and other capital; enable people to focus and specialize; provide a foundation for risk taking; yield personal, social, and political dividends; and enhance the welfare of offspring. (M. Sherraden, 1991 p. 148)

Poor families struggle to reconcile meager resources with unpredictable expenses, but often lack the education and resources to make and implement optimal decisions; therefore, significant incentives are provided to induce them to make decisions that are more likely to enhance their long-term welfare. Individual development accounts (IDAs), for example, match savings, often on a 2:1 basis for first-time home purchase, postsecondary education, or business development. Just as poor families can develop strategies in order to prosper, so low-income communities can create a constructive economic infrastructure through community development (Rubin, 2007).

The Asset-Building Paradigm is embedded in a network of primarily private organizations committed to individual and community economic development. Over time this network has leveraged two modest federal initiatives: the Community Development Financial Institution (CDFI) Loan Fund, created in 1994, and the Assets for Independence Act of 1998, which encourages poor households to establish IDAs. Capitalizing on community-based research, the Asset-Building Paradigm has secured support from private foundations, such as the Ford Foundation, and promotion by policy organizations, such as the Center for Social Development at Washington University, the Corporation for Enterprise Development, and the New America Foundation. Organizations advocating the Asset-Building Paradigm typically work collaboratively regardless of their focus on families or communities, adding synergy to the movement (M. Sherraden, 2009).

In 1991, Michael Sherraden, a professor of social development at Washington University, published *Assets and the Poor*, in which he argued that most poor families become prosperous by accruing assets. Sherraden's conclusion complemented the research of scholars who had calculated that, since the 1970s, disparities in wealth were more pronounced than disparities in income. Tax policy contributes to wealth inequality because tax expenditures favor the wealthy. Over half of the $400 billion in 2009 tax expenditures went to the top 5% of taxpayers; the top quintile of taxpayers earning $80,000 or more in 2009 received 84% of tax benefits ($5,109 per taxpayer), while the bottom quintile earning $19,000 or less received only 0.04% of tax benefits ($5 per taxpayer) (Woo, Rademacher, & Meier, 2010).

Subsequently, the Asset-Building Paradigm proceeded along dual tracks; individual- and family-based initiatives and community development efforts. First, Sherraden's IDA proposal was evaluated through the American Dream Demonstration (ADD) research project. Between 1997 and 2001, thirteen community-based organizations helped establish 2,300 IDAs, with the average participant saving $16.60 per month (M. Sherraden, 2009). IDAs established through ADD helped account holders save an average of $700 annually (Corporation for Enterprise Development, 2010). Meanwhile, IDAs became the centerpiece of the 1998 Assets for Independence (AFI) Act of 1998. Subsequently, foundations funded a demonstration of Child Development Accounts (CDAs) through SEED, savings accounts that last from childhood into adulthood, the initial deposits of which are complemented by matching funds and financial education. By 2010, 1,171 children in twelve states had established CDAs. With an average deposit of $30 quarterly, the accounts accumulated an average savings of $1,500 over three years, an amount projected to reach $6,000 upon reaching age 18 (M. Sherraden & Stevens, 2010). In 2004, legislation to universalize CDAs was proposed through the America Saving for Personal Investment Retirement and Education Act (ASPIRE) (Cramer, Huelsman, King, Lopez-Fernandini, & Newville, 2010).

Second, a network of public and private community development organizations had embraced the Asset-Building Paradigm concept for communities. Arising from the ashes of the War on Poverty Community Action Programs and catalyzed by financial reform through the Community Reinvestment Act (CRA) of 1977, which required banks to make credit available to their entire service area, including to residents of low-income, minority neighborhoods, community development advocates from the Ford and Enterprise Foundations focused assistance on initiatives that were more entrepreneurial and self-sustaining than dependent on traditional grant assistance (Sandel, 1996; Siegel, 1997). Capitalization of low-income communities was supported by researchers: Michael Porter (1995) reported that even poor neighborhoods had tens of millions of dollars in capital that could be put to constructive use, while Paul Jargowsky (1997) computed that even the poorest urban neighborhoods received more than 70% of revenue from wages and salaries. Modeled after such innovations as Shorebank in Chicago, Self-Help in Durham, and the Alternatives Credit Union in Ithaca, the Riegle Community Development and Regulatory Improvement Act of 1994 established the CDFI Loan Fund to promote community-based economic development. By 2009, 798 Community Development Financial Institutions and 3,938 Community Development Entities had been established, accounting for 6,478 IDAs established at a value of $5.9 million (Community Development Financial Institution Loan Fund, 2010). For 2011, the CDFI Loan Fund planned to award $135 million in grants (Federal Register, 2010).

The Asset-Building Paradigm is comparatively new, having been codified in federal statute less than two decades, compared to seven for the Welfare Entitlement and three for the Tax Credit Paradigms; yet a network of advocacy organizations has evolved for its promotion. The CDFI Coalition and Opportunity Finance Network are trade associations advancing community economic development, while the Corporation for Enterprise Development and Washington University's Center for Social Development have facilitated the growth of asset strategies for individuals and their families with the New America Foundation providing a forum for seminars and distributing monographs on the value of asset strategies in social policy. Together these organizations have become a dynamic network for promoting the Asset-Building Paradigm. By 2010, forty states had established savings programs that advantaged low-income households (M. Sherraden & Stevens, 2010).

A striking difference between the Asset-Building Paradigm and other anti-poverty paradigms is that the former complements community economic development. Communities prosper as they aggregate capital and deploy institutions that put it to constructive use. Similarly, by emphasizing savings as opposed to consumption, the Asset-Building Paradigm encourages families to buffer themselves against future expense shocks by building assets that can be liquidated if necessary. Moreover, households that invest in assets, such as a home, business, or postsecondary education, are more likely to be upwardly mobile (Stoesz, 2005), particularly due to the positive intergenerational effects on wealth of asset ownership. The interplay between family asset building and community capitalization creates a dynamic that is mutually beneficial.

Advantages notwithstanding, the Asset-Building Paradigm has been of limited utility in abating poverty, although its proponents would be quick to point out that their target population is not only broader than those eligible for benefits through the Welfare Entitlement and Tax Credit paradigms, but their aspirations are qualitatively different as well: moving low-income families into the middle class. Compared to the tens of billions of dollars that are spent through the Welfare Entitlement and Tax Credit Paradigms, the Asset-Building Paradigm offers much less: $135 million for CDFIs and $24 million for IDAs in 2011. A secondary problem is its novelty; comparatively new as federal and state policies, both community- and family-based asset strategies struggle for credibility vis-à-vis other anti-poverty paradigms; therefore, during a recessionary period, less funding is available to expand the Asset-Building Paradigm. Most of the programs comprising the Welfare Entitlement Paradigm and the Tax Credit Paradigm are open-ended entitlements, while those of the Asset-Building Paradigm are discretionary, subject to alteration with each Congress (Karger & Stoesz, 2010).

The lack of familiarity with, or outright antagonism toward, capitalization to accelerate economic development violates conventional ideological presumptions of the liberal Left. The Asset-Building Paradigm requires a different, unfamiliar, and possibly suspect vocabulary for traditional advocates of economic justice who may be uncomfortable with using capitalism to address poverty. Structural impediments also restrict expansion of the Asset-Building Paradigm: programs of the Welfare Entitlement Paradigm either deny poor families the opportunity to build savings or view savings as disconnected from the proper purpose of welfare, which is income maintenance (Cramer et al., 2009). The Great Recession has also hampered expansion of the Asset-Building Paradigm: lost income due to unemployment causes poor families to empty savings, and the decline in government revenues reduces funding for community economic development and savings incentives.

THE FRINGE ECONOMY

The mismatch between anti-poverty paradigms, financial deregulation in the 1980s, and stagnant family income during the last decades of the 20th century provided a verdant environment for a fringe economy. Between 1979 and 2003, the Consumer Price Index (CPI), which measures the cost of a sample of goods consumed by urban Americans, averaged *increases* of 4.2% annually, yet the pre- as well as posttax income of the poorest 40% of families actually *fell* 3.6% and 3.8% respectively (Mishel, Bernstein, & Allegretto, 2007).[2] The CPI-income gap is poignant for poor households because a 1% reduction in the CPI nets low-income families an additional $6.5 billion in spending (Fellowes, 2008). For low-income families, the stress induced by the income/expense disconnect would have been about 10% worse had not mothers entered the labor market (Mishel et al., 2007).

As a result of financial deregulation, poorer families soon found conventional financial services less accessible. Banks and savings associations abandoned low-income communities for more favorable affluent locations: between 1975 and 1995, the number of savings offices per 10,000 residents in the poorest communities dropped 39% (Avery, Bostic, Calem, & Canner, 1997). By 2008 the number of *un*banked consumers (i.e., lacking a savings or checking account) totaled 7.7 million households or 9 million Americans; *under*banked consumers (i.e., those who had a savings or checking account but relied on alternative financial services) represented 17.9% of households or 21 million Americans. In 2009, the unbanked or underbanked population included about 54% of African American households, 44.5% of Native American households, and 43.3% of Hispanic/Latino households (Federal Deposit Insurance Corporation, 2009).

Economic distress compromised the ability of low-income households to weather expense shocks. Researchers calculated that the typical family below the poverty line reported liquid assets at $400 (Barr, 2009) while lower-income households with incomes just above the poverty line reported $800, both sums insufficient to deal with a major emergency (McKernan & Ratcliffe, 2008). Unable to cover daily expenses, many families resorted to "alternative financial services" (AFS)—buy-here-pay-here auto dealers, payday loans, auto title loans, RALs, check cashing, overseas wire transfers, open-loop prepaid credit cards, and rent-to-own furniture and appliances—to extend diminishing resources. Use of AFS was higher among the minority poor who were young and less educated, and those who are unbanked (FINRA Foundation, 2010).

By 2009, the FDIC reported that AFS outlets were generating $230 billion in annual revenues through an array of financial products (Bradley, Burhouse, Gratton, & Miller, 2009). An extensive network of storefronts made the fringe economy accessible to many consumers: one scholar calculated that the number of check-cashers and payday lenders (33,000) exceeded all of the franchises of McDonalds, Burger King, Target, Sears, and J.C. Penny's (29,000) (Karger, 2005). Approximately 66% of unbanked families rely on AFS (Federal Deposit Insurance Corporation, 2009), paying annual percentage rates of interest ranging from 70% to 390% (Elliehausen, 2006), far above those paid by consumers relying on mainstream depository institutions.

Despite the high cost of fringe financial products, many low-income consumers find the terms of fringe banking institutions acceptable: locations are convenient, transactions are prompt, staff courteous, services are provided in many languages, and hours extend into the evenings and weekends (Financial Service Centers of America, 2007, p. 2). The proliferation of payday lending has been attributed to its appeal to consumers who have had negative experiences with banks. Scanning the interior of a payday loan store, a journalist observed that "it's like banking turned upside down. Poor customers are commodities, deposits are irrelevant, bad credit makes for a good loan candidate and recessions can be boom times" (McGray, 2008). The inviting ambiance of AFS providers is almost the direct opposite of public welfare. The myriad problems encountered by low-income households who seek public welfare—long waits, inhospitable staff, indecipherable applications, inconvenient hours, substandard benefits—helps explain how using AFS, high fees and interest notwithstanding, has become popular among the poor.

Functionally, the fringe economy compensates for the inadequacies of the anti-poverty paradigms that have evolved in the United States, providing quick access to cash needed by desperate families. The Welfare Entitlement Paradigm is replete with rigid eligibility requirements, time-consuming recertifications, capricious eligibility technicians, and time limits, which dissuade many poor families from accessing benefits from welfare programs. The Asset-Building Paradigm suffers from paltry funding, lack of integration with other anti-poverty paradigms, and ignorance on the part of eligible families and agents of other welfare programs. Within this context, the fringe economy exploits the spotty coverage of extant anti-poverty paradigms and the absence of constructive financial services for low-income households, effectively stripping poor families and their communities of vital income and assets. The fringe economy might be understood as a financial system that actually exacerbates poverty (Stoesz, 2010).

THE GREAT RECESSION

The Great Recession exacerbated the tenuous finances of low-income households. Between 2000 and 2008, inflation-adjusted median family income fell 4.2% from $52,500 to $50,303 (McGhee & Draut, 2009). An unemployment rate exceeding 9% added stress to families unable to meet day-to-day expenses. A survey of the unemployed revealed that many resorted to borrowing to meet routine expenses, but often found that inadequate (Borie-Holtz, Van Horn, & Zukin, 2010).

A survey of a sample of the general population found that many families had experienced a reversal of financial fortune during the recession. Of those unemployed, the median duration of joblessness was 23 months; almost half, 46%, were unemployed longer than 26 weeks, the typical span of unemployment benefits. The impact was felt disproportionately by families earning less than $30,000 per year, 55% of whom reported they were worse off due to the recession. Accordingly, between 2008 and 2010, the number of respondents who identified as "lower class" increased from 25% to 29%, while the number unable to meet basic expenses increased from 7% to 11%. The unemployed were more likely to borrow than the employed. Forty percent of families anticipated that six years or more would be necessary to restore family finances to prerecessionary levels (Pew Research Center, 2010).

The Great Recession is likely to further inflate the fringe economy with negative implications for poor families. Low-income households struggle to meet daily expenses by stretching static incomes, yet many jobless find this no longer effective and will resort to the fringe economy, particularly if they are unable to access mainstream financial services. For these families, existing anti-poverty paradigms will be virtually useless; the Welfare Entitlement Paradigm's lengthy application process and stringent means test disqualify it as a source of assistance, the Tax Credit Paradigm's offer of refunds during tax season is not well timed, and the Asset-Building Paradigm's focus on thrift requires savings that have long been exhausted. For struggling families, the last resort is the fringe economy that furthers indebtedness. Aggregated, the consequences are equally profound, and already pronounced economic inequality widens.

THE CAPABILITY PARADIGM

The lack of integration of extant anti-poverty paradigms, compounded by the rise of the fringe economy and the ravages of the Great Recession, poses fundamental problems for American social welfare. That hundreds of billions of dollars have been committed to reduce poverty through welfare entitlements, tax credits, and asset building, resulting in a tangle of conflicting eligibility rules maintained by separate bureaucracies while leaving millions of families with little recourse but to resort to the fringe economy is untenable even under normal economic circumstances. During a recession it is simply perverse.

A promising point of departure can be found in the concept of "capability" articulated in the philosophy of Amartya Sen and Martha Nussbaum. Fundamentally, capability means more than subsistence, as Nussbaum (2000) writes:

> A life has been so impoverished that it is not worthy of the dignity of the human being, that it is a life in which one goes on living, but more or less like an animal, unable to develop and exercise one's human powers. (p. 72)

Toward a more inclusive definition of capability, Nussbaum (2000) has proposed ten criteria for human development, including health, autonomy, sensuality, affluence, socialization, civil liberties, and recreation. Capability, according to Nussbaum, is multidimensional in identifying the primary factors constituting a good life and thus presuming full social, economic, and political participation, and oriented toward prosperity.

Capability is a multifaceted and dynamic concept, not one to be reduced to simple economic variables, such as the federal poverty level or per capita gross domestic product. Thus, Sen (2009) has translated his notion of "poverty as capability deprivation" into multivariable rankings of well-being, most notably through the Human Development Index produced by the United Nations, a ranking of the social development of nations according to income, longevity, and education. Sen (1999) contends that a fully amplified notion of well-being must be multidimensional: "A person's 'capability' refers to the alternative functioning combinations (or, less formally put, the freedom to achieve various lifestyles)" (p. 75). Such multifactorial studies have been employed in the United States to chart the well-being of children, as evident in Kids Count (Annie E. Casey Foundation, 2010) and the Index of Child Well-Being (Land, 2010), as well as the general population (Miringoff & Miringoff, 1999). Published in 2010, *The Measure of America, 2010–2011* applied an extensive list of variables related to child well-being to the United States (Lewis & Burd-Sharps, 2010).

Conceptually, capability charts a middle ground between the liberal preoccupation with equality and the conservative focus on opportunity. Through various institutions—voluntary, governmental, and commercial—society should make available a comprehensive array of opportunities to citizens; however, people reserve the right to select among them in order to craft an autonomous life; some choices are congruent with a good life, others suboptimal, and a few actually counterproductive. By scripting positive defaults in social policy and including incentives to engage in constructive behavior, social policy can minimize destructive impulses and maximize positive decisions (Thaler & Sunstein, 2008). A capability approach in social welfare thus requires multiple options from which people can choose to fulfill their aspirations, and the menu from which people select should include those institutions essential for prosperity. With respect to economic justice, "financial capability requires both the *ability to act* (knowledge, skills, confidence, and motivation) and the *opportunity to act* (through access to beneficial financial products and institutions)" (M. S. Sherraden, 2010, p. 2).

OPERATIONALIZING THE CAPABILITY PARADIGM

A capability approach would amplify the choice architecture of families by instituting an anti-poverty paradigm congruent with the information age, expediting benefits, crafting them in accord with the aspirations of family members, and assuring their upward mobility. As Ron Haskins and Isabel Sawhill (2009) of the Brookings Institution contend, "we need more public policies that are designed to provide incentives for individuals to make choices that will promote their own development and boost their own income" (p. 47).

The following ideas show how a capability paradigm could serve as a successor to previous anti-poverty paradigms. Optimizing the capability of low-income households requires three fundamental changes in anti-poverty policy: (1) Consolidating public funding for low-income families into a single revenue pool, (2) Replacing welfare departments with community credit unions, and (3) Using account management to optimize the resources of low-income households in order to accelerate the upward mobility of poor families.

To integrate the current anti-poverty paradigms, public funds should be pooled and available to low-income households. Income assistance programs, such as TANF and SSI, as well as in-kind supports, like SNAP, should be transferred to the US Treasury Department so that they can be integrated with existing refundable tax credits for employees, employers, and families (Cramer et al., 2010, p. 22) in order to create an American Mobility Program (AMP), the benefits of which would not be conditioned on an assets test nor subject to time limits. Over time, other public assistance programs, such as weatherization assistance and Pell grants, should be added to the core of refundable tax credits. Benefits should diminish as households become more prosperous, reducing the dependence on public support.

The primary objective would be to assure low-income households access to financial products that promote their upward mobility. Financial products geared toward poor families should be available through Community Credit Unions (CCUs), which are established as alternatives to welfare departments. CCUs would be licensed and regulated by the National Credit Union Administration (NCUA), and provide an array of traditional products, such as savings and checking, as well as innovative services, such as micro-finance and IDAs, short-term loans, and tax preparation in order to maximize tax refunds for workers and employers. Beneficiaries would select a CCU to which their benefits would be deposited electronically, thus introducing a measure of competition into the provision of financial services and reducing the need for check-cashing outlets. Consumer-friendly CCUs would prosper while those that retained the culture of the welfare department would wither.

Encouraging citizens to optimize social benefits would increase the number of eligible families who participate, approximating participation levels of social insurance programs. Some products/services, such as electronic benefit transfer and access to cash through reloadable debit cards, would improve cost-effectiveness of financial services access, while others, such as automatic deductions from pay/benefits for IDAs, would encourage thrift. Government could contract to have CCUs conduct eligibility applications or make direct deposit after eligibility is established by government employees. In communities where government is unwilling to relinquish control of public welfare, neighbors should be able to charter CCUs as alternatives to welfare departments, much as charter schools have evolved as alternatives to public schools.

Assistance to consumers would be provided by an account manager, who would not only help members maximize benefits but also assist them with other financial objectives related to home ownership, business development, and higher education/vocational training. Account management would be a core practice method, comprising not only knowledge of public benefits and wage income, but also resources related to retraining and education. Account managers would be proficient in family finance and consumer protection, and their career trajectory would lead to supervisory positions in various CCU departments. Managers would need specialized knowledge found in business schools, departments of human ecology, economic development programs, and possibly one of the few social work programs that have added financial education and capability to their curricula. An essential component of CCU services would be financial literacy education, conducted by account managers. A competitive environment of CCUs would place a premium on innovation and service, so account managers would be encouraged to pilot new ways to service low-income households, improve financial products, evaluate the effectiveness of services, adopt technological innovations to enhance productivity, and relate to local officials to advance community development initiatives. For example, account managers could facilitate the creation of affinity groups of poor families, providing them with the technology to monitor their upward mobility, as demonstrated by Oakland's Family Independence Initiative (Miller, 2011; Stuhldreher & O'Brien, 2011).[3] Account management practice would also include brokering and referring families to resources for social issues, such as child maltreatment, substance abuse, homelessness, and mental illness. To maintain competitiveness, CCUs would be encouraged to adopt state-of-the-art management information systems that would monitor accounts as well as client satisfaction with services provided and products available. A requirement for being chartered by the NCUA would be real-time reporting of financial activity to federal officials who could monitor performance of the CCU. Since members could transfer accounts to other CCUs, CCUs would be attentive to consumer satisfaction. Because accounts have market value, CCUs would seek to attain full participation of consumers in program benefits and constructive financial products. Significantly, CCUs would pilot randomized controlled trials (RCTs) in order to assess product performance. RCTs could be internal projects or collaborations involving other CCUs for purposes of testing new products. CCUs would be sought out by businesses seeking to test novel financial products in niche markets, such as single mothers.

A mature CCU could capitalize community projects through several strategies. Loan portfolios that CCUs build could be sold to capitalize community development projects. Commercial banks could make deposits in CCUs as a way to be CRA compliant. If community nonprofits used CCUs for their payrolls, significant capital would be available for community development, such as expanding daycare businesses in order to meet the needs of working parents, rehabbing deteriorated housing, and brokering the location of essential businesses in the community. A mature CCU would be well positioned to finance operations through innovations, such as social impact bonds through which government seeks funds from private organization and pays service providers according to attainment of predetermined objectives (Liebman, 2011). CCUs providing better service are likely to attract more members, expanding the accounts they manage and further capitalizing their operations. A coalition of CDFIs, the Opportunity Finance Network, reported that member credit unions in operation less than three years claimed assets of $4.6 million, while those operating at least a decade held $11.6 million in assets (National Community Capital Association, 2001), sufficient to leverage important projects in poor communities. A regional network of a handful of mature CCUs could capitalize larger projects benefiting poor communities in inner cities, rural areas, and Indian reservations. A national network of hundreds of mature CCUs would be a powerful voice for the marginalized, minority poor.

CONCLUSION

During the 20th century, divergent anti-poverty paradigms evolved. Anti-poverty paradigms now comprise sizable portions of government expenditures, yet significant numbers of families receive little or no benefit from them. In precarious economic circumstances, low-income households resort to the fringe economy during a recession, too often exacerbating their poverty. The systemic failure of anti-poverty policies has been acknowledged by welfare scholars: "People need protection when things go wrong, but also the material and moral capabilities to move through major periods of transition in their lives," noted Anthony Giddens (1999) in arguing for "investments in *human capital*" (p. 117). Ultimately, this calls for fundamental changes in a nation's response to poverty.

A 21st-century approach to poverty requires integrating extant anti-poverty paradigms in order to optimize the capability of low-income families. In 2004, only 24% of single-parent families surviving on less than 50% of the poverty level received TANF benefits; for two-parent families that were as poor, only 10% received TANF (Burkhauser, Moffitt & Scholz, 2010). The likelihood that the poorest families compensate for the inadequacy of the Welfare Entitlement Paradigm by accessing the Tax Credit Paradigm or the Asset-Building Paradigm strains credulity. Public skepticism about conventional efforts to assist the poor implies support for an anti-poverty paradigm that choreographs upward mobility for low-income households. The public would endorse anti-poverty programs that promise to boost households into the middle class, provide accountability about the return on public investment, and can be adjusted when needed.

An integrated anti-poverty policy would lessen economic inequality. For the past three decades, income and assets have been skewed increasingly in favor of the affluent, while those of low-income households have stagnated. Embedded inequality reduces upward mobility, especially among the minority poor. A report on mobility sponsored by prominent policy institutes across the ideological spectrum concluded, "Only 17% of those born to parents in the bottom quintile climb to one of the top two income groups" (Isaacs, 2006, p. 5). Many minority children actually experience downward mobility: Of Black children with middle-class parents, 45% fall to the bottom of the income distribution, compared to 16% of White children. Poor Black children fare the worst: 54% of children in families in the bottom quintile remain there, compared to 31% of White children (Isaacs, 2006). While some in the American economic stratification have claimed success, too many parents and their children have been locked in place, the promise of prosperity a chimera.

Rebuilding the opportunity structure for low-income households can bring anti-poverty policy in line with public expectations, capitalize on innovation, and accelerate the upward mobility of poor families. Far better this than continuing the contradictory paradigms that have proven irrelevant to many needy Americans, invited the contempt of taxpayers, and made public officials keep them at arm's length. In contrast, a Capability Paradigm that maximizes the aspirations of citizens would enjoy a wider spectrum of support.

NOTES

1. M. Sherraden's (1991) description of a "virtuous circle" through which low-income households use assets to improve their economic position anticipates that aspect of behavior economics related to poverty (p. 169).

2. CPI computation calculated from data downloaded June 29, 2010, from ftp://ftp.bls.gov/pub/special/requests/cpi/cpiai.txt; Income data from Mishel, Bernstein, and Allegretto (2007, p. 68). Although poor families experienced an income increase during the 1990s, this failed to compensate for income losses during the 1980s and the period between 2000 and 2006; the average cash income for the lowest and second-lowest quintiles fell 5.3% and 3.6% respectively between 1979 and 2006 (computed from House Ways and Means Committee, 2008, Table E-27).
3. Because the Family Independence Initiative is a private sector organization that emphasizes self-sufficiency and upward mobility, it illustrates how a conservative concept, "mediating structures," can address poverty (Schambra, 2010).

REFERENCES

Annie E Casey Foundation. (2010). *Kids count*. Baltimore: Author.
Avery, R., Bostic, R., Calem, P., & Canner, G. (1997, September). Changes in distribution of banking offices. *Federal Reserve Bulletin*.
Barr, M. (2009). Financial services, savings, and borrowing among low- and moderate-income households. In R. Blank & M. Barr (Eds.), *Insufficient funds* (pp. 66–96). New York: Russell Sage Foundation.
Beland, D. (2010). *What is social policy?* Malden, MA: Polity Press.
Berkowitz, E., & McQuaid, K. (1980). *Creating the welfare state*. New York: Praeger.
Borie-Holtz, D, Van Horn, C., & Zukin, C. (2010). *No end in sight: The agony of prolonged unemployment*. New Brunswick, NJ: Rutgers University, Heldrich Center for Workforce Development.
Bowler, M. (1974). *The Nixon guaranteed income proposal*. Cambridge, MA: Ballinger.
Bradley, C., Burhouse, S., Gratton, H., & Miller, R. (2009). Alternative financial services: A primer. *FDIC Quarterly*, 3(1), 39–47.
Burkhauser, R., Moffitt, R., & Scholz, J. (2010). Transfers and taxes and the low-income population. *Focus*, 27(2), 13–20.
Community Development Financial Institution Loan Fund. (2010). *Performance and accountability report 2009*. Washington, DC: Author.
Corporation for Enterprise Development (2010). *State IDA program support*. Washington, DC: Author.
Cramer, R., Huelsman, M., King, J., Lopez-Fernandini, A., & Newville, D. (2010). *The assets report 2010*. Washington, DC: New America Foundation.
Cramer, R., Rourke, O., Cooper, D., & Luengo-Prado, M. (2009). *A penny saved is mobility earned*. Washington, DC: New America Foundation.
Department of Health and Human Services. (2007). *Indicators of welfare dependence*. Washington, DC: GPO.
Elliehausen, G. (2006). *Consumers' use of high-price credit products: Do they know what they are doing?* (Working Paper, 2006-WP-02). Terre Haute: Indiana State University, Networks Financial Institute.
Epstein, W. (2010). *Democracy without decency*. University Park: Pennsylvania State University Press.
Farley, R. (1996). *The new American reality*. New York: Russell Sage Foundation.
Federal Deposit Insurance Corporation. (2009). *National survey of unbanked and underbanked households*. Washington, DC: Author.

Federal Register. (2010, October 6). Funding opportunity: Notice of funds availability inviting applications for the community development financial institutions program.

Fellowes, M. (2008). *From poverty, opportunity: Putting the market to work for lower income families.* Washington, DC: Brookings Institution.

Financial Service Centers of America. (2007, October 24). *Financial inclusion.* Washington, DC: Author.

FINRA Foundation. (2010). *Financial capability in the United States.* Washington, DC: Author.

Giddens, A. (1999). *The third way.* Cambridge, MA: Polity Press.

Gilbert, N. (1995). *Welfare justice.* New Haven, CT: Yale University Press.

Gordon, L. (1994). *Pitied but not entitled.* Cambridge, MA: Harvard University Press.

Hall, P. (1993). Policy paradigms, social learning and the state. *Comparative Politics, 25*(3), 275–296.

Haskins, R. (2006). *Work over welfare.* Washington, DC: Brookings Institution.

Haskins, R., & Sawhill, I. (2009). *Creating an opportunity society.* Washington, DC: Brookings Institution.

Holt, S. (2006). *The Earned Income Tax Credit at age 30.* Washington, DC: Brookings Institution.

House Ways and Means Committee. (1996). *Overview of entitlement programs.* Washington, DC: GPO.

House Ways and Means Committee. (2004). *Overview of entitlement programs.* Washington, DC: GPO.

House Ways and Means Committee. (2008). *Overview of entitlement programs.* Washington, DC: GPO.

Howard, C. (1997). *The hidden welfare state.* Princeton, NJ: Princeton University Press.

Isaacs, J. (2006). *Economic mobility of families across generations.* Washington, DC: Brookings Institution.

Jackson, P. (1977). The philosophical basis of the private pension movement. In D. McGill (Ed.), *Social security and private pension plans* (pp. 14–28). Homewood, IL: Richard Irwin.

Jacobs, L., & Skocpol, T. (2010). *Health care reform and American politics.* New York: Oxford University Press.

Jargowsky, P. (1997). *Poverty and place.* New York: Russell Sage Foundation.

Karger, H. (2005). *Shortchanged.* San Francisco: Berrett Koehler.

Karger, H., & Stoesz, D. (2010). *American social welfare policy* (6th ed.). New York: Pearson.

Kuhn, T. (1970). *The structure of scientific revolutions.* Chicago: University of Chicago.

Land, K. (2010). *The index of child well-being.* Durham, NC: Duke University.

Lawinski, T. (2010). *Living on the edge in suburbia.* Nashville, TN: Vanderbilt University.

Lewis, K., & Burd-Sharps, S. (2010). *The measure of America, 2010–2011.* New York: New York University Press.

Liebman, J. (2011). *Social impact bonds.* Washington, DC: Center for American Progress.

Loprest, P., & Acs, G. (1995). *Profile of disability among families on AFDC.* Washington, DC: Urban Institute.

McGhee, H., & Draut, T. (2009). *Why we need an independent consumer financial protection agency now.* New York: Demos.

McGray, D. (2008, November 9). Check cashers, redeemed. *New York Times*, p. 5.
McKernan, S., & Ratcliffe, C. (2008). *Enabling families to weather emergencies and develop: The role of assets*. Washington, DC: Urban Institute.
Mead, L. (1986). *Beyond entitlement*. New York: Basic Books.
Meyer, D., & Cancian, M. (1998). *Economic well-being following an exit from Aid to Families with Dependent Children*. Madison, WI: Institute for Research on Poverty.
Midgley, J. (1998). The American welfare state in international perspective. In H. Karger & D. Stoesz (Eds.), *American social welfare policy* (3rd ed.; pp. 388–407). New York: Longman.
Miller, M. (2011). *The uphill battle to scale an innovative antipoverty approach*. Washington, DC: New America Foundation.
Miringoff, M., & Miringoff, M. (1999). *The social health of the nation*. New York: Oxford University Press.
Mishel, L., Bernstein, J., & Allegretto, S. (2007). *The state of working America 2006/2007*. Washington, DC: Economic Policy Institute.
Moynihan, D. (1965). *The Negro family: The case for national action*. Washington, DC: Department of Labor.
Murray, C. (1984). *Losing ground*. New York: Basic Books.
National Community Capital Association. (2001). *CDFIs side-by-side*. Philadelphia: Author.
Novak, M. (1987). *The new consensus on family and welfare*. Washington, DC: American Enterprise Institute.
Nussbaum, M. (2000). *Women and human development*. Cambridge, UK : Cambridge University.
Pew Research Center. (2010). *How the Great Recession has changed life in America*. Washington, DC: Author.
Porter, M. (1995). Competitive advantage in the inner city. *Harvard Business Review, 73*(May/June), 45–62.
Quadagno, J. (1994). *The color of welfare*. New York: Oxford University Press.
Ridzi, F. (2009). *Selling welfare reform*. New York: New York University.
Rubin, J. (2007). *Financing low-income communities*. New York: Russell Sage Foundation.
Sandel, M. (1996). *Democracy's discontent*. Cambridge, MA: Harvard University Press.
Schambra, W. (2010). Conservatism and the quest for community. *National Affairs*. Retrieved November 11, 2011, from www.nationalaffairs.com
Sen, A. (1999). *Development as freedom*. New York: Knopf.
Sen, A. (2009). *The idea of justice*. Cambridge, MA: Belknap Press of Harvard University Press.
Sherraden, M. (1991). *Assets and the poor*. New York: M. E. Sharpe.
Sherraden, M. (2001). Asset-building policy and programs for the poor. In T. Shapiro & E. Wolff's (Eds.), *Assets for the poor* (pp. 302–323). New York: Russell Sage Foundation.
Sherraden, M. (2009). Individual development accounts and asset-building policy. In R. Blank & M. Barr (Eds.), *Insufficient funds* (pp. 191–217). New York. Russell Sage Foundation.
Sherraden, M., & Stevens, J. (2010). *Lessons from SEED*. St. Louis, MO: Washington University, Center for Social Development.
Sherraden, M. S. (2010). *Financial capability: What is it, and how can it be created?* (CSD Working Paper 10-17). St. Louis, MO: Washington University, Center for Social Development.

Siegel, F. (1997). *The future once happened here.* New York: Basic Books.
Skocpol, T. (1992). *Protecting soldiers and mothers.* Cambridge, MA: Harvard University Press.
Stoesz, D. (2000). *A poverty of imagination.* Madison: University of Wisconsin Press.
Stoesz, D. (2005). *Quixote's ghost.* New York: Oxford University Press.
Stoesz, D. (2010). *Quick credit.* Washington, DC: New America Foundation.
Stuhldreher, A., & O'Brien, R. (2011). *The family independence initiative.* Washington, DC: New America Foundation.
Thaler, R., & Sunstein, C. (2008). *Nudge.* New Haven, CT: Yale University Press.
Titmuss, R. (1968). *Commitment to welfare.* New York: Pantheon.
Urban Institute. (2008). *Taxation and the family.* Washington, DC: Author.
Van Oorschot, W., Opielka, M., & Pfau-Effinger, B. (2008). *Culture and the welfare state.* Northampton, MA: Elgar.
Wilensky, H. & Lebeaux, C. (1965). *Industrial society and social welfare.* New York: Free Press.
Woo, B., Rademacher, I., & Meier, J. (2010). *Upside down: The $400 billion federal asset-building budget.* Washington, DC: Corporation for Enterprise Development.

PART TWO

Innovations in Financial Capability

4

Financial Capability among Survivors of Domestic Violence

CYNTHIA K. SANDERS

Survivors of domestic violence often lack financial resources and knowledge, and many women remain with or return to an abusive partner because they are economically dependent (Sanders, 2007; Sullivan, 1991). Understanding and addressing financial dimensions of abuse is essential to helping women successfully deal with domestic violence. This chapter begins with a discussion of the role economic factors and financial issues play in domestic violence. It then describes an innovative community collaborative that provides financial and economic development services to low-income survivors of domestic violence, and provides empirical evidence on outcomes. The conclusion focuses on implications for social work practice, education, policy, and research.

INTERSECTION OF DOMESTIC VIOLENCE AND ECONOMIC WELL-BEING

Survivors of domestic violence endure various forms and degrees of abuse including physical, sexual, verbal, psychological, and emotional abuse (M. P. Johnson & Ferraro, 2000). In addition to these more commonly recognized and studied dimensions, women who experience intimate partner violence commonly deal with economic abuse. A woman's capacity to establish herself financially, independent from an abusive partner, is often severely compromised.

Feminist scholars often attribute domestic violence (or intimate partner violence [IPV]) to men's desire to control women (Davis & Hagen, 1992; Dobash & Dobash, 1979; Schechter, 1982; Yllo, 1993). In addition to physical violence, one way of maintaining power in a relationship is to control financial resources. Additionally, men's violence can restrict women's participation in economic life, thus maintaining male dominance in the economic sphere and restricting women to subordinate roles within the family (Raphael, 2000). Social norms and policy reinforce this dynamic, thus condoning male dominance and patriarchy in society (Abramovitz, 1996).

IPV, economic factors, and financial issues intersect in a variety of ways. "Economic factors" refers to broader environmental and structural factors that impact financial well-being and women's capacity to move from financial dependence on an abusive partner to financial independence. Examples include poverty, employment availability, educational opportunities, availability of affordable housing, and discrimination. "Financial issues" refers to more immediate household financial matters including a woman's access to household financial resources, knowledge of and skills to manage financial affairs, and availability of financial services and resources. Abusive behavior on the part of a partner may intersect with and impact a woman's capability in either or both spheres. Research demonstrates the intersection of economic factors, financial issues, and IPV in at least four ways. First, although domestic violence cuts across all socioeconomic classes, growing evidence suggests that low-income women are more vulnerable to abuse than more affluent women (Riger & Kreiglstein, 2000; Tolman & Raphael, 2000). According to National Crime Victimization Survey data, IPV increases as women's household income decreases. Women in households with income under $7,500 experience IPV at a rate of seven times that of women with household incomes of at least $75,000 (Rennison & Welchans, 2000). Additionally, limited economic resources have been found to predict the likelihood and severity of abuse—with lower income, fewer resources, and greater economic dependency predicting more severe violence (Kalmuss & Straus, 1982; Kurz, 1998; Smith, 1990).

Second, women are often prevented from leaving an abusive partner due to economic dependence. Lack of access to economic resources makes women dependent on abusive partners, a factor that predicts women's ability to leave an abusive relationship (Gonzalez, 2005; Barnett, 2000; I. M. Johnson, 1992; Strube & Barbour, 1983). Women who are unable to establish economic independence also find it more difficult to pursue legal charges or obtain restraining orders (Fernandez, Iwamoto, & Muscat, 1997). Moreover, insufficient housing, financial assistance, job training, and childcare prevent women from permanently escaping abusive relationships (Davis & Hagen, 1992). Women leaving shelters often return to an abusive partner because they lack alternative housing and income (I. M. Johnson, 1992; Menard, 2001; Schechter, 1982). In fact, women risk increased economic hardship, including loss of a home and possessions, when they leave an abusive relationship, increasing their vulnerability to homelessness (Zorza, 1991).

Third, economic and employment status are significantly associated with IPV (Browne, Salomon, & Bassuk, 1999; Riger, Staggs, & Schewe, 2004). Abusive partners may intentionally interfere with work efforts or career enhancing education and training through such tactics as escalating physical abuse prior to scheduled job interviews, harassing women at their place of employment, destroying textbooks or initiating conflict before an exam, and failing to fulfill child care responsibilities or provide transportation (Sanders, 2007; Swanberg, Logan, & Macke, 2005; Swanberg & Macke, 2006; Tolman & Raphael, 2000). Further, battered women may face mental health concerns such as depression or post-traumatic stress disorder (PTSD), which may affect their ability to work or pursue financial independence (Kurz, 1998; Lloyd & Taluc, 1999).

Several studies suggest when women's economic status (e.g., employment, income, external financial support) equals or exceeds that of a partner, levels of IPV decrease (Farmer & Tiefenthaler, 1997, 2003; Tauchen, Witte, & Long, 1991). Lambert and Firestone (2000) find that women who work may have a level of independence that reduces an abuser's ability to control them, and also have increased ability to escape violence. Increasing economic independence may therefore not only decrease violence within a relationship but also provide resources that allow a woman to leave an abusive relationship (Farmer & Tiefenthaler, 1997; Page-Adams, 1995).

Fourth, abusive partners engage in a variety of tactics that negatively affect women financially and undermine their efforts to become financially independent (Ptacek, 1997). Financial abuse often includes complete control of financial resources, including restricting a woman's ability to pursue education and employment (Moe & Bell, 2004) and exploiting her financial resources (e.g., incurring debt in her name, damaging credit rating, stealing her money). Financial issues may also lead to other forms of abuse including physical, sexual, and verbal (Sanders, 2007).

In sum, survivors of domestic violence often have limited financial independence. Helping battered women achieve financial independence includes increasing their knowledge and skills to pursue greater economic stability and responsibility. It also requires access to institutional structures that permit them to use their financial knowledge and skills (E. Johnson & Sherraden, 2007). For survivors of domestic violence, in particular, building financial capability must take into concern physical and emotional safety. The following section discusses a pioneering community-based initiative developed to advance the financial knowledge and skills of survivors of domestic violence and promote women's financial capability through Individual Development Accounts (IDAs).

REDEVELOPMENT OPPORTUNITIES FOR WOMEN'S ECONOMIC ACTION PROGRAM

Redevelopment Opportunities for Women's Economic Action Program (see REAP materials at http://www.row-stl.org/Content/REAP.aspx) arose out of the recognition that economic and financial issues play a critical role in domestic violence and present serious obstacles for many women who may wish to leave abusive partners. The REAP program emerged from a community collaborative of 13 domestic violence and 3 homeless service agencies that began working together in 2000 to develop economic services for low-income battered women in the St. Louis, Missouri, region (Sanders & Schnabel, 2006). This consortium of agencies works though Redevelopment Opportunities for Women (ROW), a nonprofit agency whose mission is "to empower women and their families to build safety, skills, economic security and hope for the future" (Redevelopment Opportunities for Women, n.d.). The collaboration culminated in development of formalized financial and economic development services, including economic education and credit counseling; women's individual development accounts (IDAs); and economic advocacy and support services.

With safety as the central component, the program emphasizes long-term economic development and security for low-income women, focusing on strategies that address not only basic financial skills, but also approaches that empower women and give them a sense of hope about their ability to safely plan for their future. Indeed, REAP's economic education program has been shown to increase women's levels of financial self-efficacy, improving their sense of ability to make financial decisions and reach goals (Sanders, Weaver, & Schnabel, 2007).

Financial Education and Credit Counseling

Women who experience domestic violence are commonly isolated from financial resources. They may lack knowledge of financial matters and ready access to cash, checking, or charge accounts. Women's financial status can be negatively impacted by abusive partners and restriction of their work and educational opportunities, and when leaving a relationship they often have few economic resources. "Realizing Your Economic Action Plan," REAP's 12-hour group economic education curriculum (Redevelopment Opportunities for Women, Inc., 2005) is offered in 17 emergency shelter programs and nonresidential social service programs serving low-income women in the St. Louis area. In addition to providing core financial information on money management, budgeting, credit, banking, and investing, REAP staff also provide assistance for dealing with creditors.

To begin, each woman is given an economic action plan (EAP) they will work on over the course of four class sessions. The EAP guides women as they create financial goals and learn to view themselves as competent financial actors. Safety is an important part of the curriculum, which recognizes that safety considerations may force women to deviate from financial goals.

In section one, women explore their feelings about money and begin to examine the factors that have shaped their financial situation. Many women have never had an opportunity to discuss their feelings about money. Safety considerations in this section include the need for confidentiality among participants. Participants also consider potential dangers posed by taking course materials home, and if necessary participants make alternative arrangements, including having the facilitator hold them in between classes.

Section two helps women develop a budget (cost of living plan) that meets their immediate needs as well as enables them to reach long-term goals. They organize financial and personal documents, learn about budgets and financial terms, and identify "spending leaks." Safety considerations include acknowledging that women may be limited to making only small financial decisions because they lack control over major household expenses and spending.

Section three focuses on understanding credit and debt. Women learn about their credit report. They are given specific steps that will help improve their credit and achieve personal goals. Examples of safety considerations include whether a credit report can be mailed to a safe address and whether an abuser can access her credit report (using a social security number) and learn where she is living. In such cases the class facilitator may, for example, with a woman's consent, contact a sister organization in another state to pull a woman's credit report.

Section four examines financial products and services, savings, and investments, as well as potentially predatory alternative financial services. While bank accounts may be financially optimal for many women, other women are not comfortable opening a bank account for a variety of reasons such as safety, credit history, or discrimination (Redevelopment Opportunities for Women, Inc., 2005). Safety considerations include opening new financial accounts at a financial institution other than that of an abusive partner, and using an employment address or post office box for financial mailings.

As a whole the REAP curriculum promotes women's empowerment and financial self-determination, provides hands-on skills, increases knowledge of and access to financial resources, increases women's self-confidence in managing and coping with financial issues, and assists women in identifying feasible short- and long-term financial goals through an individualized economic action plan (EAP). Throughout, the curriculum addresses safety issues.

Women's Individual Development Accounts

Upon completing the REAP curriculum, low-income participants may apply for an individual development account (IDA). IDAs are matched saving accounts that enable low-income families to save, build assets, and enter the financial mainstream. The philosophy behind IDAs is that, when appropriate structures are in place, low-income families can save and accumulate financial assets, thereby improving economic status and future financial security (M. Sherraden, 1991). Income and consumption are not enough to build a financial foundation for poor households; assets and wealth accumulation also matter (Scanlon & Page-Adams, 2001). Social and psychological effects, such as increasing personal efficacy and sense of well-being, greater future orientation, hope for one's future, and long-term planning, might be expected as well (Sanders, 2007; M. S. Sherraden & McBride, 2010). IDAs have gained national recognition as a social and economic development tool designed to help low-income families accumulate assets (M. Sherraden, 2001). While there are hundreds of IDA programs nationally (CFED, 2009), REAP is unique in its specific focus on battered women and is likely the first program to design an IDA program specifically with the needs of survivors in mind. However, such initiatives are on the rise (see for example the Kentucky Domestic Violence Association at www.kdva.org).

REAP savings accounts can be used to purchase or repair a home, acquire career enhancing education, purchase an automobile, start or support a small business, or build retirement savings. Most IDAs include a two-to-one savings match, with a $3,000 ceiling in match funds provided over 2.5 years (e.g., if a participant saves $1,500, she will receive $3,000 in match funds).

Matching funds to support REAP's IDA program come from (1) the Assets for Independence Act (AFIA), a federal program designed to provide matching funds for community-based IDA programs; (2) local community partners, such as local domestic violence service providers and local banks and foundations; and (3) United Way of Greater St. Louis Great Rivers Community Reinvestment Corporation, the largest contributor to matching funds for REAP's IDA program. Great Rivers and local partner matching funds offer greater flexibility than AFIA. For example, local funders support vehicle purchases, which are not permitted under AFIA rules. A vehicle may contribute to economic well-being by permitting women to maintain stable employment, pursue educational goals, or flee an abusive relationship. Local funders also support a limited number of "safety accounts" for women to save money and receive a savings match to implement a safety plan for immediate safety and longer term planning. Thus, a safety plan may contribute to a woman's ability to gain independence from an abusive partner.

Economic Advocacy and Support Services

Economic advocacy and support services are another critical component of the REAP program. These one-on-one services help build financial capability by assisting women to apply new financial knowledge and skills learned through the REAP curriculum. Working with an advocate, women identify action steps to accomplish their EAP, including education and employment planning, resource identification and acquisition, and continuous safety planning. Additionally, the plan addresses outstanding debt and credit concerns and other long-term goals such as asset development.

Several assumptions about building financial capability among survivors of domestic violence underlie REAP's program. Greater financial literacy is likely to translate into a greater capacity to manage one's own finances. Backup savings may prevent a woman from staying with or returning to an abusive partner for financial reasons in the event of an emergency. Acquiring assets may allow women to become more economically secure, and ultimately facilitate independent decision-making. Purchasing a home may result in greater residential stability (Scanlon, 1998). More education, job training, or starting a small business may result in greater job stability and earning potential (Pandey, Zahn, Neely-Barnes, & Menon, 2000). Purchasing a car may contribute to a woman's safety and ability to get to and from work or school (Brabo, Kilde, Peske-Herriges, Quinn, & Sanderud-Nordquist, 2003).

PROGRAM OUTCOMES

This section reports key findings from three studies conducted to evaluate REAP's economic education and IDA program (Sanders, 2007).[1] The first study is based on in-depth qualitative interviews conducted with the first 30 women to participate in REAP's IDA program. Women shared their experiences and the perceived effects of participating in REAP's economic education and IDA program. The second study (Sanders, 2011) is based on a standardized phone survey with 70 women that examines self-reported outcomes including behavioral, psychological, and economic changes; assesses financial knowledge and practices; and asks women about the relationship between REAP and their experiences of domestic abuse. Finally, the third study (Sanders, 2010) is based on quantitative account monitoring data on 125 REAP IDA accounts. Data includes demographic information about account holders and monthly account activity, including saving rates, withdrawals, and purchases.

While these are three separate studies, the 125 women represented in the savings outcome study are largely inclusive of the 30 women who participated in the qualitative study and the 70 women who took part in the phone survey. Thus, Table 4.1 provides basic demographic and economic characteristics of women at enrollment, as well as types of intimate partner violence experienced. Women in this study were mostly Black or White and averaged 37 years of age at enrollment. The women were relatively well educated, with over half having at least some college. Household size was generally small, often with the woman as the sole adult within the household and one or two children. The majority of women were single, divorced, or separated at the time of enrolling in REAP's IDA program. The most common forms of IPV experienced were physical, verbal, and economic abuse. The majority of women (91%) were employed at least part-time when they enrolled in REAP's IDA program, with about half working full-time or more. Mean and median income was about $1,400 per month and 91% of women lived at or below 150% of the poverty line.

Perceived Effects

Qualitative findings and phone survey results indicate REAP participants are overwhelmingly positive about their experiences and report positive effects of the program (Sanders, 2007, 2011). In qualitative interviews, 30 early participants in REAP discuss their experiences with economic education and the IDA program.

Economic Education

Qualitative findings regarding REAP's economic education program can be grouped into three general areas: cognitive and affective impacts, behavioral changes, and learning outcomes (Sanders, 2007).

Cognitive/Affective Impacts

Women made many comments indicating they changed the way they think about their finances as a result of participating in REAP's economic curriculum, including changes in the way they think about the importance of finances, the way they make financial decisions, how they handle their money, and a more positive outlook on their financial future and ability to achieve financial goals. Women also noted they feel more self-confident, have higher self-esteem, and greater feelings of control. Several women left classes determined to achieve financial independence,

Table 4.1. WOMEN'S CHARACTERISTICS AT ENROLLMENT (N = 125)

Characteristic	
RACE	
Black/African American	58 (46%)
White	52 (42%)
Latina/Hispanic	5 (4%)
Mixed/Biracial or Other	7 (6%)
Asian/Pacific Islander	3 (2%)
EDUCATION	
Less than High School	12 (10%)
High School or GED	25 (20%)
Some College	46 (37%)
2-Year Degree	21 (17%)
4-Year Degree	12 (10%)
Attended Graduate School	9 (7%)
Age (Mean)	37 (median 37, range 20–61)
HOUSEHOLD STRUCTURE	
Mean Number of Adults	1 (median, range 1–4)
Mean Number of Children	2 (median 1, range 0–6)
RELATIONSHIP STATUS	
Single	53 (42%)
Divorced	44 (35%)
Separated	14 (11%
Married	14 (11%)
INTIMATE PARTNER VIOLENCE	
History of Physical Abuse	
Yes	92 (74%)
No	19 (15%)
Unknown/missing	14 (11%)
HISTORY OF VERBAL ABUSE	
Yes	100 (80%)
No	11 (9%)
Unknown/missing	14 (11%)
HISTORY OF SEXUAL ABUSE	
Yes	35 (28%)
No	76 (61%)
Unknown/missing	14 (11%)

(continued)

Table 4.1. (CONTINUED)

HISTORY OF ECONOMIC ABUSE	
Yes	83 (67%)
No	28 (22%)
Unknown/missing	14 (11%)
EMPLOYMENT STATUS	
Full-time or more	60 (48%)
Part-time	43 (34%)
Working and in school	11 (9%)
In school or job training	1 (1%)
Unemployed	3 (2%)
Disabled	6 (5%)
Missing	1 (1%)
GROSS MONTHLY INCOME	
$0–$999	36 (29%)
$1,000–$2,000	65 (52%)
$2001–$3,000	15 (12%)
$3000–$3,500	6 (5%)
Missing	3 (2%)
Mean	$1,420 (median $1,385, range $0–$3500)
POVERTY STATUS (% OF FEDERAL POVERTY LINE)	
Less than 100%	53 (42%)
101–150%	35 (28%)
151–175%	14 (11%)
176–200%	12 (10%)
200%+	10 (8%)
Missing	1 (1%)

NOTE: The percentage of missing cases is reported when the value is 1% or more. Percentages may not sum to 100% due to rounding.

feeling more positive and empowered to address their finances head-on. Amber, for example, realized she was no longer under the control of her previous partner and had greater confidence that she could accomplish her goals:

> I know that I... I don't feel so limited in my life anymore. I feel like I can do whatever I want to do. I guess both financially and it makes you independent in so many other ways. The way that you think about your life and things you

thought you couldn't do before... when you've got somebody else telling you, "You can't do this. You can't do that. I don't want you to do this. I don't want you to do that." It really makes a big difference.

BEHAVIORAL CHANGES

Asked if they do anything differently after taking REAP's economic education classes, the women noted several key behavior changes. Women frequently said they consume differently, use a budget, log their spending, and were actively working on credit repair. Additionally, they indicated they are trying to reduce their debt, to save when possible, and to take active steps to achieve short- and long-term goals. Less frequently women indicated they were teaching their children financial lessons and keeping important documents in a safe place. The majority of women mentioned multiple ways they have changed their financial behavior, including Michelle:

> Well, I didn't have a safe place for all my documents, and that was an easy one to do, but I did that. I have a safety deposit box now. I am careful to budget. I am... you know, I'm saving in this IDA account, which I wouldn't be doing if I hadn't taken the class. Again, I think the class really affected my outlook in what I teach my kids about not saying I don't have enough... but saying it's not the way I choose to spend it. I know the class was part of that. But I think that that's terrifically valuable.

LEARNING

Changes in behavior clearly indicate women learned in REAP. In many cases knowledge translated into behavior changes; in other cases women said they learned about a variety of topics but had not yet implemented all they learned. Women commonly mentioned learning about how to budget, bank account and investment options, credit cards and their hidden costs, ways to cut spending, understanding their credit reports, the importance of good credit and addressing debt, community financial and social support resources, and predatory lending. The majority of women believe they learned valuable information. Dora, for example, talked about multiple things she learned in REAP classes:

> I learned the value in budgeting money, saving money... the true value of how your credit score affects the finance... the interest on bills. Take for instance, if I buy a car. My interest rate is higher if my credit score is low. So, the better my credit score the better interest. So it helps me to understand one of the reasons why you hear commercial and advertisement, "You can buy this car at 0% finance." If your credit score is lousy, they're not going to give you 0% finance. So I've learned that. I learned a little bit more about the different saving options... not that I've gotten involved in many extra ones... but the mutual funds, different money market accounts, CD's, stocks... a little bit more about that... the different types of banks and savings institutions out there. We looked at those kind of things. Different ways to generate money.

Quantitative results also suggest that women believe REAP's economic education classes are helpful. In the phone survey 70 REAP participants (Sanders, 2011) stated whether they agreed or disagreed with 20 items assessing financial knowledge. Sample questions include: payday loans can cost three times the amount borrowed in repayment; credit information only stays on your credit report for 2 or 3 years. The average and median score of correct responses was 19, ranging from 13 to 20 correctly answered. The women also answered an 11-item survey rating improvement on psychosocial outcomes on a 5-point scale of changes in their comfort level (i.e., improved significantly, improved, stayed the same, decreased, decreased significantly). Questions addressed women's sense of financial control, hope for the future, knowledge of their credit rating, comfort in dealing with financial institutions, and so forth. The mean and median score was 47, ranging from a low of 33 to a high of 55 (the maximum score).

The women also rated their level of financial knowledge on a five-point scale, ranging from "excellent" to "very poor." Seventy percent rated their knowledge as good or excellent. They were asked: "As a result of participating in REAP's economic education classes, would you say your financial knowledge has increased significantly, increased, stayed the same, decreased?" In response, 52% reported their knowledge increased, and 47% reported their knowledge increased significantly. Of course the reliability and validity of self-rated financial knowledge is limited, and future research should examine financial knowledge utilizing objective measures.

Overall, women believe economic education classes have had a very positive effect on their lives. Regarding the effect on their family, 89% stated the classes affect their families "very positively," and 11% say "somewhat positively." Since participating in REAP, 71% (50) report that their financial circumstances have improved. Seventy percent attribute the change to a "large" or "very large" extent to their participation in REAP.

Women's Individual Development Accounts

Several key themes about the perceived effects of participating in REAP's IDA program arose in discussion with women (N = 30). Similar to outcomes associated with economic education classes, the outcomes related to IDAs include behavior changes, cognitive and psychological effects, and the role that savings, and ultimately greater economic well-being, may play in women's safety (Sanders, 2007). Although women in the IDA program discussed outcomes of REAP classes, it is difficult to differentiate among the outcomes of each program component. It is likely some outcomes are a result of either program and/or of both programs together. Further research should tease out differences among program outcomes in controlled studies. Conceptually, outcomes of economic education may be reinforced by participation in the IDA program. That is, in the absence of the IDA program, sustained outcomes of REAP classes may be diminished.

BEHAVIORAL CHANGES

Women's participation in the IDA program resulted in several behavioral changes, including greater fiscal prudence and financial management; creating and sticking to a budget; saving more consistently; altering consumer habits; and teaching children lessons about saving. Nellie, for example, observed that money for her IDA is an important line item in her budget, and she is willing to forgo some purchases in order to save:

> When you think about the long run, you just have to come up with that money. You just have to. If you want the benefits, you have to budget that along with your bills. You know? Forget about the pair of jeans this month or whatever.

After joining the IDA program, Karen models saving behavior and matches her sons' savings to encourage them to save:

> I taught my boys that, don't spend everything you have. If they wanted something, they could earn it. You see something for $1 and you have 50 cents, then I will give you the other 50 cents. So I taught them that.

PSYCHOLOGICAL AND COGNITIVE EFFECTS

Among the reported psychological and cognitive effects of participating in REAP's IDA program are greater focus on setting goals and motivation to achieve goals; more self-confidence and self-esteem; and greater future orientation and hope. Overall, saving in an IDA seems to make women feel good about themselves. These outcomes have important implications for women who have experienced domestic violence. The negative psychological impacts of domestic violence, including post-traumatic stress disorder, depression, and lowered self-esteem are well documented (M. P. Johnson & Ferraro, 2000, p. 957). Thus, the positive cognitive and psychological changes noted by women as result of participation in REAP's IDA program are encouraging. Michele articulated how she thinks differently about herself and also feels more hopeful about the future:

> The IDA... because the matching funds is a huge boost to mentality... the way I think about myself. And then to experience that, is the motivation to keep saving to keep earning. It's an experience that takes place, with the acceleration of the funds, I have that I haven't experienced before. I'm going to walk away with a significant amount of cash... more than I've ever had. And I mean... there's hope in that. There's hope attached to that and hope affects people's behaviors. It affects my behavior with my kids and so I think that's how it helps.

Continuing, Michele explained the IDA program makes her feel compensated in some small way for the abuse she endured and the negative financial consequences. This sense of compensation or "justice" helped her have a more positive future orientation:

> It clicked with me that so many people haven't cared about the abuse, because well, I'll have to tell you this... when I did have the guts to share [the abuse] with some people that were in my family and in my church... there was a general discounting about that. So the people close to me discounted my experiences and then these people [at REAP] who don't know me are giving it credence and that is significant. I mean, it's part of the healing that makes me able to go on and leave it. I mean, you can't leave it completely, but you can surely walk away from it further than I had. A little bit of justice in the world.

REAP and Safety

In the phone survey with 70 women, 81% report the REAP program has had a positive impact on their experiences of domestic violence and 95% feel participation in REAP will have a positive impact on their future safety (Sanders, 2011). In the qualitative study, many women made comments indicating that, while savings and asset accumulation may not play a direct role in their safety, it plays an important indirect role (Sanders, 2007). Women believe that the positive outcomes of participating in REAP, such as improved self-esteem and self-confidence, hope about their future, focus on goals, and a desire to be financially independent from an abusing partner, will help support their future safety. As their financial stability increases, women believe their ability to stay safe and free from intimate partner violence will also improve (Sanders, 2007). Darlene, for example, believes her self-esteem has increased as a result of having savings, and this will help her stay safe:

> Well, one thing is for sure, I wouldn't have to ask a man for [money]. Just the knowledge itself... empowers you. It's just up to you what you do with it. For me, I've chosen to take what I've learned and when I have the money to do what I need to do. That will assist me in not entering into another abusive relationship because I won't have those financial issues. I'll be stable in that area.

Kate summed up her thoughts about how the IDA will add to her future financial stability and safety, stating:

> Yeah, stability would help anyone, 'cause a woman that's stable and able to obtain and take care of and financially support her family... that's all she needs. If she got that, she ain't got to rely on no man. She don't have to take Tom, Dick, and Harry... because she needs support. Or she don't have to put up with her ex-husband or an abuser or an issue because she tried to get child support or whatever little crumbs he put out on the table. Because this economy is expensive and with four kids... even one... but four, it ain't easy. I think that would make a big difference. I think that would have helped me five or six years ago.

A few women do see a direct role of assets in safety and indicate how a specific asset purchase will help provide stability and prevent them from falling back into an abusive relationship. Louise commented on the benefits of owning a reliable vehicle:

> Well, [a car] would keep me out of a run of bad luck. Well, first of all, like if I have a car, then I would be working, you know, or I would still have a car. I mean, like I don't have a car now. It would just keep me running with the car… with a job.… it just seems like it would keep me in the idea that I would be emotionally stable working in a good job.

Monique believes that purchasing a home with her IDA savings will reduce her economic dependence and make her safer:

> Well, because I wouldn't have to live with a guy to make it. I wouldn't have to rely on his paycheck and his financial status to make it in the world. [The house] would be mine. It wouldn't be his. I wouldn't have to say, "What do you like honey?" "Okay honey," because I was afraid I would be out of a place to live.

Savings Outcomes

Secondary data on saving deposits, matching funds, and withdrawals provide evidence about the extent to which survivors of domestic violence can successfully save and invest in assets in an IDA program. Evidence comes from REAP program data and monthly account activity data from financial institutions. Data are managed by REAP staff using a data management program (MIS IDA; E. Johnson, Hinterlong, & Sherraden, 2001).

As of March 2009, 125 REAP IDA participants saved a total of $1,310 on average, and net savings[2] was $1,045 (Sanders, 2010). At the time of data analysis, this included 112 closed accounts and 13 open accounts. Of the women holding open accounts, five had reached their saving goal but had not completed their asset purchases, and eight participants were still saving toward a savings goal. Among the 112 participants with closed accounts, 72 (64%) closed after meeting their saving goal, while 40 (36%) account holders did not meet their savings goal and closed prematurely. Some women were simply unable to remain in the IDA program and meet their savings goal.

Prior to closing an account women routinely met with their REAP advocate and the IDA program director to assess strategies for continuing in the program or closing the account when deemed appropriate. Reasons for premature account closure included such things as inability to regularly save each month (a violation of program rules); life circumstances such as losing a job, health events, household bills, safety issues; or running out of time to meet their savings goal.

Table 4.2 examines saving indicators including total savings accumulation, total matching funds received, unmatched withdrawals, average savings per deposit,

Financial Capability among Survivors of Domestic Violence

Table 4.2. IDA Savings Outcomes (N = 125)

IDA Outcome	Mean	Median	Min–Max	N
Participant Total Savings[a]	$1,310	$1,500	$28–$4,153[b]	125
Participant Total Savings Less Unmatched Withdrawals (net savings)[c]	$1,045	$1,471	$0–$4,153	125
Total Savings Accumulation[d]	$3,041	$4,394	$0–$7,155	112[e]
Total Unmatched Withdrawals	$447	$275	$12–$1,944	74
Total Matching Funds Received	$1,980	$2,930	$0–$4,000[a]	112[b]
Participant Savings Goal	$1,570	$1,500	$1,000–$2,000[f]	125
Monthly Savings Goal	$57	$50	$10–$333	125
Average Deposit	$87	$59	$2.33–$519	125
Average Deposit Less Unmatched Withdrawals	$74	$49	$0–$519	125
Number of Deposits	22	21	3–48	125
Months of Participation	27	27	3–58[g]	125
Months to Reach Savings Goal	19	16	3–48	79[h]

[a] While the majority of accounts allowed a maximum saving goal of $1,500 with a $3,000 match, ten AFIA accounts and three local matching partner accounts allowed a maximum saving goal of $2,000 with a $4,000 match.
[b] A few women exceeded their savings goal through lump sum deposits; other women exceeded their total savings goal due to unmatched withdrawals that were later redeposited.
[c] Net savings includes money saved by participants less unmatched saving withdrawals. It does not include match money.
[d] Total savings accumulation includes total participant savings including interest, less unmatched withdrawals, plus matching funds received.
[e] Thirteen accounts were still open and eligible for matching funds as of March 2009.
[f] While the majority of accounts allowed a maximum saving goal of $1,500 with a $3,000 match, ten AFIA accounts and three local matching partner accounts allowed a maximum saving goal of $2,000 with a $4,000 match.
[g] At the discretion of REAP staff and the matching source, a few women were given time extensions beyond the normal 30-month maximum program length.
[h] Includes five accounts that had reached the savings goal but were still open as of March 2009.

saving goals, number of deposits, months of participation, and time taken to reach savings goal.

Among 116 participants (nine accounts were still open and no withdrawals had been made yet), 88 (76%) women made at least one matched withdrawal purchase, while 28 (24%) did not receive matching funds for withdrawals made as of March 2009. The average number of withdrawals was 2.5 (median 2).[3] The average number of matched withdrawals was 2 (median 2) and number of unmatched withdrawals was 1.5 (median 1). Taken together, women made a total of 307 withdrawals, including 189 (62%) matched and 118 (38%) unmatched. The mean and median monthly deposits were $74 and $49 respectively. On average, women who achieved their savings goal did so in 19 months.

Tables 4.3 and 4.4 provide details about how participants used savings withdrawals. By and large, most matched withdrawals were for purchasing a vehicle or for education. Most unmatched withdrawals were for emergency spending such as paying bills or for safety purposes. Emergency withdrawals to maintain housing, for example, could enhance safety. Additionally, many unmatched withdrawals were balance withdrawals that closed the IDA account. Forty-two (57%) women who made at least one unmatched withdrawal also received at least one matched withdrawal.

The women's asset purchases have potential implications for long-term economic stability. The purchase of a vehicle, for example, may allow women to

Table 4.3. MATCHED WITHDRAWALS

Purchase	Total	Percent	Average Amount	Average Participant Amount	Average Match Amount
Vehicle	63	33	$2,914	$1,015	$1,900
Education	52	28	$1,003	$340	$662
Small Business	32	17	$1,117	$375	$742
Home Repair	31	16	$1,555	$546	$1,009
Home Purchase	6	3	$3,420	$1,226	$2,195
Safety/emergency	4	2	$1,190	$522	$668
Retirement	1	.5	$900	$300	$600
Total	189[a]	100%	$1,830	$637	$1,194

[a]Total is greater than 125 due to some women making multiple purchases.

Table 4.4. UNMATCHED WITHDRAWALS

Purchase	Total	Percent	Average Participant Withdrawal
Safety/emergency	59	50	$313
No Purchase balance withdrawal	55	47	$238
Other/unknown	3	3	$523
Total	118	100%	$281

reliably and safely travel to and from work and school, and take their children to school and doctor appointments (Brabo et al., 2003; Ong, 1996). More education and training could allow women to acquire higher wage jobs (Pandey, Zhan, Neely-Barnes, & Menon, 2000; Spalter-Roth & Hartman, 1991). Buying or repairing a home could give women a sense of ownership, pride, and stake in their neighborhood (Rohe & Stegman, 1994a, 1994b).

Challenges

While self-reported effects and savings outcomes of REAP suggest meaningful effects on women's lives, not all women accomplished what they had hoped. One-fourth of women in the IDA program were unable to make matched asset purchases. Most of the challenges women discussed concern daily financial struggles, including unstable and insufficient income, substantial debt, and children's needs (Sanders, 2007). Based on data available about emergency withdrawals, women who closed their accounts prematurely had difficult life circumstances that prevented them from saving consistently. The most common emergency expenditure was rent or utilities to help women maintain housing, although in a few cases women made safety withdrawals for temporary housing such as a hotel stay or a move to another city. These withdrawals may have played a positive role in women's economic stability, independence, and ability to remain safe from abuse.

Other women also made emergency withdrawals, but redeposited the withdrawn savings and eventually made matched withdrawals. Moreover, REAP staff gave extensions and exceptions to some women that allowed them to miss deposits (when funding sources permitted).

DISCUSSION AND IMPLICATIONS

Survivors of domestic violence commonly experience economic abuse, including isolation from financial knowledge and resources. Safe provision of financial education helps women become more financially independent (Sanders, 2007). However, while financial education is vital, it is not sufficient. Financial resources and access to financial services and supports make it possible for women to apply financial knowledge and skills and become financially capable (M. S. Sherraden, 2010). Teaching women the importance of keeping important documents in a safe place or having a savings account may prove fruitless without the ability to open an affordable bank account or safe deposit box. Outcomes of economic education may be reinforced by participation in the IDA program. That is, having the opportunity to act on what is learned in REAP classes, by saving money, may reinforce and sustain cognitive/affective and behavioral changes. Stated simply, having an IDA may reinforce changes women have made with regard to their financial lives and goals. Ultimately, this is likely to translate into greater economic well-being and safety, although research is needed to verify this empirically.

Although scholars have known that poverty, financial concerns, and intimate partner violence are often interrelated, few communities have designed targeted strategies to deal with this reality. The innovative work of REAP highlights the relationship between economic factors, financial issues, and domestic violence and has shown how financial services have the potential to build financial capability. The REAP collaboration that brought together domestic violence service providers offers a framework for communities to develop tailored economic interventions for survivors of domestic violence (Sanders & Schnabel, 2006).

Social Work Practice: Economic Abuse and Interventions

REAP studies have important implications for social work practice and education, social policy, and research. While women's physical safety must take precedence in dealing with issues of domestic violence, economic abuse should be addressed along with the physical, sexual, verbal, and emotional dimensions of IPV. Historically, services for victims of domestic violence have focused on individual counseling and crisis services, such as short-term shelter (Davis, Hagen, & Early, 1994). Financial knowledge and self-efficacy promote economic well-being of survivors of domestic violence (Jacob, Hudson, & Bush, 2000; Sanders, Weaver, & Schnabel, 2007). Moreover, research demonstrates the positive social, psychological, and economic implications of asset ownership (Scanlon & Page-Adams, 2001; M. Sherraden, 2001). While many women successfully saved and purchased assets, others were challenged to consistently save or were faced with financial emergencies that prevented them from meeting their savings goals. Social work practitioners and advocates for abused women have an important role in the development of economic interventions unique to the needs of survivors in order to promote successful outcomes, address challenges to saving, and identify the readiness of women to participate in a matched savings program. Assessment of economic abuse is also a critical component of intervention. Recent measures of abuse and financial issues have been developed, highlighting the economic dimension of domestic violence and providing practitioners with hands-on assessment tools (Adams, Sullivan, Bybee, & Greeson, 2008; Weaver, Sanders, Campbell, & Schnabel, 2009).

Social Work Education: Curricula Needed

Family violence is a crosscutting issue that social workers encounter in many settings; therefore, schools of social work should include curricula on the economic dimensions of domestic violence. Few schools of social work systematically integrate content on IPV that prepares social workers to practice with victims of domestic violence (Danis & Lockhart, 2003). As schools make strides toward greater integration of content on IPV, it is critical to include economic issues and interventions. Interventions should emphasize methods that build financial capability; that is, not only financial education and skill building but also inclusion and access to financial services that meet the unique needs of survivors including safety measures. Finally, social workers must understand the role of economic factors in domestic violence and acquire basic financial knowledge themselves. An emerging theme in some schools of social work is the provision of economic education classes for social workers (Birkenmaier, Kennedy, Kunz, Sander, & Horwitz, chapter 13, this volume; M. S. Sherraden, Laux, & Kaufman, 2007).

Policy Support for Building Financial Capability among Survivors

In addition to community-based initiatives, state and federal policy measures are needed that specifically address financial capability among survivors of domestic violence. Policy measures have focused largely on crisis shelter, legal assistance, and individual counseling. Economic security initiatives for battered women have not received similar policy attention. Historically, for example, the Violence Against Women Act (VAWA) emphasized the criminal justice response to domestic violence and community-based service responses to domestic violence, dating violence, and sexual assault. VAWA's reauthorization in 2005 includes greater recognition of the risk of losing housing and employment. Nonetheless, more attention should be paid to the role of financial issues in domestic violence and the need for initiatives that advance financial capability. Policy initiatives can direct funding to programs aimed at building financial capability of survivors of domestic violence. For example, IDA matching funds, including those from the Assets for Independence Act (AFIA), can target low-income women impacted by IPV. Targeting would require greater flexibility with regard to time limits, allowable asset purchases, and provisions for safety withdrawals in order to meet the unique needs of women moving toward economic independence and stability.

Programs like REAP can assist women by increasing their economic empowerment, helping them deal with daily financial tasks, and advancing their short- and long-term financial goals. However, advocacy and policy initiatives that address larger structural conditions and forces that work against low-income women are vital. These include problems associated with low wages, job discrimination, limited access to education, lack of job skills, lack of access to affordable childcare and housing, and holes in the social safety net.

Research on the Intersection of Domestic Violence and Financial Capability

Further research is needed to understand the complex relationship between financial capability and domestic violence, as well as the impact of programs such as REAP on women's long-term safety. Although self-reported experiences in REAP are overwhelmingly positive and savings outcomes remarkably successful, relatively little is known about the ways in which programs such as REAP impact women's experience of domestic violence. Controlled studies are needed to examine abuse issues as they relate to economic circumstances and participation in REAP. While existing research results are encouraging, the relationship between the provision of financial education, matched savings, asset purchases, and occurrence of abuse is unknown. Controlled studies would begin to answer these questions.

Additionally, because programs like REAP are intended to support longer-term economic development and well-being, longitudinal studies are needed to assess economic well-being and abuse outcomes over time. Fundamentally, it will be important to understand if the provision of services—such as those offered by REAP—result in improved financial capability, economic well-being, and reduction of domestic violence.

CONCLUSION

This chapter demonstrates the role that financial issues play in domestic violence and provides a framework for understanding the importance of interventions that address the economic dimension of abuse and advance women's economic knowledge, skills, and capability. The initial empirical evidence on REAP's economic education program and IDA savings outcomes are promising. However, current research is limited, calling for continued efforts to implement and evaluate programs that advance financial capability among survivors of domestic violence.

NOTES

1. Readers are encouraged to refer to additional publications by the author for a more comprehensive reporting and discussion of REAP empirical findings. See for example Sanders (2007, 2010); Sanders, Weaver, and Schnabel (2007); and Sanders and Schnabel (2006).
2. Net savings includes money saved by participant less unmatched saving withdrawals. It does not include match money.
3. Number of withdrawals among participants ranged from 1 to 9 withdrawals.

REFERENCES

Abramovitz, M. (1996). *Regulating the lives of women: Social welfare policy from colonial times to the present* (2nd ed.). Boston: South End Press.

Adams, A. E., Sullivan, C. M., Bybee, D., & Greeson, M. R. (2008). Development of the scale of economic abuse. *Violence against Women, 14*(5), 563–588.

Barnett, O. W. (2000). Why battered women do not leave, part 1. *Trauma, Violence, and Abuse, 1*(4), 343–372.

Brabo, L. M., Kilde, P. H., Peske-Herriges, P., Quinn, T., & Sanderud-Nordquist, I. (2003). Driving out of poverty in private automobiles. *Journal of Poverty, 7*(1/2), 183–196.

Browne, A., Salomon, A., & Bassuk, S. S. (1999). The impact of recent partner violence on poor women's capacity to maintain work. *Violence against Women, 5*(4), 393–426.

Corporation for Enterprise Development (CFED). (2009). *IDA directory*. Retrieved June 15, 2009, from http://www.cfed.org/ida/directory/

Danis, F. S., & Lockhart, L. (2003). Domestic violence and social work education: What do we know, what do we need to know? *Journal of Social Work Education, 39*(2), 215–224.

Davis, L. V., & Hagen, J. L. (1992). The problem of wife abuse: The interrelationship of social policy and social work practice. *Social Work, 37*(1), 15–20.

Davis, L. V., Hagen, J. L., & Early, T. J. (1994). Social services for battered women: Are they adequate, accessible and appropriate? *Social Work, 39*(6), 695–704.

Dobash, R. P., & Dobash, R. E. (1979). *Violence against wives: A case against the patriarchy.* New York: Free Press.

Farmer, A., & Tiefenthaler, J. (1997). An economic analysis of domestic violence. *Review of Social Economy, 55*(3), 337–358.

Farmer, A., & Tiefenthaler, J. (2003). Explaining the recent decline in domestic violence. *Contemporary Economic Policy, 21*(2), 158–172.

Fernandez, M., Iwamoto, K., & Muscat, B. (1997). Dependency and severity of abuse: Impact on women's persistence in utilizing the courts system as protection against domestic violence. *Women and Criminal Justice, 9*(1), 39–63.

Gonzalez, W. C. (2005). Factors in the decision of Mexican battered women to stay or leave abusive relationships. *Dissertation Abstracts International, A: The Humanities and Social Sciences (0419-4209), 65*(9), 3569.

Jacob, K., Hudson, S., & Bush, M. (2000). *Tools for survival: An analysis of financial literacy programs for lower-income families.* Chicago: Woodstock Institute.

Johnson, E., Hinterlong, J., & Sherraden, M. (2001). *Strategies for creating MIS technology to improve social work practice and research* (CSD Working Paper 01-13). St. Louis, MO: Washington University, Center for Social Development. Retrieved August 1, 2009, from http://csd.wustl.edu/Publications/Documents/84.StrategiesForCreatingMISTech.pdf

Johnson, E., & Sherraden, M. S. (2007). From financial literacy to financial capability among youth. *Journal of Sociology and Social Welfare, 34*(3), 119–146.

Johnson, I. M. (1992). Economic, situational and psychological correlates of the decision-making process of battered women. *Families in Society: The Journal of Contemporary Human Services, 73*(3), 168–176.

Johnson, M. P., & Ferraro, K. J. (2000). Research on domestic violence in the 1990s: Making distinctions. *Journal of Marriage and Family, 62*(4), 948–963.

Kalmuss, D. S., & Straus, M. A. (1982). Wife's marital dependency and wife abuse. *Journal of Marriage and the Family, 44*(2), 277–286.

Kurz, D. (1998). Women, welfare, and domestic violence. *Social Justice, 25*(1), 105–122.

Lambert, L. C., & Firestone, J. M. (2000). Economic context and multiple abuse techniques. *Violence against Women, 6*(1), 49–67.

Lloyd, S., & Taluc, N. (1999). The effects of male violence on female employment. *Violence against Women, 5*(4), 370–392.

Menard, A. (2001). Domestic violence and housing: Key policy and program challenges. *Violence against Women, 7*(6), 707–720.

Moe, A. M., & Bell, M. P. (2004). Abject economics: The effects of battering and violence on women's work and employability. *Violence against Women, 10*(1), 29–55.

Ong, P. M. (1996). Work and automobile ownership among welfare recipients. *Social Work Research, 20*(4), 255–262.

Page-Adams, D. (1995). *Economic resources and marital violence* (Unpublished doctoral dissertation). Washington University, St. Louis, MO.

Pandey, S., Zhan, M., Neely-Barnes, S., & Menon, N. (2000). The higher education option for poor women with children. *Journal of Sociology and Social Welfare, 27*(4), 109–170.

Ptacek, J. (1997). The tactics and strategies of men who batter. In A. P. Cardarelli (Ed.), *Violence between intimate partners: Patterns, causes, and effects* (pp. 48–69). Boston: Allyn & Bacon.

Raphael, J. (2000). *Saving Bernice: Battered women, welfare, and poverty.* Boston: Northeastern University Press.

Redevelopment Opportunities for Women, Inc. (REAP). (2005). *REAP—Realizing Your Economic Action Plan: An economic education curriculum for women experiencing domestic violence.* St. Louis, MO: Redevelopment Opportunities for Women, Inc.

Redevelopment Opportunities for Women, Inc. (n.d.). *About Redevelopment Opportunities for Women.* Retrieved October 28, 2010, from http://www.row.stl.org/content/about.aspx

Rennison, C. M., & Welchans, S. (2000). *Intimate partner violence.* Washington, DC: USGPO. NCJ 178247. Retrieved July 1, 2009 from: http://ojp.usdoj.gov/bjs/pub/pdf/ipv.pdf

Riger, S., & Krieglstein, M. (2000). The impact of welfare reform on men's violence against women. *American Journal of Community Psychology, 28*(5), 631–647.

Riger, S., Staggs, S. L., & Schewe, P. (2004). Intimate partner violence as an obstacle to employment among mothers affected by welfare reform. *Journal of Social Issues, 60*(4), 801–818.

Rohe, W., & Stegman, W. (1994a). The effects of homeownership on the self-esteem, perceived control, and life satisfaction of low-income people. *Journal of the American Planning Association, 60*(2), 173–184.

Rohe, W., & Stegman, W. (1994b). The impact of homeownership on the social and political involvement of low-income people. *Urban Affairs Quarterly, 30*(1), 152–172.

Sanders, C. K. (2007). *Domestic violence, economic abuse and implications of a program for building economic resources for low-income women: Findings from interviews with participants in a women's economic action program* (CSD Research Report 07-12). St. Louis, MO: Washington University, Center for Social Development. Retrieved April 15, 2007, from http://csd.wustl.edu/Publications/Documents/RP07-12.pdf

Sanders, C. K. (2010). *Savings outcomes of an IDA program for survivors of domestic violence* (CSD Report 10-42). St. Louis, MO: Washington University, Center for Social Development. Retrieved December 15, 2010, from http://csd.wustl.edu/Publications/Documents/RP10-42.pdf

Sanders, C. K. (2011). *Survey results of a program to advance the financial capability of survivors of domestic violence.* Unpublished research report. St. Louis, MO: Washington University, Center for Social Development.

Sanders, C. K., & Schnabel, M. (2006). Organizing for economic empowerment of battered women: Women's savings accounts. *Journal of Community Practice, 14*(3), 47–68.

Sanders, C. K., Weaver, T. L., & Schnabel, M. (2007). Economic education for battered women: An evaluation of outcomes. *Affilia: Journal of Women and Social Work, 22*(3), 240–254.

Scanlon, E. (1998). Low-income homeownership policy as a community development strategy. *Journal of Community Practice, 5*(1/2), 137–154.

Scanlon, E., & Page-Adams, D. (2001). Effects of asset holdings on neighborhoods, families, and children: A review of research. In R. Boshara (Ed.), *Building assets: A report on the asset-development and ID field.* Washington, DC: CFED.

Schechter, S. (1982). *Women and male violence: The visions and struggles of the battered women's movement.* Boston: South End Press.

Sherraden, M. (1991). *Assets and the poor: A new American welfare policy.* Armonk, NY: M. E. Sharpe.

Sherraden, M. (2001). Asset-building policies and programs for the poor. In T. Shapiro & E. Wolff (Eds.), *Assets for the poor: Spreading the benefits of asset ownership* (pp. 302–333). New York: Russell Sage.

Sherraden, M. S. (2010). *Financial capability: What is it, and how can it be created?* (CSD Working Paper 10-17). St. Louis, MO: Washington University, Center for Social Development.

Sherraden, M. S., Laux, S., & Kaufman, C. (2007). Financial education for social workers. *Journal of Community Practice, 15*(3), 9–36.

Sherraden, M. S., McBride, A. M., with Beverley, S. (2010). *Striving to save: Creating policies for financial security of low-income families.* Ann Arbor: University of Michigan Press.

Smith, M. D. (1990). Sociodemographic risk factors in wife abuse: Results from a survey of Toronto women. *Canadian Journal of Sociology, 15*(1), 39–58.

Spalter-Roth, R. M., & Hartman, H. I. (1991). *Increasing working mothers' earnings: Executive summary.* Washington, DC: Institute for Women's Policy Research.

Strube, M. J., & Barbour, L. S. (1983). The decision to leave an abusive relationship: Economic dependence and psychological commitment. *Journal of Marriage and the Family, 45*(4), 785–793.

Sullivan, C. M. (1991). The provision of advocacy services to women leaving abusive partners: An exploratory study. *Journal of Interpersonal Violence, 6*(1), 41–54.

Swanberg, J. E., Logan, T. K., & Macke, C. (2005). Intimate partner violence, employment and the workplace: Consequences and future directions. *Trauma, Violence, and Abuse, 6*(4), 286–312.

Swanberg, J. E., & Macke, C. (2006). Intimate partner violence and the workplace: Consequences and disclosure. *Affilia: Journal of Women and Social Work, 21*(4), 391–406.

Tauchen, H. V., Witte, A. D., & Long, S. K. (1991). Domestic violence: A nonrandom affair. *International Economic Review, 32*(2), 491–511.

Tolman, R. M., & Raphael, J. (2000). A review of research on welfare and domestic violence. *Journal of Social Issues, 56*(4), 655–682.

Weaver, T. L., Sanders, C. K., Campbell, C. L., & Schnabel, M (2009). Development and preliminary psychometric evaluation of the domestic violence-related financial issues scale (DV-FI). *Journal of Interpersonal Violence, 24*(4), 569–585.

Yllo, K. (1993). Through a feminist lens: Gender, power, and violence. In R. J. Gelles & D. R. Loseke (Eds.), *Current controversies on family violence* (pp. 47–62). Newbury Park, CA: Sage.

Zorza, J. (1991). Woman battering: A major cause of homelessness. *Clearinghouse Review, 25*(4), 421–429.

5

Low-Income Parents of Preschool Children

Financial Knowledge, Attitudes, Behaviors, and Ownership

DEBORAH D. ADAMS AND SONDRA G. BEVERLY

In this chapter, we provide a profile of the financial knowledge, attitudes, behaviors, and ownership of low-income parents with preschool children. Parents of students attending fourteen Head Start centers administered by a community-based organization in an economically distressed county in the North Central region of the United States were surveyed. About half of these parents later had the opportunity to open college savings accounts with initial deposits of $1,000 for their children's futures. However, the profile presented here is based on our analysis of data from the first survey of parents and includes those in the treatment group and similar parents in a comparison group who did not have the college savings account opportunity through the community-based organization.

Following a 4-year quasi-experimental intervention that included the initial deposit into children's college savings accounts, matching funds for parental deposits, and the opportunity to attend financial education classes, a second survey was conducted. Detailed findings from previous longitudinal studies are reported elsewhere (Loke, Clancy, & Zager, 2009; Marks, Rhodes, Engelhardt, Scheffler, & Wallace, 2009; Mason, Nam, Clancy, Loke, & Kim, 2009).

Two findings from these prior longitudinal studies with particular import for understanding asset building among low-income families with young children are: (1) very few treatment group parents in the college savings program attended the voluntary financial education sessions offered by the community-based organization that administered the program, and yet (2) most of these parents opened college savings accounts for their children when given the opportunity to do so, and about one-third made additional deposits to those accounts in the first four years after they were opened.

Do these findings, taken together, mean that low-income parents of young children who have the opportunity to participate in an inclusive asset-building program with progressive account features do not need financial education? To address this question, data from the first (preintervention) survey was used to develop a financial profile of families with preschool children who participated in the larger study. Consistent with the concept of financial capability, the findings presented here suggest the need for *both* financial education *and* real access to financial products that are appropriately structured and incentivized so that they are truly inclusive of low-income parents of preschool children.

STUDY BACKGROUND

The financial profile developed in this chapter is part of a large, multimethod research project on child development accounts (CDAs). CDAs, sometimes called child savings accounts, are asset-building accounts designed to help children and youth achieve long-term developmental goals such as attending college, buying a home, or opening a small business. A policy, practice, and research initiative was developed to test the efficacy of and inform policy for a national system of progressively funded asset-building accounts for children and youth. The initiative began in 2004 with twelve community-based organizations throughout the United States and Puerto Rico. This initiative, called Saving for Education, Entrepreneurship, and Downpayment (SEED), was the first large demonstration of CDAs in the United States.

With the help of staff members at the participating community-based organizations, a team of researchers from a number of partnering universities and firms conducted several studies of the CDA initiative. One of the community-based organizations that operated a CDA program as part of SEED was a large multiservice agency that administered Head Start centers in an economically distressed county in a North Central state. This particular SEED program was designed to build assets for postsecondary education through a state college savings (529) plan. Parents of preschool children who were enrolled in 14 Head Start centers participated in a baseline survey in 2004–2005 just as the CDA program began. The survey included items on parent financial knowledge, attitudes, and behaviors, as well as account and asset ownership. The findings reported here come from the analysis of data from this first (preintervention) survey on these topics, and may help interpret outcomes from previous longitudinal studies of the SEED program.

LITERATURE REVIEW

Most of the community-based programs in the SEED initiative focused their asset-building efforts on low-income families with young children because children in such families represent the poorest age group in the nation. In 2010, among children under the age of 6 who lived in households with related adults, one in four children (25.3%) was living in poverty. Further, one in three children (31.6%) living in households maintained solely by women were poor. Most SEED families were maintained solely by women (US Census Bureau, 2011).

In addition to income poverty, asset poverty is of particular concern because developmental goals such as higher education are nearly out of reach for children who grow up in households without wealth. Further, while income gaps by race and ethnicity are wide, asset gaps are even wider. A recent analysis of data from the Survey of Program Participation (SIPP) revealed that the gap in net worth between Whites, Blacks, and Hispanics was at a record high in 2009, with the median wealth of White households being 20 times that of Black households and 18 times that of Hispanic households (Taylor, Kochhar, Fry, Velasco, & Motel, 2011). This represents the widest asset gap since the US government began publishing such data 25 years ago.

Our interest in studying financial knowledge, attitudes, and behaviors, as well as ownership of accounts and assets in low-income families, stems from our concern about increasing poverty rates in families with young children, and growing income and asset gaps by race and ethnicity. Our interest in developing an accurate financial profile of low-income parents of young children also coincides with increasing attention to both financial education and financial capability among researchers, policy makers, and community-based social service providers and advocates.

In studies of asset-building policies and programs, like the Child Development Account (CDA) initiative that provided the context for our study, financial education has been shown to positively impact matched savings account opening and saving performance as measured by both amount of savings and frequency of deposits (Clancy, Grinstein-Weiss, & Schreiner, 2001; Schreiner & Sherraden, 2007). Further, in qualitative research, youth who participated in a matched savings program reported that financial education had a positive effect on their financial knowledge (Scanlon & Adams, 2009).

Beyond studies with participants of asset-building programs, there is empirical evidence of both the need for and the effects of financial education among various groups in the general population. Turning first to the need for such education, research demonstrates low levels of financial literacy among both teens and young adults in the United States (Lusardi, Mitchell, & Curto, 2010; Mandell, 2008b). Other groups that have been shown to have relatively low levels of financial education include college students (Markovich & DeVaney, 1997; Warnick & Mansfield, 2000) and women (Lusardi & Mitchell, 2008; Lusardi et al., 2010), as well as low-income and ethnically diverse populations (Lusardi et al., 2010; Mandell, 2008b).

Research on the effects of financial education is more mixed. Mixed results are perhaps related to a range of design and measurement difficulties in these studies (Beverly & Clancy, 2001; Hilgert, Hogarth, & Beverly, 2003; Lucey, 2005; Mandell & Klein, 2009). While some research suggests that the impact of financial education is promising, or even positive, (Bernheim & Garrett, 2003; Clancy et al., 2001; Hilgert et al., 2003), findings from other studies highlight the difficulties in achieving consistently high participation rates (Mandell, 2008a; Marks, Rhodes, Engelhardt, et al., 2009).

Further, with some notable exceptions, very little research has focused specifically on the effects of financial education for low-income and ethnically diverse communities (Lusardi et al., 2010; Schuchardt et al., 2009; M. S. Sherraden, 2010). The exceptions include studies of African American and Native youth (Anderson, Jorgensen, Brantmeier, & Mandell, 2008; Jorgensen & Mandell, 2007; Mandell & Hanson, 2008) and studies of asset-building policies and programs (Schreiner & Sherraden, 2007; Sherraden, Johnson, Elliott, Porterfield, & Rainford, 2007; M. Sherraden & Stevens, 2010; M. S. Sherraden, McBride, & Beverly, 2010). With mixed research results, and minimal inclusion of low-income and ethnically diverse populations in studies, it is difficult to speak with any confidence about the overall effects of financial education.

One thing that is clear from a review of the literature is the important role that parents play in their children's financial education and socialization. In reviewing this literature, and with particular import for the financial profile presented in this chapter, Margaret Sherraden writes, "If parents lack financial knowledge and skills, they cannot model sound financial decision making" (M. S. Sherraden, 2010, p. 4).

Indeed, one of the reasons that programs designed to build assets for children often include financial education opportunities for parents is because of the central role they can play in their children's financial education and socialization. Recently, however, some have begun to argue that financial education is a necessary but not a sufficient condition for increased social and economic well-being. The financial capability approach (Johnson & Sherraden, 2007; M. S. Sherraden, 2010) holds that real access to financial products that are designed to facilitate asset building, along with the opportunity to act on financial knowledge, are necessary *in addition to financial education* to enhance social and economic well-being. Outlining a theory of financial capability that is informed by the work of Sen (1999) and Nussbaum (2000), Margaret Sherraden (2010) writes:

> Financial literacy will undoubtedly make people more capable of managing their finances. It is unclear, however, whether it will reduce financial vulnerability in low-income households if institutional barriers to beneficial financial products are not also addressed. The concept of *financial capability* (emphasis in the original) includes financial literacy but also addresses these institutional barriers facing low-income households. (p. 2)

Such institutional barriers come into sharp relief in the financial profile that is the focus of this chapter, especially as the ownership of accounts and assets among low-income parents of preschool children is described.

Further, institutional features of asset-building initiatives such as access, incentives, and facilitation (Beverly & Sherraden, 1999; Beverly et al., 2008) are of special interest for understanding the financial profile presented in this chapter given that prior longitudinal studies involving the same treatment group parents of preschool children have revealed: (1) low levels of participation in voluntary financial education paired with (2) nearly universal asset accumulation in children's college savings accounts. Before reporting findings on baseline ownership of accounts and assets, however, we will describe our research methods, as well as findings about financial knowledge, attitudes, and behaviors among low-income parents of young children who participated in the survey.

METHODS

The data for this research come from a larger study in which 790 parents (or other primary caregivers) of children who were enrolled in Head Start centers in fall 2004 participated in a survey. These parents completed 45-minute telephone interviews conducted by RTI International[1] using a survey instrument developed by SEED research team members at the University of Kansas and the University of Michigan (Adams, 2008; Beverly & Williams Shanks, 2004).

It is important to note two things about the financial profile presented below. First, the data used in this analysis were responses to baseline, or preintervention, survey questions from low-income parents of young children in both the treatment and comparison groups. Thus the findings presented in this chapter do not compare differences between the two groups at the end of the CDA initiative, but rather present a financial profile of low-income parents of young children at the very beginning of the initiative. None of the comparison group parents (n = 409) and 85% of the parents in the treatment group (n = 323 of 381) completed the baseline survey *before* CDA outreach began, and thus had *not* received educational and promotional material about saving from agency staff.

Even so, it is important to note that many of the responses documented here may be affected by social desirability bias, which is the tendency for survey respondents to give answers that are socially acceptable. Most people who live in the United States have been told in a variety of ways that certain money management behaviors are "good," and many may be reluctant to admit that they do not budget, save, and so forth. This issue is further addressed in the discussion section following the presentation of findings below on financial knowledge, attitudes, behaviors, and ownership of low-income parents of preschool children living in an economically distressed community.

RESULTS

Demographic and Economic Characteristics of Sample

Demographic and economic characteristics of the families in this study are summarized in Table 5.1. Most of the parents are female. At the time of the 2004–2005 survey, just under half of the parents had never been married; just over one-third were currently married. Most parents are White or African American, and most were born in the United States. About 70% of the sample had at least a high school education, including 39% with more than a high school education.[2] The median family income (for the 553 parents who reported precise amounts) was about $15,000. Most families had multiple children, and most had at least one employed adult.

Table 5.1. CHARACTERISTICS OF THE SAMPLE (N = 790)

Parent Characteristics		Family Characteristics	
Female	92.0%	Number of Children	
Marital Status		One child	20.8%
Never married	47.0%	Two children	37.0%
Currently married	34.9%	Three children	24.8%
Previously married	18.1%	Four or more children	17.5%
Race		Employed	78.2%
White	46.4%		
African American	43.4%		
Other	10.2%		
Hispanic	12.1%		
US Native	87.2%		
Education			
Less than high school education	29.2%		
High school diploma or GED	31.5%		
More than high school education	39.3%		

NOTES: The sample was drawn from families with children enrolled in Head Start programs in fall 2004. Due to missing data, actual sample size varies from 742 to 790.

Financial Profile

FINANCIAL KNOWLEDGE

The baseline (preintervention) survey included six items designed to assess the financial knowledge of parents. The percentages of parents who answered the first five of these items correctly are displayed in Table 5.2. On a positive note, 75% of parents correctly identified annual percentage rate as the most important feature of a credit card contract for families that do not pay the balance in full each month. However, more than 40% *incorrectly* responded that banks usually contact customers who are about to overdraw their checking accounts or responded "don't know." Parents were even more likely to incorrectly answer specific questions about the state's college savings (529) plan, about rates of return, and about compound interest.

The sixth survey item designed to help us assess financial knowledge among parents of preschool children was worded as follows: "About how much is a year's tuition for a full-time student at a local community college?" Only seven percent (7%) of parents could roughly estimate the cost of a year's tuition at a local community college. Almost 52% answered "don't know." The vast majority of those who gave a dollar value *overestimated* the cost of tuition. For example, after "don't know," the most common answer was $10,000, about $8,500 higher than the actual cost of tuition at the local community college.

Table 5.2. FINANCIAL KNOWLEDGE AMONG LOW-INCOME PARENTS OF PRESCHOOL CHILDREN (N = 789)

Survey Question	Percent Correct
If you are comparing offers from credit cards and don't expect to pay the bill in full every month, the Annual Percentage Rate or APR is the most important thing to look at. (**true**, false)	74.7%
A bank will usually call to warn you if you write a check that would overdraw your account. (true, **false**)	58.7%
People who deposit money in the Michigan Education Savings Program can get a tax break on their Michigan state income tax. (**true**, false)	41.1%
Which of the following is most likely to make the most money over the next 18 years? (savings account, checking account, savings bond, **stocks**)	38.5%
With an account that has compound interest, you earn interest on the principal and the interest. (**true**, false)	35.5%

NOTES: Correct answers are in bold. Refusals and "don't know" were defined as incorrect responses.

Agency staff members were confident that most parents thought about the local community college when hearing this question. It is the largest community college in the state and is located in the county, which is home to all 14 of the Head Start centers. A county resident taking 12 credit hours at the community college for each of two semesters would pay just over $1,360 in tuition.[3] A county resident taking 15 credit hours at the college for each of two semesters would pay just over $1,700. Using a generous range for determining correct answers, we coded tuition estimates that we believed were "in the ballpark"—that is, estimates from $700 through $2,500—as correct.

FINANCIAL ATTITUDES

The SEED survey included several questions assessing financial attitudes. First, parents were asked about their time horizons for money management (Table 5.3). Over two-fifths of parents said they usually thought about the current month. Another 36% said that they usually thought about the next few months. Longer time horizons were much less common.

Parents were also asked what they would do with an "extra" $200 (Table 5.4). There was quite a bit of variation in the responses. The most common response was "save most," and the second most common was "spend most." About two-thirds said they would save either most or all.

In response to yes/no questions (Table 5.5), about 90% of parents said that it was important for children, and for their families, to have savings accounts. Three-quarters said that they trusted banks. About 70% said they were hesitant to spend money they had saved.

Table 5.3. MONEY-MANAGEMENT TIME HORIZONS OF PARENTS (N = 788)

When it comes to money management, do you usually think about…	Percent
The current month	41.1%
The next few months	36.4%
The next year	7.7%
The next few years	4.1%
The next five to ten years	3.2%
Longer than ten years	4.4%
Don't know	3.1%

Table 5.4. PLANNED USE OF "EXTRA" MONEY AMONG PARENTS (N = 789)

Suppose you had some extra money, say $200. What would you probably do with that money?	Percent
Spend all	10.8%
Spend most	22.3%
Save most	45.3%
Save all	19.3%
Don't know	2.4%

Table 5.5. SAVING-RELATED ATTITUDES OF PARENTS

Survey Question	N	Yes	No
It is important for a child to have a savings account while growing up.	787	90.2%	9.8%
It is important for my family to have a savings account.	789	89.0%	11.0%
I trust banks.	783	74.8%	25.2%
Are you hesitant to spend money that you have saved?	779	70.3%	29.7%

Finally, to assess baseline attitudes about the need for emergency savings, parents were asked the following question: "About how much do you think you should have saved for emergencies and other unexpected things that come up?" Thirteen people responded that no savings were needed, and 83 people said they didn't know. The most common response (given by 146 parents) was $1,000. The median amount was also $1,000, and the mean was $2,353 (SD = $3,677).

Financial Behaviors

Table 5.6 summarizes findings related to financial behaviors. Almost two-thirds of parents said they often kept track of their spending, and another 20% said they sometimes did. About 43% of survey respondents said they often set financial goals. About 37% said they often stuck to their financial plans. Over one-fourth of families said they rarely set financial goals, and a similar percentage said they rarely stuck to their financial plans.

Only 36% of parents said they had a written budget or spending plan. Two-thirds of parents said they tried to save a regular amount each month. Those who reported trying to save regularly (N = 517) were asked how much they tried to save each month. For the 459 people who answered this question, the median monthly saving goal was $100, and the mean was $166 (SD = $201). Across all respondents (including the 263 who said they did *not* try to save a regular amount each month), the median monthly saving goal was $50, and the mean was $106 (SD = $179). Only 16% of parents (or spouses/partners, if applicable) had money directly deposited into a savings account.[6]

Account and Asset Ownership

A number of questions on the baseline survey allow us to document ownership of specific accounts and assets before the CDA initiative began (Table 5.7). Most of these questions explicitly ask about ownership by parents or spouses/partners, if applicable. Just over half of families had savings accounts (54.3%), and slightly

Table 5.6. Money-Management Behaviors of Low-Income Parents of Preschool Children

Survey Question	N	Often True	Sometimes True	Rarely True
I keep track of my spending.	781	65.3%	20.1%	14.6%
My family sets financial goals for our future.	773	42.7%	30.1%	27.2%
My family sticks to the financial plans we set for ourselves.	777	36.7%	37.8%	25.5%
	N	Yes	No	
Do you have a written budget or spending plan?	782	35.5%	64.5%	
Do you try to save a regular amount each month?	780	66.3%	33.7%	
Do you (or your spouse/partner) have money from a paycheck or government program directly deposited into a savings account?	783	16.2%	83.8%	

Table 5.7. ACCOUNT AND ASSET OWNERSHIP AMONG LOW-INCOME PARENTS OF PRESCHOOL CHILDREN

	N	Percent Owning Account/Asset
Vehicle*	787	87.8%
Computer	790	62.4%
Checking account	785	57.6%
Savings account**	786	54.3%
Home	789	27.1%
Retirement account (excluding pension plans)	782	17.9%
Certificate of deposit	776	6.4%
Bond	783	6.0%
Stock or mutual fund	782	5.1%

*43% owned more than one vehicle
**72.8% had either a checking *or* savings account

more had checking accounts (57.6%). About 88% of families owned at least one vehicle, and just over 62% owned a computer. At first glance, then, the families at the beginning of the CDA initiative appear to have had some assets. However, with the exception of money in savings accounts, more than half of the parents reported assets that either tend to depreciate or do not appreciate over time. While of major importance in terms of transportation, education, and everyday financial transactions, the ownership of vehicles and computers and regular bank accounts does not mean that families are included in the financial mainstream.

Turning to assets that have historically appreciated or have the potential to appreciate over time, notably fewer families reported ownership at the beginning of this study. For example, about 27% of parents said they owned their own homes, with 75% of the homeowners reporting a home mortgage. Further, ownership rates for investment products were quite low. About 18% had retirement accounts, such as individual retirement accounts and 401(k)s. About 5% or 6% owned certificates of deposit, stocks or mutual funds, and bonds.

A careful look at Table 5.7 brings the pattern of ownership into sharp relief; as growth potential increases, ownership decreases among parents of families with young children. The percentages of parents in this study who had vehicles and computers were higher than the proportion of those who had checking accounts. The percentage of checking account owners was a bit higher than the percentage of savings account owners. Finally, the percentage of families who owned bank accounts at baseline was much higher than the percentage of parents who reported owning assets that have been historically more likely to appreciate over time.

The small percentages of families who reported investment accounts at baseline are of special concern in the study reported here. For many treatment group families, the CDA initiative may well have been their first real opportunity to open an investment account, and especially one that was dedicated to long-term future developmental uses. The implications of this finding are discussed further in the discussion and conclusion sections of this chapter.

The baseline survey also asked a number of questions related to current levels of savings (Table 5.8). Almost half of parents (47%) said that they or their spouse or partner currently had some money saved.[4] Those who reported having some savings (N = 367) were asked how much they had in savings. For the 298 who answered this question, the median amount was $700.[5] For the full sample of parents (including those without savings), the median level of current savings was $0.

Parents were asked whether they had ever saved money specifically for the child enrolled in Head Start. Those who answered affirmatively were asked how much they *currently* had saved for their child. The median value of current savings for the 50% with savings was $300; the median value for the full sample was $2.

Parents who said they had ever saved specifically for the Head Start child were asked whether they had ever saved specifically for their child's education. Those

Table 5.8. SAVINGS CURRENTLY HELD BY LOW-INCOME FAMILIES IN THE STUDY

	Percent with Savings	Amounts for Those with Savings			Amounts for Full Sample		
		N	Median	Mean (SD)	N	Median	Mean (SD)
Any savings	46.9%[a]	298	$700	$4,514 ($13,899)	714	$0	$1,884 ($9,243)
Savings for child	50.0%[b]	359	$300	$969 ($2,725)	718	$2	$484 ($1,986)
Savings for child's education	21.3%[b]	158	$900	$1,749 ($3,188)	741	$0	$373 ($1,634)

NOTE: SD = standard deviation.

[a] The SEED survey asked parents whether or not they currently had any money saved. A total of 783 people answered this question, and 367 (47%) responded affirmatively. A follow-up question asked *those with savings* how much money they currently had saved, and we computed the median and mean for the 298 people who reported positive amounts. To compute the median and mean amounts for the *full sample*, we assigned a value of $0 to the 416 people who said that they were not currently saving.

[b] For "savings for child" and "savings for child's education," the survey did not ask whether or not parents currently had any money saved for these purposes, but whether or not they had *ever* saved for these purposes. A follow-up question asked those who had ever saved for these purposes how much money they currently had saved. We computed the median and mean for the people who reported positive amounts. To compute the median and mean amounts for the *full sample*, we assigned a value of $0 to the people who said that they had never saved for these purposes.

who responded affirmatively were asked how much they currently had saved for their child's education. The median value of current savings for the 21% with savings was $900; the median value for the full sample was $0.

The fact that any of the families had savings, and that the median savings amount for those who saved was as high as it was, is somewhat remarkable given findings from another analysis of data from the same sample that detailed the financial challenges faced by the families in this study at the beginning of the CDA initiative. Beverly and Barton (2006) used several measures of household economic well-being in a study of potential barriers to asset accumulation for SEED families in Michigan before the initiative began. These measures included income poverty, housing cost burden, food insecurity, economic pressure, and social network demands.

Beverly and Barton (2006) found that 85% of the SEED families in Michigan had incomes at or below 150% of federal poverty guidelines, and that 22% of the families reported food insufficiency. In their discussion of findings, Beverly and Barton (2006) write: "Unless these families experience substantial improvements in their financial situations, we would be surprised to see them make many personal deposits into their accounts.... almost all SEED families have some genuine economic barrier to saving and accumulating assets in SEED accounts" (p. 8). They go on to say that the economic barriers they found were to be expected because the SEED preschool demonstration was targeted toward low-income families "that are most in need of subsidies and programmatic support for asset building" (p. 8).

In fact, as Beverly and Barton (2006) note, the economic barriers that low-income families face serve to highlight the importance of institutional features of child development accounts such as initial deposits, matching contributions for personal deposits, and supportive services including financial education. We discuss the roles of these institutional features of the CDA program for families with young children in the next section of this chapter.

DISCUSSION

We began this chapter with two important findings from prior studies of a CDA initiative involving low-income parents of preschool children. First, very few of the parents attended the voluntary financial education classes that were offered by the community-based organization that administered the college savings program. In fact, only 10% of surveyed parents whose children had college savings accounts through the CDA program attended *any* informational or educational events, classes, groups, parent advisory board meetings, or other gatherings sponsored by the agency during the course of the four-year initiative (Marks, Rhodes, Engelhardt, et al., 2009). Second, the CDA "initiative had a large positive impact" on the likelihood that the children in the program had accounts through the state college savings (529) plan (Marks, Rhodes, Engelhardt, et al., 2009, p. 24).

In fact, in their SEED account monitoring study, Loke et al. (2009) found that 62% of the families in the CDA program opened accounts through the state college savings (529) plan.[7] Further, Loke and his colleagues also report that about one-third of the parents made additional deposits into the accounts in the first four years following account opening. Using state 529 plan data from the full sample of low-income parents whose children had SEED accounts, we know that the median value of assets accumulated over the first four years of these accounts was $1,131 (Loke et al., 2009). Parents in the full survey sample reported a median value of $0 for children's college education at the time the CDA initiative began (see Table 5.8).

Given the economic barriers at baseline among SEED families as detailed by Beverly and Barton (2006) and described above, in concert with the near absence of financial education for parents during the four-year CDA initiative, the accumulation of assets in children's college savings accounts may appear difficult to understand. Do these findings, when considered together, suggest that parents did not need financial education in the context of a progressive asset-building program? We do not believe that the evidence supports this interpretation. As the analyses of baseline data presented in this chapter demonstrate, there were many low-income families in this study who may well have benefited from parental financial education.

The overwhelming majority of families in the study were both income- and asset-poor. The finding of low levels of asset holding was especially stark when we focused on assets that have the potential to appreciate over time. It is worth noting that opening a children's college savings account was likely the first real opportunity for many of the families in the CDA program to hold assets that were meant to appreciate over time and help achieve a developmental goal for a family member. Consistent with the concept of financial capability then, the findings presented in this chapter suggest that most families in this study demonstrated the need at baseline for *both* financial education *and* real access to financial products that are appropriately structured and incentivized so that they are truly inclusive of low-income parents of young children.

CONCLUSIONS

The findings reported here may provide useful information to staff in community-based organizations that are planning children's savings account programs or otherwise working to increase the social and economic well-being of low-income families with preschool children. For example, findings indicate the importance of choosing or designing account features that are progressive and, thus, incentivize participation in asset building for children and youth. Further, knowledge of the preintervention characteristics of low-income parents with preschool children may help both scholars and practitioners interpret findings related to outcomes of longitudinal studies of SEED as well as future CDA research.

It is important to note that most of the responses to items in the baseline, or preintervention, survey may be affected by social desirability bias. As a result, for example, findings may overestimate current savings levels and overestimate the prevalence of "desired" financial attitudes and behaviors. It is not possible to rigorously assess the severity of this bias. However, the fact that 40% of parents reported a money-management time horizon of one month and almost two-thirds said they did not have a written budget suggests that many families were willing to admit that they did not follow recommended financial behaviors.

Despite the limitations of self-report methods, some conclusions that flow from findings in this chapter are as follows. First, the low-income parents with young children in this study appear to have needed financial education but, for the most part, did not attend the voluntary classes and events offered by the agency administering the CDA program. Perhaps one of the most disturbing examples in the context of a study of children's college savings accounts was the finding that only a small proportion of parents (7%) knew the approximate cost of their community college. The vast majority of those who gave a dollar value *overestimated* the cost of tuition.

This lack of knowledge suggests that the families in our study had little access, opportunity, or other connections related to community colleges. For example, they may not have relatives or close friends who have attended community college, be exposed to advertising or other formal sources of information about tuition, or have taken any action to educate themselves about costs. The latter would certainly not be surprising for parents of very young children. The fact that most overestimated tuition costs may mean that many parents believe they will not be able to afford to send their children to community college. Without additional information, many low-income parents with preschool children may conclude that community college is not an option for their children. As a result, parents may not encourage their children to consider college or guide them to take advantage of college-related opportunities at school. For example, parents may ignore outreach by their children's guidance counselors, choose not to explore options for financial aid, and choose not to open or make deposits to college savings accounts even when they are incentivized as was the case in the SEED initiative.

On a positive note, lack of knowledge about tuition is something that can be corrected. Staff members at community-based agencies and organizations can actively work to educate families about the cost of a community college education. For example, when financial education materials show how savings and interest in accounts can accumulate over time, asset accumulation might be compared to the cost of tuition at particular local colleges, including community colleges. Research on the impact of seventh grade classroom presentations on college suggests that adolescents who received information on financial aid availability in addition to the cost of college expected higher grades in their current classes and planned to spend more time on homework than their peers who received information on college cost only (Destin & Oyserman, 2009).

If information on how to finance a college education works in somewhat the same way for parents, such research provides some guidance for CDA programs serving low-income families with young children. When working one-on-one with parents, staff might help develop a deposit plan that would allow them to accumulate enough in their savings accounts to finance two years of community-college tuition. These suggestions are consistent with findings from a study of CDA programs in the United States on the importance and value of community-based programs to parents who were saving for their children, especially their committed and knowledgeable staff members (Marks, Rhodes, Wheeler-Brooks, & Adams, 2009; Sherraden & Stevens, 2010).

Second, most low-income parents in the study aspired to save and have assets at baseline, but actual financial behaviors and outcomes fell short of recommended practices as well as the parents' own desired outcomes. When parents were asked how much they should have saved for emergencies, the vast majority of responses implied that parents aspired to have precautionary savings. When asked what they would do with an "extra" $200, about two-thirds of parents said they would save either most or all. Two-thirds said they tried to save a regular amount each month. About 70% said they were hesitant to spend money they had saved.[8] About 90% of parents said that it was important for children, and for their families, to have savings accounts. Although it is impossible to know the extent of social desirability bias, these responses suggest that most low-income parents of preschool children in this sample place a high value on saving and asset holding.

Conventional financial wisdom encourages families to set financial goals, to have written spending plans, to keep track of actual spending, and to have strategies for regular saving. The evidence from this study regarding families' adherence to these recommendations is mixed. Most parents said they sometimes or often kept track of their spending. However, less than half of parents said they often set financial goals, and less than half said they had a written budget. Less than one-fifth had money directly deposited into a savings account.

Conventional financial wisdom also encourages families to think about short-term, medium-term, and long-term financial needs. However, the majority of parents interviewed in this study said they considered only the current month or the next few months when thinking about money management. This finding suggests that many parents in this study are not currently preparing for medium- and long-term financial needs (e.g., saving for children's education, homeownership, retirement).

There are also reasons to be concerned about short-term financial needs. Although the vast majority of families seem to value saving, less than half (47%) reported having any current savings. The median amount of savings—*even for those with savings*—was only $700, $300 less than the median and modal precautionary savings amount desired by parents, and less than a family would need to cover one month of household expenses. There is a clear savings shortfall, even for short-term financial needs.

This second conclusion may have implications for financial education and related social services designed to increase social and economic well-being among low-income families. If such families are led by parents like those in this study, they may already aspire to save and there may be relatively little need for "motivational" efforts. At the same time, staff members might encourage and help parents to set specific and realistic financial goals. In addition, parents may benefit from receiving concrete information, guidance, and support about finding resources that can be saved rather than spent and about choosing appropriate financial vehicles that can facilitate building and holding assets for short-term, medium-term, and long-term financial goals.

Third, most low-income parents in this study were only modestly integrated into the financial mainstream at baseline, making the children's college savings accounts the first real access to a financial product designed to hold assets with the potential to appreciate over time for family developmental goals. Some of the evidence from the analysis of baseline data regarding financial integration is positive. On the one hand, three-fourths of families had either a savings account or a checking account, and a similar proportion said they trusted banks. More than one-fourth of the families were homeowners. On the other hand, very few had "investment-oriented" financial products, such as retirement accounts, stocks, bonds, or even certificates of deposit. It is important to note that low ownership rates for investment products reflect more than limited household resources. Limited household resources are directly tied to high unemployment and underemployment, low wages, part-time positions with hourly pay, and seasonal work. Products that are designed to appreciate, such as retirement accounts with employer contributions, are not widely available to part-time, low-wage, hourly, or seasonal workers. Further, parents like the participants in this study may lack access to certain products such as retirement accounts through work with employer contributions.

Looking first at individual-level barriers to integration into the financial mainstream, some low-income families may manage to set aside emergency savings in basic bank accounts but may not have additional resources to invest in less liquid vehicles. Low-income families may also be uncomfortable with products requiring a fair degree of financial sophistication. This suggests that low-income parents of young children may have reservations about saving for future developmental goals as part of a strategy to increase their families' social and economic well-being. Such reservations may be a particular barrier to financial mainstream integration if savings accounts or other financial products are viewed as illiquid, complex, or risky. Through financial education, staff members working with such families can make efforts to present a full range of materials and examples that can help overcome individual-level barriers to asset building.

It is important to note that despite all of the challenges to the social and economic well-being of families with young children in this study, more than half of the survey families who had the opportunity to open children's college savings accounts did so, and one-third of these families made additional deposits to those accounts within the first four years of account opening. Beverly and Barton (2006) detailed a number of household economic challenges for these families at baseline. The analysis in this chapter documents the need for financial education at the beginning of the CDA initiative, as well as the differences between the parents' goals and attitudes as compared with actual financial behaviors. This analysis also documented very limited ownership of or experience with investment products or assets that have the potential to appreciate. Even with all of these challenges, the majority of SEED parents in this study opened CDAs and a sizable minority managed to make deposits within the first four years of opening college savings accounts for their preschool children.

Taken together, these findings suggest support for a financial capability approach that encompasses not only financial education but also real access to asset ownership in accounts that are designed to appreciate over time and are dedicated to developmental goals. A financial capability approach takes individual-level challenges to social and financial well-being into account while also focusing on barriers to such well-being that are "built in" to our economic structures and institutional arrangements.

Turning to implications for practice, it will be harder for community-based agencies and organizations to address the structural and economic barriers that make it difficult for low-income families to save and invest (Beverly & Barton, 2006; Johnson & Sherraden, 2007; M. S. Sherraden, 2010). But, consistent with the financial capabilities perspective, findings from this study suggest the need for *both* increased financial education *and* enhanced access to financial opportunities, products, and resources.

Perhaps the most striking of our findings on the need for financial education was the very low percentage of low-income parents of preschool children at baseline who could correctly estimate the annual cost of tuition at the local community college. Without additional financial education on college affordability, such parents may believe that college is simply out of the question for their children regardless of any financial efforts that they make to prepare for developmental goals.

In addition to the need for financial education, we find evidence of very limited prior access to and experience with asset-building structures, programs, products, opportunities, and institutional arrangements among the low-income parents of young children in this study. For example, less than one in five of the parents used direct deposit, very few had investments of any kind, and the minority who had any savings did not have enough money saved, on average, to cover household expenses for one month. These examples of limited access to institutional arrangements that facilitate savings and asset building represent structural barriers to social and economic well-being.

We conclude that both financial education and real access to financial products and incentives are needed if parents like those in our study are to be truly integrated into the financial mainstream and, therefore, become financially capable in their efforts to improve the social and economic well-being of their families. The incentives built into the CDA program studied here, namely initial and matching deposits into accounts that are both secure and dedicated to developmental goals for higher education, clearly represented real access to the majority of low-income families with preschool children in this study.

NOTES

1. Parents entered the sample in one of two ways. First, in fall 2004, all parents with children enrolled in the 14 centers were invited to participate in a research study. A total of 732 parents consented and completed interviews. After these interviews ended, agency staff began outreach for the CDA program at the seven treatment centers. Staff at the agency (like staff in many CDA programs that were part of the

national initiative) found recruitment to be much more difficult than expected. To increase the size of the research sample and to achieve program goals, eligibility for the CDA program was extended to families enrolled in the seven treatment centers in fall 2005. A second round of baseline interviewing occurred in fall 2005; all families whose children had been in Head Start the prior year (2004–2005) and who had enrolled in the CDA program after the original round of baseline interviewing were invited to participate. A total of 58 families completed interviews in fall 2005. Thus, the sample includes a total of 790 parents, with 381 parents in the treatment group and 409 comparison group parents. The analysis in this chapter does not distinguish between these two subsamples, however, because the aim is not to document differences between the treatment and comparison groups, nor to investigate the impact of the CDA program. Instead, we provide descriptive findings using data from the sample as a whole. For a report on the impact assessment itself, see Marks, Rhodes, Engelhardt, Scheffler, and Wallace (2009).
2. The "more than high school" category includes those with vocational diplomas as well as those with some college credits or college degrees.
3. We gathered information on tuition for the 2006–2007 academic year as we were analyzing the data for this study. Thus, tuition may have been somewhat less at the time of the parent interviews.
4. The 656 families that did not use direct deposit included 359 (55%) that did not have savings accounts.
5. Respondents were prompted to consider money at home and money being held by others, as well as money in formal saving products.
6. Mean values for current savings levels are presented in Table 5.8. Means are not discussed in the text because all three distributions have large positive skews. (For example, for "any savings," 28 parents reported savings of $10,000 or more, including 6 who reported savings of $50,000 or more.) When a distribution is highly skewed, the median is more representative of the sample than the mean.
7. While we do not have direct comparative data on account opening for the comparison group, 8% of the parents in the comparison group reported in a survey that they had opened children's college savings accounts (Marks, Rhodes, Engelhardt, et al., 2009). As Marks and her colleagues report, only half of the surveyed parents of preschool children who had opened college savings accounts through the SEED program reported that they had done so (31% based on survey responses vs. 62% based on state 529 plan data). In the account monitoring study, Loke and his colleagues (2009) worked with data that came directly from the state 529 plan administrator, so we know that 62% of parents in the treatment group opened accounts. It is possible that comparison group members also underreported the opening of children's college savings accounts. Even if this was the case, we feel confident that such underreporting would not fully close the gap between the comparison group's reported rate of opening children's college savings accounts as per survey data (8%) and the treatment group's rate of account opening (31% based on survey responses; 62% based on state 529 plan data).
8. Some or all of the remaining 30% may also value saving and asset holding. Many people save for short-term goals (e.g., to finance particular goods and services or to maintain consumption during financial crises). It is not obvious that people "should" be hesitant to spend their savings to meet these short-term goals.

REFERENCES

Adams, D. (2008). *SEED pre-school demonstration and impact assessment* (Research brief). Lawrence: University of Kansas School of Social Welfare.

Anderson, W., Jorgensen, M., Brantmeier, N., & Mandell, L. (2008). *Deepening our understanding of the financial education of native youth: An in-depth look at native students in Montana, New Mexico, and South Dakota*. Rapid City, SD, and Washington, DC: First Nations Oweesta Corporation and Jump$tart Coalition for Personal Financial Literacy. Retrieved October 18, 2011, from http://www.oweesta.org/youthreport2008

Bernheim, B. D., & Garrett, D. M. (2003). The effects of financial education in the workplace: Evidence from a survey of households. *Journal of Public Economics, 87*, 1487–1619.

Beverly, S., & Clancy, M. (2001). *Financial education in a children and youth savings account policy demonstration: Issues and options* (Research Background Paper 01-5). St. Louis, MO: Washington University, Center for Social Development.

Beverly S. G., & Barton, J. (2006). *Barriers to asset accumulation for families in the SEED Pre-School Demonstration and Impact Assessment* (SEED Research Report). Lawrence: University of Kansas School of Social Welfare.

Beverly, S. G., & Sherraden, M. (1999). Institutional determinants of saving: Implications for low-income households and public policy. *The Journal of Socio-Economics, 28*(4), 457–473.

Beverly, S. G., Sherraden, M., Cramer, R., Shanks, T. R., Nam, Y., & Zhan, M. (2008). Determinants of asset holdings. In S.-M. McKernan & M. Sherraden (Eds.), *Asset building and low-income households* (pp. 89–151). Washington, DC: Urban Institute Press.

Beverly, S. G., & Williams Shanks, T. (2004). *SEED impact survey: Baseline instrument in English and Spanish* (SEED Research Instrument). Lawrence: University of Kansas School of Social Welfare.

Clancy, M., Grinstein-Weiss, M., & Schreiner, M. (2001). *Financial education and savings outcomes in Individual Development Accounts* (CSD Working Paper No. 01-2). St. Louis, MO: Washington University, Center for Social Development.

Destin, M., & Oyserman, D. (2009). From assets to school outcomes: How finances shape children's perceived possibilities and intentions. *Psychological Science, 20*(4), 414–418.

Hilgert, M. A., Hogarth, J. M., & Beverly, S. G. (2003). Household financial management: The connection between knowledge and behavior. *Federal Reserve Bulletin* (July), 309–322.

Johnson, E., & Sherraden, M. S. (2007). From financial literacy to financial capability among youth. *Journal of Sociology and Social Welfare, 34*(3), 119–213.

Jorgensen, M., & Mandell, L. (2007). *The financial literacy of Native American youth*. Rapid City, ND: Oweetsa Corporation.

Loke, V., Clancy, M., & Zager, R. (2009). *Account monitoring research at Michigan SEED* (CSD Research Report 09-62). St. Louis, MO: Washington University, Center for Social Development.

Lucey, T. A. (2005). Assessing the reliability and validity of Jump$tart survey of financial literacy. *Journal of Family and Economic Issues, 26*(2), 283–294.

Lusardi, A., & Mitchell, O. S. (2008). Planning and financial literacy: How do women fare? *American Economic Review, 98*(2), 413–417.

Lusardi, A., Mitchell, O. S., & Curto, V. (2010). Financial literacy among the young. *Journal of Consumer Affairs, 44*(2), 358–380.

Mandell, L. (2008a). *Financial education in the workplace: Motivations, methods, and barriers.* Washington, DC: New America Foundation, Asset Building Program. Retrieved October 18, 2011, from http://www.newamerica.net/files/nafmigration/Financial_Education_in_the_Workplace.pdf

Mandell, L. (2008b). Financial literacy in high school. In A. Lusardi (Ed.), *Overcoming the saving slump: How to increase the effectiveness of financial education and saving programs* (pp. 257–279). Chicago: University of Chicago Press.

Mandell, L., & Hanson, K. O. (2008). *The financial literacy of young African-American adults: Results of the 2008 Jump$tart surveys* (Report for Operation Hope). Retrieved October 18, 2011, from http://5millionkids.org/reports.php

Mandell, L., & Klein, L. (2009). The impact of financial literacy education on subsequent financial behavior. *Journal of Financial Counseling and Planning, 20*(1), 15–24.

Markovich, C. A., & DeVaney, S. A. (1997). College seniors' personal finance knowledge and practices. *Journal of Family and Consumer Sciences, 89,* 161–166.

Marks, E. L., Rhodes, B. B., Engelhardt, G. V., Scheffler, S., & Wallace, I. N. (2009). *Building assets: An impact evaluation of the MI SEED Children's Savings Program.* Research Triangle Park, NC: RTI International.

Marks, E. L., Rhodes, B. B., Wheeler-Brooks, J., & Adams, D. (2009). *A process study of the SEED Community Partners Initiative.* Research Triangle Park, NC: RTI International.

Mason, L. R., Nam, Y., Clancy, M., Loke, V., & Kim Y.-M. (2009). *SEED account monitoring research: Participants, savings, and accumulation* (CSD Research Report 09-05). St. Louis, MO: Washington University, Center for Social Development.

Nussbaum, M. (2000). *Women and human development: The capabilities approach.* Cambridge, MA: Cambridge University Press.

Scanlon, E., & Adams, D. (2009). Do assets affect well-being? Perceptions of youth in a matched savings program. *Journal of Social Service Research, 35*(1), 33–46.

Schreiner, M., & Sherraden, M. (2007). *Can the poor save? Saving and asset building in individual development accounts.* New Brunswick, NJ: Transaction.

Schuchardt, J., Hanna, S. D., Hira, T. K., Lyons, A. C., Palmer, L., & Xiao, J. J. (2009). Financial literacy and education research priorities. *Journal of Financial Counseling and Planning, 20*(1), 84–95.

Sen, A. (1999). *Development as freedom.* New York: Anchor Books.

Sherraden, M., & Stevens, J. (Eds.). (2010). *Lessons from SEED: A national demonstration of Child Development Accounts.* St. Louis, MO: Washington University, Center for Social Development.

Sherraden, M. S. (2010). *Financial capability: What is it, and how can it be created?* (CSD Working Paper No. 10-17). St. Louis, MO: Washington University, Center for Social Development.

Sherraden, M. S., Johnson, L., Elliott, W. III, Porterfield, S., & Rainford, W. (2007). School-based children's savings accounts for college: The I Can Save program. *Children and Youth Services Review, 29,* 294–312.

Sherraden, M. S., McBride, A. M., & Beverly, S. G. (2010). *Striving to save: Creating policies for financial security of low-income families.* Ann Arbor: University of Michigan Press.

Taylor, P., Kochhar, R., Fry, R., Velasco, G., & Motel, S. (2011). *Twenty-to-one: Wealth gaps rise to record highs between Whites, Blacks, and Hispanics*. Washington, DC: Pew Research Center, Pew Social and Economic Trends.

US Census Bureau. (2011). *Current population survey, 2010 and 2011 annual social and economic supplements*. Washington, DC: Author.

Warnick, J., & Mansfield, P. (2000). Credit card consumers: College students' knowledge and attitudes. *Journal of Consumer Marketing, 17*, 617–626.

6

Financial Issues and an Aging Population

Responding to an Increased Potential for Financial Abuse and Exploitation

PHILLIP MCCALLION, LISA A. FERRETTI AND JIHYUN PARK

Financial capability in this text is conceptualized as comprising both knowledge and financial inclusion and as focused on the building of financial futures (Sherraden, chapter 1, this volume). For older adults there are somewhat similar concerns but with a greater focus on the maintenance rather than the building of financial lives. The FINRA Investor Education Foundation definition of financial capability captures this maintenance focus by seeing capability as a combination of banking and asset status, access to pensions and retirement funds, and effective management of debt burden (FINRA, 2009), and as highly influenced by financial literacy and financial behaviors. An added feature of the consideration of financial capability among older adults is their exposure to financial abuse and exploitation.

In terms of resources, trends have been noted of growing wealth among older populations (Lusardi & Mitchell, 2007a), but there are also challenges in their lives that place many older adults and their finances at risk. Many older adults would benefit from improved financial literacy and changed behaviors as well as financial protections. This chapter will consider the issues in financial exploitation and abuse and offer a systematic review of available aging-focused financial education materials, the evidence to support their effectiveness, and gaps identified in such educational resources. Finally, the chapter will discuss the roles of social work and adult protective services in prevention and management of financial concerns including social work support of legal remedies and the treatment of psychosocial consequences.

RISKS TO FINANCIAL CAPABILITY

Among the risks to financial capability are additional financial needs arising from extended retirement years, uncertainty about Social Security and Medicare (despite assurances that they are sufficiently funded), new older generation (Boomer) issues, health concerns, and financial exploitation and elder abuse.

Extended Retirement Years

Employer incentives and the availability of limited Social Security benefits at age 62 have all contributed to the growth of a group of early retirees (Korczyk, 2004). Even when individuals choose the traditional retirement age of 65 years they will often spend an additional 25–30 years in retirement and potentially more years in retirement than they did in prior employment (Bronstein, McCallion, & Kramer, 2006). Quality of life during those extended retirement years will be greatly influenced by the availability of resources and their effective management and protection (McCallion & Ferretti, 2008). Older age may not be a period in people's lives where the attainment of additional resources is possible; financial literacy and supports for the better management and protection of available financial resources are a critical concern.

Social Security and Medicare

Social Security and Medicare are critical components of retirement "wealth," but fears for the viability of Social Security, Medicare, and indeed Medicaid (see Glossary in Table 6.1) have contributed to older persons feeling less sure about the value of those resources (Korczyk, 2004; Wan, Sengupta, Velkopf, & DeBarros, 2005). Such concerns encourage the pursuit of greater financial literacy so that available resources are better managed, but some argue that limited financial literacy may actually encourage more aggressive investment and management approaches in which the associated risks are poorly understood (Lusardi & Mitchell, 2006). Such experiences and concerns suggest that more concerted efforts are required to build financial literacy among the retiree population (Lusardi & Mitchell, 2007b)

Being a Boomer

"Baby Boomers," those born between 1946 and 1964, appear overall to have more resources than prior generations, but their assets are mainly in home equity (Lusardi & Mitchell, 2007a). Moreover, their planned or actual retirement income is often based on greater risk than older retirees because it largely comprises 401(k) plans and IRAs (see Table 6.1), rather than the defined benefit pensions of prior generations (McCallion & Ferretti, 2008). For example, the 2007 Survey of Consumer Finances found that 36.5% of workers had an employer pension plan, with an additional 17% having both an employer supported pension plan and an IRA, but 10.3% only had a self-funded IRA, and 36.2% had no provision for retirement resources beyond Social Security. Deliberate corporate and, to some extent, public efforts to place responsibility for the funding of retirement on the individual (for a discussion, see Hacker, 2006) has increased such dependence on

Table 6.1. Glossary of Programs Key to Financial Stability for Older Adults

Income Supports for Older Adults
Defined Benefit versus Defined Contribution Pension Plans
In a defined benefit pension plan, usually funded by the employer, an employee receives a set monthly amount (based on salary and length of service) once they reach retirement. Retirees will continue to receive that amount (plus cost of living increases) every month for the rest of their lives. In a defined contribution pension plan like a 401k, employees contribute a portion of their salary into a retirement account, where it can be invested in stock, bonds, mutual funds, and so forth. Often employers make a matching contribution up to a certain percentage. There are no guarantees of how much (if any) of the money contributed will be available at retirement; value depends on investment choices. Most private employers have moved from offering defined benefit to defined contribution pension plans.
Social Security
Social Security is a federal, mandated, supplemental retirement system intended to ensure a threshold subsistence level below which any worker who had paid into the program cannot fall. Social Security is funded out of payroll taxes.
Supplemental Security Income (SSI)
This program pays benefits to adults and children with disabilities who have limited income and resources. SSI benefits also are payable to people 65 and older without disabilities who meet the financial limits.
Survivor Benefits
The widow or widower of a person who worked long enough to qualify for Social Security can receive full benefits at full retirement age, or reduced benefits as early as age 60, or can begin receiving benefits as early as age 50 if they are disabled.
Health Care Supports for Older Adults
Medicare
Medicare covers most people 65 or older and those with long-term disabilities. Part A, a hospital insurance plan, also pays for home health visits and hospice care. Part B, a supplementary plan, pays for doctors' services, tests, and other services. Part C Medicare Advantage Plans, offered by private companies approved by Medicare, provide all Part A (Hospital Insurance) and Part B (Medical Insurance) coverage and may offer extra coverage, such as vision, hearing, dental, and/or health and wellness programs. Part D offers prescription drug coverage (those enrolled in Part C may get drug coverage as part of their plan). Requirements and benefits have become increasingly complex, and individuals usually pay deductibles and co-payments.
Medicaid
A joint federal-state program, Medicaid covers low-income people under age 65 and those over 65 who have exhausted Medicare benefits. It pays for hospital care, doctors' services, nursing-home care, home health services, family planning, and screening. Participating states must offer Medicaid to all persons on public assistance but decide their own eligibility guidelines. Medicaid has become a primary funder of long-term care for older adults, resulting both in spend-down of assets in order to qualify and in individuals seeking assistance in sheltering assets while still being able to qualify.

(continued)

Table 6.1 CONTINUED

State Pharmaceutical Assistance Programs
Many states offer older adults help in paying drug plan premiums and/or other drug costs.
Service Supports for Older Adults
Older Americans Act Services
Home- and community-based supportive services and nutrition services are funded by the federal government, managed by the state, and implemented through local area agencies on aging. A broad array of services that enable older adults to remain in their homes for as long as possible are funded, including access services such as transportation, case management, and information and assistance; congregate and home-delivered meals; personal care, chore, and homemaker assistance; and legal services, mental health services, and adult day care. Multipurpose senior centers are also funded and they coordinate and integrate services for the older adults such as congregate meals, community education, health screening, exercise/health promotion programs, and transportation.
Adult Protective Services
Adult Protective Services (APS) vary by state but are usually mandated case management programs that arrange for services and support for physically and/or mentally impaired adults who are at risk of harm. There is particular concern for persons who are unable to manage their own resources, carry out the activities of daily living, or protect themselves from abuse, neglect, exploitation, or other hazardous situations without assistance from others. APS workers who may or may not be certified social workers seek to resolve the risks faced by eligible clients with service plans that enable these individuals to live independently and safely within their homes and communities.
Elder Justice Act
Greater standardization of APS supports and tools to address exploitation are likely to increase with the recent federal funding of the Elder Justice Act.

personal resources and self-directed plans for retirement years. The recent recession and its impact on stock market values (stocks and the mutual funds that hold them are often key financial instruments underpinning IRAs and 401ks) have meant dramatic drops in the value of many of these self-directed plans. There are also mounting concerns that when there are changes in economic circumstances and related retirement income, many in the Boomer generation will not have sufficient personal savings to fall back on (Lusardi & Mitchell, 2006).

There is also growing concern about the potential for retirement assets and income to be dramatically reduced by growing health care costs (Gist, 2006; McCallion & Ferretti, 2008). Regardless, many people have poor understanding, that is, low literacy, on the value of retirement assets held (Gustman & Steinmeier, 2005). This concern was confirmed by Lusardi and Mitchell (2007b) in their review of multiple financial literacy surveys in the United States and in other developed countries; the majority of older adults were found to be poorly informed about financial products and practices, and this was particularly true for the most financially vulnerable.

Health Concerns Raising Financial Vulnerability and Potential for Abuse

Maintenance of health is critical to quality of life in older age (WHO, 2008) and raises concerns as to whether retirement resources will be sufficient to both sustain lifestyles and pay health care costs. Although levels of disability and chronic illness as one ages have been declining overall, 80% of people aged 65 and older have one chronic condition, 50% have two, and approximately 40% have some type of disability (Wan et al., 2005). Among adults over 40 interviewed in a national survey, 85% did not believe they could rely on government to pay for their long-term care needs, 25% hoped Medicare would be sufficient (see Table 6.1 for what Medicare actually pays for), and two-thirds did not feel they had sufficient personal resources to cover these costs (Metlife, 2001).

Changes in retiree health care plans have added to the uncertainty. Retiree health care costs increased by 16% in 2002 and then at double-digit rates through 2005 (Kaiser-Hewitt, 2006). Also, changes in accounting rules moved corporate costs of postretirement benefits from being a footnote on financial reports to having to be addressed directly on employer balance sheets, incentivizing the capping or elimination of these costs. Many employers have responded to these financial realities by limiting benefits, increasing cost shares, and ending coverage (Kaiser-Hewitt, 2006). Those who thought they had health care plans in retirement may therefore have lost them or may be concerned that they will lose them in the future or that the co-pays for the plans will become too expensive to maintain coverage.

Several reviews have concluded that financial education will improve literacy and financial behaviors in the face of what, for many, are unexpected or unplanned for financial challenges in older age (Collins & O'Rourke, 2009; Martin, 2007). However, a major additional threat to financial well-being among older persons is financial exploitation and abuse, a threat that may be actually increased by individual financial vulnerability concerns. This suggests that preventive financial literacy interventions are potentially an important addition to the small grouping of evidence-based interventions to identify, prevent, and/or rectify the financial abuse of older adults.

FINANCIAL EXPLOITATION AND ELDER ABUSE

Of substantiated cases of elder abuse, approximately 20% are financial in nature (Teaster et al., 2006), but it is widely acknowledged that the actual numbers are higher and the amounts involved underreported (US Department of Justice, 2005). Definitions vary but essentially financial exploitation of older adults involves the illegal or improper use by another person of an older adult's resources; the abusive nature of this exploitation includes negative financial impact on the older adult, a threat to the older adult's independence, and negative psychosocial consequences for the older adult (McCallion, Ferretti, & Benoit, 2008). A particular form of exploitation on the increase is the "scam," which involves tricking/convincing an older adult to give a stranger or a trusted advisor money for false investments, vacations, or other goods.

Financial exploitation perpetrators particularly target older adults because, although their income may be reduced, their accumulated assets tend to be higher in value and are more likely to include "portable" assets such as antiques, bonds, cash, jewelry, and collectables. Abuse and exploitation may be perpetrated by family members, persons charged with assisting with the older adult's care, and/or by strangers (NCEA, 2006).

Financial exploitation and abuse carry a number of consequences. First, they often leave retirees destitute who were well provided for financially prior to the abuse. Older people have little ability to replenish their savings and even successful prosecution of the perpetrator, on the rare occasions when it occurs, frequently does not lead to restitution (McCallion et al., 2008). Second, there may be physical consequences due to the potential unaffordability of medications or health insurance. Third, mental health consequences related to shame, guilt, or general mistrust may be experienced, escalating into paranoia or depression (McCallion et al., 2008; McCallion & Ferretti, 2008; Metlife, 2009). Last, increased physical health concerns may occur, including high blood pressure, heart disease, and digestive problems (Fisher & Regan, 2006).

Risks for Financial Abuse

Financial abuse among older adults is underresearched, but existing findings are instructive. The "typical" victim, as reported in 1998, was aged 70–89, white, female, frail, and cognitively impaired. She was trusting of others and may have been lonely or isolated, and have chronic illness issues (NCEA, 1998). More recent data suggest that the 1998 profile has not changed very much (Metlife, 2009; NASD, 2006), but there are changes in the scope and frequency of fraud efforts with more scam and stranger-based fraud attempts than noted previously, all of which encouraged reconsideration of the Rabiner, O'Keeffe, and Brown (2004) model, as will be explained later.

While gender-based stereotypes should be avoided, there appear to be some gender-based patterns that should be considered in an effort both to identify vulnerability and to intervene. Women needing caregiving assistance appear particularly vulnerable to theft and to the interception of mail, credit card numbers, and bank information. Also, when a spouse/partner dies among current older generations, a woman may become responsible for household finances for the first time in many years and by necessity may be more trusting of "advice" by family members or others. Such advice can become undue influence encouraging changes in beneficiary, and the transfer of legal rights, for example, by signing or changing a power of attorney (Metlife, 2009; NASD, 2006).

Equally unaccustomed perhaps to managing home repairs, large purchases, and financial affairs, the individual may overly trust a "professional" who then takes funds inappropriately. Finally, if largely alone, an individual may develop predictable patterns in their finances and daily routines that catch the attention of perpetrators. A further area of concern for older women occurs for some when they continue the role of mother and caregiver. There are reported patterns of older women providing funds to a troubled child in an effort to change the life of that family member, when instead such funding is supporting growing drug, alcohol, and gambling habits and feeding a sense of entitlement. Finally, to protect their relatives from prosecution, women often do not report the financial abuse perpetrated by their children or family members (Metlife, 2009; NASD, 2006).

Men are also well represented among those exploited. They too may experience the loss of spouses and friends as they age, become dependent on children or other family members because their primary caregiver is no longer in their lives, and may become lonely to the point of facilitating victimization by people who claim to befriend them but instead coerce financial gain. Men too are victims of "experts" such as home repair "professionals" but also investment advisors, entrepreneurs, and other strangers who persuade them that there is an investment or lottery opportunity that will provide financial security and greater comfort. Indeed, compared to women, men (1) tend to take more risks in making financial investments, (2) are sometimes more vulnerable to advisors and friends promising unrealistically high returns (Sechrest, Shichor, Doocy, & Geis, 1998), and (3) often more willingly provide critical identity theft personal information.

A Model for Understanding Financial Vulnerability

Rabiner et al. (2004) proposed a conceptual framework comprising micro and macro factors to (1) understand the financial vulnerability of older adults and documented characteristics of victims, perpetrators, and the larger environment that place older adults at risk; (2) explain some of the processes and reasons for exploitation offenses and issues in the environment that made it difficult to identify; and (3) support appropriate responses to such abuse of older people.

As can be seen in Figure 6.1, the key concerns at the micro process level in the original model identify who is more likely to be a victim and what characteristics of the perpetrator and of the relationship between perpetrator and victim increase the likelihood of exploitation:

Social networks (victim): The presence of a social network offers monitoring and the potential for reporting of problems. The absence of a network, a network that is more of a loose association, or the loss of key network members (e.g., through death) all increase the risk of being exploited.

Social networks (perpetrator): Presence of a social network may act as a social control, but membership may also provide an opportunity for financial exploitation of an older person.

Individual factors (victim): Being White, older, female, isolated, lonely, and having experienced a recent loss all increase risk of being exploited.

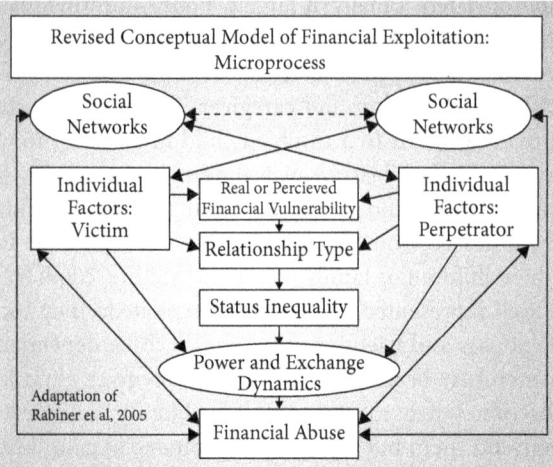

Figure 6.1 Revised Conceptual Model of Financial Exploitation: Microprocess

Individual factors (perpetrator): Substance abuse, mental health, gambling, or financial problems all increase risk of being an exploiter. A poor past relationship with the potential victim may also increase risk.

Status inequality: Differences in age, gender, race, education, and wealth all contribute to a sense of dependence or inequality, increasing resentments that may lead to exploitation.

Relationship type: The nature and purpose of the relationship (well established or newly acquired) between the potential victim and suspected perpetrator, both in its historic nature and changes in that relationship over time, may help explain why abuse may have occurred.

Power and exchange: The degree of dependency and vulnerability of the victim is directly related to the potential for exploitation. Sudden or dramatic increases in dependency and vulnerability, e.g., from the death of a loved one or onset of major illness, may increase exploitation.

At the macro level (see Figure 6.2), concerns identified in the original model speak to what society needs to do either to prevent or respond to financial exploitation of the elderly. In financial capability terms, these macro level concerns address the external structural resources with potential to facilitate actions that help maintain financial opportunities and well-being for older adults.

Prevention initiatives: There are largely untested beliefs that if isolation of older adults were decreased and their financial education increased, if there were better education of attorneys and bank officials, and if greater use were made of direct deposit and automatic payments, then there would be increased likelihood that financial abuse could be prevented and that abuse that has occurred would be more readily identified.

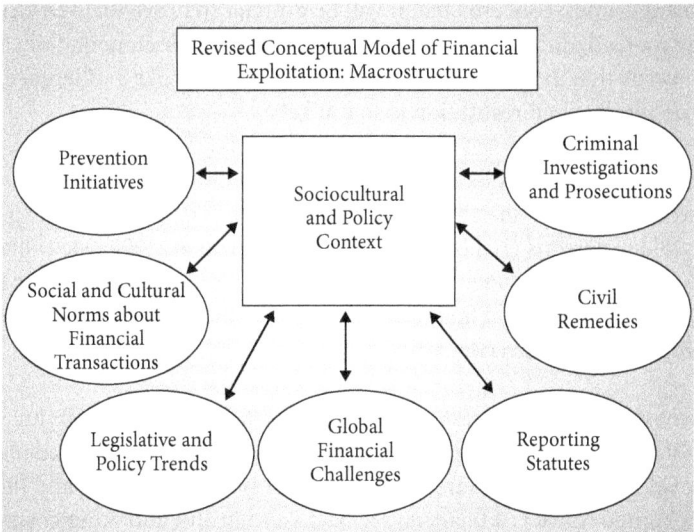

Figure 6.2 Revised Conceptual Model of Financial Exploitation: Macrostructure

Social and cultural norms about financial transactions: Financial transfers and gifts from older adults to children, friends, and caretakers that are viewed as normal and acceptable contribute to difficulties in discerning the incidences where such transactions are abusive.

Legislative and policy trends: There has been differential and limited policy and legislative impact at the state level with differences in roles and support for adult protective agencies, definitions of exploitation, and requirements for reporting. The passage and recent funding for The Elder Justice Act at the federal level offers more promise of standardization in approaches, but this is yet to be realized.

Reporting statutes: Almost all states specifically mention financial abuse in their reporting requirements, but few have specific procedures for the reporting, processing, and investigation of financial abuse.

Civil remedies: Protective orders (legal requirements that a perpetrator stay away from a victim), powers of attorney (voluntarily appointing another individual to act on one's behalf for a limited set of activities on a time limited basis or a durable basis, that is, continuing when the person is no longer competent to make decisions), and guardianship (appointed when there is evidence that the person lacks decision-making capacity) are all potential tools for protection against future financial abuse. However power of attorney and guardianship may potentially be tools for abuse when they are mistakenly granted to a perpetrator.

Criminal investigations: There are several challenges to be addressed if criminal investigation processes are to more effectively address perpetrated financial abuse: lack of expertise in identifying the transactions that represent financial abuse; a view that such crimes are not as serious as violent crimes; concerns that it will be difficult to prove that the victim was coerced; difficulties in assembling the needed documentation; and concerns that the process will move too slowly to make a difference, particularly when restitution is so unlikely.

The model is expanded in this chapter to incorporate additional salient financial issues and to offer insights into the sense of financial concern experienced by many older persons (Bailly, Loewy, Bomba, & Lynch, 2007; McCallion et al., 2008). As can be seen in Figures 6.1 and 6.2, these issues and insights have been addressed by adding global financial challenges to the macro issues and financial vulnerability to the micro concerns:

Global financial challenges that encourage risk-taking: Less certain financial resources given movements from defined benefit to self-directed plans, the need to stretch resources over a greater number of years, and the unplanned impact of financial set-backs and health and other costs.

Real or perceived financial vulnerability: A perception (founded or unfounded) that Social Security, Medicare, and other retirement resources will not be enough and are under threat of depletion, and/or the actual experience of financial reversals.

With these additions, a model emerges that recognizes that there are behaviors and concerns of individuals themselves that increase their vulnerability (micro model), and that there are also larger societal forces and activities that create troubling financial risk for older adults (macro). In financial capability terms, resources are reduced or are perceived at risk, there are problems with financial literacy around new "opportunities" being offered, and/or financial behaviors change including giving management/spending powers to others. These micro and macro level factors may make older adults more vulnerable to and poorly prepared for scams; as a result, they may make catastrophic financial decisions they would not otherwise consider. The revised model is intended to help prepare social workers to better understand and respond to financial concerns among older adults.

INTERVENTIONS

Interventions tend to fall into educational prevention efforts and the identification of at-risk situations. General financial literacy and targeted scam and exploitation awareness programs are the primary educational prevention interventions. Risk assessment considers characteristics of the person at risk and their living situation.

Financial Literacy

Financial literacy is the ability to make informed judgments and to take effective actions regarding the current and future use and management of money and other assets. Many adults, including older adults, have been found not to have high levels of financial literacy (Lusardi & Mitchell, 2006, 2007b), but financial education programs appear to improve the behavior and outcomes for the most financially vulnerable, particularly those with low incomes and levels of education (Lusardi, 2008).

Scam Awareness

The National Consumers League (2009) reports that scams cost the American public $40 billion annually with a growing number of victims over age 55. In 2009, the top scams were fake checks (42%), Internet merchandise (25%), prizes and sweepstakes (10%), phishing messages (7%), and various money offers, loans, auctions, and friendship swindles (16%) (National Consumers League, 2009). Most educational programs offer increased general information with only a small number more specifically focused on risk assessment and/or encouraging behavioral change to reduce susceptibility to victimization.

Risk Assessment

All professionals working with older persons are encouraged to be aware of generally agreed on signs of financial exploitation (see Table 6.2). In 1998, 60% of substantiated Adult Protective Services (APS) cases of financial abuse were reported to involve an adult child, compared to 47% for all other forms of abuse. Grandchildren and other relatives were also well represented, and male and female relatives were equally likely to abuse. More recent figures garnered from a review of NAPSA/NCEA Newsfeeds (over a 1-year period) identified family perpetrators as involved in 40% of cases; a sizable group of financial professionals, attorneys, and fiduciary agents were also represented (Metlife, 2009).

The Metlife (2009) findings regarding the involvement of professionals in abuse underscore that the focus of interventions should be on both trusted family members and trusted "professional" groups of potential abusers, even though there are many family members, friends, and trusted professionals who defend the older individual's best interests. In addition, evidence is emerging that newly acquired "friends" and "supporters" (Rabiner, O'Keeffe, & Brown, 2004) are also potential abusers. Finally, together with telephone scams, the Internet has introduced new exploitation tools—identity theft, lotteries, money transfers to and from other countries, inheritances from purported distant relatives, and investment schemes—that may victimize older adults as their Internet usage increases (Mouallem, 2002).

Also supported by the Metlife (2009) findings is the need for the micro factors in the Rabiner et al. (2004) model to better accommodate the phenomenon of scams. The inclusion of the interaction of real or perceived financial vulnerability will support the development of interventions that better address family-initiated, expert/friend/advisor-initiated, and online/telephone-based financial abuse and exploitation.

Table 6.2. SIGNS OF FINANCIAL ABUSE AND EXPLOITATION

Transaction Warning Signs	Behavioral Warning Signs
Numerous withdrawals from accounts and inconsistent spending	Noticeable change in appearance and grooming
Accompanied by a stranger, an older person appears to look to that person for guidance or appears pressured to withdraw money	Disorientation, often asking the same question over and over
Signature appears forged, unusual, or suspicious	
Pattern of "out-of-sync" check numbers	Change in mood
Acquaintance/family member overly interested in elder's finances	
Older person concerned or confused about missing funds from his or her account	Changes in willingness to make eye contact with bank staff
Older person applies for a credit card for the first time	Withdrawn
Credit card statements that are sent to an address other than the older person's home	Hesitancy to enter into conversation
Changes in account beneficiaries	Appearing nervous around or fearful of the person accompanying
Changes in property titles, deeds, or other documents	
Refinancing of mortgages	
Abrupt changes in wills, trusts or powers of attorney	Not being allowed to speak or make decisions on their own

SOURCE: McCallion, Ferretti, and Benoit (2008).

INTERVENTION EFFECTIVENESS

The revised Rabiner et al. (2004) model encourages attention to both micro and macro level issues and should therefore be reflected in the interventions available. Although web searches and a specific review of the databases Ageline and PsychINFO found hundreds of financial literacy and older adult resources, interventions that included or specifically targeted older adults were rarely evaluated. Newberger and Paulson (2009) confirm this conclusion, highlighting that much work is going on in terms of the development of financial literacy curricula and educational materials, and the dissemination of educational efforts is now more targeted; however, there have only been a small number of efforts to systematically evaluate outcomes, with only one longitudinal study noted.

Interventions with evaluation data fall into five categories (see Table 6.3): telemarketing fraud prevention, financial behavior and confidence, money management and consumer skills, multidisciplinary team responses, and the "do not call registry." The telemarketing fraud prevention, financial behavior and confidence, and money management and consumer skills interventions address micro-level concerns and the telemarketing fraud intervention specifically targets the relationship between victim and perpetrator where the perpetrator is usually a stranger. No evidence-based interventions were found that addressed the relationship between victim and perpetrator where the perpetrator is a family member or other caregiver. Macro-level concerns were addressed by the multidisciplinary team intervention (e.g., criminal investigations and prosecutions) and the "do not call registry" (prevention).

Types of evaluation design varied from case studies to exploratory and descriptive, quasi-experimental and experimental. Table 6.3 contains key information about these interventions and the associated studies.

Telemarketing Fraud Prevention

Telemarketing fraud prevention was targeted by the AARP (2003) through a series of peer counseling approaches (prevention information, a charity fraud emphasis, enhanced messaging, a "gotcha" intervention, and a monetary incentive), and tests of both the persistence of intervention effects and the usefulness of strategies. Data were supplemented by interviews with professionals who work with targeted older adults. Overall, in comparison to nonrandomly selected control groups, older adults completing training or receiving information on fraud prevention strategies were more successful in thwarting efforts to obtain personal/identify theft information and in resisting scams. Perhaps surprisingly, those offered a $5 incentive to ignore such messages were no less likely to hang up when the offer is a prize. Also, despite the educational message not to, there were still older adults in the experimental group who provided personal information and accepted sting offers (AARP, 2003).

Financial Behavior and Confidence

The most systematic data for a financial literacy program is offered by the FDIC's *Money Smart* program, which consists of a series of in-person and computer-assisted modules on a range of financial behavior and confidence topics. About 10% of 226 participants in the study were older adults, and they had similar results to others in terms of savings, increased comparison shopping, reduction of debt, reported sustained levels of financial comfort at six and 12 months, and movement to using and sustaining the use of a budget and to paying more of their bills on time (FDIC, 2007).

Money Management and Consumer Skills

The Daily Money Management Study (NCEA, 2003) described in Table 6.3, is a program for teaching consumers money management skills. Outcomes measured

Table 6.3. Financial Literacy Programs: Rationale, Development, and Effectiveness

Telemarketing Fraud Prevention	Peer Counseling	Quasi-Experimental	General prevention information	Intervention Group: General information about telemarketing fraud - Different types of intervention tactics in forms of telephone messages. - Peer counseling using scripts and messages to victims and potential victims. - "Sting" solicitation to both groups to purchase a rare coin.	The prevention message delivered by volunteers was effective in reducing rates of victimization. ($x^2(1,119) = 17.20$ (p < .01). 75% in control group accepted the sting offer but only 37% in exp. group accepted the offer.	AARP (2003). *Off the Hook: Reducing Participation in Telemarketing Fraud*. Washington, DC. Retrieved on June 6, 2009 from www.aarp.org.
			Prevention information with a charity fraud emphasis	Intervention Group: Specific information about charity fraud and questions to ask to determine if solicitation is for a bona fide charity - "sting" solicitation to both groups involved agreeing to make a small contribution to a hypothetical charity	Forewarning message about charity fraud was effective (X^2 (1.55) = 7.73, p < .01). 50% of control group pledged to donate but only 15% of exp. group pledged to donate after receiving prevention message.	
			Enhanced prevention information message	Three intervention groups: i) Explained the nature of telemarketing fraud ii) Requested that the listener assume the role of a fraud fighter. iii) Requested that the listener suggest what he or she would tell victims about not responding to fraudulent pitches and how others should make a plan for getting off the phone. - "sting" solicitation tests participants' willingness (all three groups) to purchase a rare coin after receiving the intervention messages.	Only Group 3 was successful in reducing fraud participation rate. X^2 (1,44) = 2.17 (p < .01(one-tail test).	

	"Gotcha"	-Helping listeners overcome any lingering belief that they are not susceptible to the tactics used by fraudulent telemarketers and not vulnerable to victimization. i) experimental group: forewarned to avoid giving out personal information over phone ii) control group: received call only to verify their television program preference, - "sting" solicitation after 3 days tested if listener would give out personal information to caller posing as telemarketer.	The Gotcha intervention was effective. Only 38% in exp. group gave out personal information after they received the intervention compared to 53% in control group $-X^2(1,77) = 1.88, p < .01$, (one-tailed test).	
	"Pot of Gold" Offer	-offered a monetary incentive ($5) to hang up on telemarketing callers the minute personal information was solicited i) experimental group: the monetary incentive was mentioned in recruitment script for half the exp. group; other half was notified by mail ii) control group received no monetary incentive or forewarning	- This intervention was not successful in reducing fraud participation rates. 32% of exp group gave out personal information compared with 37% in control treatment $- X^2 (1,64) <1$, not significant.	
	- "sting" solicitation was a guarantee of one of five prizes if the potential victim answered personal questions			

(continued)

Table 6.3. CONTINUED

		Persistence of Intervention Effects	-received "forewarned is forearmed" message delivered by volunteers -"sting" solicitation was a call two weeks and five weeks later with a free prize offer	-The effects of the forewarning intervention did persist across the 5-week delay at both the 2-week and 5-week delay with participants receiving the forewarning message less likely to reveal banking information than those in the control group, but forewarning effects were not statistically significant at follow-up.
Telephone Interviews	Exploratory and descriptive	self-evaluation of telephone related behaviors by random sample of general population age 45+ and two samples (lottery fraud and investment fraud) of victims of telemarketing fraud age 45+	Questions on Phone answering behaviors, use of answering machines Feelings about unsolicited telephone calls and callers Dealing with telemarketing calls Responses to telephone solicitations for money Experience being swindled or scammed	Most frequent strategies for resolving problematic telephone-related behaviors were use of answering machine or some form of caller ID.
Professional Interviews	Exploratory and descriptive	18 interviews with attorneys and other professionals who work with victims of telemarketing fraud, or who supervise telemarketing fraud investigations to understand how these professionals work with chronic victims	Determination of: How victims come to professionals' attention How professionals approach and work with victims Professionals' opinions of what works and what does not work in modifying victim behavior Professionals' suggestions for combating tele-fraud	Findings that: There is no "typical" victim. Assisting chronic victims is challenging because they often are reluctant to recognize they have been defrauded. Working with trusted family members and using a multidisciplinary, long-term approach appears most successful in breaking the cycle.

| Financial behavior and confidence levels | Financial education "Money Smart" | Experimental Pre/Post test; -Phase I: pretraining survey(paper) -Phase II: posttraining survey(paper) -Phase III: follow-up survey (telephone) | - Ten 60–120 minute modules - Instructor-led version/Computer-Based Instruction (CBI) version - Multilanguage | The "Money Smart" curriculum modules: - Bank On it: an introduction to bank services - Borrowing Basics: an introduction to credit - Check It Out: how to choose and keep a checking account - Money Matters: how to keep track of your money - Pay Yourself First: why you should save - Keep It Safe: your rights as a consumer - To Your Credit: how credit history will affect your credit future - Charge It Right: how to make a credit card work for you - Loan To Own: know what you're borrowing before you buy - Your Own Home: what home ownership is all about Instructor-led format includes: - An instructor's guide: including prompts for tasks such as distributing handouts, using overheads, asking questions of the audiences, or facilitating group discussion - A participant's guide: resources for after class - Overhead slides | Significant support for the effectiveness of Money Smart training in improving financial behaviors. Reported positive changes were found in: - Level of savings (69%) - Amount of debt (53%) - Likelihood to comparison shop for financial products (58%) In addition, telephone follow-up surveys at 6 and 12 months found that financial comfort levels increased over time. By the end of the training: - 43% of those without a checking account opened a checking account - 37% of those without a savings account opened a savings account - 28% of those with checking accounts, and 22% of those with savings accounts began using direct deposit for the first time. - 61% of those not using a spending plan/budget used one by the time of follow-up; - 95% of those who used a spending plan/budget at the end of course still used it at the time of follow-up. | FDIC (2007). *A longitudinal evaluation of the intermediate-term impact of Money Smart financial education curriculum upon Consumers' behavior and confidence*, Washington, DC. |

(continued)

Table 6.3. CONTINUED

Money management and consumer skills				- While 55% of respondents indicated they "always" pay bills on time, 12% indicated that they increased their on-time payments by the end of the course.	
	Daily Money Management (DMM)	Descriptive/ Survey - no control group	Soliciting information about experience with financial abuse and targeted to service providers, case management, and health care provider	A how-to manual on Daily Money Management: for care management agencies. - Distributes information about victims' experiences and resources and guidelines on financial literacy and fraud - Training for service providers on assisting with balancing checkbooks, paying bills, and sorting mail.	Survey of trained service providers, case management, and health care providers, revealed - 83.9% of the participating agencies had encountered cases of financial abuse. - Fewer than 30% of service providers had previously offered daily money management information and resources about financial abuse. - Most participants agreed that surrogate financial services and safeguards helped preserve elder clients' assets. - Agreed that elder financial abuse could be reduced by promoting resources and guidelines for financial literacy.	National Center on Elder Abuse. (2003, June). *Daily Money Management Programs: a protection against elder abuse.* Washington, DC, Nerenberg, Lisa.

Multi-Disciplinary Teams (MDTs)	Financial Exploitation	Descriptive and Qualitative study	-Multidisciplinary Team (MDT) trainings and services at both state and local level with Adult Protective Services (APS) workers	MDTs consist of professionals within a community who review cases of alleged adult/elder abuse, exploitation or neglect, and make recommendations regarding possible treatment alternatives and resources	MDT training on financial exploitation of vulnerable adults: 30 states Qualitative rating by APS workers of responses to cases of financial exploitation (1-no response, 2-average, 3-above average, 4-outstanding) State Attorneys General: 2.9 Law Enforcement (police/staff): 2.7 Bank officials: 2.4 District Attorneys: 2.2 Judges: 2.2 County/Parish Attorneys: 1.9 Response to financial abuse (out of 33 states) - Cross training with other disciplines: 29 states - More staff resources for APS programs: 28 states - Collaborative support: 13 states - Training for other agencies: 32 states	Otto, J, Stanis, P.I., & Marlatt, K.W. (2003). *Report on state adult protective services response to financial exploitation of vulnerable adults.* National Center on Elder Abuse, Washington, DC. Retrieved on June 9, 2009, from www.elderabusecenter.org.

(continued)

Table 6.3. CONTINUED

			Areas for improvement in working relationship between APS and law enforcement - Cross training and training materials - Creation of specialized law enforcement financial exploitation units - Cooperation across state lines on interstate cases - Training for law enforcement staff on interviewing victims - A national database of perpetrators - Prosecutions for smaller financial losses - More APS staff with financial exploitation training.	
Elder financial abuse prevention (Financial Abuse Specialist Team-FAST, multidisciplinary personnel team)	Case study	*FAST (Financial Abuse Specialist Team)* -A rapid-response system.	County-level *FAST* team program: - Visit victims promptly, investigate emergencies, freeze assets, and refer to law enforcement - Immediate response to reports of financial abuse - Preventing future incidents or losses by creating a seamless system of collaboration - Teams of two or more persons trained in the prevention, identification, and treatment of abuse of elderly.	- Rapid response team shown to more quickly intervene to protect client's safety and assets - Team members see how they are making a difference in victims' lives. - Greater mutual understanding of professional roles and responsibilities - Resulted in law enforcement protocol for uniform response to all elder and dependent adult abuse.	Malks, B., Schmidt, C., and Austin, M. J. (2002). Elder abuse prevention: a case study of the Santa Clara county financial abuse specialist team (FAST) program. *Journal of Gerontological Social Work*, 39(3), 23–40.

| "Do Not Call" registry | Descriptive study | The National "Do Not Call" registry | -The National Do Not Call Registry offers choice on receiving telemarketing calls at home. Managed by the Federal Trade Commission (FTC), the nation's consumer protection agency. Enforced by the FTC, the Federal Communications Commission (FCC), and state law enforcement officials. | 40% of consumers—getting very few telemarketing calls
17%—getting fewer calls from legitimate telemarketers, but the same number of fraudulent calls as before
8%—no decrease in either legitimate or fraudulent telemarketing calls
21%—wanted to enroll but did not know how
6%—heard about "do not call" but decided not to place their numbers in one
8%—never heard about the federal or state "do not call" registries | Lusardi, A. (2008). *Financial Literacy: An essential tool for informed consumer choice?* National Bureau of Economic Research, working paper 14084. Retrieved on June 9, 2009, from www.nber.org/papers/w14084. |

focused not on participants but on the professionals likely to implement the program. Such an approach reflects a legitimate concern that interventions are less likely to be successful if staff and agencies working with the persons targeted do not value what a program is trying to achieve and if they are unlikely to adopt the program after training. The survey data established that 84% of participating agencies (which included senior centers, community education programs, chapters of AARP, and for-profit financial services organizations) were not agencies that usually offered this type of program but believed that the strategies and information offered would increase literacy and preserve assets and were therefore committed to program adoption.

Multidisciplinary Teams

The complexities (as described in the component of the macro portion of the revised model) of addressing financial abuse and exploitation after they have occurred has encouraged the use of multidisciplinary teams to investigate abuses, seek redress, prosecute perpetrators, and support the victim (Bailly et al., 2007). A survey by Otto, Stanis, and Marlatt (2003) established that multidisciplinary training was ongoing in 30 states, but there was a need for additional training, a database identifying perpetrators, cooperation across state lines, and a willingness to prosecute in cases where smaller amounts of resources are involved. Malks, Schmidt, and Austin (2002) in a case study of the Financial Abuse Specialist Team (FAST) in Santa Clara County found that such a multidisciplinary team improved responses and was more likely to protect the client and his/her assets.

The "Do Not Call" Registry

The "Do Not Call" Registry was established by the Federal Trade Commission (FTC) in partnership with the Federal Communications Commission (FCC) to reduce the number of telemarketing calls by creating an option to opt out of receiving such calls. The Do Not Call Registry is the closest in financial terms to a public-health-like preventive intervention offered regardless of actual abusive or exploitive acts and designed to change societal circumstances that support the targeted acts to be prevented. Lusardi (2008) found that many of those who signed up reported fewer calls. With time, there will likely be more evidence both of the Registry's effectiveness in reducing calls and of any corresponding reduction in abusive and exploitive events.

NEXT STEPS IN THE DEVELOPMENT OF INTERVENTIONS

The revised Rabiner et al. (2004) model also suggests areas where additional interventions need to be developed and/or existing interventions need to be more rigorously tested and pursued. Some examples are legal remedies, advocacy and investigative roles for social workers and adult protective workers, and psychosocial responses by social workers.

Legal Remedies

Considering further the criminal investigations and prosecutions and the civil remedies components of the Rabiner et al. (2004) model, there are legal remedies available when financial abuse or exploitation has occurred. However, intervention at the point of a completed abuse is sometimes too late because the older adult may not recover from the losses incurred. Bailly et al. (2007) review the steps both in the use of trusts and representative payees to build in protections as well as the use of orders of protection, power of attorney, and guardianship to prevent further exploitation. However, where fraud, abuse, and exploitation have been the result of misrepresentation, failure to adequately investigate, or the hope to make a quick profit, they conclude that it can be difficult to successfully prosecute. Equally, victims themselves are often poor witnesses, feeling embarrassed to have been deceived and wishing to protect and support family members despite their deceit and injury; or fearful of loss of affection from family and friends. Victims have also demonstrated an inability to maintain adequate records and documentation needed for successful prosecutions. The onset of chronic illness, losses in visual acuity, reliance on others, and the onset of dementia symptoms further compound difficulties.

Taken together, there are many reasons why perpetrators are not pursued and why the prosecutions that do occur often fail (McCallion et al., 2008). Prosecutors and researchers alike are reliant on anecdotal information, as there has been little investigation of rates of prosecution or their success. As mentioned earlier, there is some beginning evidence that the development of multidisciplinary approaches such as forensic centers and dedicated teams of social work, medical, and legal staff has the potential to increase such success, but their availability remains limited (Navarro, Wilber, Yonashiro, & Homeier, 2010; Wiglesworth, Mosqueda, Burnight, Younglove, & Jeske, 2006). At a minimum, there is a need for training interventions focused on successful investigative techniques; collaborative approaches between legal, police, and adult protective staff; and preparation for prosecution of perpetrators (McCallion et al., 2008).

Advocacy and Investigative Roles for Social Workers and Adult Protective Workers

Kosberg, Rothman, and Dunlop (2006) argue that there is a growing need for advocacy and protection activities for older adults and that these are critical roles for social workers. The challenges posed to financial capability by vulnerability of older adults to financial exploitation and abuse, low levels of financial literacy, the growing incidence of fraud and abuse noted here, and the absence of a body of evidence-based interventions means the clinical skill and experience of social workers remain a valuable resource to support older adults when there are financial concerns. To that end, social work education initiatives that focus on tools for identification of potential financial abuse by family members and scams, and counseling potential victims may go a long way toward improving prevention efforts. However when such social workers are playing an adult protective services role, they also have an obligation to support self-determination and may not initiate involuntary interventions (Kosberg et al., 2006; McCallion et al., 2008). To the extent that social workers can play macro- and micro-level preventive roles to encourage financial literacy and more effective management of real and perceived financial vulnerability, they are likely to be most successful in balancing their protective and self-determination roles.

As well as self-determination concerns, the adult protective role is made more difficult by the differences in adult protective legislation at the state level. In most states, but not all, reporting of elder abuse is mandatory. Investigation and substantiation of cases is increased when reporting is mandatory, but definitions and practices vary and also influence successful pursuit of cases. For example, in some states, reporting is based on actual evidence and in others, reasonable cause to believe is sufficient (Rodriguez, Wallace, Woolf, & Mangione, 2006). Community awareness and public education, the content of the relevant state statutes, and professional knowledge of those statutes all appear to influence protective success (Jogerst et al., 2003). At a macro level there is a need for attention by social workers to improve reporting statutes and to advance legislation and policy that are more responsive to the changing nature of financial exploitation. As mentioned above, the Federal Elder Justice Act offers opportunities for greater advocacy at the state level for standardization of practices.

There is wide variation in the training and education of adult protective services staff. Social work educators have an important role to play in standardizing education and advancing multidisciplinary approaches that better engage health and, in particular, legal resources. This call for more multidisciplinary approaches reflects the need for social workers in legal settings such as elder law practices and the courts to advance: (1) appropriate determinations on the management of the assets of "at risk" older adults, (2) guardianship proceedings guided by comprehensive and multidimensional assessments, and (3) multidisciplinary responses such as the FAST program (see Table 6.3) and other types of multidisciplinary forensic centers responding to incidences of financial abuse (Kosberg et al., 2006; Navarro et al., 2010). Social work education may also play a role in better preparing social workers and other adult protective workers in documentation practices likely to support more successful prosecutions of perpetrators (Bailly et al., 2007).

Psychosocial Responses by Social Workers

As well as responding to the legal and financial issues when abuse and exploitation occur, social workers are uniquely equipped to respond to the trauma issues often experienced by the older victim, which in some cases can reach criteria for post-traumatic stress (McCallion et al., 2008). At a minimum, the role of social workers is to:

- Meet immediate support, financial, and care needs—social networks were probably impaired already and will be disrupted by the exploitation situation.

- Pursue legal protections—exploitation may continue otherwise.
- Ensure safety—when the perpetrator has power over the victim, the victim continues to be at risk.
- Investigate the potential for recovery of resources—loss of resources may increase the sense of financial vulnerability and place the victim at risk for exploitation by other "helpers."
- Engage the person in educational counseling, cognitive therapy, and linkage to health, legal, and/or other professionals to begin addressing stress-related symptoms and concerns (McCallion et al., 2008).

CONCLUSION

The addition of both "global financial challenges" and "real or perceived financial vulnerability" to the Rabiner et al. (2004) conceptual model of financial exploitation helps to identify that becoming more active in both the delivery and the assessment of financial literacy and prevention interventions is an important, if new, role for social workers. Too often financial literacy and prevention interventions are targeted at those who least need them and fail to address the issues of greater relevance, or represent initiatives that wane with the ending of the initiating grant funds. Instead, the growing financial risks and challenges to their financial capability faced by older adults require that the most vulnerable be reached, effective programs be established and successfully implemented, and then adopted and maintained by agencies regardless of grant funds. Such success requires professional champions, and social workers are uniquely qualified to take on this role.

Further, the examination of the macro and micro elements of the Rabiner et al. (2004) conceptual model helps to illustrate that only some elements are currently being addressed through evidence-based interventions, mostly prevention efforts. With additional effort, multidisciplinary and forensic interventions may be extended to better address the macro issues that often prevent successful resolution of exploitation incidents. There is a training and education requirement around investigation and preparation for prosecution that social work educators need to better address and that should be subjected to testing.

On a micro level, there continues to be a need for the development and testing of interventions that interrupt the cycles among individual factors, relationship type, status inequality, and power and exchange dynamics that support financial exploitation (Rabiner et al., 2004); facilitate healing after exploitation (McCallion et al., 2008); build confidence not to be victimized again because of real or perceived financial vulnerability; and restore the elements of financial capability in older age: adequate financial resources, financial literacy, and thoughtful and informed financial behaviors.

REFERENCES

AARP . (2003). *Off the hook: Reducing participation in telemarketing fraud*. Conducted for the United States Department of Justice, Office of Justice Programs. Washington DC: AARP.

Bailly, R. M., Loewy, E., Bomba, M. A., & Lynch, J. J. (2007). *Financial exploitation of the elderly*. Kingston, NJ: CRI.

Bronstein, L., McCallion, P., & Kramer, E. (2006). Developing an aging prepared community: Collaboration among counties, consumers, professionals and organizations. *Journal of Gerontological Social Work, 48*(1-2), 193-202.

Collins, M., & O'Rourke, C. (2009). *Evaluating financial education and counseling: A review of the literature*. Madison: University of Wisconsin-Madison.

FDIC . (2007). *A longitudinal evaluation of the intermediate-term impact of Money Smart financial education curriculum upon consumers' behavior and confidence*. Washington, DC: FDIC.

Finra (2009). *Financial Capability in the United States: National Survey*. Washington, DC: FINRA Investor Education Foundation.

Fisher, B. S., & Regan, S. L. (2006). The extent and frequency of abuse in the lives of older women and their relationship with health outcomes. *The Gerontologist, 46*(2), 200-209.

Gist, J. (2006). *Boomer wealth—Beware of the median*. Washington, DC: AARP Public Policy Institute.

Gustman, A. L., & Steinmeier, T. L. (2005). Imperfect knowledge of Social Security and pensions. *Industrial Relations, 44*(2), 373-397.

Hacker, J. (2006). *The great risk shift: The assault on American jobs, families, health care, and retirement—And how you can fight back*. New York: Oxford University Press.

Jogerst, G. J., Daly, J. M., Brinig, M. F., Dawson, J. D., Schmuch, G. A., & Ingram, J. G. (2003). Domestic elder abuse and the law. *American Journal of Public Health, 93*(12), 2131-2136.

Kaiser-Hewitt, J. (2006). *Retiree health benefits revisited*. Menlo Park, CA: The Henry J. Kaiser Family Foundation.

Korczyk, S. M. (2004). *Is early retirement ending?* Washington, DC: AARP Public Policy Institute.

Kosberg, J., Rothman, M., & Dunlop, B. (2006). Advocacy and protection of older adults. In B. Berkman (Ed.), *Handbook of social work in health and aging* (pp. 355-362). New York: Oxford University Press.

Lusardi, A. (2008). *Financial literacy: An essential tool for informed consumer choice?* (National Bureau of Economic Research Working Paper 14084). Retrieved September 30, 2011, from www.nber.org/papers/w14084

Lusardi, A., & Mitchell, O. S. (2006). *Financial literacy and planning: Implications for retirement wellbeing* (WP2006-01). Philadelphia: Pension Research Council.

Lusardi, A., & Mitchell, O. S. (2007a). Baby boomer retirement security: The role of planning, financial literacy, and housing wealth. *Journal of Monetary Economics, 54*, 205-224.

Lusardi, A., & Mitchell, O. S. (2007b). Financial literacy and retirement preparedness: Evidence and implications for financial education. *Business Economics, 42*(1), 35-44.

Malks, B., Schmidt, C., & Austin, M. J. (2002). Elder abuse prevention: A case study of the Santa Clara County financial abuse specialist team (FAST) program. *Journal of Gerontological Social Work, 39*(3), 23-40.

Martin, M. (2007). *A literature review of the effectiveness of financial education* (WP 07-03). Richmond, VA: Federal Reserve Bank of Richmond.

McCallion, P., & Ferretti, L. A. (2008). Retirement. In T. Mizrahi & L. E. Davis (Eds.), *Encyclopedia of social work* (pp. 533-536). Washington, DC & New York: NASW Press and Oxford University Press.

McCallion, P., Ferretti, L.A., & Benoit, L. (2008). *Facing the challenges: Addressing financial literacy and exploitation issues for PSA workers* [CD-ROM]. Albany, NY: NYS OCFS.

MetLife . (2001). *The MetLife survey of American attitudes towards retirement.* New York: Metropolitan Life Insurance Company.

MetLife . (2009). *Broken trust.* New York: Metropolitan Life Insurance Company.

Mouallem, L. (2002). Oh no, grandma has a computer: How Internet fraud will take the place of telemarketing fraud targeting the elderly. *Santa Clara Law Review, 42*(2), 659–687.

NASD . (2006). *Investor fraud study: Final report.* Los Angeles: NASD Investor Education Foundation.

National Center on Elder Abuse [NCEA]. (1998). *National elder abuse incidence study.* Retrieved September 30, 2011, from http://www.aoa.gov/eldfam/Elder_Rights/Elder_AbuseAbuseReport_Full.pdf

National Center on Elder Abuse [NCEA]. (2003). *Daily money management programs: A protection against elder abuse.* Washington, DC: NCEA.

National Center on Elder Abuse [NCEA]. (2006). *The 2004 survey of state adult protective services: Abuse of adults 60 years of age and older.* Washington, DC: National Center on Elder Abuse.

National Consumers League. (2009). *Top 10 scams of 2009.* Retrieved September 30, 2011, from http://nclnet.org/images/PDF/2009_top_scams.pdf

Navarro, A. E., Wilber, K. H., Yonashiro, J., & Homeier, D. C. (2010). Do we really need another meeting? Lessons from the Los Angeles County Elder Abuse Forensic Center. *The Gerontologist, 50*, 702–711.

Newberger, R. G., & Paulson, A. L. (2009). Strategies of success in financial education. *Chicago Fed Letter,* 267a.

Otto, J., Stanis, P. I., & Marlatt, K. W. (2003). *Report on state adult protective services response to financial exploitation of vulnerable adults.* Washington, DC: National Center on Elder Abuse. Retrieved September 30, 2011, from http://www.ncea.aoa.gov/main_site/library/cane/CANE_Series/CANE_EAScope.aspx

Rabiner, D. J., O'Keeffe, J., & Brown, D. (2004). A conceptual framework of financial exploitation of older persons. *Journal of Elder Abuse and Neglect, 16*(2), 53–73.

Rodriguez, M. A., Wallace, S. P., Woolf, N. H., & Mangione, C. M. (2006). Mandatory reporting of elder abuse. *Annals of Family Medicine, 4*(5), 403–409.

Sechrest, D. K., Shichor, D., Doocy, J. H., & Geis, G. (1998). A research note: Women's response to a telemarketing scam. *Women & Criminal Justice 10*(1), 75–89.

Teaster, P. B., Otto, J. M., Dugar, T. D., Mendiondo, M. S., Abner, E. L., & Cecil, K. A. (2006). *The 2004 survey of state Adult Protective Services: Abuse of adults 60 years of age and older.* Report to the National Center on Elder Abuse, Administration on Aging, Washington, DC.

US Department of Justice. (2005). *Financial crimes report to the public.* Retrieved September 30, 2011, from http://www.fbi.gov.gov/publications/financial/fcs_report052005/ fcs_report052005.htm

Wan, H., Sengupta, M., Velkopf, V. A., & DeBarros, K. A. (2005). *Current population reports: P23-209, 65+ in the United States.* Washington, DC: US Government Printing Office.

Wiglesworth, A., Mosqueda, L., Burnight, K., Younglove, T., & Jeske, D. (2006). Findings from an elder abuse forensic center. *The Gerontologist, 46*, 277–283.

WHO . (2008). *The World Health Report 2008 – Now more than ever.* Geneva: World Health Organization.

7

Improving Financial Capacity among Low-Income Immigrants

Effects of a Financial Education Program

MIN ZHAN, STEVEN G. ANDERSON AND JEFF SCOTT

Utilization of mainstream financial services is an important step for the economic and social integration of immigrants. Despite the rapid growth of immigrant populations and their increasing role in the labor force (Malone, Baluja, Costanzo, & Davis, 2003; Migration Policy Institute, 2010; US Census, 2010), immigrants are less likely to use a variety of mainstream financial services compared to their nonimmigrant counterparts. For example, they are much less likely to own bank accounts (Rhine & Greene, 2006), and their access to credit and other mainstream financing also is limited (Newberger, Rhine, & Chiu, 2004). As a result, immigrants are less likely to save and invest, and they have substantially lower levels of wealth accumulation compared to nonimmigrants (Cobb-Clark & Hildebrand, 2002; Hao, 2004; Osili & Paulson, 2004). They consequently are more susceptible to unfair or predatory lending practices (Paulson, Singer, Newberger, & Smith, 2006).

The important link between financial service access and social and economic well-being, along with the increasing economic potential of immigrants, has generated growing interest in strategies to improve the financial management capacity of immigrants (Lutheran Immigration and Refugee Service, 2008; National Council of La Raza, 2004). Financial management programs targeted toward low-income immigrants are emerging as one promising program response. However, two important issues have yet to be addressed. First, while some studies have examined factors related to low bank account ownership among immigrants (Paulson et al., 2006), there is limited systematic research on their financial knowledge levels. Even less is known about the substantive areas in which financial knowledge may be deficient. Thus, specific training needs of this population have not been as well defined. Second, few studies exist on the effects of financial management programs on the financial knowledge of immigrants (Zhan, Anderson, & Scott, 2009), and studies on whether such training results in changes in actual financial practices are nonexistent. These gaps in the current research literature have resulted in the growth of financial management programs accompanied by only vague and anecdotal evidence regarding the financial education needs of immigrants and the potential of training to address these needs. To improve curriculum development and financial management program implementation, it is important to obtain more detailed information on knowledge levels about a wide range of financial management issues, and also about the extent to which financial management training leads to knowledge gains and behavioral changes.

This study addresses these issues by examining pre- and posttraining surveys on financial knowledge and a follow-up survey on posttraining financial practices of immigrant participants in a large financial management training program targeted at low-income persons. Analyses are conducted to assess the initial knowledge as well as knowledge improvement among immigrant participants in comparison to nonimmigrant participants. Changes in selected financial practices after the training are also examined and compared among these two groups. The implications for developing effective financial management training for low-income immigrants are discussed.

BACKGROUND

Immigrants in the United States

As of 2008, immigrants represent about 12.5% of the total population and almost 16% of the total civilian labor force. Compared to nonimmigrants, the immigrant population, especially those from Latin America, who represent about 53% of the total immigrant population, are more likely to have lower educational status, earn lower wages, and live in poverty. For example, about 16% of immigrant families lived in poverty in 2008 (Migration Policy Institute, 2010), compared to the overall poverty rate of 13% in the United States in that year (Bishaw & Macartney, 2010).

Immigrants are also less likely than their US counterparts to use a wide variety of mainstream financial services (Rhine & Greene, 2003). This can have negative repercussions, particularly for low-income immigrants, because access to formal financial services can provide them with useful tools for effectively managing finances and for building financial assets, and can also protect them from discriminatory financial practices. Financial service access of low-income immigrants, which is very important to their social and economic well-being and integration, consequently has become an increasingly important public policy and research issue (Newberger, Rhine, & Chiu, 2004).

Financial Service Use and Asset Building among Immigrants: Needs and Challenges

Immigrants, low-income immigrants, and especially new and undocumented immigrants face a series of unique challenges in financial service utilization due to their limited language skills, cultural factors, immigration status, experiences of financial institutions in their home country, and international financial transactions that they often need to conduct. In the following sections, these challenges are discussed in terms of immigrants' access to bank accounts, home ownership, sending remittances, and their vulnerability to predatory lending services.

ACCESS TO BANK ACCOUNTS

A number of studies have examined why so many immigrant households do not use mainstream financial institutions. Studies have found that many of the characteristics associated with the decision to be unbanked by US-born citizens, such as education, income, family structure, and net worth, are also linked to immigrants' decisions to be unbanked (Rhine & Greene, 2006).

Immigrants also face particular language, legal status, and cultural barriers to accessing mainstream financial services. For example, Bleakley and Chin (2004) found that immigrants who were more likely to speak English, who came from countries where English is an official language, and who were likely to speak English at home were more likely to have checking accounts. Furthermore, many immigrants fear that the failure to produce valid immigration papers at a bank will jeopardize their ability to stay in the United States (Suro, Bendixen, Lowell, & Benavides, 2002).

Country of origin also plays an important role in bank account ownership of immigrants. Paulson et al. (2006) found that among the top 10 immigrant source countries, the percentage of immigrants who have a savings or a checking account ranges from a high of 78% (Chinese immigrants) to a low of 40% (Mexican immigrants). Similarly, Rhine and Greene (2006) found that compared to European or Asian immigrants, Mexican and other Latin American immigrants have the highest rates of being unbanked. Some studies further suggested that the immigrants who have negative experiences or perceptions of banks in their home country are less likely to have bank accounts in the United States (Hernandez-Coss, 2005; Hilgert et al., 2005; Paulson et al., 2006).

HOME OWNERSHIP

Immigrants are also less likely to own homes. In 2008, 53% of immigrant-headed households owned their homes, compared to 70% among native-born headed households (Kochhar, Gonzalez-Barrera, & Dockterman, 2009). In addition to the lack of access to bank accounts, immigrants face a variety of other barriers to homeownership including little or no credit history (Lutheran Immigration and Refugee Services [LIRS], 2008); and housing affordability (Ray, Papademetriou, & Jachimowicz, 2004). Moreover, many first-generation immigrants, as well as low-income immigrants, do not receive help with home purchases through intergenerational transfers of assets (Migration Policy Institute, 2010).

SENDING REMITTANCES

One of the common and important financial practices conducted by immigrants is sending remittances, that is, sending payments to their home countries.

Remittances sent from the United States grew from about $4 billion in 1981 to $25.5 billion in 2003 (Congressional Budget Office, 2005). Despite the rapid growth of remittances, banks and other formal financial institutions only have a very small share of this market. Instead, immigrants typically use money transfer operators, which often are located in check-cashing outlets, to send remittances (Marcuss, 2005; Orozco, 2004; Suro, 2003). Even among the remitters with a bank account, only about 20% used a bank to send their remittances (Hilgert et al., 2005).

Studies have examined why immigrants rely heavily on alternative financial sectors to send remittances. In addition to immigrants' lack of familiarity with and distrust of banking institutions (Orozco, 2004), geographic convenience for both remittance senders and recipients is an important factor, because money transfer operators are often located in immigrant neighborhoods and close to public transportation (Suro et al., 2002).

Predatory Financial Services

Immigrants, especially low-income immigrants, often rely on high cost and poorly regulated financial sectors, such as check-cashing services, to conduct financial transactions (Paulson et al., 2006). While this is due in part to these sectors' geographic convenience, anonymity, quick delivery time, fewer language barriers, and immigrant-friendly support services and products (Hernandez-Coss, 2005; Hogarth, Anguelov, & Lee, 2005; Suro et al., 2002), it may also be that many immigrants are not able to identify unfair practices (NCLR, 2004). Thus, it may be difficult for them to make optimal financial choices, especially since they face consistent exposure to predatory financial practices.

Financial Knowledge Needs and Financial Education of Immigrants

Financial Literacy of Immigrants

While no large-scale assessments on the financial literacy of immigrants have been conducted, program and research experience have generated information on their financial literacy needs in several areas. Lack of access to bank accounts for immigrants may contribute to their low financial knowledge on basic banking practices. Owning assets such as bank accounts and housing is one of the efficient ways to obtain financial knowledge. For example, there is evidence that bank account ownership is positively related to higher scores in financial knowledge tests (Baker & Dylla, 2007; Choi, 2009). Studies have found that immigrants often overestimate the minimum account balance requirements (Suro et al., 2002) and lack knowledge and information about bank account management and loan requirements (Schoenholtz & Stanton, 2001), partially due to the fact that they are not familiar with the mainstream banking system. Similarly, an evaluation of financial management training programs for low-income people in Illinois found that low-income immigrants had low knowledge about banking and alternative financial services, and they also expressed difficulties and skeptical attitudes related to bank use (Zhan et al., 2009).

EFFECTS OF FINANCIAL EDUCATION

As assessments of the financial education needs of immigrants require further refinement, the potential benefits of financial training programs also need to be evaluated. Some evaluations of financial education programs for low-income populations have indicated that these programs improve financial knowledge and behaviors of participants (Anderson, Zhan, & Scott, 2007; DeVaney, Gorham, Bechman, & Haldeman, 1996; Hirad & Zorn, 2001; Hogarth & Swanson, 1995; Shelton & Hill, 1995; Zhan, Anderson, & Scott, 2006). However, there have been very few studies that report on such effects specifically for immigrant groups. The aforementioned study (Zhan et al., 2009) found that the knowledge about banking and alternative financial services of immigrant participants improved substantially after they completed financial management training. Their attitudes also became significantly more favorable with respect to the use of mainstream financial institutions. Furthermore, immigrants exhibited more substantial attitudinal changes than nonimmigrant participants (Anderson, Zhan, & Scott, 2007).

Some financial programs for low-income people also couple education with asset accumulation incentives. This approach is exemplified by individual development account (IDA) programs, which provide matched savings to low-income persons who save for home or vehicle purchases, postsecondary education, or start-up of small businesses (Schreiner, Clancy, & Sherraden, 2002; Sherraden, 1991). Some IDA programs are specifically targeted to immigrant populations (Frank, 2004; Office of Refugees Resettlement [ORR], 2002; Robles, 2003). For example, the IDA programs offered by the Office of Refugee Resettlement provide matched savings and financial literacy savings to refugee families. Over 7,000 refugee families opened accounts through this program, and the majority of these families saved for vehicle purchases (ORR, 2002). In addition, the evaluation of a demonstration project of IDAs found that the programs are effective in increasing savings for Latino participants (Schreiner et al., 2002).

PURPOSE OF THIS STUDY

This study builds on previous literature related to immigrant financial practices in several ways. First, it employs actual tests of financial knowledge before and after receipt of financial management training, instead of relying solely on the subjective measures (e.g., self-reported financial behaviors) employed in most previous studies. Second, this study includes more clearly defined substantive knowledge and practice areas, such as banking knowledge, saving and investment strategies, and utilization of public and work-related benefits. Third, not only will the effects of training on knowledge be assessed, but also how training affects subsequent financial behaviors. Finally, the pretraining knowledge levels as well as changes in financial knowledge and behaviors after the training between immigrant and nonimmigrant participants will be compared. This will contribute to a better understanding of the unique information and program needs for immigrants.

METHODS

Data Collection

The data for this study were collected from participants at 10 training sites in Illinois operated through the Financial Links for Low-Income People (FLLIP) program (Anderson, Scott, & Zhan, 2004). FLLIP contracts with nonprofit community-based agencies in Illinois to provide a 12-hour package of basic financial management training to persons earning less than 200% of the poverty level. The program is supported by state and private foundation funds.

The analyses are primarily based on two sources of data collected at FLLIP training sites. First, pre- and posttraining tests designed to measure the financial knowledge of participants were administered. The pretest was administered in the beginning of the first training session, and the posttest was administered at the end of the last training session. The time lapse between the two tests was usually between 1 to 4 weeks. Since different sites had different starting dates and scheduling of the 12-hour training, data on pre- and posttraining tests were collected between January 2002 and May 2003.

The test instrument was developed by evaluation project staff based on a thorough review of the financial management training curriculum used in the program (Chan et al., 1997, 2001), and subsequently revised based on the feedback received from FLLIP Coalition members and community contractors as well as field testing of an initial version of the survey instrument.

The instrument contained 48 true-false and multiple choice questions in five aforementioned content areas that are important to the low-income population: predatory lending practices; public and work-related benefits; banking practices; savings and investing strategies; and credit use and interest rates. The pre- and posttraining tests were administered by the program trainers and generally took 20–30 minutes to complete. Because of concerns about the reading skills of program participants, the questions were designed to be very basic and to be comprehensible to persons with limited reading ability. Some of the sites offered the training in Spanish, and a Spanish translation of the test was administered at these sites. The testing served two principal purposes. First, the pre-test results were intended to indicate the extent to which this type of training might be needed. Second, pre-training test scores could be compared to posttraining scores to measure knowledge changes associated with the FLLIP training. In addition, information on demographic and socioeconomic characteristics was obtained as participants entered the program.

The second data source for this analysis was a follow-up survey with program participants. Specifically, program graduates were surveyed by telephone 6–12 months after training completion to ascertain whether those who completed the training subsequently changed their financial management behavior in selected ways. This time period was considered sufficient to allow graduates to incorporate desired behaviors into their financial lives, as well as to provide perspectives on the training they had received.

The follow-up survey included questions designed to determine whether graduates engaged in selected financial behaviors related to budgeting and bill-paying, savings and asset accumulation, use of banks and fringe financial institutions, and access to benefits. Because of the lack of available information on participant financial behaviors prior to training, the assessment of behavior changes related to the training relies primarily on retrospective self-reports of graduates. In particular, respondents were asked if they had changed selected financial behaviors as the result of completing the training. By specifically linking the questions on behavior changes to the training, the intent was to tie respondent perceptions as closely as possible to the training received. For most questions on which respondents indicated that their behavior had changed, open-ended follow-up questions were included that asked them to identify the specific changes they had made.

Study Sample and Data Analysis

The analysis includes a total of 302 participants (87 primary non-English speakers and 215 primary English speakers) who completed both pre- and posttraining knowledge tests, and a total of 121 participants (17 primary non-English speakers, and 104 primary English speakers) who completed follow-up surveys. Given the consideration of the languages that these participants speak, and the communities and agencies from which the samples were drawn, it is believed that almost all of the primary non-English speakers are either first- or second-generation immigrants. Hereafter in this study, the primary non-English speakers are referred to as "immigrant" participants, and primary English speakers are referred to as "nonimmigrant" participants.

Both pre- and posttraining knowledge tests were coded according to whether a correct response was given to each question. This allowed for the calculation of total correct answers for each participant, as well as the number of correct answers within each of the five substantive knowledge areas. Participant characteristics are presented first. Results from the data analysis are presented second. Independent sample t tests and nominal cross-tabulations were utilized to assess whether pretraining knowledge and changes in financial knowledge and behaviors after the training were different between immigrant and nonimmigrant participants.

RESULTS

Sample Characteristics

Table 7.1 presents the descriptive statistics of the total sample, as well as for immigrants and nonimmigrants. Considerable demographic diversity exists within the sample. Nearly half of the participants (46%) were African American, 26% were White and 22% were Hispanic. The vast majority of the participants (about 90%) were women, and the average age was 33. The educational attainment of participants overall was low. About 40% had less than a high school degree, 26% had a high school diploma, and only 36% had completed some postsecondary education. In general, the economic circumstances of participants were quite disadvantaged. Only one-third of the sample was employed, and about one-quarter of participants was receiving TANF at the time of enrollment.

Immigrant and nonimmigrant participants differed in several important respects (Table 7.1). Nearly two-thirds (62%) of immigrants identified themselves as Hispanic, while nonimmigrant participants were heavily African American (65%). Compared to the nonimmigrants, immigrants were much more likely to be married

Table 7.1. SAMPLE CHARACTERISTICS

	All Participants (N = 302)	Immigrants (N = 87)	Nonimmigrants (N = 215)
Gender (%)			
Male	12.9	17.2	11.2
Female	87.1	82.8	88.8
Race/ethnicity (%)**			
African American	46.0	1.0	65.0
Hispanics	22.0	62.0	6.0
Caucasian	26.0	23.0	27.0
Other	6.0	14.0	3.0
Age (yrs)	33.1	35.8	32.1
Marital Status (%)**			
Single, never married	53.2	17.3	67.5
Married	26.4	67.9	9.9
Separated, divorced, widowed	20.4	14.8	22.7
Percent who are parents	76.5	78.6	75.6
Number of children	1.8	1.7	1.8
Education (%)*			
Less than high school	37.5	39.5	36.7
High school or GED	25.8	24.7	26.2
Some college	27.8	19.8	31.0
Graduated college	8.9	16.0	6.2
Percent employed*	30.2	39.5	26.4
Percent receiving TANF**	25.3	2.6	33.8
Percent having Checking Account	38.1	40.0	37.3
Percent having Savings Account	20.9	21.2	20.8
Percent Home ownership	10.0	14.0	8.0
Number of debts**	1.5	0.8	1.8
Percent filing taxes last year**	55.0	39.0	62.0

NOTE: Due to small amounts of missing data, N varies slightly for certain characteristics.
* Differences between immigrants and nonimmigrants are significant at the .05 level.
** Differences between immigrants and nonimmigrants are significant at the .01 level.

(68% vs. 10%). Educational levels in general were similar for the two groups, except that immigrants were more likely to graduate from college (16% vs. 6%).

There also were differences on economic-related variables. Not surprisingly, immigrants were much less likely to receive TANF than nonimmigrants (3% vs. 34%), and they also were more likely to be employed (40% vs. 26%). Immigrants were also less likely to file tax returns (39% vs. 62%) compared to nonimmigrant participants (see Table 7.1 for a complete descriptive results).

Pretraining Financial Knowledge

Table 7.2 presents pretraining knowledge levels of training participants and compares average knowledge levels between immigrants and nonimmigrants. The data show that participants overall had low basic financial knowledge levels before the training. On average, they answered only about 52% of the questions correctly. The average percentages of correct answers were especially low in the areas of "savings and investing" (45%) and "public and work-related benefits" (48%).

Immigrants had statistically lower pretraining knowledge scores than nonimmigrants, both overall and in each of the five content areas. Immigrant participants averaged only about 33% correct responses overall, as compared to 59% correct responses by nonimmigrant participants. Both immigrants and nonimmigrants demonstrated the greatest pretraining knowledge deficiencies in the area of

Table 7.2. Pretraining Knowledge Test

	Number of test items	Average number and percentage correct		
		ALL PARTICIPANTS (N = 302)	IMMIGRANTS (N = 87)	NONIMMIGRANTS (N = 215)
All items**	42	24.8 (51.7%)	15.9 (33.2%)	28.4 (59.2%)
Content area				
Predatory lending**	8	4.4 (54.8%)	2.7 (33.2%)	5.1 (63.6%)
Public and work-related benefits**	9	4.3 (47.7%)	2.5 (27.5%)	5.0 (55.9%)
Saving and investing**	10	4.5 (45.0%)	2.7 (27.2%)	5.2 (52.1%)
Banking practices**	7	4.5 (64.1%)	2.8 (39.9%)	5.2 (73.8%)
Credit and interest rates**	8	4.6 (58.1%)	3.3 (41.1%)	5.2 (64.9%)

** Differences between immigrants and nonimmigrants are significant at the .01 level.
NOTE: We didn't include 6 of the 48 questions that do not belong to any of the 5 content areas.

"public and work-related benefits" and "savings and investing." Immigrants had low levels of knowledge in each of the five content areas, ranging from 27% correct responses for public and work-related benefits and savings and investing to 41% correct responses for credit and interest rates. The range for nonimmigrants was somewhat wider, from 52% for savings and investing to 74% for banking practices (see Table 7.2 for complete pretraining knowledge results).

Knowledge Changes after Training

Table 7.3 reports the extent to which financial knowledge improved overall and in each of the five content areas. The data demonstrate an average increase of 9.3 additional questions answered correctly, or a gain of nearly 20 percentage points in financial knowledge test scores. When differences in the total number of test items in each content area are taken into account, the knowledge improvements were fairly consistent across the content areas, with the greatest average percentage improvements made in the public and work-related benefits, predatory lending, and savings and investing areas.

Table 7.3 also compares the differences in knowledge improvement between immigrants and nonimmigrants. Compared to nonimmigrant participants, immigrant participants exhibited significantly greater overall knowledge improvements (an average of 12.3 more answers correct) than nonimmigrants (8.1 more correct) in four of the five content areas.

Table 7.3. KNOWLEDGE IMPROVEMENT

	Number of test items	Change in average number correct		
		ALL PARTICIPANTS (N = 302)	IMMIGRANTS (N = 87)	NONIMMIGRANTS (N = 215)
All items**	42	9.3	12.3	8.1
Content area:				
Predatory lending**	8	1.9	2.5	1.6
Public and work-related benefits**	9	2.1	2.3	2.0
Saving and investing**	10	2.0	2.6	1.8
Banking practices**	7	1.0	1.7	.7
Credit and interest rates**	8	1.2	2.0	.9

** Differences between immigrants and nonimmigrants are significant at the .01 level.
NOTE: We didn't include 6 of the 48 questions that do not belong to the any of the 5 content areas.

Despite these gains, it should be noted that the financial knowledge levels of participants, especially immigrants, remained relatively low after the training. That is, immigrants averaged only about 59% correct response overall after training was completed, compared to 76% among nonimmigrant participants (see Table 7.3 for complete knowledge change results).

Changes in Financial Behaviors

Table 7.4 presents findings from the questions on reported behavior changes among immigrant and nonimmigrant participants. The findings are grouped into four categories of behavior: household budgeting and bill-paying practices, savings and asset accumulation, use of mainstream financial institutions and credit, and access to government and work benefits. While the small sample size of immigrants who participated in the follow-up surveys suggests caution in interpreting findings, the results appear promising.

Table 7.4 shows that about three-fourth of immigrants (n = 13) thought they were doing a better overall job of keeping track of expenses, or had changed their household budgeting practices in important ways since completing the training. A smaller but still substantial percentage (53%, n = 9) of immigrants reported changing the ways in which they paid their bills.

Changes in savings and asset development behaviors also followed the training. About 71% (n = 12) of the responding immigrants reported that they had been able to save more in a typical month after completing the training, and about half (n = 8) indicated that they had been able to save at least some money in the last three months. Substantial numbers of immigrants also took steps toward enhancing housing assets. For example, about one-fourth (n = 4) purchased a home after the training, or stated that they had begun saving for a home down payment; about 18% (n = 3) had made a major improvement to their home.

Selected improvements in use of mainstream institutions and credit also were found. For those who did not already have bank accounts, the data show that nearly one-fifth (n = 3) of immigrants opened a new checking account, and one-third (n = 5) opened a new savings account. Substantial numbers of immigrant respondents likewise reported decreases in the use of fringe financial services. In particular, 70% (n = 12) reported improved management of their credit cards.

Finally, several differences in the changes in financial practices experienced by immigrants and nonimmigrants can be observed in Table 7.4. Due to the very small number of follow-up immigrants compared to nonimmigrant graduates, the differences between these groups should be interpreted very cautiously. Nevertheless, a few statistically significant group differences were found. For example, immigrants were less likely to improve their budgeting behaviors than nonimmigrants, although immigrant improvements in these areas were very common. Immigrants were also less likely than nonimmigrants to begin receiving government benefits or tax benefits, which may be at least partially related to eligibility restrictions facing some immigrants. (See Table 7.4 below for results of the follow-up survey).

Table 7.4. PERCENTAGE OF RESPONDENTS REPORTING CHANGES IN FINANCIAL BEHAVIORS AFTER FLLIP TRAINING COMPLETION

Financial practice	Immigrants (N = 17)	Nonimmigrants (104)
BUDGETING AND BILL-PAYING		
Doing a better overall job of tracking expenses**	76.5	87.5
Changed household budgeting in important ways*	70.6	81.7
Changed the ways that bills are paid	52.9	62.5
SAVINGS AND ASSET ACCUMULATION		
Save more in a typical month	70.6	74.0
Saved any money in last three months	50.0	55.9
Purchased a home**	23.5	2.9
Began saving for down payment for home	35.3	24.0
Made major improvement to home	17.6	23.1
Made long-term investment other than home purchase	23.5	38.5
Began saving for retirement	23.5	23.1
Purchased insurance*	29.4	20.2
USE OF BANKS AND FRINGE FINANCIAL INSTITUTIONS		
Opened new checking account	17.6	19.2
Opened new savings account	29.4	16.3
Changed an existing checking or savings account	23.5	16.3
Used currency exchanges less often	29.4	52.9
Used payday loans less often	41.2	38.5
Improved management of credit cards	70.0	79.2
ACCESS TO BENEFITS		
Started receiving government benefits or tax credits**	5.9	27.9
Applied for government benefits or tax credits	20.0	14.7
Started receiving job related benefits	23.5	10.6

* Differences between immigrants and nonimmigrants are significant at the .05 level.
** Differences between immigrants and nonimmigrants are significant at the .01 level.

DISCUSSION

As financial management programs for low-income immigrants proliferate, the findings from this study are helpful in considering the need for, as well as potential benefits of, such programs for immigrant populations. First, with regard to financial information needs, the belief that low-income immigrants lack basic financial knowledge has been an important impetus for the development of training programs. However, empirical evidence to support this has been mostly anecdotal or based on self-reported financial behaviors. The findings from this study make an important contribution by measuring basic knowledge levels through actual tests and across a wide range of knowledge domains.

Results indicate that immigrants entering this training program exhibited very limited knowledge about important financial issues across each of the five content areas on which knowledge was measured. These low knowledge levels were found despite the fact that the test was intended to measure very basic financial matters. Together with the findings from previous research, the findings from this study suggest that the difficulties immigrants express in using mainstream financial institutions, in making savings and investment decisions, and in accessing public and work-related benefits derive at least partially from their limited knowledge about these issues.

The fact that immigrants exhibited substantially lower levels of pretraining knowledge than nonimmigrants is interesting and merits further research attention, particularly given that immigrant and nonimmigrant participants all had low incomes and relatively similar levels of education. It may be that immigrants face unique challenges in terms of cultural factors, more limited experiences with American economic systems and social institutions, or language difficulties, which inhibit their accumulation of relevant knowledge. Further research studies could usefully explore whether these or other factors are important in understanding these differences between nonimmigrants and immigrants.

Despite the fact that training included immigrants with low incomes and educational limitations, financial knowledge increased significantly overall and in each of the five content areas after the training. In addition, findings indicate that immigrants experienced significantly greater knowledge increases from the training than nonimmigrant participants, both overall and in four of the five training content areas. Again, these greater gains for immigrants are especially pertinent given the comparable educational levels for immigrants and nonimmigrants in the study. Further research could seek to determine if such differences result primarily from lower initial knowledge bases, possible differences in quality between training sites, or other factors.

It should be noted that posttraining knowledge remained quite low among immigrant participants (they averaged about 59% correct response overall after the training). This suggests the need for continued experimentation with alternative training approaches. For example, it would be useful to determine if knowledge gains varied if a longer training period were provided or more individualized training were offered. These results also suggest the need for developing programs with training content and delivery methods to respond to the unique financial information needs of low-income immigrants. Although several sites in this training program offered training in Spanish, research on learning differences linked to use of primary or secondary language also merit attention.

In addition to improvement in financial knowledge, immigrants also reported many useful changes in financial practices after the training, including budgeting practices, savings behaviors, applying for and obtaining benefits, and utilization of mainstream financial institutions. Although our financial practice information is limited by small sample size and exclusive reliance on self-reporting, these findings are promising and point to a need for further research on actual financial practice behaviors of immigrants after completing training.

Study Limitations and Further Research

Several limitations in this study point to useful future research directions. First, the sample size of immigrants in the pre- and posttraining knowledge surveys was relatively small, and very small for the follow-up surveys on financial practices. Thus, the interpretation of relevant findings should be very cautious. Conducting similar research with a larger immigrant sample would be useful, both in further testing findings and in allowing more sophisticated analyses. One such analysis would be to examine immigrant groups with different employment and educational status. Second, it may be important to tailor financial training programs to consider the varying financial knowledge, attitudinal, and practice patterns among immigrants from different countries. Country of origin differences could not be examined in this study due to the small sample size and limited variation among participants in countries of origin. It would be worthwhile to conduct similar analyses on immigrant groups from different countries in the future. Finally, the FLLIP training program did not specifically target immigrants; thus, some financial issues that are particularly relevant to immigrants, such as remittances and predatory lending in the housing market, could not be included in the study. Evaluations of programs that target immigrants, therefore, may be important in further identifying their unique financial needs and determining program effectiveness.

IMPLICATIONS AND CONCLUSION

Despite these limitations, the study results point to several social work practice and policy implications with respect to the development of financial management training programs for immigrant populations. By collaborating with community-based social service agencies, and incorporating other income and employment support services, social workers can contribute their expertise in working with disadvantaged populations to design more effective programs for low-income immigrants. For example, given the diversity of immigrant populations in terms of their culture, language, and immigrant experiences, there is a need to carefully tailor training materials to the specific needs of different groups. Social work principles related to empowerment and responsiveness to client-defined needs are very useful in this respect, especially in the spirit of working with program participants to define their most important needs. This may pertain not only to content, but also to the strategies in which training can most effectively be delivered.

The findings from this study indicate that, in addition to being deficient in knowledge about banking practices and savings and investment, low-income immigrants also are in great need of information on public and work-related benefits. Since the welfare systems reforms of the 1990s, immigrant eligibility for public benefits has become more complicated, and there are variations by state and local jurisdictions (Dunkelberg, 2007). As a result, misinformation, outdated information, and concerns over their legal status may prevent many immigrant families from accessing public benefits. Because social workers often have a depth of understanding about public programs, their perspectives are helpful in information dissemination and outreach efforts to inform immigrants of available benefits. Social workers also are important actors in most of the agencies that distribute such benefits, so enhancing their knowledge about financial issues facing immigrants, as well as barriers impeding their access to services, is very important. In addition, given the fact that large proportions of immigrants are in the labor force, social workers could usefully work with employers, especially those with a large number of immigrant employees, to provide information on work-related benefits.

There has been little systematic government support for financial management training programs, let alone for such programs targeted at immigrants. Therefore, advocacy to extend governmental funding is critical for developing large-scale training programs. Social work program developers and researchers can also encourage private foundations and financial institutions to support financial management training for immigrants, as foundations have been among the leaders in providing support for financial training programs more generally. Because banks may be able to use financial management training participation to meet public service requirements mandated under the Community Reinvestment Act, the involvement of financial institutions in providing management training to immigrants also holds promise. Further, involving bankers appears particularly useful not only in terms of their specialized expertise, but also in providing immigrants with exposure to banking officials in a more friendly and supportive setting.

Finally, social work educators and community advocates should further encourage mainstream financial institutions to reach immigrant markets by developing more suitable services and products for this population. These services and products could include opening special bank branch offices that are conveniently located for immigrant neighborhoods, as well as increasing access to low-cost money orders for making long-distance payments (Caskey, 2000). Some banks also are experimenting with products designed to help Hispanics and other ethnic minorities send money to family members in their home countries (Barr, 2004). Offering bilingual financial services could be another effective strategy (Schoenholtz & Stanton, 2001). These efforts can help banks and other financial institutions become a better vehicle for serving low-income immigrants, and thus help bring this population into the mainstream financial system.

REFERENCES

Anderson, S., Scott, J., & Zhan, M. (2004). *Financial Links for Low-Income People (FLLIP): Final evaluation report.* Chicago: Sargent Shriver National Center on Poverty

Law. Retrieved September 30, 2011, from http://www.povertylaw.org/advocacy/publications/2004-06-fllip-evaluation.pdf.

Anderson, S., Zhan, M., & Scott, J. (2007). Improving the understanding of low-income families about banking and predatory financial practices. *Families in Society, 88*(3), 443–452.

Baker, C., & Dylla, D. (2007). *Analyzing the relationship between account ownership and financial education.* New American Foundation, Washington, DC. Retrieved June 24, 2012 from: http://www.newamerica.net/files/Microsoft%20Word%20-%20Account%20Ownership%20and%20Financial%20Education-Elec.pdf.

Barr, M. S. (2004). Banking the poor. *Yale Journal on Regulation, 21*(1), 121–237.

Bishaw, A., & Macartney, S. (2010). *Poverty: 2008 and 2009.* Retrieved October 14, 2011 from http://www.census.gov/prod/2010pubs/acsbr09-1.pdf

Bleakley, H., & Chin, A. (2004). Language skills and earnings: Evidence from childhood immigrants. *The Review of Economics and Statistics, 86*(2), 481–496.

Caskey, J. P. (2000, September). *Reaching out to the unbanked.* Paper presented at Inclusion in Asset Building: Research and Policy Symposium, Center for Social Development, Washington University, St. Louis, MO.

Chan, K., Fitzsimmons, V., Hardy, R., Kimmel, M., Stiles, S., & Tayor, S. (1997). *All my money: A financial management curriculum for persons working with limited-resource audiences.* Urbana: University of Illinois at Urbana-Champaign, Cooperative Extension Service.

Chan, K., Fitzsimmons, V., Hardy, R., Kimmel, M., Stiles, S., & Tayor, S. (2001). *Your money and your life.* Urbana: University of Illinois at Urbana-Champaign, Cooperative Extension Service.

Choi, L. (2009). *Bank accounts and youth financial knowledge: Connecting experience and education.* Working Paper 2009-07. Federal Reserve Bank of San Francisco, San Francisco, CA. Retrieved June 24, 2012, from: http://www.frbsf.org/publications/community/wpapers/2009/wp2009-07.pdf.

Cobb-Clark, D. A., & Hildebrand, A. (2002). The wealth and asset holdings of U.S.-born and foreign-born households: Evidence from SIPP data. *Social and economic dimensions of an aging population (SEDAP)* (Research Paper No. 89). Retrieved September 30, 2011, from http://socserv2.socsci.mcmaster.ca/~sedap/p/sedap89.pdf

Congressional Budget Office. (2005). *Remittances: International payments by migrants.* A series on immigration. Washington, DC: Author.

DeVaney, S. A., Gorham, L., Bechman, J. C., & Haldeman, V. (1996). Cash flow management and credit use: Effect of a financial information program. *Financial Counseling and Planning, 7,* 71–80.

Dunkelberg, A. (2007). *Immigrants and public benefits in Texas.* Immigration and Board Security Hearing, House Committee on State Affairs, House Committee on Board and International Affairs. Retrieved September 30, 2011, from http://www.cppp.org/files/3/Briefing%20on%20Immigrants%20and%20Public%20Benefits%203%2028%2007-1.ppt

Frank, V. (2004). *Islamic financing and IDAs.* Washington, DC: Institute for Social and Economic Development (ISED) Solutions.

Hao, L. (2004, April). *Immigration and wealth inequality in the U.S.* Paper presented at the Annual Meetings of Population Association of America, Boston, MA.

Hernandez-Coss, R. (2005). *The U.S.-Mexico remittance corridor: Lessons on shifting from informal to formal transfer systems* (World Bank Working Paper No. 47).

Retrieved September 30, 2011, from http://www-wds.worldbank.org/external/default/WDSContentServer/WDSP/IB/2005/02/28/000090341_20050228151447/Rendered/PDF/31671.pdf

Hilgert, M. A., Hogarth, J. M., Howell, S., Lucio, E. J., Sanchez, J., Smith, W.,... Farr, J. L. (2005, April). *Banking on remittances: Increasing market efficiencies for consumers and financial institutions*. Paper prepared for Federal Reserve System Community Affairs Research Conference. Washington, DC.

Hirad, A., & Zorn, P. M. (2001). *A little knowledge is a good thing: Empirical evidence of the effectiveness of pre-purchase homeownership counseling* (low-income homeownership working paper series, LIHO-01.4). Cambridge, MA: Harvard University, Joint Center for Housing Studies.

Hogarth, J. M., Anguelov, C. E., & Lee, J. (2005). Who has a bank account? Exploring changes over time, 1989–2001. *Journal of Family and Economic Issues, 26*, 7–30.

Hogarth, J. M., & Swanson, J. (1995). Using adult education principles in financial education for low income audience. *Family Economics and Resources Management Biennial*, 139–146.

Kochhar, R., Gonzalez-Barrera, A., & Dockterman, D. (2009). *Through boom and bust: Minorities, immigrants, and homeownership*. Washington, DC: Pew Hispanic Center.

Lutheran Immigration and Refugee Service (LIRS). (2008). *Financial literacy for newcomers: Weaving immigrant needs into financial education*. Retrieved November 17, 2011, from http://www.refugeeworks.org/downloads/rw_financial_literacy.pdf

Malone, N., Baluja, K., Costanzo, J., & Davis, C. (2003). *The foreign-born population: 2000* (Census 2000 Brief). Washington, DC: US Department of Commerce, Economics and Statistics Administration, US Census Bureau.

Marcuss, M. (2005, July). *International remittances: Information for New England financial institutions* (Public and Community Affairs Discussion Papers). Boston, MA: Federal Reserve Bank of Boston.

Migration Policy Institute. (2010). *U.S. immigrants*. Retrieved September 30, 2011, from http://www.migrationinformation.org/datahub/usimmigration.cfm

Newberger, R., Rhine, S. L. W., & Chiu, S. (2004). Immigrant financial market participation: Defining research questions. *Chicago Fed Letter, 199*. Retrieved September 30, 2011, from http://www.chicagofed.org/digital_assets/publications/chicago_fed_letter/2004/cflfebruary2004_199.pdf

National Council of La Raza (NCLR). (2004). *Financial education in Latino communities: An analysis of programs, products, and results/effects*. Retrieved September 30, 2011, from http://www.radicalmath.org/docs/FinancialEducationLatinos.pdf

Office of Refugee Resettlement (ORR). (2002). *Annual report to Congress 2002*. Washington, DC: Office of Refugee Resettlement, Administration for Children and Families, Department of Health and Human Development.

Orozco, M. (2004). *The remittance marketplace: Prices, policy and financial institutions*. Washington, DC: Georgetown University, Institute for the Study of International Migration.

Osili, U. O., & Paulson, A. (2004). *Prospects for immigrant-native wealth assimilation: Evidence from financial market participation* (Working Paper 20040-18). Chicago: Federal Reserve Bank of Chicago. Retrieved September 30, 2011, from http://www.chicagofed.org/digital_assets/publications/working_papers/2004/wp2004_18.pdf

Paulson, A., Singer, A., Newberger, R., & Smith, J. (2006). *Financial access for immigrants: Lessons from diverse perspectives*. Retrieved September 30, 2011, from http://www.brookings.edu/~/media/Files/rc/reports/2006/05demographics_paulson/20060504_financialaccess.pdf

Ray, B. K., Papademetriou, D., & Jachimowicz, M. (2004). *Immigrants and homeownership in urban America: An examination of nativity, socio-economic status, and place.* Washington, DC: Migration Policy Institute.

Rhine, S. L. W., & Greene, W. H. (2006). The determinants of being unbanked for U.S. immigrants. *The Journal of Consumer Affairs, 40*(1), 21–40.

Robles, B. J. (2003, June). *Low-income families and asset building in the U.S.-Mexico border* (Session Report). Austin: University of Texas, Lyndon B. Johnson School of Public Affairs, Tax and Financial Services on the Southwest Border; Baltimore, MD: Annie E. Casey Foundation.

Schoenholtz, A. I., & Stanton, K. (2001). *Reaching the immigrant market: Creating homeownership opportunities for new Americans.* Washington, DC: Fannie Mae Foundation; and Georgetown University, Institute for the Study of International Migration.

Schreiner, M., Clancy, M., & Sherraden, M. (2002). *Saving performance in the American Dream Demonstration* (Final Report). St. Louis, MO: Washington University, Center for Social Development.

Shelton, G. G., & Hill, O. L. (1995). First-time home buyers programs as an impetus for change in budget behavior. *Financial Counseling and Planning, 6,* 8391.

Sherraden, M. (1991). *Assets and the poor: A new American welfare policy.* Armonk, NY: M. E. Sharpe.

Suro, R. (2003, November). *Remittance senders and receivers: Tracking the transnational channels.* Washington, DC: Pew Hispanic Center and Multilateral Investment Fund. Retrieved September 30, 2011, from http://idbdocs.iadb.org/wsdocs/getdocument.aspx?docnum=548518.

Suro, R., Bendixen, S., Lowell, B. L., & Benavides, D. C. (2002). *Billions in motion: Latino immigrants, remittances and banking.* Washington, DC: The Pew Hispanic Center and the Multilateral Investment Fund.

US Census Bureau. (2010). *Place of birth of foreign-born population: American Community Survey Briefs.* US Department of Commerce, Economics and Statistics Administration, US Census Bureau. Retrieved September 30, 2011, from http://www.census.gov/prod/2010pubs/acsbr09-15.pdf

Zhan, M., Anderson, S., & Scott, J. (2006). Financial knowledge of the low-income population: Effects of a financial education program. *Journal of Sociology and Social Welfare, 33*(1), 53–74.

Zhan, M., Anderson, S. G., & Scott, J. (2009). Banking knowledge and attitudes of immigrants: Effects of a financial education program. *Social Development Issues, 31*(3), 15–32.

8

Developing Financial Capability through IDA Saving Clubs

JONAS PARKER

In the past two decades, the financial education movement has grown into a set of policies and programs that aim to empower individuals and families with the attitudes, knowledge, and skills necessary to make and act on informed financial decisions. However, despite its popularity, the evidence that financial education results in long-term behavior change for low-income adults remains mixed—leading some to question its viability as an effective antipoverty strategy (Financial Literacy and Education Commission, 2008; Lyons, Chang, & Scherpf, 2006; Willis, 2008a, 2008b).

The evidence from the individual development account (IDA) field is more promising. As opposed to a "stand-alone" model of financial education that emphasizes classroom learning without providing the resources to convert knowledge into action, IDAs bundle financial education with incentives, in particular, a matched savings account and access to mainstream financial institutions (Beverly et al., 2008; Shockey & Seiling, 2004). The research on IDAs demonstrates that financial education works iteratively with these incentives to promote saving and asset development (Baker & Dylla, 2007; Clancy, Grinstein-Weiss, & Schreiner, 2001). In this sense, IDAs may provide lessons for the larger financial education field.

While most of the financial education research in the IDA field focuses on the 6- to 10-week course that is typically required upon program enrollment (Anderson, Zhan, & Scott, 2004; Schreiner & Sherraden, 2007; M. S. Sherraden, McBride, & Hanson, 2005; Willis, 2008b), many IDA programs also offer financial education in the form of saving clubs—monthly meetings that provide ongoing support to participants as they save for an asset.[1] While most IDA practitioners may not identify such meetings as saving clubs, they are in fact connecting to a tradition of "money circles" with a deep history of financial empowerment throughout the developing world. Drawing from research on IDAs in Community Action

Agencies (CAAs) in Massachusetts, the goal of this chapter is to better understand the role and potential of saving clubs in promoting financial capability.

The chapter proceeds as follows. The next section reviews the research on saving clubs in both IDAs and the larger financial capability field. The chapter then grounds the discussion with a brief overview of theory from the experiential education and adult education fields before describing the research methods with which the data were collected. The data are then presented and discussed, including a demographic description of saving club participants, an overview of the basic structure common to the saving clubs found in this research, and the role of the saving club in promoting learning and positive financial behaviors through regular, informal conversations about money. The chapter concludes with recommendations for future practice, research, and policy.

PREVIOUS RESEARCH ON SAVING CLUBS

The research from the American Dream Demonstration (ADD)—the first, large-scale test of IDAs—demonstrates that both general financial education and saving club participation are associated with higher saving outcomes for IDA participants. Clancy et al. (2001) show that participants increased their savings for every hour of general financial education that they attended, up to 12 hours. Curley (2004) confirms and expands on these data in terms of the positive effects of saving clubs, which she calls "peer mentoring groups": she finds that IDA programs that offer saving clubs are significantly associated with higher measures of saving. She explains:

> The positive association with the peer mentoring groups is an indication that peer encouragement, support, and sharing the challenges and experiences of the saving process with other participants may be useful. (Curley, 2004, p. 100)

Further, utilizing hierarchical multivariate analysis, Curley (2004) finds that, of the five institutional constructs that are bundled within IDA programs, the information construct—operationalized by hours of financial education and the presence of peer mentoring groups—produces the largest significant effect on saving. These quantitative findings are complemented by in-depth interviews from the ADD, which find that IDA participants are able to learn behavioral and psychological strategies for saving with their peers through experiential learning in a supportive group format (M. S. Sherraden & McBride, 2010; M. S. Sherraden et al., 2005).

Although IDA saving clubs are relatively new and small-scale in the United States, they share essential features with a more established format, the rotating savings and credit association (ROSCA), which is among the oldest and most prevalent savings institutions in the world (Ardener & Burman, 1996; Rutherford, 2001). The core principle of ROSCAs is for a group of individuals to regularly meet to help each other save and invest money to reach financial and community goals. Its club format serves as a social commitment device for self-control and saving; as its participants say, "you can't save alone" (Gugerty, 2005, p. 3).

Throughout the developing world, ROSCAs have historically served as a tool of social and political empowerment for those who have not traditionally had access to credit or mainstream financial institutions, particularly women (Armendáriz & Morduch, 2010). In recent decades, as ROSCAs evolved and became embedded in more formal organizations, they helped spawn the microfinance field, popularized by the Grameen Bank in Bangladesh, which has found peer support as an important component for program success (Armendáriz & Morduch, 2010; Ghatak & Guinnane, 1999; Stiglitz, 1990; Woolcock, 1999). In the United States, ROSCAs were popularized by 20th-century immigrants who were unable to access credit; ROSCAs, in turn, helped catalyze the credit union movement (Low, 1995). Such informal peer associations continue to be utilized by low-income and marginalized groups in the United States, both as a replacement for and complement to mainstream financial products and services (Butler, 2004; Hung, 2006).

The saving club model has been implemented in other contexts beyond IDAs and ROSCAs. For example, *America Saves*, a national savings campaign of the Consumer Federation of America (CFA), promotes saving clubs as part of a social marketing approach to financial education (Brobeck, 1999; Kiss & DeConcini, 2002). Further, components of the saving club model are beginning to be adapted by online services that aim to promote financial capability through combinations of financial education, commitment devices, and social media. For example, stickk.com allows users to set and track financial goals, receive electronic reminders through e-mail or text messaging, and then recruit friends for support or to "referee" their progress. Emerging research demonstrates the promise of utilizing online and mobile technology delivery channels for financial education and peer support (Langan & Sledge, 2010; Meier, 2010).

EXPERIENTIAL EDUCATION AND ADULT EDUCATION THEORY

Johnson and Sherraden (2006) posit that applying the financial capability framework to financial education requires an approach that "enables people to convert knowledge into action... which includes linking individual functioning to social institutions, and *pedagogical methods* [italics added] that enable people to practice and gain competency in this functioning" (p. 6). This section highlights how saving clubs can implement such pedagogical methods through a discussion of adult and experiential education, providing the theoretical framework that underlies the empiricial evidence presented in the chapter.

As the financial education field advances, policymakers and practitioners have increasingly emphasized integrating adult education principles into program design and delivery. Specific recommendations include: customizing the program to the needs of participants, making learning practical and goal-oriented, and replacing traditional lecturing with more informal methods, such as small group and peer learning (National Endowment for Financial Education, 2005; Parrish & Servon, 2006). The core theme of such recommendations is the primacy of experience, learning from both past experiences (including mistakes) and reflection on new experiences (Gregory, 2006; Hogarth & Swanson, 1995; Knowles, Holton, & Swanson, 2005). In this sense, adult education is closely aligned with experiential education theory.

Experiential learning—which Kolb (1983) defines as "the process whereby knowledge is created through the transformation of experience"—allows individuals to test their understanding and explore new ideas through interaction with the environment (p. 38). This theory can be represented as experiential learning cycles, illustrated in Figure 8.1 below, that require the adult learner to move through an inquiry process of action, reflection, conceptualization, and testing (or practice) (Gregory, 2006; Kolb, 1983). As Kolb, Boyatzis, and Mainemelis (2000, p. 3) explain:

> The model portrays two dialectically related modes of grasping experience—Concrete Experience and Abstract Conceptualization—and two dialectically related modes of transforming experience—Reflective Observation and Active Experimentation. According to the four-stage learning cycle, immediate or concrete experiences are the basis for observations and reflections. These reflections are assimilated and distilled into abstract concepts from which new implications for action can be drawn. These implications can be actively tested and serve as guides in creating new experiences.

In this model, learning does not automatically happen through experience, but requires reflection to create knowledge, and then opportunities to test that knowledge in a new cycle of experience. This model often emphasizes learning with peers to facilitate reflection and provide feedback on practice (Gregory, 2006). Given the chapter's focus on financial capability, it is worth noting that the model of learning through cycles of action and reflection is analogous to the concept of praxis in empowering education, which focuses on the possibilities of education for social transformation (Freire, 1970).

This model of a dynamic relationship between experience and action is reflected in some financial education research, which has begun to transcend simple, unidirectional models of causality, instead hypothesizing that the flow of causality

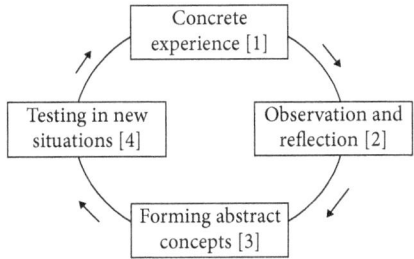

Figure 8.1 Experiential Learning Cycles
SOURCE: *Frontiers: The Interdisciplinary Journal of Study Abroad*

between financial knowledge and behaviors runs both ways. For example, using data from the University of Michigan's monthly Surveys of Consumers and the Survey of Consumer Finances, Hilgert, Hogarth, and Beverly (2003) provide dual causality as an explanation for correlations among knowledge and behavior scores in questions dealing with credit, saving, and investment.

> This pattern may indicate that increases in knowledge and experience can lead to improvements in financial practices, although the causality could flow in the other direction—or even both ways. One way to increase knowledge is to gain experience. And one way to gain additional education is to learn from the experiences of others, as can happen in classes and seminars and through conversations with family and friends (Hilgert et al., 2003).

Others researchers and practitioners have similarly hypothesized that the flow of causality runs both ways (Baker-Sabino, 1999; Beverly et al., 2008), while M. Sherraden (1991) proposes a virtuous circle between asset accumulation and financial knowledge. In interviews with national practitioners and experts in the asset development field, Baker and Dylla (2007) find that financial education has a positive, iterative relationship with savings accounts that leads to improvements in financial knowledge, attitudes, and behaviors. They suggest that the positive, iterative relationship between accounts and financial education rests on the fact that consumers need practical experience and application to assimilate financial education, and that accounts are an example of making financial education more practical, providing an avenue by which consumers can apply new knowledge and skills. IDA saving clubs may generate a similar dynamic, making financial education more practical and tangible by providing the structure for participants to go through experiential learning cycles, collectively reflecting on and analyzing their own financial behaviors as they apply new knowledge and skills. Before presenting data on the potential and limits of IDA saving clubs to foster such experiential learning cycles, the next section will first provide a brief overview of the methods used to collect and analyze the data presented in this chapter.

METHODS

The research presented in this chapter was developed as a community-based participatory research (CBPR) project, based at the Institute on Assets and Social Policy, and conducted in collaboration with nine Community Action Agencies (CAAs) in Massachusetts, and with the Massachusetts Association for Community Action (MASSCAP), their statewide association. The research emerged from the Asset Formation Initiative (AFI), an applied research and policy project that ran from 2006 to 2008, with the goal of expanding and improving free tax preparation, financial education, and IDA programs at the network of CAAs in Massachusetts.[2]

Given the applied orientation of the AFI, the CBPR methodology was utilized to explicitly draw the connection between research and practice (Bhana, 2008;

LeCompte, 1995). This approach prioritized the development of collaborative partnerships with the CAA staff that coordinate financial education programming within their respective agencies, and aimed to both maximize their participation during the key decision points in the research process and connect the research back to practical program improvements.

The research utilized a mixed-methods design. The quantitative data consist of a baseline survey (n = 94), administered during the first or second class of the general financial education course that is typically required at the start of IDA program enrollment, and a follow-up survey (n = 45), administered six to nine months later, primarily at saving club meetings.[3] The surveys gathered data on demographics, measured changes in financial attitudes and behaviors, and identified areas for further exploration in the qualitative components of the research. Survey data analysis was conducted with SPSS to provide descriptive statistics and cross-tabulations.

The qualitative data consist of interviews with 12 IDA coordinators and eight focus groups with 52 IDA participants. Interviews were conducted before saving club meetings, and focus groups were run during club meetings as an official item on the evening's agenda. Both methods used prepared keys, developed from survey responses, conversations with staff, and previous research. A semistructured format was utilized to provide the flexibility to both explore preidentified topics and to allow for emerging issues and insights.

The researcher audiorecorded and transcribed the interviews and focus groups, and used ATLAS.ti for the coding and memoing, which applied both content analysis and grounded theory. The content analysis was focused on themes previously identified from conversations with staff, the baseline surveys, and the literature, while the grounded theory was inductive, allowing for descriptive and explanatory theory to emerge from the data (Bernard, 2000; Charmaz, 1983).

BASIC COMPONENTS OF THE IDA SAVING CLUB

This section first provides an overview of the basic components of the saving clubs, before presenting detailed data on the dynamics of the saving clubs at the research sites.

Monthly Meetings

As mentioned above, most IDA programs require that participants take a basic, 6- to 10-week financial education course when they enter the program.[4] After successfully completing this course, the monthly saving club is offered to provide ongoing support and education. In this way, the saving club serves as the logical next step to the general course. Asset-specific financial education (for example, homeownership education) is usually offered through the saving club, although some agencies refer participants to partner organizations for this service. The monthly saving club meeting is typically structured around an informal conversation about budgeting, which is further elaborated on below.

The CAA

The Community Action Agency (CAA) hosts the saving club, providing meeting space, food, childcare, and other technical and logistical support. The saving club facilitates the referral of participants to programs and services within the CAA—such as free tax preparation, fuel assistance, job skills training, and Head Start—that increase their income and/or decrease expenses, and provide work support. Several of the clubs use meeting time to prepare members' taxes, encouraging them to precommit a portion of their refund to their matched accounts. Similarly, several clubs also invite a staff person from the CAA's fuel assistance department to explain eligibility requirements—or even enroll participants—during club meetings.

The IDA Coordinator

At least one CAA staff person serves the role of the IDA coordinator, who typically organizes and facilitates the monthly saving club meetings. This person must juggle many responsibilities: she collects and reports program data, promotes the program to funders and potential participants, manages institutional partnerships, teaches many of the financial education classes, and handles the logistics for all classes and meetings. In addition, the IDA coordinator provides case management, in the form of one-on-one meetings, to encourage participants to save, provide referrals, help handle financial emergencies, and assist with the asset purchase process. In most of the interviews, IDA coordinators note that, due to the intensive nature of this role, they are often overworked and "stretched thin."

Strategic Partnerships

To enhance their IDA programs, CAAs often develop strategic partnerships, of which the two most common types are financial institutions and the "home buying team" of realtors and home inspectors. In addition, CAAs also partner with credit counseling and debt consolidation agencies, other community-based organizations, and local government agencies. These partners provide guest speakers for club meetings, offering participants a structured opportunity to ask questions directly from financial and other professionals, sometimes resulting in valuable relationships and opportunities.

SURVEY FINDINGS

Although there is not a perfect overlap between the group of IDA participants who completed the surveys and those who participated in the focus groups, the surveys provide a general snapshot of the demographics and trends in financial behaviors.

The demographics of the research sample are very similar to those of the over 2,300 participants in ADD and the over 43,000 participants in the Assets for Independence Program (Office of Community Services, 2008; Schreiner & Sherraden, 2007).

The majority of participants are single mothers, 25–45 years old, who rent and work full-time. In terms of income and education, participants are primarily "working poor," but not the "poorest of the poor" (Schreiner & Sherraden, 2007, p. 81), and possess a higher education level than that of the overall low-income population.

While only half of survey respondents report that they "regularly save or put money away for the future" in the baseline survey, all except one report that they had saved some money into their matched accounts in the follow-up survey. An additional data point, gathered from administrative data on 32 IDA participants after 12–15 months, found that most continued to save, with 12 reaching the maximum amount that can be matched.

Using a retrospective self-assessment, the follow-up survey found that participants report statistically significant improvements on a range of attitudinal and behavioral measures related to budgeting, such as opening and paying bills on time, comparison shopping, and using a budget to track the previous month's expenses. These data are summarized in Table 8.1.

Table 8.1. RETROSPECTIVE SELF-ASSESSMENT OF BUDGETING BEHAVIORS (N = 39)

Budgeting Statement		Mean	Statistic
I make money management an important part of my life	Before	3.2	$Z = -4.62$
	After	4.5	$p < .001$
I think about needs vs. wants when spending money	Before	2.9	$Z = -4.79$
	After	4.4	$p < .001$
I open my bills and keep track of them	Before	3.7	$Z = -3.92$
	After	4.6	$p < .001$
I pay my bills on time	Before	3.9	$Z = -3.70$
	After	4.6	$p < .001$
I talk with my family about money issues	Before	2.6	$Z = -3.63$
	After	3.4	$p < .001$
I use coupons	Before	2.7	$Z = -3.48$
	After	3.4	$p < .001$
I comparison shop to find the best price	Before	3.7	$Z = -3.70$
	After	4.4	$p < .001$
I use a budget to track my expenses from last month	Before	2.2	$Z = -4.26$
	After	3.9	$p < .001$
I use a budget to plan for the future	Before	2.2	$Z = -4.67$
	After	4.0	$p < .001$

NOTE: Participants completed a retrospective pretest for each budgeting statement. Values are based on differences in scores from a 5-point scale (1 = never, 5 = always). The Wilcoxon signed-rank test was used to account for both the frequency and the value of the positive and negative ranks.

INTERVIEW AND FOCUS GROUP FINDINGS

While the survey data show increased savings and improved budgeting behaviors, what role does the saving club play in promoting improvements in financial attitudes and knowledge, and translating these cognitive changes into improved financial behaviors? This section presents the data from the interviews and focus groups to address this question, explicating how IDA coordinators and participants conceptualize the role and impact of the saving club.

A Regular, Informal Conversation about Money

As mentioned above, a regular conversation about money is typically structured into monthly meetings as a standard saving club activity in which participants are expected to discuss their monthly budget, focusing on successes and challenges they had in saving and controlling their spending over the past month. IDA coordinators and saving club participants praise these informal budgeting conversations for several reasons.

First, the conversation is valued because it is a rare opportunity to discuss a sensitive subject that is often taboo or repressed. Many participants point out that talking provides stress relief, especially for single mothers who do not have a partner with whom to discuss difficult money issues. Further, talking about money in a supportive group format helps participants gain perspective on their day-to-day money habits, which in turn gives them a sense of control and future orientation. The following passage from a focus group of ten low-income women enrolled in an IDA savings club highlights these themes:

KARRI: What I've gotten from this group is not being afraid of my money, in the sense of my bills. I know that throwing them away or not looking at them doesn't make them go away. And having a positive attitude towards money instead of having a negative attitude towards money. And I think that comes from growing up poor, where you're afraid of money, money is not to be discussed, it's hidden, it's unavailable... But you come here everything is brought above board, you have to really be conscious of it, you have to take a look at it, taking money seriously, you can't shy away from it, or be afraid of it. And that's everyday, that's going to the mailbox, taking the bills out of the mailbox, looking at them.

DEB: The accountability, you knew you were coming here and you had to look at it. You had to face it. And when you have to face it, like Karri was saying about opening the bills, when you face it, you have to look at it head on, you're forced to work on it.

KARRI: Consciousness. Bringing it to consciousness.

DEB: It's not just, "I don't have to think about that until the bill comes with the red around it."

RESEARCHER: So it's a matter of putting it on the front burner?

DEB: Well yeah, and knowing you were coming here every month, you have to be prepared for what you're gonna to talk about here, and what you were gonna learn, and you had to be aware of your budget and what your bills were, and how to look at your credit report, that it existed and what the impact was...I think it was in your face a lot more and you couldn't walk away from it.

KARRI: Actually the talking about it. Having it be a point of conversation is really important. When we grew up we didn't talk about money because it was so stressful, so just having it be a normal conversation between grownups...that's done a lot in terms of depressing the heightened anxiety around it, making it just a normal conversation.

DEB: Well, a lot of us in this room are single parents...and the stress level is extreme...I work an eleven hour day and have two children, and yes, my parents do watch them, but I still have to make sure that their clothes are still clean, and their lunches are made, and I check their homework when I get home at nine o'clock at night, make sure it's correct, get them up in the morning, still make sure they know I love them. And on top of that, still run the errands, still do everything for the household. There's a lot of stress there. And then you add the stress of your job.

CHRISTINE: That's definitely true, at my house I'm the only adult...Who wants to keep telling the kids, "OK, we got this bill and we have no money?" There's no point in making them stress about it...there's nothing they can do about it.

RESEARCHER: So what is about this conversation here that makes it less stressful and helpful?

CHRISTINE: Sometimes just to know that you're not the only one.

KARRI: The camaraderie.

CHRISTINE: Sometimes you just feel like you're the only one with a million bills.

KATIE: And we've been really lucky, this group is really vocal, none of us are afraid of each other, and we're more than willing to throw everything out on the table, the horrors and the highlights. And just knowing that the conversation is going to be there...we're talking about money...if you have a problem, knowing that you can talk to [the IDA coordinator], you can talk to any of us, it's not gonna go beyond these walls.

In addition, the regular budgeting conversation helps participants prioritize saving and reinforces their commitment to achieving their financial goals. The quotes below, from participants at three different saving clubs, illustrate this point, highlighting themes of motivation, discipline, and sacrifice:

> I just never really thought about it that much before... so it never really occurred to me. But once I started attending the meetings... I really started thinking about putting money away and saving it for the future, now that I'm like a grown up, you know, in the real world. (Lindsey, a white woman in her early-20s)

For me, it's motivation. For me, it's "OK, I can save money" and there's a purpose to it, for me to reach my goal, to buy a home one day. That is something I want to do. And now, having this type of support... it's something that gets me to think, to go ahead with it. (Donna, an African American woman in her mid-40s)

The first thing was the principle of the importance of saving, and how simple saving can be if you have a goal. And it made me more goal-oriented, because goals are, for me, just personally really important... even if it's sometimes just an effort to make [the meetings]... they really just help to bring that into focus, and be more self-disciplined... And especially for me, my family is growing. I have a two year-old and six month-old twins... so this has become a lot more personal. So when we first started, I was in school, and the idea of saving was not even something I said I was gonna be able to accomplish. Honestly, I was like "How am I gonna save ten thousand dollars? I can't even make my car loan payment sometimes. How am I gonna do this?" So when we got serious, and we finally realized that this is what we want to do, we have to sacrifice... and also they instilled in me that sacrifice is also part of what this is all about, you know? (Joanna, a Hispanic woman in her mid-40s)

Budgeting Conversations as Cycles of Experiential Learning

The regularity of the informal budgeting conversations hold potential to develop financial capability by fostering *cycles of experiential learning*, illustrated in Figure 8.2 below. As opposed to teaching the principles of budgeting *in the abstract* and then expecting participants to apply them on their own after program completion, the sav-

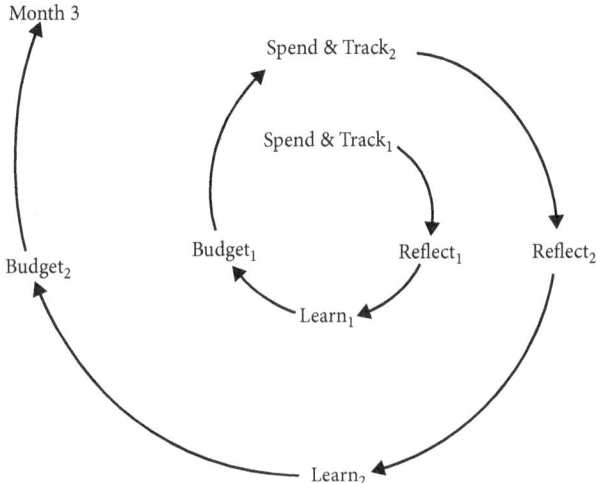

Figure 8.2 The Iterative Cycles of Budgeting

ing club allows for participants to learn how to budget by actually doing it repeatedly, with their own financial behaviors as the object of study and critical reflection.

The iterative budgeting cycle begins with the participant spending and tracking her expenses, designated as Spend & Track$_1$. She then reflects on her money management decisions, designated as Reflect$_1$, during the saving club meeting. The data from this research demonstrate that such reflection in a supportive and collective format both develops financial knowledge and increases commitment to translate knowledge into behavior change. This is designated as Learn$_1$.

The next step in the cycle is for the participant to make a projected budget for the next month, designated as Budget$_1$. As the next month begins, she again tracks spending and expenses (Spend & Track$_2$), and then reflects on them (Reflect$_2$) again at the next saving club meeting. As Steve, a white man in his mid-30s who is in the program with his wife, puts it:

> We made a commitment to do this: to be in this program. We are gonna save and budget. And then, after doing this process of budgeting and saving over and over again, and thinking about it and being reminded at these meetings, it becomes habit. That is the idea.

The iterative dynamic that occurs between budgeting and learning over time is an example of the experiential learning cycles discussed earlier, in which the adult moves through an inquiry process of action, reflection, conceptualization, and practice. In this way, conversations about budgeting in the saving club format represent the integration of adult and empowering education principles into financial education.

The Potential and Limits of Peer Support

Because participants are expected to track and discuss their budget every month, the saving club meetings help them focus on targeted behavior change, such as controlling and reducing their spending. In this respect, participants commonly mention the value of the peer support they receive from each other, as illustrated in the following quote from Jada, an African American woman in her 30s:

> We're all in this kind of beginning stage of wanting more and trying to figure out how to get more… For me, it really was nice to sit in a room with co-workers, and other people, friends or whatever, and know that they understand your struggle. Because it makes it a lot easier to talk about your struggle when you feel like the people in the room understand it, and you're more willing to take in the information or act on the recommendations when you feel like "these people understand my struggle."

However, although peer support from other club members is helpful, both IDA coordinators and participants agree that accountability for behavior change primarily derives from the one-on-one relationship with the IDA coordinator—both during the saving club meeting and through one-on-one case management. As one IDA coordinator puts it:

> Group dynamic plays an important role, but case management has more influence on success... They know they will meet with us, and we put them on the spot: "Did you make your deposit? Did you fill out your budget?"... It's you and them, they can't turn to other people to answer their question.

Similarly, in discussing the value of the saving club, another IDA coordinator talks about how participants become accountable to her and to themselves:

> It gets people talking about money, you know, and talking about it in a realistic way, that's really important for people. Because it's the first time that they actually had to sit down for any period of time I think and sort of be accountable to themselves... and to someone else about their money. I don't pry a ton, but they become accountable to me, which I think is a good thing.

As these quotes illustrate, IDA coordinators can put saving club members "on the spot" and hold them accountable for targeted behaviors, such as saving, reducing spending, tracking expenses, and paying off debts. However, while members greatly appreciate such intensive support, IDA coordinators report that filling this role requires considerable time and energy, and becomes unsustainable as the program grows.

Implications for Practice: Increasing Commitment and Accountability by Democratizing the Saving Clubs

In summary, this research finds that the monthly IDA meeting serves as a saving club that provides sustained, experiential financial education. The saving club format works in synergy with case management and other institutional features of the IDA program to facilitate ongoing learning and to promote the implementation of specific saving strategies, such as budgeting to reduce expenses, focusing on the asset goal, and increasing income through CAA services. However, although saving clubs provide general peer support, the accountability to behavior change primarily derives from the one-on-one relationship with the IDA coordinator, which is extremely time and energy intensive.

The fact that the IDA coordinator has almost all of the responsibility for facilitating the saving club and holding participants accountable to behavior change is a challenge in two ways. First, locating the power of authority within the IDA coordinator represents a top-down approach to service delivery that conflicts with the empowered learner at the center of the adult education model, which emphasizes active participation and small group learning. Second, IDAs remain small-scale and expensive in large part because of the costs associated with staffing (Schreiner, Ng, & Sherraden, 2006).

CAAs and other community-based organizations may be able to run IDA saving clubs more cost-efficiently and more in alignment with contemporary education theory by *democratizing* them. This would entail shifting more responsibility and ownership of the saving club meetings to its members. Democratizing the saving clubs would help address the cost and accountability challenges identified above, as well as build on and strengthen the positive peer support element.

For example, clubs often include "veteran" participants who have been attending meetings for several months (or years) and undergone significant attitudinal and behavioral changes in this time. Several participants mention being motivated by and learning from these individuals. Such veteran members could receive the support to take a greater leadership role in the saving club. In addition to relieving the IDA coordinator, this approach would further develop such veteran members' financial literacy—as the maxim goes, "If you want to learn something, teach it." Further, training local leaders is in alignment with principles of adult and empowering education, and engages CAA's history and mission of connecting meaningful participation of poor people to poverty reduction (Hogarth & Swanson, 1995; Nernon, 2007).

The saving club could increase accountability around spending behaviors if participants reviewed each other's budgets in pairs or small groups, rather than depending on the IDA coordinator. However, the data from this and related research indicate that saving club members are more likely to commit to such an enterprise if they have existing social capital to leverage. For example, writing about saving clubs in developing countries, Vonderlack and Schreiner (2001) point out that strangers cobbled together by the implementing organization will not trust each other enough to hold each other accountable (Vonderlack & Schreiner, 2001). This is a core challenge to IDA saving clubs: participants are often strangers upon program entry. With this in mind, CAAs may consider enrolling participants with existing social capital to leverage, such as coworkers, couples, and family members, although engaging these close relationships must be handled with sensitivity. Additional options include enrolling cohorts from schools, employers, religious organizations, neighborhoods, and affinity clubs.

Future Directions for Research: Community-Based Participatory Research in Saving Clubs

The saving club format is particularly well suited for future CBPR projects, investigating *generative themes* for collective research, education, and social action (Freire, 1970). The focus groups highlighted this potential when participants engaged in critical reflection on the personal and structural financial issues that affect their lives. Two examples of generative themes that emerged from this research are the stress of raising a child in a consumerist society and the lack of affordable housing.

When discussing these issues as a group, participants began to make the connection between their own personal experiences and larger social phenomena, transcending the individual-level focus that typically characterizes financial education. Future CBPR projects could collectively investigate the causes of and potential responses to these challenges, which in turn could lead to organized action. Such an educational enterprise would not be a diversion from the IDA program goals of saving and homeownership, but would actually help participants reach these goals by empowering them to better analyze, understand, and improve their own financial lives. Further, by building client and staff capacity collaboratively, CBPR holds special potential for CAAs to foster meaningful client participation that contributes to reducing poverty, a perennial challenge for the community action field (Nernon, 2007).

CONCLUSION

As Americans have been encouraged to take greater individual responsibility for the management of their personal finances, financial education will continue expanding as a major social policy. While the dominant discourse around financial education often emphasizes self-reliance and self-sufficiency, the financial capability framework challenges these ideals, focusing on a beneficial linking of individuals to social institutions. All Americans depend on social policies that ensure a fair financial system and provide opportunities and incentives to save and build wealth. For example, in regards to curbing predatory lending, financial education is best considered a complement to substantial consumer protection laws, not a replacement (Schloemer, 2004). Financial education policy can promote financial capability for low-income families by fostering sustained and experiential learning environments—such as the saving club format—that increase financial knowledge and skills while supporting positive financial norms and behaviors. However, to be effective, such a policy must be situated within a larger agenda that ensures a fair financial system, and connects financial education to meaningful opportunities for its participants.

NOTES

1. For example, saving clubs were offered to almost half of all IDA programs funded through the Assets for Independence (AFI) Program in 2009, the largest source of IDA funding in the United States (Office of Community Services, 2010)
2. The nine agencies that participated in the CBPR research were self-selected from the larger pool of agencies in the AFI. The researcher approached each agency through the personal contacts developed during the first year of the project. Incentives for participation were not offered to either CAA staff or clients.
3. Of the 45 participants that completed the follow-up survey, 39 enrolled in the IDA program. The survey data on changes in saving and budgeting behaviors are provided only for these 39 participants, given the chapter's focus on financial education in IDA programs.
4. This course typically meets once per week, and uses a combination of two main curricula: FDIC's *Money Smart* and CFED's *Finding Paths to Prosperity*.

REFERENCES

Anderson, S. G., Zhan, M., & Scott, J. (2004). Targeting financial management training at low-income audiences. *The Journal of Consumer Affairs, 38*(1), 167–177.

Ardener, S., & Burman, S. (1996). *Money-go-rounds: The importance of ROSCAs for women.* London: Berg.

Armendáriz, B., & Morduch, J. (2010). *The economics of microfinance.* Cambridge, MA: MIT Press.

Baker, C., & Dylla, D. (2007). *Analyzing the relationship between account ownership and financial education.* Washington, DC: New America Foundation.

Baker-Sabino, C. (1999). *Financial fitness education for potential homebuyers: A start-up guide for Neighborworks® Organizations.* Washington, DC: Neighborhood Reinvestment Corporation.

Bernard, H. R. (2000). *Social research methods: Qualitative and quantitative approaches.* Thousand Oaks, CA: Sage.

Beverly, S. G., Sherraden, M., Zhan, M., Shanks, T. R., Nam, Y., & Cramer, R. (2008). *Determinants of asset building* (Urban Institute Poor Finances Series). Washington, DC: Urban Institute.

Bhana, A. (2008). Participatory action research: A practical guide for realistic radicals. In M. T. Blanche, K. Durrheim, & D. Painter (Eds.), *Research in practice: Applied methods for the social sciences* (2nd ed., pp. 429–442). Rondebosch: University of Cape Town Press.

Brobeck, S. (1999). *Making household savings a priority.* Retrieved October 18, 2011, from http://www.americasaves.org/about/household.asp#2

Butler, J. S. (2004). *Immigrant and minority entrepreneurship: The continuous rebirth of American communities.* Santa Barbara, CA: Praeger.

Charmaz, K. (1983). The grounded theory method: An explication and interpretation. *Contemporary field research: A collection of readings* (pp. 109–126). Prospect Heights, IL: Waveland Press.

Clancy, M., Grinstein-Weiss, M., & Schreiner, M. (2001). *Financial education and savings outcomes in individual development accounts* (CSD Working Paper 01-2). St. Louis, MO: Washington University, Center for Social Development.

Curley, J. (2004). *The role of institutions in the saving participation and performance of low-income households in individual development accounts* (Unpublished dissertation). George Warren Brown School of Social Work, Washington University, St. Louis, MO.

Financial Literacy and Education Commission. (2008). *Research priorities: Results from the national research symposium on financial literacy and education.* Washington, DC: US Department of the Treasury and US Department of Agriculture.

Freire, P. (1970). *Pedagogy of the oppressed* (Vol. 15). London: Continuum International.

Ghatak, M., & Guinnane, T. W. (1999). The economics of lending with joint liability: Theory and practice. *Journal of Development Economics, 60*(1), 195–228.

Gregory, J. (2006). Principles of experiential education. In P. Jarvis (Ed.), *The theory and practice of teaching* (2nd ed., pp. 114–129). London: Kogan Page.

Gugerty, M. K. (2005). *You can't save alone: Commitment in rotating savings and credit associations in Kenya.* Seattle: University of Washington, Daniel J. Evans School of Public Affairs.

Hilgert, M. A., Hogarth, J. M., & Beverly, S. G. (2003, July). Household financial management: The connection between knowledge and behavior. *Federal Reserve Bulletin*, 309–322.

Hogarth, J. M., & Swanson, J. (1995). Using adult education principles in financial education for low income audiences. *Family Economics and Resource Management Biennial, 2*, 139–146.

Hung, C. R. (2006). Rules and actions: Determinants of peer group and staff actions in group-based microcredit programs in the United States. *Economic Development Quarterly, 20*(1), 75–96.

Johnson, E., & Sherraden, M. (2006). *From financial literacy to financial capability among youth* (CSD Working Paper 06–11). St. Louis, MO: Washington University, Center for Social Development.

Kiss, E., & DeConcini, D. (2002). *America saves—cooperative extension: A program guide*. Washington, DC: The Consumer Federation of America.

Knowles, M., Holton, E., & Swanson, R. (2005). *The adult learner: The definitive classic in adult education and human resource development* (6th ed.). Oxford, UK: Butterworth-Heinemann.

Kolb, D., Boyatzis, R., & Mainemelis, C. (2000). Experiential learning theory: Previous research and new directions. In R. Sternberg & L. Zhang (Eds.), *Perspectives on thinking, learning, and cognitive styles* (pp. 227–247). Mahwah, NJ: Erlbaum.

Kolb, D. A. (1983). *Experiential learning: Experience as the source of learning and development* (1st ed.). London: Prentice Hall.

Langan, A., & Sledge, J. (2010). *Looking to the future: Improving financial services for underbanked consumers, highlights of the fifth annual underbanked forum*. Chicago, IL: Center for Financial Services Innovation.

LeCompte, M. D. (1995). Some notes on power, agenda, and voice: A researcher's personal evolution toward critical collaborative research. In P. L. McLaren & J. M. Giarelli (Eds.), *Critical theory and educational research* (pp. 93–112). Albany: State University of New York Press.

Low, A. (1995). *A bibliographical survey of rotating savings and credit associations*. Oxford: Oxfam.

Lyons, A. C., Chang, Y., & Scherpf, E. (2006). Translating financial education into behavior change for low-income populations. *Financial Counseling and Planning, 17*(2), 27–45.

Meier, S. (2010, November 18). *What works in financial education?* Paper presented at the First Annual Conference of the Financial Literacy Research Consortium, New Insights and Advances in Financial Literacy: Translation, Dissemination, Change, Washington, DC.

National Endowment for Financial Education. (2005). *Closing the gap between knowledge and behavior: Turning education into action*. Denver, CO: National Endowment for Financial Education.

Nernon, H. (2007). Community action: Lessons from forty years of federal funding, anti-poverty strategies, and participation of the poor. *Journal of Poverty, 11*(1), 1–22.

Office of Community Services. (2008). *Report to Congress: Assets for independence program: Status at the conclusion of the eighth year*. Washington, DC: Administration for Children and Families, US Department of Health and Human Services.

Office of Community Services. (2010). *Report to Congress: Assets for independence program: Status at the conclusion of the tenth year*. Washington, DC: Administration for Children and Families, US Department of Health and Human Services.

Parrish, L., & Servon, L. (2006). *Policy options to improve financial education: Equipping families for their financial futures*. Washington, DC: New America Foundation.

Rutherford, S. (2001). *The poor and their money*. New York: Oxford University Press.

Schloemer, E. (2004). *Financial education: No substitute for predatory lending reform*. Durham, NC: Center For Responsible Lending.

Schreiner, M., Ng, G. T., & Sherraden, M. (2006). Cost-effectiveness in individual development accounts. *Research on Social Work Practice, 16*(1), 28–37.

Schreiner, M., & Sherraden, M. (2007). *Can the poor save: Saving and asset building in individual development accounts*. New Brunswick, NJ: Transaction.

Sherraden, M. (1991). *Assets and the poor: A new American welfare policy*. New York: M.E. Sharpe.

Sherraden, M. S., & McBride, A. M. (2010). *Striving to save: Creating policies for financial security of low-income families*. Ann Arbor: University of Michigan Press.

Sherraden, M. S., McBride, A. M., & Hanson, E. (2005). *Saving in low-income households: Evidence from interviews with participants in the American dream demonstration*. St. Louis, MO: Washington University, Center for Social Development.

Shockey, S. S., & Seiling, S. B. (2004). Moving into action: Application of the transtheoretical model of behavior change to financial education. *Financial Counseling and Planning, 15*(1), 41–52.

Stiglitz, J. E. (1990). Peer monitoring and credit markets. *The World Bank Economic Review, 4*(3), 351–366.

Vonderlack, R., & Schreiner, M. (2001). *Women, microfinance, and savings: Lessons and proposals* (CSD Working Paper 01–5, Spanish). St. Louis, MO: Washington University, Center for Social Development.

Willis, L. E. (2008a). *Against financial literacy education* (Public Law Research Paper No. 08–10). Philadelphia: University of Pennsylvania Law School.

Willis, L. E. (2008b). *Evidence and ideology in assessing the effectiveness of financial literacy education* (Public Law Research Paper No. 08–08). Philadelphia: University of Pennsylvania Law School.

Woolcock, M. J. (1999). Learning from failures in microfinance: What unsuccessful cases tell us about how group-based programs work. *American Journal of Economics and Sociology, 58*(1), 17–42.

9

Income Tax Time as a Time to Build Financial Capability

JENNIFER L. ROMICH, NICOLE KEENAN,
JODY MIESEL AND CRYSTAL C. HALL

The federal income tax system delivers more cash assistance to low- and moderate-income working families than any other public program. Parents earning below $50,000 per year qualify for several tax credits that reduce or eliminate federal income tax owed and, in many cases, provide a cash refund even when no tax is owed. For instance, a two-adult, two-child family with earnings equal to the federal poverty guideline of $23,050 in 2012 would owe no taxes and receive tax credits totaling $6,800. This is the cash equivalent of more than three extra months of earnings. Despite the importance of federal tax credits in dollar terms to low- and moderate-income families' budgets, many social service practitioners and social welfare scholars pay more attention to and are more knowledgeable about other means-tested programs such as cash welfare, nutrition assistance, or other state and local programs for the poor.

To bring attention to the importance of the federal income tax system to practitioners and scholars interested in facilitating family financial capability, this chapter presents a case study and a cross-case analysis. These are interwoven with an overview of the federal income tax system's treatment of low- and moderate-income tax filers, and an analysis of the connections between the major elements of financial capability—capacity and access—and the income tax system. The chapter concludes with a discussion of how this tax knowledge can be applied to practice and policy to enhance low-income families' financial capability.

CASE STUDY: "SALLY"

The circumstances of a research study participant provide an example of how some low-income filers experience tax time. A member of the research team spoke with Sally (a pseudonym), a 39-year-old, White English-speaking woman who was waiting to have her taxes prepared in early 2010. A single parent to one daughter, Sally works in a call center and made just over $24,000 in the prior year. She describes herself as the "kind of person who works every day" and jokes she would "have to be dying" to skip work. Further describing her financial life, she adds, "I don't make a lot of money and all my money goes to the bills."

Sally tells us that she has filed her federal taxes yearly for the last ten years. She came to the tax preparation site with the necessary form from her employer as well as her and her daughter's Social Security numbers. She expects a refund, estimated as about $2,000–$2,800 because that is what she has received in the past. She explained that tax refund amounts depend on the number of jobs one holds within a year, basing her guess on the fact that she had just one job in the prior year. When pressed, she admitted she was not that sure about her estimate; it could easily be $500 more or less. Although, beginning in 2010, tax filers had the option of buying savings bonds with their refund, Sally was not interested because she has other investments in the form of a 401K from a job that she has rolled over into an IRA. She is happy with this saving ("With that I've got myself established for when I get old") although she noted that her account had recently lost value with the economic downturn.

After Sally had her tax return prepared by one of the volunteers at the nonprofit agency, she learned that her refund was higher than she had guessed, about $3,500. At the time of the interview, she planned to get a new couch set and clean the carpets in her apartment after receiving the money in her account. She also planned to pay off part of her truck and save some as an emergency fund for car repairs because she has spent so much to fix her truck in the past.

BACKGROUND: FEDERAL INCOME TAXES AND LOW-INCOME FAMILIES

Low-income tax filers like Sally experience the same basic structure of the federal income tax system as filers with higher incomes. This chapter focuses on the federal income tax system. Most states also have state income tax systems, and these systems tend to mirror the federal rules and procedures. The next section provides basic background about the operation of the tax system, while the following section provides a discussion about the tax system relative to the dimensions of financial capability.

Income Tax Basics

Tax is paid on most income that is earned (through working for pay) or received from investments or similar sources. Most workers pay income tax over the year in the form of withholding from their pay. Employers submit withheld wages to the US Department of the Treasury's Internal Revenue System (IRS) and report taxes paid on employees' pay stubs. Taxes are calculated based on the calendar year. In January or February, employers issue the federal W2 forms showing total earnings, withholding, and select other information for the prior year. Other institutions such as banks similarly issue tax forms reporting relevant transactions. Individuals and households then prepare their taxes to figure out whether they have paid enough or too much in the withholding process. If not enough has been paid, the taxpayer is supposed to remit the outstanding amount to the IRS. Conversely, if the person or household paid too much over the course of the year, the Treasury issues a refund.

Less Taxable Income and Substantial Tax Credits

Unlike higher earning households, low-income households are likely not to owe any income tax and, in many cases, may get money back even when they do not pay income tax. This is due to both the progressive structure of the income tax system and the tax credits for which low-income persons and families are eligible. Income tax is levied on income minus certain deductions and exemptions. A single person with a straightforward financial life does not pay income taxes on the first $9,350 of income in 2010 (from the $5,700 standard deduction plus the $3,650 personal exemption). A married couple with two children would not pay any income tax on the first $26,000 of income (standard deduction of $11,400 plus four personal exemptions). For low-income families with earnings not far above this, most of their income is untaxed.

Low- and moderate-income tax filers also qualify for one or more available tax credits. Tax credits typically reduce taxes owed for persons who qualify based on some status or behavior, such as having children in the household or saving for retirement. Some credits reduce tax owed but do not provide money back if no tax is owed; others transfer money to the filer regardless of whether any tax is owed.

The largest and most-claimed tax credit for low-income families is the Earned Income Tax Credit (EITC). The EITC is calculated as a supplement to "earned income," money received from working for pay, including self-employment. Politically, the EITC is a popular tool for raising the income of the poor—particularly families with children—while also encouraging employment (Holt, 2011; Ventry, 2000). Whereas welfare or other forms of public assistance often entail meeting with a caseworker, claiming the EITC requires only filing a tax return, resulting in lower administrative costs and less stigma for recipients.

The EITC is fully refundable, which means that it is paid even if the tax filer does not owe any income taxes. In 2010, the EITC was worth up to $5,666 for families with three or more children. Low- and moderate-income tax filers can also claim the Child Tax Credit (worth $1,000 per dependent child in most cases), as well as credits for money spent on childcare, postsecondary education expenses, and retirement savings.

Sally's earnings and family status suggest that she may have benefited from both tax credits. Table 9.1 displays one possible accounting of her earnings and tax situation. Her employer withheld tax from her paycheck throughout the year, likely remitting about $1,500 to the IRS on her behalf. With $24,000 in earnings, Sally owed just over $800 in federal income tax. However, she would also qualify for about $1800 in EITC as well as the child tax credit and the "Making Work Pay

Table 9.1. SALLY'S TAX OWED AND REFUND AMOUNT ESTIMATES FOR TAX YEAR 2009[*]

Income tax calculation	
Total income from wages	$24,050
Subtractions from income	
Standard deduction	-$8,350
Personal exemption (Sally)	-$3,650
Exemption for daughter	-$3,650
Taxable Income	$8,400
Income tax owed	$840
Refund calculation	
Income tax owed	-$840
Credits and payments	
Taxes withheld by employer	$1,500
Child Tax Credit	$840
Refundable Making Work Pay Credit[+]	$160
Earned Income Tax Credit	$1,824
Total Refund	$3,484

[*]All amounts are estimated and rounded. The first author calculated amounts using Taxsim. Feenberg, D., & Coutts, E.. (1993). An Introduction to the TAXSIM Model. *Journal of Policy Analysis and Management, 12*(1),189–194.
[+]The Making Work Pay Credit was created as part of the American Recovery and Reinvestment Act of 2009, commonly known as the economic stimulus package. Designed to counteract the recession of 2007–2009, this credit applied for the 2009 and 2010 tax years only.

Credit" available for 2009 and 2010. Taken together, these figures account for her refund of about $3,500, equivalent to about two months of take-home pay.

Tax Preparation Options and Financial Products

Tax time brings a choice about whether or not to engage a financial services firm for tax preparation. Although it is possible to prepare one's own taxes using IRS instructions, many persons choose to use a commercial preparer. Low-income tax filers more often use paid preparers than higher-income filers (Berube, Kim, Forman, & Burns, 2002). Sally's choice to have volunteers at a nonprofit agency prepare her taxes reflects an increasingly common third option.

FOR-PROFIT TAX SERVICES

Low- and moderate-income tax filers who seek a commercial tax preparer have many options. Local franchises of large national firms such as H&R Block and Jackson Hewitt have substantial presences in low-income neighborhoods

(Berube et al., 2002), often opening five months of the year for tax preparation. Regional franchises and small "mom and pop" firms also offer tax preparation.

Many commercial tax preparers sell additional financial services or products, including accounting services, savings and investment vehicles, and loan products. Since tax time is a time when customers are thinking about financial matters and may have money from a refund to invest, these product offerings can provide opportunities for wealth building. However, consumer advocates have also criticized commercial firms for using the tax filing process to sell costly products with little or no long-run benefit for consumers. One example of the latter is refund anticipation loans (RAL), which are short-term, high-interest loans whereby firms loan customers their expected refund amount and then recoup the loan minus processing costs when the refund arrives. Widespread in the 2000s, RALs allow tax filers to get their refund quickly and—in most cases—pay for the cost of tax preparation services from their refund. Consumer advocates have criticized RALs based on their high costs (up to 10% or more of a tax refund); annualized interest rates of well over 100%; and deceptive marketing claims that they are "quick refunds" rather than loans. Over the past few years, the combination of legislative action and voluntary industry compliance has changed regulation and practices to make RALs more transparent to consumers, less profitable for preparers, and less likely to be available in the future (Wu & Fox, 2011). However, innovation in the financial services industry may bring other similarly controversial products to the commercial preparation market.

Nonprofit Community Tax Programs

Tax filers in certain locations can also choose—as Sally did—to have their taxes prepared for free by trained community volunteers. The IRS supports a nationwide program of volunteer tax preparers through the Volunteer Income Tax Assistance (VITA) programs. VITA is supported by the IRS and delivered locally by nonprofits including legal services clinics, community agencies, and other groups interested in helping low-income consumers. Similar sites operated by AARP are supported by the IRS's Tax Preparation for the Elderly program. Most sites receive technical assistance and software from the IRS and are locally funded through foundation or other support. Individuals and working-age families making less than about $50,000 per year are typically the primary customers at these sites. In 2010, VITA programs affiliated with the National Community Tax Coalition, the organizing network for such sites, completed just over one million returns, which is about one out of every 25 EITC returns nationwide (NCTC, 2011a).

Some community tax centers prepare returns during tax season as one part of a larger asset-building agenda. The filing of tax returns can provide relatively large lump sums of money, and provide an opportunity for families to acquire assets. Early research established that many EITC recipients use their money for durable good purchases or savings (Romich & Weisner, 2000; Smeeding, Phillips, & O'Connor, 2000), and efforts have been made to encourage families to save part of their tax refunds either in specially created accounts or by diverting some of their refund to purchase US Savings Bonds (see, for example, Beverly, Romich,

& Tescher, 2003). Some programs supported by the national coalition offer assistance in other matters, such as helping families complete federal student aid forms, connecting households to unclaimed public benefits, or serving as a recruiting location for financial education or coaching (NCTC, 2011b). Table 9.2 lists some community tax sites and their associated asset-building activities.

A FRAMEWORK OF TAX TIME AND FINANCIAL CAPABILITY

As presented by Sherraden (chapter 1, this volume), a financially capable person has the capacity ("knowledge, skills, confidence and motivation") to act and access "products and institutions" that support economic well-being. Three dimensions important to financial capability at tax time are fair value from preparer method or servicer, predictability of refund or liability, and net impact on family financial well-being. This section describes each in turn.

Table 9.2. EXAMPLE VITA SITES WITH ASSET-BUILDING COMPONENTS

VITA Program	Returns per year[a]	Asset-building services
Boston EITC Coalition, Boston, MA	12,000	benefit screening, financial coaching, financial education
Cerebral Palsy Research Foundation of Kansas	1,800	benefit screening, financial education, financial counseling, savings bond and account promotion
Cook Inlet Tribal Council, Cook Inlet, AK	65	individual development accounts (IDAs) including vehicle purchase program
RealSense Prosperity Campaign, Jacksonville, FL	9,900	financial education, IDAs, account promotion
Southern Good Faith Fund, Rural AR and MS	2,000	referrals to microlending, IDAs, homebuyer and credit counseling, children's savings accounts, bank product promotion
United Way of Snohomish County, Snohomish, WA	4,400	IDAs, savings bond promotions, financial education classes

SOURCE: National Community Tax Coalition (2011b) [a] Figures shown for year reported by NCTC, typically 2007 through 2010.

One question is whether the tax filer is able to make a satisfactory decision about how to prepare the return. Whether someone chooses to file his or her taxes directly with the IRS or uses a third-party paid or unpaid preparer is a function of the available products and institutions. Work to promote financial capability can be supported by fair and functional public institutions, private institutions, and for-profit institutions. Information is one marker of good institutions. Tax filers need knowledge about the costs, services, and competency of different options to make a good decision. Costs include both fees for preparation and time costs spent waiting for the return to be prepared. Services include completing forms, filing the return electronically, and offering or facilitating linkage to associated financial products such as IRAs or IDA options for the investment of the return. Another aspect is follow-up service for clients whose returns are disputed or not accepted by the IRS. Financial capability is best served when persons can choose from a range of providers with clear up-front information about pricing, time, energy, commitment, and quality.

A second dimension of capability at tax time is whether the year-end tax filing results in a refund amount or amount owed that is reasonably expected and manageable. That is, there are no substantial surprises; the filer does not unexpectedly owe a great deal nor receive an unanticipated large refund. This is not to imply that a person needs to be able to accurately predict their refund amount exactly far in advance, but rather that the net refund or liability is within an expected and manageable range. Unanticipated liabilities could be destabilizing, as a filer has either to scramble to come up with the money owed or fall into arrears with the IRS. On the other extreme, the exciting surprise of a higher-than-expected refund might create a windfall mentality in which money is directed toward discretionary consumption rather than long-term goals.

Third, tax preparation work should be examined in light of a broader question about how the work serves overall family financial well-being. Certainly, unreasonably high fees or an unexpected liability could hurt financially. However the structure of the income tax system could also support financial capability. Some parts of financial capability are intrinsic parts of tax time. First, the data on the tax forms provides a review of annual earnings, providing some overview information that is not always visible on a week-by-week basis. Second, the filing process requires interaction with one or more institutions including the IRS, and, in many cases, a private-sector tax preparer. Since access to financial institutions is a part of financial capability, these forced interactions provide one avenue to connect consumers who are not using or making full use of services with potentially helpful new products or options. Finally, the income tax system can help families achieve financial goals through accumulating money. For many families, tax time also means the largest lump sum payment received during the year, meaning that this is a time that funds may be available for investment or other nonroutine purposes.

EMPIRICAL RESEARCH: THE SEATTLE TAX STUDY

This section presents new empirical data about the second aspect of financial capability, the predictability of refunds or liabilities. As part of a larger study on cognition and tax filers (see, for example, Hall, Romich, Keenan, & Miesel, 2010; Hall, Romich, Miesel, Arevalo, & Bae, 2009), clients of a community-based VITA tax preparation service responded to questions about their tax-time thinking and experiences. Hearing about whether and how tax filers predict their refund amounts gives insight into whether the income tax return process might lead to unexpectedly large windfalls (or liabilities) and provides a basis for further supporting financial capability at tax time.

Findings reported here are from interviews of a racially diverse group of 38 tax filers, just over half of whom lived with dependent children. (See the appendix for a more complete description of the sampling strategy, respondent demographics, data collection, and analysis.) Tax filers were asked to predict their refund amounts and queried about their estimating process. The findings are presented in two parts, describing first the explanations offered for the estimated amounts, and then examining the sources of information used.

Findings: Respondents Explain Refund Predictions

All but one of our 38 study participants expected to receive refunds. The average amount predicted was $2,844 (Hall et al., 2010). In explaining why they expected the estimated amount, participants offered two broad types of explanations: factual and social. Factual explanations describe how refunds are calculated, such as outlining the factors that go into the formulas. In contrast, social explanations focus on the larger meaning of receiving money back from a system designed to serve societal or policy goals. Sometimes specific factors have both factual and social dimensions. For instance, the most common factor mentioned was income level. Factually, tax and credit amounts are calculated based on earned income. Existentially, low-income workers are seen as worthy, or deserving, under the work-based social contract that characterizes American antipoverty policy around the turn of the 21st century.

INCOME

Fifty percent of the participants (19 of 38) referenced their income when offering rationales for their anticipated tax refund amounts. We found that when people talked about their income in relation to their tax refund, they tended to do so in one of three ways. They either referenced that (1) they were low-income, (2) their income had increased in the past year, or (3) their income had decreased in the past year. These categories are not mutually exclusive and some of our participants talked about their income in multiple ways.

"I make such a low income," said Kelli, a 27-year-old woman with two children. She continued, "and then I don't, I don't own anything, like we rent an apartment and things, so we've typically gotten a refund back." Kelli is very explicit about her low-income status and reinforces this statement by offering what she considers to be evidence of her status: she does not own anything and rents an apartment. Some participants reference these kinds of "symbolic markers" when discussing their income, particularly when discussing decreases in income or low-income status. Kelli's use of homeownership as evidence of low-income status is an excellent example. To Kelli, homeownership serves as a symbol of something that low-income people cannot have, so using it serves to buttress her claim that she should expect a refund.

"I got laid off last year," said May, a 32-year-old woman with no children, offering up one of the reasons why she thought she would get a refund. Those who reported that their income decreased rarely stated so explicitly; only one person stated directly that she was making less money this year than in years past. Others presented changes in their employment status, which served to represent the change in income. Lina, a 40-year-old woman, said "I lost my job. Yeah. And but I don't know how much it will get this year. Last year it was a different amount because...I had a job but this year [is] a little bit different."

"My income is higher this year," said Stephanie, a 43-year-old woman with one child who had received a small raise, as she offered reasons why she estimated that her refund could be higher than she initially estimated. Stephanie's explanation is consistent with prior findings from a study of EITC claimants (Romich & Weisner, 2000). Respondents commonly use "more work, more money" as the rule of thumb, but in most cases this understanding does not adequately capture the complexities of the income tax calculation rules.

Changes in income make it harder for tax filers to estimate their refunds. The relationship between earnings and refund is not straightforward. Refund amounts depend on household composition, how much the filer's employer or employers withheld, and the exact level of earnings. When asked how her refund might change if she were to earn $5,000 more, Lina said, "I don't have any idea. I don't have a lot of knowledge about how it works. Or what the percentage is, how much I earn and how much I will have returned. Yeah? Returned money. I just add it." Lina demonstrates how she knows that her earnings are related to her tax refund, but also how little she knows about how the system works.

In contrast, Sara, a 40-year-old mother of two, had taken on a second job and was fearful that the increase in income would reduce her refund amount. She said, "In 2008 I picked up a second job, because of the economy and I was in quite a bit of debt...if I had earned $5,000 more, then I know I wouldn't be eligible for [the] Earned Income Credit and my additional tax credit would go down. And that's what I'm afraid of this year. Get less money which is really going to be devastating to me."

Features of the Tax System

Nearly 40% of our participants (15 of 38) made some sort of reference to specific features of the tax system at least once during their interviews. These comments were in reference to withholding, the EITC, the child tax credit, claiming dependents, and the IRS. Sasha, a 36-year-old woman with two children, offers an example of a typical reference to withholding. When Sasha was asked how she came up with her specific refund estimate, she said, "I just looked on my tax form and see what I put in...you know, the W2 form. I just look at that like I look and see what federal income tax [was] withheld."

Of the twenty participants with dependents, thirteen stated that they expected to receive a refund because they had children or were claiming a dependent when filing their taxes. Gail, who has three adult children and two whom she still claims as dependents, stated that she knew that she would receive the "Earned Income Credit for the two children at home." This statement demonstrates her knowledge of the fact that children claimed for the credit must be dependents. "I am the only one working, I claim my kids," says Jonathan, a 35-year-old man with two dependents, when asked why he expects to get a tax refund.

Another participant, Lisa, made reference to knowledge of a credit per child when she said, "I'm under the impression that it's like, $1,300–$1,500 per kid." However, her use of the word "impression" suggests that Lisa is not absolutely confident in her knowledge of the amount of the credit or how it works. Despite this uncertainty, Lisa is clearly drawing on a factual explanation about the rules and rates underlying the tax system.

Social Contract

A second major theme in respondents' comments concerns how the tax system carries out social policy goals of redistribution and supporting work among low- and moderate-income filers. These explanations reference an implicit social contract, in which persons—particularly parents—work for pay, but receive some public support if their wages are not sufficient for meeting expenses.

Jen is a 53-year-old woman with one child living in her household. Throughout her interview, Jen spoke in ways that suggested a structural understanding of the tax system and social problems. While most participants would talk about their personal circumstances while considering reasons that their refund might vary, Jen cited the economy, changes in the structure of the tax system, as well as a difficult job market. However, this structural perspective begins with her understanding of the social contract. When asked why she thought she would get a refund this year, she said "Well because I work. And I do have children. And I'm a citizen, and I earned my taxes." Jen suggests that she has upheld her end of the social contract, her "duties" of working and raising children. Through this good behavior, she judges herself to be deserving of the "rights," including her tax refund.

This sort of understanding of deservingness or "right to a refund," was evident in five interviews. Participants usually cited some combination of work, children, student status, or even their child's citizenship status. For example, to explain why she expects to get a tax refund, Lina suggested that in addition to anticipating a refund because she was employed this year, that she also anticipates getting a refund because "I'm a student now and I think the government can help me." Her statement communicates an understanding of the "citizen as worker" and also an expectation that the government will help someone who is engaging in the social good of education.

Findings: Sources of Information

People gain knowledge and develop beliefs about financial capability in a variety of ways. This research sought to explore the sources that tax filers use to form their understanding of tax refunds, and the ways in which beliefs develop. Personal experience was cited as the most common teacher. A few others also relied on family, trusted friends, or formal tax providers.

Twenty of the 38 respondents spontaneously referenced their own past experience when anticipating the potential for receiving a refund this year. Gail, a 57-year-old mother with two dependent children, described why she anticipated getting a refund by saying, "Last year it was close to $5,000, a little over $5,000 so I'm looking for that much again this year." Drawing on past experience served as the starting point for many refund estimates, even if participants understood reasons why their refund might be different than in years past. For example, Vicky is a 21-year-old mother with one child, who states that she expects to receive a refund of about $2,000 although she received $1,800 last year, saying, "I think it's going to be higher because I make less money than last year."

Two participants drew on their personal networks, made evident when they cited family knowledge or experience as a source of information when anticipating tax refund amounts. Jay is a 19-year-old man who was filing taxes for the first time and cited his mother as a source of information. "My mom said when I put on, like my W2... put in 0 and they are gonna take the most out but I am guaranteed not to owe at the end then I should get a refund so based on that information that's how I came up with that 1,000 dollars." It is clear from this quote that Jay trusts his mother's instruction and draws on her knowledge to make an estimate about how much he anticipates receiving as a refund. Stacy, a 50-year-old woman, cited her sister's experience with taxes after winning some money, "My sister won money and she got some money back. She got back more than she expected, so I think okay, maybe I'll get more back." In both of these instances, participants without personal knowledge or experience of their own drew upon the knowledge and experience of people close to them whom they trusted.

Another source of information that three of our participants cited was formal providers. Sandy, a 38-year-old woman with one dependent, thought that she was going to break even on her taxes this year, stating that she thought this "because I went over to H&R Block and they did my taxes but it was too much. So I came over here. But they already told me how much it was going to cost." Juan, a 30-year-old man with one dependent, described how he used the internet to determine what his refund amount would be prior to coming to the free tax site. "Well I just did my research you know online. I looked online. I went to Turbo Tax." Whether initially the intent or not, these formal providers ended up serving as a resource to gain information about the expected tax refund amount. The formal sources did not appear to enhance knowledge of how the tax system worked, but rather to simply provide an estimate.

SUMMARY AND LIMITATIONS

The low- and moderate-income tax filer respondents entered the tax preparation site with general ideas about the size of their refund. When asked to make estimates of their anticipated refund amounts, participants relied, first, on past personal experience and, second, on second-hand experience and knowledge of those they trust. Most intuitively referenced several parts of the complex relationship between their household circumstances, yearly earnings, and anticipated refund. However, it was less clear that low-income tax filers understood how all the moving pieces fit together. This study examines respondents' reasoning, not whether or not their estimates were correct. Future work will cross-walk estimates with calculated refunds.

The tax filers in the current study are a select group, and our findings cannot be generalized to all low- and moderate-income filers. The respondents in this study are clients of a free tax service staffed by volunteers (a VITA site), and no respondents who utilize a for-profit preparer or who prepared their own return were included. Whether or how well someone understands the federal income tax system may influence the choice of preparation method. VITA sites are typically aligned with social service providers in the nonprofit sector, and VITA tax clients are often recruited through their connections with other private or public service or benefit receipt. Clients of for-profit preparers may be more or less knowledgeable about their refund amounts. Persons who prepare their own taxes likely understand the system better.

DISCUSSION AND IMPLICATIONS FOR SUPPORTING FINANCIAL CAPABILITY AT TAX TIME

Consider again Sally, the tax filer profiled in the case study. What has this exposition taught us about how tax time can be a time to build financial capability for Sally and other low-income tax filers like her? This section discusses some implications for direct practice resulting from the study of tax filers' predictions as well as some agenda items for advancing financial capability at tax time more broadly.

Social workers and others who work with low- and moderate-income families should, at a minimum, be aware of the importance of tax time. Talking about tax preparation with constituents and disseminating information about different tax preparers (including for-profit, nonprofit, and free online filing providers) helps create awareness of options (Beverly, 2002).

Discussing prior years' experiences can yield information about financial goals, plans, and practices. Our current study shows that most filers anticipate they will get a refund more or less like that of prior years. One question is whether asset-building practitioners should try to help filers better understand the tax system. Insofar as household circumstances, earnings, and the tax code provisions remain relatively stable, relying on past experience makes sense. However, alerting tax filers to life changes that may trigger tax changes will support their financial planning. For example, tax refunds will likely decrease if dependent children turn 18, cease being full-time students before the age of 24, or move out of the household. Holding down a second job will often increase taxes owed due to withholding practices, and increases in earnings—particularly above the poverty line—will often decrease refund amounts. Finally, marriages, divorces, or separations affect tax status. Because not receiving an expected refund could be financially destabilizing, education efforts that focus on events that change these tax situations are important.

Practitioners working with clients to build financial capability should also bear in mind that most persons will get refunds, these refunds are largely expected, and people plan uses for the refunds. Many low-income workers receive refunds equal to as much as two or more months of earnings sometime in the first four months of the year. For example, Sally's refund of $3,500 was equivalent to receiving an extra month and a half of paychecks. For situations requiring down payments (such as for housing rental or purchase) or investments, tax time can provide start-up capital. However, accumulating debt or delaying purchases in anticipation of refunds can limit the use of funds for asset accumulation.

Building on the language used by tax filers themselves may be one way to encourage savings or other uses that align with larger goals. In explaining why they expected substantial refunds, Sally and the 37 other respondents most often mentioned their low income level. The respondents understood that their large tax refunds were linked to their status as low-income workers, parents, and citizens. Communication strategies could incorporate these ideas. For instance, consider Sally's interest in establishing an emergency fund. Noting that tax time is a time when she can create some measure of financial security can echo the "deservedness" theme noted by respondents.

Reforms should recognize that tax filers bring a limited and impressionistic view of tax decisions. Policy and advocacy efforts are needed to make sure consumers are offered options that are transparent and support well-being. The campaign against RALs, which included grassroots activists and think-tanks, is a good example of consumer protection. Although the nonprofit sector may not be a natural home for developing new financial services, the sector can provide vigilance against wealth stripping. Combinations of increasing necessary knowledge and advocating for wealth-supporting products and industry practices will best support family financial capability at tax time.

ACKNOWLEDGMENTS

Partial support for this research came from a Eunice Kennedy Shriver National Institute of Child Health and Human Development research infrastructure grant, 5R24HD042828, to the Center for Studies in Demography & Ecology at the University of Washington. The authors thank the survey respondents, Courtney Noble of the United Way of King County EITC campaign, and the VITA site managers and volunteers. We also thank April Arevalo who oversaw project logistics; Makeba Greene, Claire Miccio, Alejandra Guillen, Debbie Caruso, Therese Fialko, Megan Farwell, Ranae Desouza, and Radka Enriquez, who volunteered to collect and transcribe data; and Abe Bae and John Oh, who helped with analysis.

APPENDIX: DATA COLLECTION AND ANALYSIS

The empirical findings in this chapter are part of a larger study on cognition and tax filers. This appendix describes the data collection and analysis process. Readers interested in the framework of the larger study should consult Hall, Romich, et al. (2009). Hall et al. (2010) describe the qualitative analysis process in greater detail. All study procedures were approved by the University of Washington Human Subjects Division.

Participants were recruited at two free community-based tax preparation sites in Seattle suburbs in January through April 2010. In collaboration with the volunteers at the tax-prep site, interviewers approached individuals in the order they had signed up to have their taxes prepared and inquired if they were interested in participating in the study. A total of 48 low-income tax filers agreed to be interviewed and were compensated for participating in the study with a $10 retail gift card.

Five graduate students conducted semistructured interviews with participants at the tax-prep site while they waited to file taxes. Each interview lasted approximately 15 minutes and was audiotaped after obtaining verbal informed consent from the participant. Interviewers adhered to predetermined interviewer questions and probed for clarification as appropriate.

For the purposes of this analysis, researchers limited the sample to those participants who were English-speaking, thereby excluding five interviews. One participant declined to have her interview audiorecorded and another four audio records of interviews were unable to be transcribed due to equipment failure. Hence results in this paper are based on the 38 tax filers with complete English audio files.

Thirty of the respondents were women. Most (21 of 38) had dependents. Self-reported race and ethnicity information showed 16 participants were non-Hispanic White, 9 Black, 2 Asian, and 6 Hispanic. Five used other descriptions such as "mixed" or specific combinations of the major categories. A majority (20 of 38) reported at least some college or career training. An additional 11 said they were high school graduates or GED holders, and 4 reported not finishing high school.

Data consist of interview notes, live recordings, and verbatim transcriptions. With input from the entire research team, authors Miesel and Keenan analyzed these data using techniques including case summaries, exploratory and systematic coding, and cross-case analysis.

REFERENCES

Berube, A., Kim, A., Forman, B., & Burns, M. (2002). The price of paying taxes: How tax preparation and refund loan fees erode the benefits of the EITC. *Progressive Policy Institute: Survey Series*. Washington DC: The Brookings Institution.

Beverly, S. G. (2002). What social workers need to know about the Earned Income Tax Credit. *Social Work, 47*(3), 259–266.

Beverly, S. G., Romich J. L., & Tescher, J. (2003). Linking tax refunds and low-cost bank accounts: A social development strategy for low-income families? *Social Development Issues*, 25(1/2), 235–246.

Hall, C., Romich, J., Keenan, N., & Miesel, J. (2010, November). *Mis/under-estimating: How EITC-eligible tax filers estimate their refunds*. Paper presented at the Association of Public Policy Analysis and Management Annual Research Meeting, Boston, MA.

Hall, C., Romich, J., Miesel, J., Arevalo, A., & Bae, A. (2009, November). *Psychological insights into how low-income tax-filers view the EITC*. Paper presented at the Association of Public Policy Analysis and Management Annual Research Meeting, Washington, DC.

Holt, S. (2011). Ten years of the EITC movement: Making work pay then and now. *Metropolitan Opportunity Series*. Washington, DC: Brookings Institution.

National Community Tax Coalition (NCTC). (2011a). *State of the field report*. Retrieved September 30, 2011, from http://tax-coalition.org/about-us/state-of-the-field-reports/2010-state-of-the-field-report/view

National Community Tax Coalition. (2011b). *Program profiles*. Retrieved September 30, 2011, from http://tax-coalition.org/our-coalition/our-coalition/program-profiles.

Romich, J. L., & Weisner, T. (2000). How families view and use the EITC: Advance payment versus lump sum delivery. *The National Tax Journal*, 53(4.2), 1245–1265.

Smeeding, T. M., Phillips, K. R., & O'Connor, M. (2000). The EITC: Expectation, knowledge, use, and social and economic mobility. *The National Tax Journal*, 53(4.2), 1187–1210.

Ventry, D. J. (2000). The collision of tax and welfare politics: The political history of the Earned Income Tax Credit, 1969–1999. *The National Tax Journal*, 53(4.2), 983–1026.

Wu, C. C., & Fox J. A. (2011). *End of the rapid rip-off: An epilogue for quickie tax loans*. Washington, DC: National Consumer Law Center & Consumer Federation of America. Retrieved September 30, 2011, from http://www.consumerfed.org/pdfs/RAL-report-2011-final.pdf.

10

Building Financial Capability of Native American Households

The Role of the EITC

KRISTEN WAGNER

The Earned Income Tax Credit (EITC) has been shown to alleviate poverty in low-income households. For Native American households, among the poorest in the United States, the EITC has the potential to make an important contribution to economic well-being. This chapter examines the financial behaviors and needs of low-income Native American families and the potentially critical role of the EITC in improving the financial situation of underserved Native American families. It begins with an overview of the social and economic circumstances of Native Americans in the United States, followed by a review of the EITC and its potential contribution to building financial capability in Native American households. Next, the chapter presents evidence on the role of the EITC in financial capability among Native American households. Suggestions for social work education, practice, research, and policy that may improve financial capability among low-income Native American families are provided.

SOCIAL AND ECONOMIC WELL-BEING IN NATIVE AMERICAN HOUSEHOLDS IN THE UNITED STATES

The historical, social, and economic context impacts the current financial capability of Native American [hereafter, Native] households. Native nations are sovereign nations that reside within the borders of the United States. Therefore, treaty-protected rights and rights related to the governance of institutions on that land have a direct effect on economic improvement for Native people (Anderson, 1995). Despite these protections, Native people have been systematically excluded from economic opportunities afforded to other Americans, such as homeownership, employer-sponsored contribution plans (e.g., 401(k)s, 403(b)s, etc.), and loan programs to support business development. Many of these opportunities are available through employer-sponsored programs, and the lack of employment opportunities for Native people living on or near reservations excludes them from these financial investment opportunities. Exclusions from these investment programs and others are also a direct result of both discriminatory practices and confusion regarding the sovereignty status of Native nations (Adamson, 2003; Anderson & Parker, 2009). As a result, Native households are among the poorest in the United States, and Native communities lack institutional structures and opportunities to support their members.

Native communities in the United States currently face multiple economic challenges. There are approximately 3.4 million Native people—including American Indians, Alaska Natives, and Hawaiian Natives—in the United States, comprising 2.1% of the population (US Census, 2011). In 2009, poverty among Native households reached 21.4%, nearly twice the national average (American Consumer Survey, 2011). Median income in Native households is approximately $36,520 (American Consumer Survey, 2011). Among racial and ethnic groups, only African American households have lower income: median household income for African Americans is $34,445, for Latinos is $40,946, and for Whites is $54,535 (American Consumer Survey, 2011). For Native people living on reservations, the most economically disadvantaged, median household income is substantially less, averaging $16,718 (American Consumer Survey, 2011). Prior to the economic crisis, unemployment rates averaged 49% in Native communities compared to an average of 5% nationally (US Department of Labor, 2005). Furthermore, almost one-third of employed Native Americans live below the poverty line (Bureau of Indian Affairs, 2005). These statistics suggest a need for programs and policies that strengthen financial circumstances in Native households.

FINANCIAL CAPABILITIES APPROACH

The financial capability framework provides guidance in examining the role of the EITC in financial well-being and development among low-income Native families. For purposes of this discussion, financial capability is defined as the ability of people to understand and assess financial options while making financial choices that will help them live the life they choose (Johnson & Sherraden, 2006). Critical components of financial capability include the following: (1) means with which to make economic choices; (2) knowledge, skills, and opportunities related to money and its function; and (3) the ability to make financial choices that support life goals (HM Treasury, 2007; SEDI, 2004).

Financial capability efforts among Native households should be considered within historical/political and cultural context. The resources of Native people have been subject to social, economic, and legal exploitation throughout history (Anderson & Parker, 2009; Cornell, 2007). Policies under colonization stripped and redistributed social, financial, and natural resources, eliminating opportunities for future generations to access and manage community assets. Tribes did not regain control over their financial affairs until the Indian Self-Determination and Educational Assistance Act was enacted in 1975 (P.L. 93–1638, 1975). Culturally, financial capability defined as individual wealth building may not resonate with the experience or goals of Native households (Miller, 2001; Pickering, 2000; Pickering & Mushinski, 2004). Though each tribe is unique, many Native cultures value collective resource ownership and management over individual wealth accumulation (FNDI, 2004). The ways that financial capability is approached may vary based on individual choice and structural differences that include social institutions such as norms, traditions, and culture. Building financial capability of Native households can be pursued by strengthening the economic circumstances of Native households in ways that make it possible to share their resources with others in need. Leveraging the EITC, as will be discussed below, offers one promising approach.

EITC CONTRIBUTIONS TO FINANCIALLY VULNERABLE NATIVE FAMILIES

The federal EITC is the largest cash income support program contributing to improved economic circumstances for low-income families in the United States (Bartolomei-Hill, 2000; Berube & Forman, 2001; Eissa & Liebman, 1996; Lim, Livermore, & Davis, 2009; Llobrera & Zahradnik, 2004).[1] The EITC, created in 1975, provides a refundable tax credit, administered through the Internal Revenue Service (IRS). The amount of the tax credit is based on a percentage of taxpayer earnings, marriage status, and number of dependent children. The EITC is a "refundable" credit, meaning that it may be more than the amount of money the taxpayer paid in taxes during the prior year. The taxpayer receives the credit in the form of a check mailed to them or by direct deposit into their bank account. The IRS allows for splitting of the refund so that portions of the tax refunds can go into multiple accounts (Beverly, Schneider, & Tufano, 2006). In addition to the federal EITC, 24 states have implemented state EITC programs (Internal Revenue Service, 2010).

The increase in income through the EITC contributes to a number of economic opportunities for working families (Berube & Forman, 2001; Meyer & Rosenbaum, 2001). Families utilize EITC resources in a variety of ways, including as an initial balance to establish bank accounts, maintain basic purchasing needs, pay down debt, make substantial investments in durable goods such as transportation, or make long-term investment decisions like home ownership. Each of these investments helps move individuals toward a higher level of economic well-being (Mammen & Lawrence, 2006; Romich & Weisner, 2000; Smeeding, Ross-Phillips, & O'Connor, 2000).

EITC AS A FOUNDATION FOR FINANCIAL CAPABILITY AMONG NATIVE HOUSEHOLDS

Tax time presents an opportunity to build financial capability (Lim et al., 2009). The act of filing taxes is one way of exercising capability: individuals interact with institutions such as a paid tax preparer, a free tax service, or via the Internet directly to the IRS. Workers gain access to an earned benefit and have an opportunity to make decisions about how they will utilize this resource. Tax time may be the only time all year when some households consider their current and future financial plans or talk with someone about money issues. In addition, it may be the only time families have access to liquid funds and an opportunity to leverage them for savings or investment (Brown, 2005). The size of an EITC refund provides a substantial economic resource that provides an opportunity for people to make choices about how to reach their financial goals. In the 2008 tax year, the maximum credit for a working family with two or more qualified children (including biological, foster, permanently and totally disabled, step, and adopted children), and a family income of less than approximately $41,646 ($38,646 for a single-parent household) was $4,824 (IRS, 2008).

Research findings suggest that EITC involvement can influence financial behaviors. Evidence from a pilot savings program paired with the EITC suggests that when given an opportunity to save, particularly through direct deposit, individuals were more likely to save the money or to spend it slowly over time rather than spending it all at once and were more thoughtful about how they planned to use the money (Beverly, Tescher, & Marzahl, 2000; Beverly, Tescher, & Romich, 2004; Beverly, Tescher, Romich, & Marzahl, 2005; Hilgert, Hogarth, & Beverly, 2003).

Access to Tax Information

In addition to income, including the EITC, increasing awareness of financial concepts and financial choices is also needed to build financial capability (HM Treasury, 2007; Johnson & Sherraden, 2006; Lim et al., 2009; Romich, Keenan, Miesel, & Hall, chapter 9, this volume; Sherraden, 2008). In the case of the EITC, eligible households must file their taxes in order to receive the benefit. Yet, each year, between 15% and 25% of US households who qualify for the EITC do not claim their credit (Berube, 2003).

In Native households, confusion about tax filing obligations is a particularly relevant issue. Tribal members with qualifying income are usually eligible for the EITC, yet many do not file. A study of five Native communities discovered that, on average, 20% of eligible recipients in these communities do not claim their EITC dollars (Lui, Robles, Leonard-Wright, Brewer, & Adamson, 2006). In some cases, where treaties have been established between the US government and a tribe to protect fishing rights or other activities, Native people are exempt from federal income tax. They are sometimes unaware of this exemption. When Native taxpayers do not claim a tax credit, they forfeit dollars that could help them meet basic needs or provide future development opportunities. For these reasons, EITC outreach and education is a critical first step in building financial capability of low-income Native households.

Tax Preparation Services

Many tax filers use commercial preparers who offer refund anticipation loans/ checks (RALs or RACs) because they believe they will receive their refunds faster through this venue, but these services can prove to be quite costly.[2] Native American EITC recipients use RALs/RACs at a higher rate than others, at an average cost of $250 per RAL (Berube, Kim, Forman, & Burns, 2002; First Nations Development Institute and Center for Responsible Lending, 2008; Tumulty, 2007).

An alternative to these more costly services is volunteer income tax assistance (VITA) services. In Native communities, VITA sites serve as a gateway to other financial services connecting customer needs and financial services. These access points are particularly important for Native communities where financial opportunities have been substantially limited throughout US history. These sites have improved Native livelihoods by connecting them to EITC benefits, providing free tax preparation, and contributing to financial capability. VITA sites offer financial education, typically outside of tax time, about how EITC recipients can leverage EITC dollars. Increasingly, VITA sites also serve as a bridge to other financial services for unbanked households. For example, it is common for VITA site volunteers to share information about the option to receive a refund via a check in the mail or through direct deposit to a bank account. If taxpayers do not have a bank account, VITA volunteers may connect them to financial institutions through a referral or through an on-site consultation with a bank or credit union representative. Sites have also begun to offer financial counseling and assist consumers in building relationships with financial institutions.

Access to Financial Services in Native Communities

Access to financial services is a key component of building financial capability (HM Treasury, 2007; Johnson & Sherraden, 2006; Sherraden, 2008). However, Native households tend to have less experience with financial institutions, more limited credit histories, and fewer assets compared to other US households, mostly due to the absence of financial services available in Native communities (Pickering, 2000; Pickering & Mushinski, 2001, 2004). A study by the US Department of the Treasury finds there are financial institutions located in only 14% of reservation communities. Among those with financial services, 50% offer automated teller machines (ATM) as their primary service (CDFI Fund, 2001). In a CDFI study of Native American access to capital and financial services, 33% of respondents reported that the nearest ATM or bank branch was over 30 miles from their home. Additionally, 6% indicated that the nearest financial services are located more than 100 miles away (CDFI Fund, 2001).

Participation in the economic marketplace is largely dependent on social relationships where trust is a central element. Native communities have dealt with a history of racial tension and discrimination in the economic marketplace, which has translated into limited relationships between Native households and banks (Pickering & Mushinski, 2004; Wagoner, 2002), and further distrust and misunderstandings (CDFI Fund, 2001; Pickering & Mushinski, 2004). Many Native reservations are bordered by communities that are linked to mainstream commodity and commercial financial markets. Yet, due to historical exclusion and discrimination, Native people have had limited connections to mainstream markets (Pickering & Mushinski, 2004). In many reservation communities, banking services are unavailable or located great distances from the community (CDFI Fund, 2001). Limited access to financial institutions has led to a reliance on cash transactions in Native communities and limited exposure to banking processes. As a result, Native people have few opportunities to acquire financial knowledge, experience, and skills needed to achieve financial capability.

Account Ownership

Bank account ownership has been linked to a number of positive economic outcomes for low-income families. Those with an account are more likely to save and accumulate financial reserves that can buffer economic crises such as illness or job loss. Furthermore, those who own a bank account are more likely to hold assets providing further economic protection (Sherraden & Barr, 2005; Sherraden, Schreiner, & Beverly, 2003), and take advantage of direct deposit for receipt of EITC funds (Beverly et al., 2000; Beverly et al., 2004; Beverly et al., 2005; Zhan, Anderson, & Scott, 2006).

However, a substantial percentage of Native households do not have bank accounts. A study conducted by the FDIC (2009) revealed that approximately 45% of Native people had limited access to banking services, 16% were more likely to be unbanked, and 39% were more likely to be underbanked compared to the general population. Many factors, including high minimum balances, fees associated with falling under these balances, credit checks, and accessibility to banks, inhibit account ownership (Barr, 2004).

Limited access to banking services encourages many Native households to use alternative financial services, often referred to as fringe services, many of which are predatory and charge high transaction fees (Rhine, Toussaint-Comeau, Hogarth, & Greene, 2001). Such fringe services take advantage of the unbanked and underbanked and market their services to this group (CDFI Fund, 2001). There is a large presence of fringe banking services, especially on or near Native communities served by VITA sites.

Financial Utilization

Savings cushion families against income shocks and unexpected expenses, offering greater personal financial security (Oliver & Shapiro, 1995; Shapiro, 1998; Sherraden, 2008; Tufano & Schneider, 2009). The lump-sum nature of the EITC provides an opportunity for saving. Hotz and Scholz (2001) find that 98% of eligible households view the tax system as a potential savings mechanism and opt to receive the EITC as a lump sum when they file their taxes. However, even though households describe EITC receipt as part of their savings plan, they clarify that the "savings" will be used to purchase large, durable goods such as washing machines, vehicles, and other large ticket items. Contrary to these findings, additional evidence suggests that EITC recipients balance consumption with short and long-term savings goals such as home ownership and retirement investments (Beverly & Dailey, 2003; Romich & Weisner, 2000; Smeeding et al., 2000).

Another critical step in the development of financial capability is the ability to plan for a financial future. The EITC provides an opportunity to engage families in formal and informal planning about their utilization and investment options. Most families use EITC for three primary purposes: basic needs, financial security, and asset building. In some cases, all of the EITC dollars are allocated to one of these purposes; others decide to divide the benefit among multiple uses (Mammen & Lawrence, 2006; Romich & Weisner, 2000; Smeeding et al., 2000).

EITC and Asset Building

In addition to helping households meet basic needs, the EITC may contribute to long-term household development, thus helping to build household financial capability. Recipients may invest the EITC in buying a home, paying for college tuition, or investing in a business (Federal Reserve Bank of San Francisco, 2005; Smeeding et al., 2000). For many Native American households, home ownership is not possible due to legal, economic, and social constraints on owning property within reservation land (e.g., land trust laws between tribal and US governments, limited household resources, and a communal value of collectively owned assets) (CDFI Fund, 2001; HUD, 2009; Miller, 2001). Therefore, in Native communities, EITC may more likely be invested in asset-building opportunities such as educational expenses or business investment as will be discussed the next section.

A STUDY OF WAYS NATIVE HOUSEHOLDS UTILIZE THE EITC

The Native Community EITC Survey (NC-EITC) utilized data from a sample of 1,847 Native American taxpayers who filed taxes at VITA sites during the 2008 tax-filing season. The sample includes 18 sites that served widely diverse households from over 80 Native communities, both rural and urban, across 10 states,[3] including Native American reservations, Alaska Native communities, and Native Hawaiian villages. The NC-EITC survey was developed for this study to assess household utilization of EITC and access to VITA and other financial services. VITA sites were selected using purposive sampling to ensure the selection of sites primarily serving Native communities, and to ensure that both urban and rural sites were included from a variety of regions across the United States. Respondent selection was based on convenience sampling at each of the study sites.

Surveys were administered in hard copy during tax preparation hours at VITA sites. Upon entrance to the VITA site, volunteers offered taxpayers the opportunity to participate in the survey. They were informed that participation was voluntary and their responses would be kept confidential. In addition, respondents were assured that a decision not to participate would not affect their tax preparation service in any way. Most participants completed the survey in approximately 15 minutes prior to their tax preparation appointment. At the end of tax preparation season (around April 15), VITA site coordinators mailed completed anonymous surveys to the research team for analysis.

Survey items included questions on planned use of the EITC including saving and consumption intentions, use of formal and informal financial services, and participation in financial education and related financial education classes. With a goal to produce useful community-relevant research, local VITA site coordinators were actively involved at all stages of the project, from survey development to data collection and interpretation. This is the first study of EITC receipt in Native households and makes a unique contribution to literature on EITC utilization and ways that financial capability may be approached in Native communities.

STUDY RESULTS

The respondent sample in this study (see Table 10.1) was comprised of 81% individual filers (42% female and 39% male) and 18% joint married filers. The sample included a fairly even age distribution, including a fifth who were young and a fifth over the age of 50. Households claimed approximately $4 million in refundable tax credits for 2008. Overall, educational attainment among filers was low, with a majority holding only a high school degree or equivalent (44%) or some

Table 10.1. DEMOGRAPHICS OF STUDY SAMPLE (N = 1,847)

Variable	Percentage of Respondents
Tax Filer	
Female	42%
Male	39%
Married-joint filers	18%
Age	
16–20	9%
21–30	22%
31–40	17%
41–50	23%
51–60	17%
61+	13%
Education Level	
< High school or GED	15%
High school graduate or GED	44%
Some college or tech school	26%
Associate Degree	7%
Undergraduate Degree	3%
Graduate Degree	5%

college (26%). Respondent demographics are comparable to other VITA sites, but are not generalizable because of the sampling method.

Access to EITC Information and Tax Services

This study of Native communities identified sources of information that were most effective for learning about the EITC and VITA services. Although the primary marketing tool was poster advertisements on bulletin boards of grocery stores, banks, community centers, and churches, the primary source of information identified by Native EITC recipients was word-of-mouth. More than one-third (38%) heard about EITC from family and friends, followed by interaction at the site during the previous tax season (36%) and media advertisements such as flyers, newspapers, and posters (21%) (see Table 10.2). These findings suggest that outreach efforts used in non-Native communities (e.g., television and newspaper advertisements) may not work as well in Native communities.

Over one-quarter of households in this study (26%) who used commercial preparers in prior years reported paying an average of $196 (range, $20–$400) for tax preparation services. Using the VITA sites saved this group an aggregate $113,000. Results from this study suggest that once a tax filer is aware of and interacts with a free tax filing service, they continue to utilize the service in subsequent years. Moreover, nearly half of the respondents (46%) used the same VITA site as in the previous year, discontinuing their use of commercial preparers. The fact that these individuals sought VITA services multiple times indicates a notable level of knowledge of and trust in VITA services (see Table 10.3).

Table 10.2. How Tax Filers Heard about VITA Sites (N = 1,847)

Information Source	Percentage of Respondents
Word of Mouth	38%
Filed here last year	36%
Flyer/Newspaper/Poster	21%
Radio or TV	5%
Envelope stuffer in paycheck	1%

Table 10.3. How Respondents had Taxes Prepared in the Past (N = 1,847)

Tax Preparation Method	Percentage of Respondents
Had them done at same VITA site	46%
Did not file	17%
Paid a commercial tax preparer	16%
Another free service	12%
Relative or friend prepared my taxes	7%
Did my own	3%

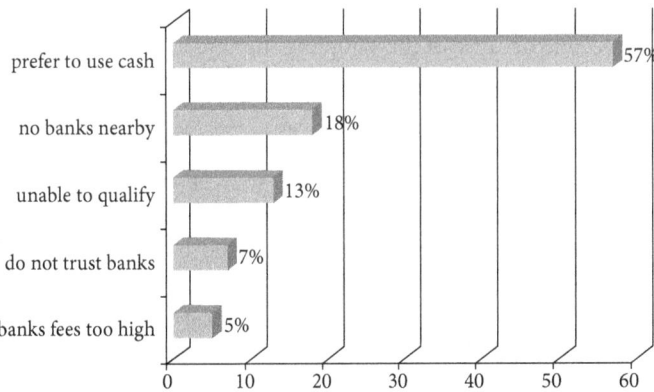

Figure 10.1 Reasons Why Native Americans Report They Do Not Have Bank or Savings Accounts

Access to Financial Services

Respondents were asked to indicate whether they currently have a checking account, savings account, or both.[4] A relatively high percentage of households have bank or credit union accounts (66%), but a substantial percentage with no type of transaction account remains (33%). It is important to note that these data vary substantially by Native community, often depending on accessibility of financial services. In some communities, numerous banks and credit unions are located on or near the community but in others, it was not uncommon to hear about individuals driving over 100 miles to reach a bank. In addition, ATMs are not commonly located in Native communities and access to online banking services is also limited due to little or no Internet connectivity (CDFI Fund, 2001).

To better understand the banking status of Native households, respondents without accounts were also asked to indicate why they do not have an account. The overwhelming response was that individuals prefer to use cash (57%). Others noted they were unable to qualify for a bank account (13%) or that there are no banks nearby (18%). Some respondents indicated that bank fees associated with either opening an account or maintaining one were too high (5%), while others noted that they do not have a bank account because they do not trust banks (7%) (see Figure 10.1).

In communities lacking banks, credit unions, or other types of financial services, respondents indicated that they often conduct financial activities at alternative providers including grocery stores (36%), check cashing facilities (8%), and pawn shops (2%)—all costly alternatives to mainstream services.

Financial Education

Customer experience with financial education over the past three years was also assessed. Survey results found that participation in basic financial management courses increased from 6% to 12% between 2005 and 2007. Home ownership class

Table 10.4. FINANCIAL EDUCATION REPORTED BY NATIVE AMERICAN TAXPAYERS (N = 1,597)

Class Type	Percentage of Respondents		
	2005	2006	2007
Basic financial management	6%	8%	12%
Credit repair	1%	3%	5%
Home ownership	6%	7%	11%
Small business development	1%	5%	6%

Note: This subsample who had participated in a financial education class represents 86% of the total sample.

participation rates increased similarly from 6% to 11% in the same time period. Rates of participation in programs designed to improve credit history and scores (1% to 5%) and small business classes (1% to 6%) had only modest increases (see Table 10.4). Furthermore, when asked about the type of financial education they would like to see offered, 23% requested basic financial management classes, 26% requested credit counseling services, 21% requested classes related to homeownership, 20% requested small business classes, and 19% requested more information about retirement planning.

How Native Families Use the EITC

Another critical step in the development of financial capability is the ability to plan for the future. Receipt of the EITC provides an opportunity to examine consumption and saving choices among Native households when they receive a lump sum of capital such as EITC dollars.

BASIC NEEDS
A significant percentage of respondents reported that they plan to allocate their EITC dollars to cover basic needs such as groceries (49%), utilities (44%), clothing (23%), and rent (22%) (see Figure 10.2). Approximately 32% of Native respondents indicated that they anticipate using at least half of their refund dollars for necessities such as those listed above. Nearly a fourth of respondents (22%) plan to allocate 75% or more of their total refund to cover essential expenses, and 18% plan to put all of their refund toward daily living expenses. Others report they plan to use their tax refund dollars for emergency expenses such as car repairs (9%) and medical bills (7%). For these individuals, the EITC serves as an important safety net that buffers them from severe financial hardship.

FINANCIAL SECURITY
A smaller proportion of participants use the EITC to protect from economic shock and build financial security by paying auto insurance premiums, property taxes, licensing fees, and other larger bills (11%). Results also indicate investments

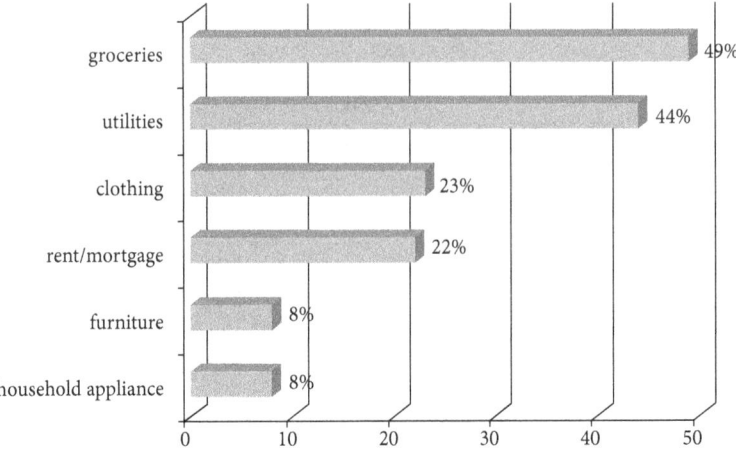

Figure 10.2 Ways the EITC Is Utilized for Basic Needs

in areas such as helping a family member (8%) and saving for traditional ceremonies (3%). These are considered social obligations that may result in financial returns in the future through reciprocal giving processes in some communities (see Figure 10.3).

Saving and Asset Building with the EITC

Among respondents in this study, 14% plan to save their entire refund, and 16% plan to save at least a portion of their EITC dollars. Many have already established savings accounts with an average personal savings amount of $1,500. A number of respondents indicated specific savings goals that include auto and home repair, auto and home purchase, school-related expenses for themselves and their children, and investment in their small business. Other long-term savings goals for

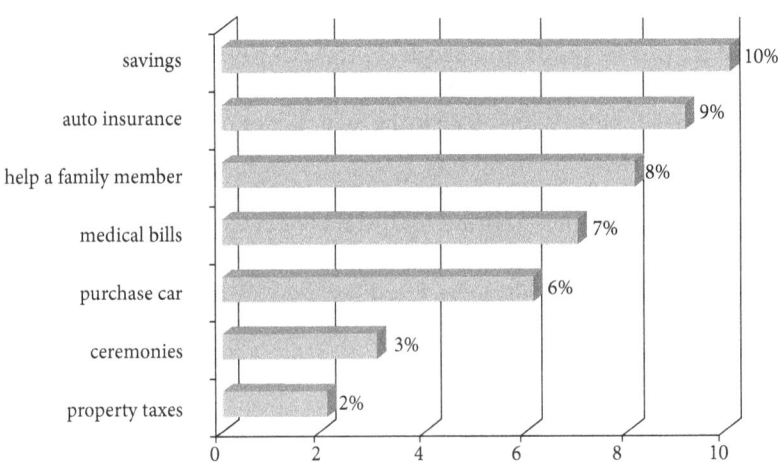

Figure 10.3 Ways Native American Taxpayers Plan to Use EITC for Financial Security

the EITC refund include homeownership, education, retirement, or simply to establish an emergency fund (see Figure 10.3).

In recent years, policy-makers have encouraged the use of the EITC toward asset-building goals for low-income families as a way to further contribute to financial capability. Respondents in this study indicate that they plan to invest their EITC dollars in education for themselves or a family member (5%), a computer for both education and small business purposes (3%), down payment on a home (3%), and small business start-up (1%) (see Figure 10.3). Even though very few respondents planned to invest in small business start-up, they are investing in other livelihood activities. Communities in Alaska, Hawaii, Wisconsin, and Minnesota included in this study are particularly reliant on subsistence living activities for meeting their food and income needs. A relatively large proportion of respondents (18%) indicate that they will invest at least half of their tax refund dollars in income-generating items such as tools, hunting and fishing gear, and vehicles. Among this group, approximately 6% of respondents also listed payment of professional licenses and training as ways that build human and financial capital.

DISCUSSION AND IMPLICATIONS

Findings suggest that a number of factors are involved in building financial capability among low-income Native households. The following sections address the empirical results and implications for policy and practice in the context of Native communities.

Improved Access to Free Tax Preparation Services and Information

Outreach efforts that increase knowledge among eligible recipients would go a long way toward providing a bridge from welfare to economic self-sufficiency and therefore, financial capability. Results from this study suggest that Native households continue to have limited access to information and services regarding their taxes that would improve their economic well-being. Improved access could best be facilitated through improved outreach and information about tax policy benefits and financial service and product options. As noted earlier, word-of-mouth is one of the primary ways that people in Native communities receive information about EITC. Efforts to reach key Native institutions and leaders in these communities would effectively start that information flow.

VITA sites serve as an important institution for leveraging the financial capability effects of EITC for Native households. Results from this study suggest that Native-serving VITA sites are improving customers' livelihoods by connecting them to the EITC benefits they have earned and reducing costs associated with tax preparation, which increases the potential for reinvestment of these dollars in the household and local economy. Continued and expanded support for VITA sites in and near Native communities would allow EITC recipients and other low-to-moderate income tax filers to access VITA services. Furthermore, the number of VITA sites located in more convenient and trusted locations for Native Americans should be expanded to increase utilization among this population. Linking VITA site consumers with financial information or referrals to other financial service providers may inform Native households of their financial options, and increase the likelihood that they will open a bank account. With additional opportunities to manage their money, individuals may be more likely to save. Connections to these types of services would increase opportunities for working families to plan for their financial future, explore financial services options, and leverage the EITC resource toward their asset-building goals.

Development and Delivery of Financial Services to Native Households

Study findings indicate that a substantial number of Native households also have limited to no access to banking or credit union services. Furthermore, when banking services are available, individuals often choose not to utilize them for a number of reasons (e.g., high bank fees, trust of banks, prefer to use cash). These findings suggest that more services could be located on or near reservation lands at tribal housing authorities, tribal colleges, tribal business centers, and Native Community Development Financial Institutions (CDFIs). Locating services in familiar places could build on existing relationships within the community between institutions and tribal members, improving trust and increasing the likelihood that utilization of financial products and services would be maintained over time.

Although the preference for cash was not fully explored in the study, this may be directly linked to issues of trust between Native households and formal banking institutions. One possible way of addressing this concern is to allow tribes to choose which financial institutions operate on their land and afford them regulatory authority over financial institutions that do locate on reservation land. For example, a formal partnership between tribes and financial institutions could provide opportunities to create and customize financial services that meet the specific needs of tribal members. Some of these services may include general banking, investments, and mortgage financing. In addition to partnerships with mainstream financial institutions, increased funding to support Native CDFIs tribal credit unions, and community banks would increase access to financial services and products to Native households.

Role of Social Workers

In addition to VITA sites, social service programs in which social workers are involved could serve as economic access points for Native households. During intake processes, social workers have an opportunity to assess the household economic situation and goals of their clients along with their current banking practices and views regarding financial institutions. Taking the time to gain a deeper understanding of the financial needs, wants, and goals of Native households is a worthwhile investment toward the development of more effective programs and policies that are not only more tailored to meet their needs, but also more accessible. With this information, financial services and products can be designed so that the result is increased economic security and financial capability among Native households. For those families who want to save all or part of their EITC, social workers can connect them to a number of savings options such as traditional savings accounts, IDAs, or retirement savings plans, all of which could be facilitated through the split refund option.

In addition to providing education about money management for individuals, it is important to provide education and awareness to financial institutions regarding financial product and service needs of Native households. In this way, social workers can serve as "social brokers" facilitating relationships between Native communities and financial institutions. For example, financial institutions could be located closer to reservation communities or online banking made accessible to Native households.

Inclusion of Financial Issues Facing Native Households in Social Work Education

Native households face some of the most challenging economic circumstances in the United States due to historic and sustained exclusion from financial institutions and opportunities. One of the most important components to include in social work curricula is the role of historically structured economic systems in the inclusion or exclusion of Native populations in the mainstream economy. The effects of the history and systems continue today and determine the level of access Native households have to services and benefits. Social workers are uniquely positioned to examine these issues and advocate for improved access for Native populations.

One critical finding from this study is a desire among Native households for more financial education. Social workers may be in a position to offer formal financial education courses or simply provide a basic level of financial counseling to Native households as part of another social service program. Regardless of the setting, some of the key components of financial education programs should comprise: basic money management to include goal-setting, planning, and implementation of financial plans through saving, investing, and spending decisions; asset development as relevant to Native household goals; and information about the role of tribal sovereignty and tribal government in both individual and community asset building. A recent policy report of the National Congress of Native Americans and the Department of Interior calls for the development of financial education curricula for Native youth and adults to not only build personal financial skills among tribal members but also develop future economic development leaders (NCAI & DOI, 2007). Financial education could include information about the tax laws that apply to Native people working and/or living on a reservation so they are clearer about their tax liabilities and potential tax credits.

In addition, social workers could provide information about effects of the EITC on benefit eligibility to Native households and assist them in taking steps to increase economic stability by connecting them to information and resources. For example, some tribes receive TANF grants to run their own programs. Therefore, when working with Native families, it is important that social workers confirm income and resource eligibility rules specific to the household's tribal affiliation (Edwards & Wagner, 2007).[5] Furthermore, to better resonate with and meet the needs of Native households, efforts should be made to incorporate the unique values and cultural teachings passed down from tribal elders for each tribe.

FUTURE RESEARCH ON FINANCIAL CAPABILITY IN NATIVE HOUSEHOLDS

This study provides an initial understanding of Native EITC recipients' financial decisions and the types of financial services used for these purposes. However, VITA sites continue to innovate by adding services and education. More research is needed to examine the effectiveness of these efforts; particularly how many Native people utilize these opportunities, demographics of those who choose these options, and long-term effects on financial security of Native households.

The extent to which receipt of the EITC converts access and opportunity to actual utilization of services or changes in decision-making processes deserves further examination. Although research has examined outcomes associated with the EITC, there is limited knowledge about how Native Americans view the EITC. It is unknown whether the EITC is considered a financial safety net, part of the household's annual income, or as a resource for asset investment. This type of research requires qualitative examination of how people think about the EITC and whether that view changes given expanded opportunities for financial education and utilization of financial services and products.

In addition, a better understanding of culture related to financial resources and decisions could inform development of finance-related policies and programs that may be more relevant for Native households. Much of the research on EITC has focused on how people intend to use it, but due to unpredictable employment, weak safety nets, and little to no savings to protect against income shocks and emergencies, Native families are often unable to reach their goals. Instead, they must make alternative financial decisions to survive. A better understanding of these financial choices would inform program and policy design that could assist Native people in building their ability to plan and manage their EITC and other resources.

Data for this study were collected from respondents who chose to utilize tax preparation services at VITA sites. Self-selection may be correlated with other outcomes related to financial choices (e.g., bank account ownership, use of direct deposit, and utilization of the EITC). Also, the choice to use VITA services may indicate a higher level of knowledge about financial service availability compared to EITC recipients who chose not to use VITA services and were therefore not part of this study. In order to better understand financial capability among Native households, future research should seek samples of households who do not use VITA sites.

CONCLUSION

The EITC, when it is linked with financial information and access to financial services and products, assists households to make informed decisions and take action that maximizes the contribution of the EITC to meet short-and long-term needs. In this way, EITC helps households meet their financial needs, and incorporates them into the economic mainstream.

These relationships can be facilitated by social workers directly involved in outreach efforts that help low-income Native people claim their EITC benefits and connect to low-cost, flexible financial services. Considering the ever-changing economic context in the United States, social workers must become more adept at assessing the financial capacities and needs of low-income households, the range of economic options available, and ways to navigate the financial services world that may help clients overcome their financial challenges.

Most importantly, low-income Native households will only be able to participate in the economic mainstream and build financial capability if they have the opportunity to access financial services and products that meet their needs. In addition, they must have the opportunity to build financial knowledge and skills that are relevant to their financial goals.

NOTES

1. For purposes of this discussion, household income is broadly defined as "earnings from wage work." Individual studies cited throughout this paper constructed income based on a varying definitions some of which include nontaxable income.
2. RALs/RACs are loans based on taxpayer's expected tax refund. The loan process is facilitated by tax preparers in partnership with banks, which secure the refund. They are marketed as "rapid refunds." In reality, taxpayers usually receive these loans only five to ten days faster than they would have received their refund directly from the IRS if they had been filed electronically. These loans result in substantial costs to the taxpayer.
3. The states included in this study include Alaska, Arizona, Hawaii, Minnesota, Montana, New Mexico, Oklahoma, South Dakota, Texas, and Wisconsin.
4. In this discussion, "banked" refers to owning a transaction account or savings account in a bank or credit union, while "unbanked" refers to customers who do not currently utilize any type of financial transaction account or service (Berke, Lopez-Fernandini, & Herrmann, 2008).
5. Tribes have some authority to create their own eligibility rules with the exception of Food Assistance and Medicaid programs. Rules for these programs are determined at the state and federal levels.

REFERENCES

Adamson, R. (2003, Summer). Land rich and dirt poor: The story of Indian assets. *Native Americas*, 26–47.

American Consumer Survey. (2011). *American Consumer Survey 2005–2009 five year estimates*. Factfinder, US Census. Retrieved from http://factfinder.census.gov

Anderson, T. (1995). *Sovereign nations or reservations: An economic history of American Indians*. San Francisco: Pacific Research Institute for Public Policy.

Anderson, T. & Parker, D. (2009). Economic development lessons from and for North American Indian economies. *Australian Journal of Agricultural and Resource Economics, 53*, 105–127

Barr, M. (2004). Banking the poor. *Yale Journal on Regulation, 21*(1), 121–237.

Bartolomei-Hill, S. (2000). *Investing in families: Opportunities for using Maryland's welfare surplus*. Silver Spring, MD: Maryland Budget and Tax Policy Institute.

Berke, S., Lopez-Fernandini, A., & Herrmann, M. (2008). *Highlights from the 3rd annual underbanked financial services forum: New approaches, new understandings, new relationships*. Chicago, IL: Center for Financial Services Innovation.

Berube, A. (2003). *Rewarding work through the tax code: The power and potential of the earned income tax credit in 27 cities and rural areas*. Washington, DC: The Brookings Institution.

Berube, A., & Forman, B. (2001). *A local ladder for the working poor: The impact of the earned income tax credit in the U.S. metropolitan areas*. Washington, DC: The Brookings Institution.

Berube, A., Kim, A., Forman, B., & Burns, M. (2002). *The price of paying taxes: How tax preparation and refund loan fees erode the benefits of EITC*. Washington, DC: The Brookings Institution.

Beverly, S., & Dailey, C. (2003). *Using tax refunds to promote asset building in low-income households: Program and policy options* (Policy Report). St. Louis, MO: Washington University, Center for Social Development.

Beverly, S., Schneider, D., & Tufano, P. (2006). Splitting tax refunds and building savings: An empirical test. *Tax Policy and the Economy, 20*, 111–162.

Beverly, S., Tescher, J., & Marzahl, D. (2000). *Low-cost bank accounts and the EITC: How financial institutions can reach the unbanked and facilitate savings*. St. Louis, MO: Washington University, Center for Social Development.

Beverly, S., Tescher, J., Romich, J., & Marzahl, D. (2005). Linking tax refunds and low-cost bank accounts to bank the unbanked. In M. Sherraden (Ed.), *Inclusion in the American dream: Assets, poverty, and public poverty* (pp. 167–184). New York: Oxford University Press.

Beverly, S. G., Tescher, J., & Romich, J. L. (2004). Linking tax refunds and low-cost bank accounts: Early lessons for program design and evaluation. *Journal of Consumer Affairs, 38*, 332–341.

Brown, A. (2005, September). *Expanding financial services to underbanked consumers: How tax preparation partnerships can help bridge the gap*. Chicago, IL: The Center for Financial Services Innovation.

Bureau of Indian Affairs (BIA). (2005). *2005 Native American population and labor force report*. Washington, DC: United States Department of the Interior, Bureau of Indian Affairs, Office of Indian Services.

Community Development Financial Institutions Fund (CDFI). (2001). *The report of the Native American lending study*. Retrieved from http://www.cdfifund.gov/docs/2001_nacta_lending_study.pdf

Cornell, S. (2007). Remaking the tools of governance: Colonial legacies, indigenous solutions. In M. Jorgensen (Ed.), *Rebuilding native nations* (pp. 57–77). Tucson: University of Arizona Press.

Edwards, K., & Wagner, K. (2007). Putting the earned income tax credit (EITC) to work in Native communities. In *Integrated asset-building strategies for reservation-based communities: A 27-year retrospective of First Nations Development Institute* (Report). Longmont, CO: First Nations Development Institute.

Eissa, N., & Liebman, J. B. (1996). Labor supply response to the Earned Income Tax Credit. *Quarterly Journal of Economics, 111*(2), 606–637.

Federal Reserve Bank of San Francisco. (2005). *From refunds to assets: Leveraging the benefits of the earned income tax credit*. San Francisco: Author.

FDIC. (2009). *FDIC National survey of unbanked and underbanked households*. Retrieved from http://www.fdic.gov/householdsurvey/executive_summary.pdf

First Nations Development Institute (FNDI). (2004). *Family economic success in Native communities: Adapting the Annie E. Casey family economic success framework to rural and reservation-based Native communities*. Fredericksburg, VA: Author.

First Nations Development Institute and Center for Responsible Lending. (2008). *Borrowed time: Use of refund anticipation loans among EITC filers in Native American Communities*. Longmont, CO: First Nations Development Institute.

Hilgert, M., Hogarth, J., & Beverly, S. (2003, July). Household financial management: The connection between knowledge and behavior. *Federal Reserve Bulletin, 89*, 309.

HM Treasury. (2007). *Financial capability: The Government's long-term approach*. Norwich, UK: Crown.

Hotz, V. J., & Scholz, J. (2001). *The earned income tax credit* (NBER Working Paper No. W8078). Cambridge, MA: National Bureau of Economic Research.

Internal Revenue Service. (2008). *EITC eligibility*. Retrieved from http://www.irs.gov/

Internal Revenue Service. (2010). *State and local governments with earned income tax credit*. Retrieved from http://www.irs.gov/individuals/article/0,id=177866,00.html

Johnson, E., & Sherraden, M. S. (2006). From financial literacy to financial capability among youth. *Journal of Sociology and Social Welfare, 34*, 119–145.

Lim, Y., Livermore, M., & Davis, B. C. (2009). Knowledge of the earned income tax credit and financial behaviors among low- and moderate-income consumers. *Journal of Consumer Education, 26*, 58–69.

Llobrera, J., & Zahradnik, B. (2004). *A hand up: How state earned income tax credits help working families escape poverty in 2004*. Washington, DC: Center for Budget and Policy Priorities.

Lui, M., Robles, B., Leondar-Wright, B., Brewer, R., & Adamson, R. (2006). *The color of wealth: The story behind the U.S. racial wealth divide* (pp. 67–68). New York: The New Press.

Mammen, S., & Lawrence, F. (2006). How rural working families use the earned income tax credit: A mixed methods analysis. *Financial Counseling and Planning, 17*(1), 51–63.

Meyer, B., & Rosenbaum, D. (2001). Making single mothers work: Recent tax and welfare policy and its effects. In B. D. Meyer & D. Holtz-Eakin (Eds.), *Making work pay: The earned income tax credit and its impact on America's families* (pp. 69–115). New York: Russell Sage Foundation.

Miller, R. (2001). Economic development in Indian Country: Will capitalism or socialism succeed? *Oregon Law Review, 80*(3), 757–859.

National Congress of Native Americans (NCAI), and the Department of Interior (DOI). (2007). *Developing tribal economies to create healthy, sustainable, and culturally vibrant communities* (Native American Economic Policy Report). Retrieved from http://www.ncai.org/Economic-Policy-and-Research.292.0.html

Oliver, M. L., & Shapiro, T. M. (1995). *Black wealth/White wealth: A new perspective on racial inequality.* New York: Routledge.

Pickering, K. (2000). Alternative economic strategies in low-income rural communities: TANF, labor migration, and the case of the Pine Ridge Reservation. *Rural Sociology, 65*(1), 148–167.

Pickering, K., & Mushinski, D. (2001). Cultural aspects of credit institutions: Transplanting the Grameen Bank credit group structure to the Pine Ridge Indian Reservation. *Journal of Economic Issues, 35*(2), 459–467.

Pickering, K., & Mushinski, D. (2004). Locating the cultural context of credit: Institutional alternatives on the Pine Ridge Reservation. In C. Werner & D. Bell (Eds.), *Values and valuables: From the sacred to the symbolic* (pp. 185–205). Lanham, MD: Altamira Press.

Social and Enterprise Development Innovations (SEDI). (2004, July). *Financial capability and poverty discussion paper.* Canada: Policy Research Initiative. Retrieved from http://www.horizons.gc.ca/doclib/Poverty_SEDI_final_E.pdf

Rhine, S., Toussaint-Comeau, M., Hogarth, J., & Greene, W. (2001). *The role of alternative financial service providers in serving LMI neighborhoods.* Paper presented at the Federal Reserve System Community Affairs Research Conference, Washington, DC.

Romich, J., & Weisner, T. (2000). How families view and use the EITC: Advance payment versus lump sum delivery. *National Tax Journal, 4*(2), 1245–1265.

Shapiro, T. (1998). *Assets and the poor: An introduction.* Paper presented to the Ford Foundation Conference on Assets and the Poor, New York.

Sherraden, M. (2008). *IDAs and asset building policy: Lessons and directions* (CSD Working Paper No. 08–12). St. Louis, MO: Washington University, Center for Social Development.

Sherraden, M., & Barr, M. (2005). Institutions and inclusion in saving policy. In N. Retsinas & E. Belsky (Eds.), *Building assets, building credit: Bridges and barriers to financial services in low-income communities* (pp. 286–315). Washington, DC: Brookings Institution Press.

Sherraden, M., Schreiner, M., & Beverly, S. (2003). Income, institutions, and saving performance in individual development accounts. *Economic Development Quarterly, 17*(1), 95–112.

Smeeding, T., Ross-Phillips, K., & O'Connor, M. (2000). The EITC: Expectation, knowledge, use, and economic and social mobility. *National Tax Journal, 53*(4), 118–210.

Tufano, P. & Schneider, D. (2009). Using financial innovation to support savers: From coercion to excitement. In R. Blank & M. Barr (Eds.), *Insufficient funds: Savings, assets, credit and banking among low-income households* (pp. 149–190). New York: Russell Sage.

Tumulty, B. (2007, March 14). *Tax refund anticipation loans prevalent on Indian Reservations.* McLean, VA: Gannett News Service.

US Census Bureau. (2011). *Overview of race and Hispanic origin: 2010*. Retrieved from www.census.gov/prod/cen2010/briefs/c2010br_02.pdf.

US Department of Housing and Urban Development (HUD). (2009). *Section 184 Indian home loan guarantee program.* Retrieved from http://www.hud.gov/offices/pih/ih/homeownership/184/index.cfm

US Department of Labor (2005). *The employment situation: July 2005*. Retrieved from http://www.bls.gov/news.release/archives/empsit_08052005.pdf.

Wagoner, P. (2002). *They treated us just like Indians: The worlds of Bennett County, South Dakota*. Lincoln: University of Nebraska Press.

Zhan, M., Anderson, S. G., & Scott, J. (2006). Financial knowledge of the low-income population: Effects of a financial education program. *Journal of Sociology and Social Welfare*, *33*(1), 53–74.

11

Financial and Asset-Building Capabilities of Southwest Border Working Families

An Action Research Approach to Culturally Responsive Economic Resiliency Behaviors

BÁRBARA J. ROBLES

INTRODUCTION

The 2010 Census reports 50.5 million Hispanics in the United States, comprising 16.3% of the total population (Pew Hispanic Center, 2011). Over 52% of the 50.5 million Hispanics in the United States reside in four states with a contiguous border with Mexico: Texas (37.6%), New Mexico (46.3%), Arizona (29.6%), and California (37.6%) (Pew Hispanic Center, 2011).[1] Local, state and national non-governmental community-based organizations (NGOs/CBOs) and government agencies, as well as nonprofit foundations forming support coalitions and networks in this region, offer free or low-fee tax preparation services. In addition, tax awareness campaigns in hard-to-reach and vulnerable communities increase the tax filing participation rates of qualifying families. As working families face escalating financial stress and limited labor market opportunities, the earned income tax credit (EITC) crucially contributes to family financial stability and asset building for low-income and limited-English-speaking populations.

The research literature assessing the impact of the EITC on vulnerable populations and as a crucial poverty reduction program is well established (Berube, 2005; Mammen & Lawrence, 2006; Romich & Weisner, 2000; Smeeding, Phillips, & O'Connor, 2000). Differences between rural and urban low-income families as well as cultural behaviors toward asset building bring an additional research lens to policy assessment and policy innovation. Geographical regions with high immigrant and immigrant-legacy communities create a further layer of complexity for program delivery and outreach. Community-based organizations operating in hard-to-reach and underserved communities such as the southwest border of the United States have developed effective financial inclusion strategies that remain below the research radar and yet offer a possible outreach template for replication in new and growing gateway regions. This region is similar in poverty indicators and isolation to Native American reservations and Appalachia (Esparza & Donelson, 2008).

This study employs data that document the financial behaviors of border working families over a 5-year period. An overview of the socioeconomic characteristics of the US-Mexico borderlands is presented in the first section of this chapter. The chronology of the *Frontera*[2] Asset Building Network (FABN) and the action research collaboration are described in the second and third sections of the chapter. The data collection and methodology are discussed in section four. Section five presents descriptive data and response analysis and interprets the findings in the context of working poor border families. The conclusion offers alternative policy directions and suggests future research issues that may provide further support for culturally responsive community tax and financial inclusion outreach in the context of asset-building initiatives as the transnational nature of borderlands families grows.

A SOCIOECONOMIC SNAPSHOT OF THE BORDERLANDS

The recent media attention directed at the southwestern border of the United States focuses almost exclusively on drug trafficking and migration flows. The borderlands are much more than merely a geographical line that extends 2,000 miles from the Gulf of Mexico to the Pacific Ocean dividing six Mexican states (Tamulipas, Nuevo Leon, Coahuila, Chihuahua, Sonora, and Baja California Norte) from four US states (Texas, New Mexico, Arizona, and California). The borderlands are a confluence of recent migrant and historical legacy peoples. The US-Mexico border region consists of a rich geographical landscape and a cultural blending that captures the old and the new in a continuous dynamic mapping of traditions and language among and between diverse ethnic and racial communities.

In 2009, the population of the four border states totaled 70.4 million people with 63.4% reporting non-Hispanic status and 36.6% reporting Hispanic identity. The diversity of the border's inhabitants is reflected in the 40 million (56.8%) of the 70.4 million who self-identify as: Hispanic, African American, Native American, Asian American, and Native Hawaiian and Pacific Islander. The poverty rates for the border region (counties contiguous to the Mexico northern frontier) are higher than national US averages or the four border state averages. The median incomes of the region are also lower than those of the border states and national U.S. medians (US Census, 2008).

Other southwest border economic indicators reflect the chronic and concentrated poverty metrics of Appalachia, the deep South, and select Native American reservations: high unemployment, noncompletion of high school, chronic health conditions, low public transportation infrastructure, a high incidence of contract-for-deed homeownership financing, and the proliferation of unincorporated townships known as *colonias*.[3] Due to these regions' long growing seasons, legacy ranching, and agricultural characteristics, they are the anchored home location of a large number of the US migrant farm laborers, predominantly Latino.

BRINGING BORDER VOICES TO THE RESEARCH/POLICY TABLE

Two learning dialogues sponsored by the Annie E. Casey Foundation's Border Portfolio convened participants engaged in researching, managing, funding, and delivering community services that impact the well-being and financial stability of border families (primarily Latino) residing on the US-Mexico border. The participants involved in the two roundtable convenings represented national, regional, state, and local foundation officers; executive directors of national, state, and local nonprofit community-based organizations (CBOs) whose service area included border communities, national, state, and local governmental public sector representatives; and university professors and graduate students.

Many of the foundation and government agency participants did not have intimate field knowledge of the borderlands. For the learning dialogue to move beyond the usual media images of the US-Mexico border, local CBO representatives with long-term presence in the borderlands shared experiential knowledge and provided perspectives that have been missing from policy debates and program design. The dialogues provided an opportunity for those not familiar with the daily lives of the border working poor, their communities, and *colonias*[4] to become familiar with the unique characteristics of cultural legacy communities of the US-Mexico border region (Yankelovich, 2001).

Several obstacles to healthy economic behaviors, community capacity building, and family financial stability emerged from the learning dialogues, including financial nonliteracy in *colonias* and working poor border communities. Other important issues included institutionalized "business as usual" practices hindering working poor Latino families from accessing and participating in mainstream asset-building markets such as housing, financial and tax services, education, and health services, which were identified as important barriers. Culturally responsive financial and economic behaviors were discussed as asset and wealth "leveraging" resources in *colonias* and other metropolitan and adjacent metro areas along the US-Mexico border.

At the close of the learning dialogues, a new collaborative coalition formed: the Frontera Asset Building Network (FABN). The FABN members identified affordable and reliable tax preparation services as a focal program for linking border families to the following asset-building and financial capability services: (1) public assistance eligibility services; (2) homeownership preparation and counseling; (3) culturally responsive financial and tax education; (4) individual development accounts (IDAs); (5) down payment assistance programs for homeownership; (6) leadership and self-advocacy development training; (7) small and micro business incubator programs; and (8) self-help and affordable housing programs.

One additional proposal that FABN members believed was necessary for successful coalition and individual organization capacity building was a commitment *to collect and control data on their own communities.* Currently, membership in FABN centers on providing tax preparation services during tax seasons with a subset of FABN members participating in survey administration and participatory research projects. Membership in FABN covers all four border states spanning eight coalitions and over 75 individual community-based organizations with local, state, and federal government agency partners as well as local, regional, and national foundation support, and local and regional private corporate and nonprofit sponsorship.[5]

FROM LISTENING AND LEARNING TO ACTION RESEARCH

Many poverty researchers and community-based organizations serving hard-to-reach populations acknowledge the contradiction in employing only "objective" and "empirical" data as success indicators for programs and services.[6] Qualitative indicators convey deeper information about social change and capture more nuanced community characteristics than aggregated data and indicators (Jones & Woolcock, 2007). These hard to quantify, community-identified success metrics include: increased trust of community-based organization staff by community members; increased self-confidence and self-advocacy of residents; and increased networking and maintenance of social capital among community members, families, and communities who are engaging in shared knowledge– and cultural asset–building activities.[7]

Incorporating and documenting cultural behaviors such as the incidence of "pooling" of family and extended family resources to increase wealth and asset accumulation provide a deeper understanding of family, fictive and extended kin, and collective community resources and provide a measure of success for program and service delivery that supports such self-generating community safety nets. Nontraditional cultural-legacy indicators provide guidance to researchers and policy makers in crafting policies supportive of family wealth-building behaviors in ethnic/racial enclaves and in culturally isolated locales. Employing mixed methodological approaches[8] to understanding borderlands' "hidden" assets, family resiliency, and survival strategies requires an inclusive and egalitarian partnership with community-based organizations in prioritizing community services and programs. A key element of such inclusive approaches to mapping community resources and uncovering community preferences is to incorporate cultural assets and behaviors into the choice of research method.

The role of culturally inclusive data collection centers on revealing the cultural capital of border communities as well as the anchoring role of legacy communities in the region. Studies have demonstrated that socially embedded community research provides the community with access to data that deconstructs and dispels media-driven "stereotypes" by tapping into emerging voices and organic community leadership (Markham & Diaz-Funn, 2009; Mora & Diaz, 2004). Additionally, communities can advocate based on data that is place-based and includes historical and cultural legacy information. Border culture and language play a large role in family economic security and financial resiliency behaviors. The community data capture this aspect of border family life. Multigenerational, multi-earner border family units engage in shared asset building (a form of economic resiliency), and the data uncover border family and community assets (informal savings circles) not previously documented (Markham & Diaz-Funn, 2009; Robles, 2007).

SURVEY DATA COLLECTION AND METHODOLOGY

The key research question for this study can be formulated as follows: Do working poor southwest border families display financial capabilities? Financial capabilities are defined as resilient behaviors (making ends meet), planning for the present and the future, and asset building connected to economic mobility aspirations within the context of a geographical area rooted in cultural and linguistic legacies. To shed light on this question, survey questions were generated in consultation with grassroots CBOs within a participatory research framework specifically oriented to capture information about borderlands residents' financial behaviors and aspirations. The survey captures the following financial capabilities of working poor border families: Where do they engage in financial transactions? How do they pay their bills? Do they save formally and/or informally? Do they build assets when receiving a lump-sum amount (tax refund)? Do they send money to family members not living with them? Do they lend to or borrow from family members in emergencies? How aware are they of savings and asset development programs, such as the individual development accounts program? What types of financial products and services do they want to know more about?

FABN members offer free tax preparation services to qualified low-income working individuals and families as well as those members of the community that are English-limited proficient, elderly and/or disabled. The survey respondents voluntarily completed paper surveys, in either English or Spanish, as they were waiting for free tax preparation services at the grassroots FABN organizations. All the original members of the Frontera Asset Building Network (FABN) helped design and craft the survey instrument. In addition, several other interested border community-based organizations joined the FABN initiative with each new cycle (year) of data collection.

The survey instrument was designed to be short in order to increase response rates and to piggy-back on the tax preparation information and services offered. For example, two research questions that were identified as important areas of concern with respect to understanding border communities' financial capabilities were:

Do border low-income workers employ their tax refunds in asset-building and wealth-enhancing opportunities?
Do border residents aspire to learn more about financial products and asset-building services?

Several survey questions were designed to capture the affordability and accessibility of financial services used by border families. Survey questions capturing these issues were framed as follows:

1. Where do you cash your paycheck? This question seeks to capture the actual usage of financial transaction entities as opposed to wanting to know if the community resident owns a bank or savings account. The question provides information on the "comfort" level that community residents have with respect to frequenting particular financial transaction locales.
2. Do you use money orders to pay your bills? This question in combination with question 1 provides evidence that despite frequenting banks or credit unions, or using direct deposit, border community residents may be limited to the use of money orders because they live in communities where mainstream products such as checks are not honored (e.g., cash-based economies).
3. Have you ever received your tax refund the same day (or within the week) from a commercial tax preparer? This question helps to capture information concerning use among community residents of rapid anticipation loans (RALs) that are prevalent in low-wealth communities, where pay stubs are used to provide these products to community residents during the Christmas season in advance of the usual tax filing season. It is also an indicator of how well the community-based tax preparation service outreach campaign works if this particular question has low response rates.
4. Do you lend to or borrow from family members in emergencies? This question provides evidence of family members as "lenders of first resort" during emergencies. It further provides information on how family members retain helping ties and provide safety nets for immediate and extended family members during emergency life-events.
5. Do you send money to family members not residing with you? This question captures the continued support family members provide each other despite constrained income and geographical distance. In addition, the question focuses not only on the international flow of funds among family members with transnational ties but also on "family-resource-leveraging," an important form of reciprocal support.

Finally, to better understand how border families engage in asset-building and savings behaviors, a survey question designed to capture "informal savings circles" (known as rotating savings and credit associations, or ROSCAS, in the development economic literature) was included in the survey instrument. This particular question captures savings behavior displaying a communal-trust component since it occurs outside mainstream financial institutions, does not have an interest rate attached to it, and relies on a high degree of trust among the savings participants.[9]

Working with community-based organizations helps frame culturally responsive survey questions revealing how border residents access financial transactions services while living in a cash-based, binational, bicultural, and bilingual economy. A significant aspect of designing community-based survey instruments is the inclusion of open-ended responses capturing community voices and community defined issues.

The various members of the FABN Border coalition agreed to administer the surveys during tax season (January 15 to April 15) at the participating border community-based organizations that offer either low-fee tax preparation services or free tax preparation services affiliated with VITA (Volunteer Individual Tax Assistance) programs. The surveys were administered in English and Spanish, and each community-based organization used individual intake protocols for serving community residents during tax season.

EMPIRICAL ANALYSIS AND FINDINGS

The aggregate impact data collected for 2009 (tax year 2008) is presented in Table 11.1 and captures the flow of impact funds that benefit border families. Through the work of the tax services, over 58,397 tax returns were filed by free or low-fee tax preparation services, resulting in $23 million dollars in EITC (an average of $399 per household) and $45 million in federal returns (an average of $776 per household) claimed by border families. This work saved over three million dollars in tax preparation fees. Additionally, 6% of the households completed homebuyer workshops, 5% opened savings accounts, and 10% completed

Table 11.1. FRONTERA ASSET-BUILDING NETWORK, 2008–2009 (N = 58,397)

Type of Asset Building Activity	Totals
Amount of EITC Claimed	$23,322,994
Amount of $ Federal returns	$45,287,726
Number of returns filed by free or low-fee tax preparation	58,397
Completed IDAs	315
Enrolled IDAs	1,738
IDA Matching Ratio	Ranges from 1:1 match to 4:1
IDA Maximum	Ranges from $1,000 to $7,000
Completed Homebuyer Workshops	3,707
Number of Homes Purchased	444
Savings Accounts Opened	3,362
Checking Accounts Opened	696
Completed Financial Education	5,876
Number of Improved Credit Scores	459
Tax Prep Fees Saved	$3,158,225
Small Business Opened/Expanded	70

financial education. These data reveal that tax services and education can provide an entry point to an array of financial capability-enhancing programs such as homeownership counseling, financial education, credit-score repair programs, small business incubator programs, and IDA programs.

Individual response rates are generally high and attributable to the long-term presence and reputation of the community-based organizations (CBOs).[10] As Table 11.2 indicates, over the 5 years of data collection, the total survey response rate ranged from a low of 34% to a high of 77%, for a total of 32,694 respondents. Each individual survey administration site experienced a variety of service delivery issues: volunteer churning, tax season coordinator turnover, changes in their software or IT system, key program personnel changes, and funding changes. Despite these various challenges, few sites dropped out over the 5-year collection effort, and new sites were added during the time frame.

Although the data were collected over several years, there are no unique identifiers for individual respondents that can be tracked over time. Thus, the data collected does not constitute a "longitudinal" panel whereby observations of the same individual over time are collected in repeated surveys. Rather, the data consist of a cross-sectional panel of tax filers (families and individuals) choosing to respond to the paper survey and contain a large number of observations per time period. This allows for an in-depth analysis of a single year of data that capture survey respondents' engaging in asset-building and economic resiliency behaviors. Many of the questions allowed for multiple responses (such as "circle or check off all that apply") and therefore individual responses add up to more than 100% for particular survey questions. Additionally, since surveys were voluntary, many respondents answered only selected questions.[11]

Table 11.3 provides respondent summaries of income, filing status, and demographics for the tax years of 2004 to 2008. The data demonstrate an increase

Table 11.2. FRONTERA ASSET-BUILDING FINANCIAL BEHAVIORS SURVEY, TAX YEARS 2004–2008 (N = 32,694)

Survey Years	Number of Total Survey Respondents	Total Aggregated Response Rates	Number of Spanish Survey Respondents
TY2004	4,551	34%	1,080 (24%)
TY2005	7,068	77%	1,973 (28%)
TY2006	6,450	59%	2,141 (33%)
TY2007	7,377	74%	1,871 (25%)
TY2008 (Prelim)	7,248	54%	2,272 (33%)

SOURCE: FABN Financial Behaviors Survey, all border sites, tax years 2004 to 2008. Response rates are calculated from a baseline count of total tax returns filed at each survey administration site. Surveys are administered on a voluntary basis. Raw aggregated response rate = (# of Financial Behavior Paper Surveys)/(# of Tax returns filed at participating survey administration sites).

Table 11.3. RESPONDENT SUMMARY OF INCOME, FILING STATUS, AND DEMOGRAPHICS, TAX YEARS 2004–2008

Adjusted Gross Income, Filing Status, and Dependents	All Respondents				Prelim
	TY2004	TY2005	TY2006	TY2007	TY2008
	n = 4,550	n = 7,068	n = 6,450	n = 7,377	n = 7,248
Avg Adjusted Gross Income	$12,210	$13,842	$13,281	$14,848	$17,120
Median AGI	$10,126	$11,269	$11,082	$12,456	$15,095
Avg EITC	$768	$1,150	$881	$1,274	$1,375
Max Sch C/SE	–	$19,543	$16,666	$30,840	$23,941
Avg federal tax refund	$1,335	$1,607	$1,231	$1,533	$1,851
Avg state tax refund	–	$115	$83	$85	$76
Filing status:					
Single	51.6%	48.2%	43.6%	50.5%	47.9%
Married	22.3%	25.3%	30.0%	25.5%	25.1%
Head of household	24.0%	24.6%	21.6%	21.3%	25.2%
Filing with dependents	60.8%	57.6%	59.9%	56.9%	59.3%
Filing with one W-2	–	–	–	55.8%	60.4%
Filing with more than one W-2	–	–	–	44.2%	39.6%
Avg years of education	11.2	11.3	10.5	11.3	11.5
Avg age	–	–	–	45.4	41
Homeowner	–	44.5%	35.0%	41.9%	52.8%
Renter	–	53.8%	45.7%	57.6%	48.3%

SOURCE: FABN Survey, Tax Years: 2004, 2005, 2006, 2007, and 2008 data collected in CA, AZ, NM, and TX

in average income over the study years: the average adjusted gross income increased from $12,210 in 2004 to $17,120 in 2008, and the median adjusted gross income increased from $10,126 in 2004 to $15,095 in 2008. Additionally, the average EITC return also increased from $768 in 2004 to $1,375 in 2008. Approximately 50% of the respondents were single. The average years of education remained constant at 11 years, and more respondents were homeowners in 2008 (53%) than in 2005 (45%). Border families have unusually high incidence of dependents, with 60% of the sample filing with dependents. Given the low-wage rates of the border region, the frequency responses of the number of W-2 forms reported when filing tax returns are captured for the last two years (56% in 2007 and 60% in 2008).

Table 11.4 reports the financial behaviors and transactions for the sample, including the racial/ethnic self-identification frequency counts of respondents for tax years 2007 and 2008.[12] The data show that the sample was overwhelmingly Latino (73% both years), with the next largest groups being Native American (12% in 2008) and non-Hispanic Whites (10% in 2008). The data show that the majority of respondents utilize a formal financial institution, as evidenced by the 81% and higher rates of those that use a bank, credit union, and/or direct deposit.

However, despite high rates of financial mainstream attachment, close to half of the respondents utilize money orders to pay their bills (with a range of 47% in 2006 and 2007 to 48% in 2008). This usage of a higher-cost product may occur for a number of reasons. First, border families often reside in "cash-economy" communities (e.g., landlords only accept cash or money orders for rent, or local convenience stores take only cash). Second, just like middle-class, suburban families, low-income families pass on intergenerational money management habits. Growing up watching family members pay bills with money orders (left over from an agricultural past where *giros*, or money orders, from the local post office were the only reliable substitutes for cash) can be part of inherited money management skills, as well as engendering familiarity and comfort with an easy-to-understand financial product. Third, safety issues propel many low-income community residents to employ money orders as an alternative to cash as well as a relatively safe "savings" vehicle.

The southwest border has a legacy of concentrated multigenerational households[13] with deep cultural roots that value extended family proximity and family sharing and leveraging of resources. This can be empirically ascertained from the high frequency counts in Table 11.4 for the questions related to lending to or borrowing from family members across all years. Nearly half of the respondents (range of 45% to 49%) lend to and/or borrow from family members in emergencies; and 20% to 30% send money to relatives not living with them. These frequency counts reveal that sharing resources among and between family members is part of border families' financial behaviors and capabilities.

Saving and savings knowledge, (e.g., awareness of particular programs meant to increase savings opportunities in low-wealth communities such as IDAs) are also elements of financial capability. Over half of the respondents (51% to 56%) have a savings account. The data in Table 11.4 indicate an increasing awareness of IDAs (generally, spread by word of mouth in isolated, low-income communities) over the data collection years, from a 7.6% response frequency count in tax year 2004 to 10.6% in tax year 2008. Only two years of data contained specific queries on owning a savings account, but this data show that the rate of saving account ownership increased from 51% in tax year 2007 to 56% in tax year 2008. Additionally, informal savings participation has a relatively low response frequency (a range of 2% to 3%) but remains steady across the data collection years. The aggregated informal savings "amounts" reported are substantial (with a range from a total of $44,180 to $68,015) which is generally the case in "goal-specific" neighborhood savings circles (most "savings pots" or "turns" are anywhere from $500 to $10,000). The

Table 11.4. FINANCIAL AND ECONOMIC RESILIENCY BEHAVIORS, TAX YEARS 2004–2008

Financial Behaviors and Transactions	All Respondents				Prelim
	TY2004	TY2005	TY2006	TY2007	TY2008
	n = 4,550	n = 7,068	n = 6,450	n = 7,377	n = 7,248
Race/Ethnicity:					
Latino	–	–	–	72.9%	73.1%
Native American	–	–	–	5.4%	11.6%
Non-Hispanic White	–	–	–	13.3%	10.1%
African American	–	–	–	5.2%	3.5%
Asian American	–	–	–	1.3%	1.0%
Other	–	–	–	2.4%	2.7%
Do You Have A Savings Account?					
Yes	–	–	–	51.0%	56.0%
No	–	–	–	47.7%	44.0%
where do you cash your paycheck?					
Grocery store	11.4%	9.9%	11.2%	11.8%	10.8%
Check cashing outlet	7.8%	7.5%	7.8%	7.2%	7.5%
Bank	62.7%	54.6%	51.7%	48.5%	48.4%
Credit union	15.1%	9.9%	9.6%	9.3%	11.1%
Direct deposit	5.1%	21.1%	19.4W%	22.7%	26.0%
Financial institution (Bank + C.U. + Direct Deposit)	82.9%	85.6%	80.7%	80.5%	85.5%
Do You Use Money Orders To Pay Your Bills?					
Yes + Sometimes	49.0%	48.1%	46.5%	46.6%	47.5%
No	50.2%	52.5%	49.8%	53.7%	53.2%
Do You Participate In Informal Savings:					
Yes	2.4%	2.3%	2.9%	3.2%	2.3%
Total Amount of Border Informal Savings	$44,180	$57,011	$48,620	$68,015	$55,068

(continued)

Table 11.4. CONTINUED

Have You Heard of IDAs?					
Yes	7.9%	9.6%	9.1%	12.5%	10.6%
Do you send money to relatives not living with you?					
Yes + Sometimes	20.5%	27.1%	25.1%	28.5%	29.7%
No	77.9%	73.1%	71.2%	71.7%	70.5%
Do you lend to/borrow from family members in emergencies?					
Yes + Sometimes	47.9%	48.1%	45.3%	46.8%	48.5%
No	51.1%	52.3%	50.9%	53.3%	51.9%

SOURCE: FABN Survey, Tax Years: 2004, 2005, 2006, 2007, and 2008 data collected in CA, AZ, NM, and TX. Entries do not total to 100% due to multiple responses.

participation in savings circles also provides evidence of financial planning and future orientation. Yet, because this financial capability behavior does not appear familiar to mainstream financial educators and policymakers, it rarely is incorporated into financial literacy and support programs meant to encourage savings behaviors in distressed bicultural or cultural legacy communities.

The density of fringe banking and commercial tax services in low-income areas has been escalating in the South and Southwest for the last 25 years. The proliferation of RALs has served to erase some of the positive effects of the earned income tax credit (EITC) lump-sum tax refund for many low-wage qualifying working families (Berube, 2005; Romich & Weisner,2000). The presence of free and low-fee tax preparation services in grassroots CBOs and NGOs has provided an alternative to more expensive commercial tax preparers with their end-of-tax-year, holiday (December 15–January 15) high-pressure marketing of RALs to many working families. The frequency counts for RAL usage in Table 11.5 indicate that approximately 9%–12% of border respondents have used RALs but are clearly aware of and using free tax filing services in their communities.

A cautionary note is in order here; the border families that use CBO free tax preparation services are only a fraction of those continuing to use commercial tax preparers offering RALs. The estimated savings for border working families by using free tax preparation services at border CBOs for 2008–2009 was $3.1 million (see Table 11.1).

Table 11.5 also provides information on how working border families allocate their lump-sum tax refunds. It is not surprising that the majority of respondents (from 52% to 66% frequency counts) over the entire data collection period indicate that personal expenses are the bulk of how they expend their tax refunds. Getting ahead of monthly bills and current debts is part of financial capability practices. Correspondingly, the expending of tax refunds on items other than immediate household expenses provides insight into how border residents plan financially and engage in asset building, indicating financial capabilities despite extraordinarily low incomes.

Table 11.5. FINANCIAL AND ECONOMIC RESILIENCY BEHAVIORS, TAX YEARS 2004–2008

Economic Resiliency and Asset Building	All Respondents				Prelim
	TY2004	TY2005	TY2006	TY2007	TY2008
	n = 4,550	n = 7,068	n = 6,450	n = 7,377	n = 7,248
Have you used an RAL?					
Yes	12.3%	12.5%	11.6%	9.4%	11.7%
No	86.2%	87.2%	82.8%	90.5%	88.1%
Have you ever used your tax refund for:					
Down payment on a home/mobile home	3.8%	4.2%	4.3%	4.4%	5.8%
Car/truck purchase	10.8%	10.0%	9.6%	16.1%	20.4%
Household appliance (washer/dryer)	8.0%	8.1%	8.4%	13.1%	15.8%
Computer/laptop	4.3%	4.9%	5.1%	8.2%	10.0%
Home furniture	9.8%	9.6%	9.7%	14.1%	18.4%
Help family member w/ immigration fees	3.0%	2.7%	3.3%	2.6%	3.7%
Property taxes	11.2%	11.9%	10.7%	10.3%	12.0%
Medical bills	13.6%	13.8%	13.4%	14.1%	17.5%
Auto insurance	–	12.0%	11.8%	11.0%	19.9%
Small/micro business/self-employment	1.8%	1.3%	2.6%	1.4%	1.5%
Personal bills/expenses	64.6%	66.4%	52.3%	57.4%	58.3%
School expenses (for you or dependent)	14.9%	14.2%	12.3%	11.2%	16.1%
Cell phone	–	–	–	–	8.7%
Pay off a pay day loan	–	–	–	4.1%	6.0%
Savings/saving account	–	–	11.4%	11.0%	14.2%
Other	8.9%	10.6%	8.4%	15.8%	12.7%

SOURCE: FABN Survey, Tax Years: 2004, 2005, 2006, 2007, and 2008 data collected in CA, AZ, NM, and TX. Entries do not total to 100% due to multiple responses.

Public transportation infrastructure in the southwest metropolitan and rural areas has a limited presence. Increasingly, job maintenance depends on owning a vehicle and having access to a phone. Border residents indicate that using their tax refunds as a down payment or purchase of a car has increased in tax years 2007 and 2008 (from a low of 9.6% in 2006 to 20.4% in 2008). Correspondingly, auto/vehicle insurance also increased (from 11% in 2007 to 19.9% in 2008). Tax refunds expended on cell phone plans has a frequency count of almost 9%.

Over the data collection horizon, paying medical bills is an important tax refund expenditure (tax year 2008, 17.5%). Expending tax refunds on school-related expenses (16.1% in 2008) and owning a computer (10% in 2008) are essential for accessing educational opportunities and securing future asset-building opportunities. Without allocating resources on school tuition, supplies, and computers, performing well in formal educational settings is especially difficult for low-wealth youth as well as low-wage-earning adults seeking to gain living-wage employment. This result indicates that expending tax refunds on acquiring access to schooling opportunities and computer ownership constitutes asset building for low-income respondents in the short, intermediate, and long run.

Other important financial and asset-planning activities can be ascertained from the frequency counts that capture border residents' allocation of tax refunds toward savings (14.2% in 2008), property taxes (12% in 2008), paying off payday loans (6% in 2008), down payments on a home or mobile home (5.8% in 2008), helping family members standardize their immigration status (many mixed-status families reside in the region; 3.7% in 2008), and the "other" category (see Appendix C for write-in responses to this category, which include resource sharing and asset-building activities especially among extended family members generally not addressed in mainstream studies).

Table 11.6 captures border respondents' desire to learn more about particular financial products and services that provide families with entry into asset building and financial planning. This question along with the category "other" provides a time-horizon snapshot in each year of data collection of border families' economic aspirations. In 2008, wanting to learn more about job opportunities takes precedence over all other categories in terms of frequency counts (32.1%). This finding is not surprising given the current economic conditions facing many families, especially families with fewer education credentials.

The entries displaying a steady financial aspiration over time include buying a home (range from 19.1% to 35%) and IDAs (range from 15.7% to 27%). Both entries have consistently strong frequency counts and are followed in order of magnitude by school financial aid (range from 17.3% to 22.2%). Clearly, free tax preparation sites or low-fee tax preparation sites operated by CBOs are the ideal location to provide information to border families on how to navigate the school financial aid and college scholarship application process. Additionally, a "window" presents itself for intensive educational campaigns and outreach during tax season to familiarize border families with programs such as IDAs. Such awareness campaigns with clear messaging provide an opportunity to engage community members and advocate to funders (private and public sector) for more IDA program delivery in hard-to-reach and isolated communities. Linking IDA programs to school financial aid would provide an important "comprehensive" financial planning and aspirational economic mobility feature into program awareness and outreach. However, IDA program modifications are necessary for southwest border family uptake.[14]

Table 11.6. ECONOMIC MOBILITY ASPIRATIONS, TAX YEARS 2004–2008

Economic Mobility Aspirations	All Respondents				Prelim
	TY2004	TY2005	TY2006	TY2007	TY2008
	n = 4,550	n = 7,068	n = 6,450	n = 7,377	n = 7,248
Would you like to know more about:					
Buying a home	19.1%	35.0%	22.2%	26.0%	25.6%
Car/truck loans	10.0%	17.0%	10.9%	14.7%	12.8%
Credit cards/debit cards	7.9%	12.0%	7.3%	10.9%	8.6%
Property taxes	6.0%	10.6%	7.7%	9.0%	8.8%
Children's saving accounts	8.5%	16.8%	10.8%	11.8%	11.8%
Bank/credit union account	5.1%	8.1%	5.0%	7.6%	5.5%
Credit/budgeting	8.1%	13.7%	8.8%	11.3%	11.7%
Small/micro business/self-employment	8.1%	14.1%	9.2%	10.2%	10.2%
Individual development accts (IDAs)	15.9%	27.0%	17.9%	18.7%	15.7%
School financial aid (Loans or Grants)	–	–	17.3%	20.9%	22.2%
Retirement accounts	–	–	–	15.0%	12.4%
Credit repair	–	–	–	–	20.6%
Insurance products (funeral, life, etc.)	–	–	–	–	10.5%
Job opportunities	–	–	–	–	32.1%
Other	–	7.5%	9.1%	18.6%	9.1%

SOURCE: FABN Survey, Tax Years: 2004, 2005, 2006, 2007, and 2008 data collected in CA, AZ, NM, and TX. Entries do not total to 100% due to multiple responses.

Many respondents have seasonal and erratic income flows (see Table 11.3 for frequency counts that capture multiple W-2 income forms used in tax filing), which can hinder participation in available IDA programs unless they allow "lump sum" deposits in lieu of time-oriented deposits (e.g., weekly or monthly savings contributions). Another barrier to successful IDA program participation and completion by many border families is the "allowed goals and use" of IDA programs. Perhaps rethinking the usual "three" goals of (1) home ownership down payment, (2) tuition/expenses for higher education, and (3) small/micro business capitalization, to allow other practical and pragmatic goals for low-wealth families such as "used car purchases," "yearly auto insurance premiums," or "school or microbusiness-related computer purchases" is warranted.

For tax year 2008, the survey question categories were expanded to include questions about whether the respondents were interested in information about credit repair (20.6%), insurance products (10.5%), and retirement accounts (12.4%). These additions were the most frequent responses to previous year's "other" categories (fill-in-the-blank narrative space). Many financial education campaigns focus on transactions products and services, and staff may fail to understand the concerns of low-income communities with respect to protecting their families from future financial burdens by acting in the present (i.e., the participants want to know more about insurance products and retirement accounts).

In sum, the key empirical findings from the survey indicate that "family" is a far more fungible definition among border community members (sharing resources among extended kin and fictive kin) and that asset building in communities with high ethnic and cultural legacies does not conform to the individualized consumer prototype or the nuclear family unit of middle-class America. Rather, border communities encompass multigenerational family compositions not based on proximity or same-household status. The unique regional data provide an opportunity to explore the basic research question proposed: Do border families display financial capabilities? Examining the frequency counts for each survey question summarized in Tables 11.4, 11.5, and 11.6, information emerges on culturally driven financial behaviors engaged in by working border families. Despite the stark average and median adjusted gross income of the border region's low-income residents, the capacity and capabilities of impoverished border families to make ends meet (an economic survivalist definition of financial capability) are reflected in their responses to the survey questions. In addition, the data provide evidence of future financial planning and economic mobility aspirations, which are related to financial capability.

CONCLUSIONS AND FUTURE RESEARCH ISSUES

This study framed the significant research question to be addressed as follows: Do working poor southwest border families display financial capabilities? For the purposes of this study, financial capabilities are defined as economic resiliency behaviors such as making ends meet, planning both for the present and the future, and engaging in asset-building activities connected to economic mobility aspirations *within the context of a geographical area rooted in cultural and linguistic legacies*. Given the unique geographical specificity and culturally anchored traditions of many border communities, an action research approach relying heavily on trusted and long-serving community-based organizations allowed entry into hard-to-reach populations with formerly minimal ties to university researchers and resources. The 8-year research project (2002 to 2009) involved partnership building through university roundtable convening, retreats, and regular site visits by university researchers as well as collaborative survey design, CBO survey administration and data collection, university researchers' analysis of data, and reporting to network members the results of each year's data findings. The significance of connecting an action research approach with capturing culturally responsive financial capabilities of ethnic, racial, and immigrant legacy communities creates an opportunity for community values and hidden economic resiliency behaviors to emerge. These features of hard-to-reach populations often remain below the radar in mainstream surveys of economic indicators and financial behaviors. The critical information uncovered in this study leads to a deeper understanding of the contextual and cultural forces that border families negotiate as they seek financial and economic security. Future research on financial resiliency and asset-building behaviors in low-income communities and among vulnerable populations requires an equal understanding of the availability of affordable products and services supplied with what consumers desperately need. Such a balance may reveal the stark and limited choices available to cash-economy low-income neighborhoods and community residents (Prager, 2009). Field observations in low-income communities can reveal an entirely different consumer economy with respect to a variety of financial markets and services. This lived-reality for border residents (and other established ethnic enclave and new gateway immigrant communities) has obvious supply effects for economic inclusion policies such as financial education and culturally responsive asset building.

Research initiatives from inclusive and culturally responsive community development initiatives in New Zealand, Australia, Asia, Africa, and Canada among indigenous populations and vulnerable ethnic/racial communities indicate that despite isolation and public investment neglect, communities treasure their cultural traditions and rely on cultural narratives and experiential knowledge as important resource leveraging and economic resiliency buffers (Findlay, 2003; Lassiter, 2005; McGee & Brock, 2001; Pfohl, 2004; Waldgrave, Stuart, & Stephens, 1996). Foundations seeking to sponsor inclusive funding and program initiatives in isolated and hard-to-reach communities need to remain attentive to the culturally responsive approaches that resonate with culturally and racially diverse communities. Additionally, researchers require field experience in understanding the interconnectedness between transnational families with recent and legacy immigrant attributes, which are often part-and-parcel of cash-oriented low-income communities. Financial activities are often "rational" within the context of nonmainstream US markets, and our knowledge of survival-oriented financial capabilities and culturally driven behaviors is limited when predicated on norms that are not practiced in ethnic, racial, and immigrant legacy communities with high-density populations in specific geographies (e.g., southwest border, Deep South, Appalachia, and Native American reservations).

If culturally responsive community development initiatives are to succeed, our community building policies must begin to deconstruct the silos between social services, economic initiatives, and community development practices. Research is emerging that highlights the interconnected consequences of missing support structures in one area of community and family well-being creating spillover impacts on other areas of family economic resiliency and community vitality. Our recent national experience has heightened our awareness that financial capabilities permeate all aspects of community and family well-being: housing, retirement, vocational and higher education, public services, nutrition, workforce development and transportation. Financial planning and asset building may look different in various parts of the United States. By recognizing the range of culturally anchored and geographic-specific features of financial capabilities and economic resiliency behaviors among our diverse communities, pragmatic "best practices" and "replicable models" that have long been exercised in isolated corners of the United States may be found to be efficacious and effective. Ultimately, our 21st-century challenge as community development researchers and practitioners centers on our willingness to remain open to diverse partnerships in coproducing knowledge and success narratives.

NOTES

1. For Hispanic children under 18 years of age the population counts for the border states are striking: California (51.2%), Arizona (43.2%), New Mexico (58.2%), and Texas (48.3%).
2. The term "frontera" is the Spanish word for border.
3. The term "colonia" is a Spanish word for neighborhood or community. However, *colonia* conveys a unique meaning along the US-Mexico border. *Colonias* are areas of nonincorporated townships that may lack basic water and sewage systems, paved roads, safe and sanitary housing conditions, phone service, and school and public health facilities (Federal Reserve Bank of Dallas, 2001) and are comparable to Appalachian "hollers."
4. For a deeper understanding of *colonia* cultural life and socioeconomic characteristics, see Vélez-Ibañez (2004) and Esparza and Donelson (2008).
5. See Appendix A and B for a full description of the dynamic feedback process all participating survey administrating FABN members engaged in through the action research cycle as well as the total number of coalition partners.
6. McGarvey (2006) identifies collaborative inquiry as an important component in mutual learning and recognizes that community organizations are instrumental to coproducing knowledge. However, he asserts that in established fields of inquiry where "practices and methods" have a mainstream consensus, collaborative inquiry may be erroneously applied. He does not raise the issue of "cultural competency." Organic philanthropy differs from the collaborative inquiry approach in that it stems from and incorporates cultural responsiveness.
7. Hard to quantify success metrics that are community identified generally do not look like "mainstream" middle-class success metrics. For example, increased participation in savings circles among neighborhood mothers, aunts, and grandmothers often result in increased trust in other domains (e.g., childcare, emergencies, food sharing, and emergency short-term loans). The closest parallel would be a women's investment club that captures soft-success metrics like shared knowledge of a particular stock or mutual fund, shared narratives of how the

women will spend the investment proceeds, and increased reliance on particular voices of knowledge after establishing a successful "pick" rate of investments. What is absent in hard-to-reach community research studies, is an assessment of success metrics from the point of view of the community as opposed to an imposed middle-class or affluent standard such as capturing the "consistency" of weekly savings deposits per *individual*, or *individual* membership in the local Parent-Teachers Association (PTA). In immigrant and high-density ethnic and racial communities, the success metrics often take on a "pooled-resource" aspect, with minimal emphasis on the "individual," which is often absent in White middle-class communities.

8. Mixed methodological approaches in an action research framework employ qualitative textual analysis of the open-ended responses on a short multiple-choice one-page survey capturing both the voices of the community (qualitative) and the empirical (quantitative) aspects of the survey responses. In addition, rapid appraisal methods and videography were used in the action research project. Indigenous research methods combined with action research approaches have established a variety of pragmatic practices that are often collaborative in nature and provide a richer assessment of communities that do not fit traditional research methodological approaches (Galt, 2009).
9. In high density immigrant or immigrant-memory communities, savings circles take on a variety of names. In Latino communities they are known as: "cestas," "tandas," "cundinas," "rondas," or "sans."
10. Paper survey response rates greater than 50% are deemed high.
11. Many of the community-based organizations held grievances toward university researchers and external evaluators for being invasive and bringing "outside" surveys into isolated communities as opposed to working with community-based organizations in designing surveys that would capture the types of information that would be useful for community-based organizations to employ in creating new programs and for providing improved services to residents based on resident responses/voices as captured in the surveys. The long-run nature of the data collection effort as well as community "owning" the data provided a context of full-collaboration with community research partners.
12. Community-based organizations deemed some of the questions (age, ethnicity/race, savings) as too invasive or too sensitive for community residents. As more financial programs were planned, more information concerning life-cycle behaviors and aspirations were revisited, and additional demographic information was considered desirable.
13. Some 18.8% of people living in immigrant households in the United States live in a multigenerational family household, compared with 14.2% of people in native-born households, according to a Pew Research analysis of data from the Census Bureau's 2009 Current Population Survey. Interestingly, however, among the nation's two largest immigrant groups by race and ethnicity—Hispanics and Asians—the native-born households of these groups have a slightly higher tendency to be multigenerational families than the foreign-born households. (Taylor et al., 2010)
14. Sherraden and Stevens (2010) indicate that being Hispanic is associated with saving less when participating in IDAs.

REFERENCES

Berube, A. (2005). ¿Tienes EITC? A study of the Earned Income Tax Credit in immigrant communities. The Brookings Metropolitan Policy Program: Survey Series. Washington DC: Brookings Institution.

Environmental Protection Agency. (2012). *U.S.-Mexico Border 2012*. Retrieved September 30, 2011, from http://www.epa.gov/Border2012/bordermap.html

Esparza, A., & Donelson, A. (2008). *Colonias in Arizona and New Mexico: Border poverty and community development solutions*. Tucson: University of Arizona Press.

Federal Reserve Bank of Dallas. (2001). *Texas Colonias: A thumbnail sketch of the conditions, issues, challenges, opportunities, and community affairs*. Retrieved September 30, 2011, from http://www.dallasfed.org/ca/pubs/colonias.html

Findlay, I. M. (2003, May). *Re-imagining co-operative research futures: Co-operation as decolonizing theory and practice*. Paper presented at the Mapping Co-operative Studies in the New Millennium: Joint Congress of the International Co-Operative Alliance Research Committee and the Canadian Association for Studies in Co-Operatives, University of Victoria, Canada.

Galt, K. A., (2009). *Qualitative, quantitative and mixed methods approaches to research and inquiry*. Presentation: August 26, 2009. Retrieved June 19, 2012, from http://spahp2.creighton.edu/OfficeOfResearch/share/sharedfiles/UserFiles/file/Galt_SPAHP_Methods_Presentation_082609.pdf

Jones, V. N., & Woolcock, M. (2007). Using mixed methods to assess social capital in low income countries: A practical guide (Working Paper #12). Manchester, UK: University of Manchester, Brooks World Poverty Institute.

Lassiter, L. E. (2005). Collaborative ethnography and public anthropology. *Current Anthropology, 46*(1), 83–106.

Mammen, S., & Lawrence, F. C. (2006). How rural working families use the earned income tax credit: A mixed methods approach. *Financial Counseling and Planning Education, 17*(1), 51–63.

Markham, M., & Diaz-Funn, N. (2009). *Strengthening southwest border and native families: Portfolio reflection 2008*. Washington, DC: Annie E. Casey Foundation. Retrieved September 30, 2011, from http://www.aecf.org/~/media/Pubs/Topics/Special%20Interest%20Areas/SW%20border%20and%20American%20Indian%20Families/StrenghteningSWBorderNativeFamilies/FINALLearningAssessment10%2029%2009.pdf

McGarvey, C. (2006). Learning together: Collaborative inquiry among grant makers and grantees. *GrantCraft*. Retrieved September 30, 2011, from http://grantcraft.net/index.cfm?fuseaction=Page.ViewPage&pageId=1541

McGee, R., & Brock, K. (2001). *From poverty assessment to policy change: Processes, actors and data* (Working Paper 133). Brighton, Sussex, UK: Institute of Development Studies.

Mora, J., & Diaz, D. (2004). *Latino social policy: A participatory research model*. Binghamton, NY: Haworth Press.

Pew Hispanic Center. (2011). *Census 2010: 50 million Latinos*. Washington, DC: Pew Research Center. Retrieved September 30, 2011, from http://pewhispanic.org/files/reports/140.pdf

Pfohl, S. (2004). Culture, power, and history: An introduction. *Critical Sociology, 30*(2), 191–205.

Prager, R. (2009). *Determinants of the locations of payday lenders, pawnshops and check-cashing outlets* (Working Paper 2009-33). Finance and Economics Discussion Series. Washington, DC: Federal Reserve Board, Divisions of Research and Statistics and Monetary Affairs.

Rambaldi, G., Chambers, R., McCall, M., & Fox, J. (April 2006). Practical ethics for PGIS practitioners, facilitators, technology intermediaries and researchers. *Participatory Learning and Action Series, 54*, 106–113. http://pubs.iied.org/pdfs/14507IIED.pdf

Robles, B. (2006). *Asset accumulation and economic development in Latino communities: A national and border economy profile of Latino families*. Madison, WI: Filene Research Institute.

Robles, B. (2007). Tax refunds and microbusinesses: Expanding family and community wealth building in the borderlands. *Annals of the American Academy of Political and Social Sciences, 612*, 178–191.

Romich, J., & Weisner, T. (2000). Earnings, refund, windfall or equity: How families view and use the EITC. *National Tax Journal, 53*(4.2), 1245–1265.

Sherraden, M., & Stevens, J. (Eds.). (2010). *Lessons from SEED: A national demonstration of Child Development Accounts*. St. Louis, MO: Washington University, Center for Social Development. Retrieved September 30, 2011, from http://csd.wustl.edu/Publications/Documents/SEEDSynthesis_Final.pdf

Smeeding, T., Phillips, K., & O'Connor, M. (2000). The EITC: Expectation, knowledge, use, and economic and social mobility. *National Tax Journal, 53*, 1187–1203.

Taylor, P., Parker, K., Kochhar, R., Lopez, M., Passel, J., Fry, R., et al. (2010). *The return of the multi-generational family household* (A Social and Demographic Trends Report). Washington, DC: Pew Research Center. Retrieved September 30, 2011, from http://pewsocialtrends.org/assets/pdf/752-multi-generational-families.pdf

US Census Bureau. (2008). *American Community Survey: 1-year estimates*. Table B03001. Retrieved from http://factfinder2.census.gov/faces/tableservices/jsf/pages/productview.xhtml?pid=ACS_08_1YR_B03001&prodType=table

Vélez-Ibañez, C. (2004). Regions of refuge in the United States: Issues, problems and concerns for the future of Mexican-Americans in the United States. *Human Organization, 63*(1), 1–20.

Yankelovich, D. (2001). The magic of dialogue. *Non-Profit Quarterly, 8*(3). Retrieved from September 30, 2011, from http://www.nonprofitquarterly.org/index.php?option=com_content&view=article&id=8701:the-magic-of-dialogue&catid=150:from-the-archives&Itemid=351

Waldgrave, C., Stuart, S., & Stephens, R. (1996). Participation in poverty research: Drawing on the knowledge of low-income householders to establish an appropriate measure for monitoring social policy impacts. *Social Policy Journal of New Zealand, 7*. Retrieved September 30, 2011, from http://www.msd.govt.nz/about-msd-and-our-work/publications-resources/journals-and-magazines/social-policy-journal/spj07/participation-in-poverty-research.html

PART THREE

Social Work Education, Practice, and Curriculum Development

12

Financial Capabilities of Service Providers in the Asset-Building Field

VERNON LOKE, JULIE L. WATTS AND SALLY A. KAKOTI

Building long-term wealth is critical for economic security and it represents a pathway out of poverty for low-income families. Yet to effectively build long-term wealth, it is crucial to possess the knowledge and ability to make healthy financial choices (Johnson & Sherraden, 2007). However, low- and moderate-income populations often face financial challenges such as accessing alternative financial services that carry higher costs than conventional services (Barr, 2004; Caskey, 2006; Fellowes & Mabanta, 2008), lacking savings for emergencies (Brobeck, 2008a, 2008b; Bucks, Kennickell, Mach, & Moore, 2009; Jacob, Hudson, & Bush, 2000), and underutilizing tax benefits (Caputo, 2006, 2009). In addition, financial literacy among low- and moderate-income individuals tends to be lower compared to those with higher incomes (Bernheim, 1998; Jacob et al., 2000; Zhan, Anderson, & Scott, 2006).

Despite the different interpretations of what constitutes financial capability, there is growing consensus that it encompasses both the ability to act (knowledge, skills) and the opportunity to act (through access and engagement with the financial markets) (Sherraden, 2010). In addition, it involves multiple aspects of behaviors relating to how financial decisions are made and resources managed (FINRA, 2009), such as actively budgeting and keeping track of expenses. In other words, financial capability is about what you do as well as what you know (Sledge, Tescher, & Gordon, 2010).

However, many community programs that work with clients to promote financial knowledge and asset development, primarily focus on financial literacy, rather than financial knowledge, skills, and opportunities to act. The need to study the financial capabilities of low-income people and the relationship between such capabilities and asset-building outcomes may seem self-evident. So why then study the financial capabilities of *frontline service providers*?

First, the financial capabilities of service providers can have a direct relationship on outcomes for clients. A frontline worker's own financial knowledge and practices may influence how the client's economic situation, needs, and strengths are assessed and the worker's subsequent decisions about necessary intervention and/or referral. They are therefore uniquely positioned to help increase the financial capabilities of these populations (Anderson, Scott, & Zhan, 2004; Birkenmaier & Curley, 2009; Sherraden, Laux, & Kaufman, 2007). However, little is known about the financial capabilities of service providers and the extent to which their own financial knowledge and skills may represent a benefit or a barrier to their clients' ability to build assets. Less-than-ideal financial capabilities among service providers may represent a significant challenge to their clients' abilities to build long-term wealth and achieve higher levels of economic security.

Second, frontline workers' financial capabilities may influence the effectiveness of systems and policies designed to promote asset development for people with lower incomes. If indeed the financial capabilities of service providers affect the development of clients' financial assets, as those on the frontlines of implementation, the success of the policies and programs may be significantly affected as well. Such findings could have implications for future research, policy, and program development.

In Washington State, asset-building services are typically provided by multiservice, social service agencies. Such agencies provide a range of services for low-income individuals and families, including state-funded housing counseling programs, Low Income Home Energy Assistance (LIHEAP), food banks, and case management for the homeless. Most are either connected to local asset-building coalitions or receive funds from the State of Washington to engage and organize asset-building efforts in their local communities, bank the unbanked, provide financial literacy and debt management services, and administer IDA programs. Frontline service providers in the asset-building field may or may not have any specialized training in social work, counseling, or finance. Many come from a variety of different educational backgrounds and educational levels, yet their financial capabilities and the skills and tools they employ in their work with clients is of great importance. They serve as an entry point into social service systems, the primary or secondary level of relationship to the client and a critical point of referral and/or direct engagement into asset building programs and tools. Assessing their financial capabilities and the impact on asset-building outcomes for clients may have significant implications for the future development of strategies to support low-income people in long-term wealth building.

BACKGROUND

The asset-building field began with the passage of the Assets for Independence Act in 1998 when Individual Development Accounts (IDAs) were introduced, supported, and funded by the federal government. According to the Center for Social Development at Washington University in St. Louis, there are over 500 IDA initiatives across the United States, with 35 states, Washington, DC, and Puerto

Rico having some form of IDA legislation passed by their legislatures. In addition, another 30 states have also included IDAs in their state Temporary Assistance for Needy Families (TANF) plans (Center for Social Development, n.d.).

Washington State is one such state. In 1997, when the state of Washington was crafting its WorkFirst welfare program in response to the Personal Responsibility and Work Opportunity Reconciliation Act (PWORA), then-governor Gary Locke established a pilot IDA program for WorkFirst participants. The program tapped TANF funds and was established for five years. After the WorkFirst funding expired, the state legislature expanded the program to residents living at or below 80% of area median income (AMI) or 200% of the federal poverty line, whichever was greater (Washington State Department of Commerce, 2008).

While the asset-building field started with IDAs, it has now moved beyond IDA programs to include a plethora of programs and services. These asset-building programs and services could broadly be grouped into the classifications of asset creation, asset management, and asset protection and preservation.

Asset creation programs and services focus on helping individuals and families create additional assets and financial resources through a combination of interventions at the institutional and individual levels. Institutional-level interventions include the creation of structures to enable individuals to acquire, build, and grow assets. Examples of such structures range from long-term savings plans with initial endowments and/or a savings match (e.g., IDAs, Maine's NextGen 529 plan with an initial contribution of $500 by the Alfond Foundation for every newborn in Maine) and prize-linked saving accounts, to providing access to productive assets, such as machinery or vehicles, that could be deployed to generate income. At the individual level, these asset-creation programs and services aim to connect individuals to the various asset-creation structures; increase the income potential and earning capacities of individuals; and help individuals create assets through helping them establish savings, investment, and retirement accounts.

Such asset-creation programs have achieved mixed success in Washington State. While Washington's IDA program led to the creation of over 512 accounts and $1.2 million in savings for working poor families, funding for the program was discontinued in 2009 (Burst for Prosperity, 2011). Washington's Guaranteed Education Tuition (GET) program also provides the opportunity for working families to prepay future college tuition at today's rates. However, the take-up rate for these accounts is extremely low among middle- and low-income families, perhaps due to fees for opening accounts and a lack of incentives or matches for low-income individuals (Burst for Prosperity, 2011).

A second focus of asset building is that of asset management. Being able to manage, stretch, and grow one's existing and newly acquired assets is just as important as having assets and being connected to asset-creation structures. Yet studies have found Americans to have relatively low levels of financial literacy, especially among the lower-income and racial minority groups (Applied Research & Consulting LLC, 2009; FINRA, 2009). However, individuals who received support services to increase their financial literacy, in addition to being connected to asset creation structures, have better economic outcomes compared to those who received one or the other or neither (Clancy, Grinstein-Weiss, & Schreiner, 2001; Rand, 2004; Schreiner, Clancy, & Sherraden, 2002). With the loss of state funding for IDAs, much of the asset-building work among service providers in Washington State now revolves around asset management, often in the form of financial education classes or financial counseling. More recently, a new financial coaching approach has been implemented and is being tested across the state.

Asset protection and preservation is the third focus of the asset-building approach. Here, the concern is how assets that have been accumulated could be protected for the individual's long-term development needs, as well as for intergenerational transfers. It is estimated that about 50% to as high as 60% of Americans lack emergency savings or rainy day funds that could cover expenses for three months in case of income disruptions due to illness or other emergencies (FINRA, 2009, n.d.). In addition, 30% of US households have no life insurance coverage (LIMRA, 2010), while 16.7% of Americans (50.7 million) have no health insurance (Denavas-Walt, Proctor, & Smith, 2010). There are also anecdotal indications that individuals are discouraged from accumulating assets due to the fear that they will lose their public benefits, or that the assets they have accumulated will be seized by their creditors. Furthermore, having easily accessible assets can increase one's obligation to give financial assistance to family and friends.

Developments have begun in some segments of the asset-building field to address the disincentives for asset accumulation and emphasize the importance of asset protection. Examples include providing restricted access to the assets accumulated; stronger consumer protections in lending; advocating for policies that would remove impediments to asset accumulation such as the modification of asset limits and perhaps the exemption of certain classes or amount of assets from creditor proceedings; and introducing the various forms of insurance in existing financial education classes.

This study is one phase of a multiphase research effort in Washington State by Burst for Prosperity to understand what most effectively leads low-income individuals toward long-term wealth building. The initiative seeks to identify personal and structural barriers to building assets that will lead to the development of better tools and resources to improve asset-building outcomes for the working poor and to guide the development of future asset-building policies. Ultimately the goal of studying the financial capabilities of service providers is to affect positive change in outcomes for clients. The next phases of this research project will be to examine the effectiveness of a financial coaching tool and whether or not its application results in increased financial capabilities for clients and greater success in building long-term wealth.

The purpose of this study is to examine the financial capabilities of service providers as a possible structural barrier to asset building and the development of financial capabilities among the populations they serve. Toward that end, this study seeks to describe the level of financial capability of frontline service providers and their supervisors in the asset-building field as well as to explore service providers' perceptions of their comfort levels and preparedness in delivering finance-related services to their clients.

METHODOLOGY

Participants

The participants of this study consist of a subsample drawn from a larger study. For the larger study, a list of 353 names and e-mail addresses of service providers representing 117 agencies providing asset-building services to low-income individuals and families in Washington State was compiled. This list of agencies included both private and state agencies, for-profit and nonprofit organizations, and agencies from the social service and financial sectors. In addition, this list consists of individuals with different roles and responsibilities in their organizations, from senior management personnel with little or no direct contact with clients, to frontline staff and volunteers who interact directly with clients in their regular work. Based on the self-identified designations of participants, different sections of the survey instrument were administered to answer a broad range of research questions.

E-mail invitations were sent to all 353 service providers on the list in early April 2010, and a total of 184 service providers responded to the invitation for the larger study. These respondents came from 84 different agencies, representing 71.8% of agencies in the sampling frame.

Of the 184 service providers in the overall sample, a subsample of 155 participants was drawn for this study. These participants were volunteers, frontline staff, and their supervisors, who provide a wide range of direct asset-building services to their clients, including financial counseling, financial literacy training, debt management, housing counseling, working with clients to develop personal and family budgets, and other related forms of case management. Participants come from not-for-profit multiservice agencies such as Community Action Agencies, state and federal public agencies such as the housing authorities of various cities, mental health agencies, institutes of higher education, consumer counseling programs, job readiness centers, agencies working with domestic violence victims, religious organizations, and financial institutions such as banks and credit unions. Excluded from this study were participants who did not interact directly with clients. As information on participants' roles and designations at their agencies was not available a priori, calculation of response rates based on designation was not possible.

Procedures

A self-administered survey instrument was created for this study, and was deployed using the SurveyMonkey online survey service. The online survey instrument included items that explored respondents' self-assessed financial knowledge and abilities, as well as items that assessed respondents' financial and debt literacy, their financial behaviors, and their ownership of financial products. Respondents were also asked to rate their perceived level of comfort and preparedness to work with clients on their financial matters. Information on respondents' work and sociodemographic background such as their work designations, length of service in the asset-building field, gender, and highest educational level, was also collected. In addition, respondents were asked about their perceptions of the adequacy of the asset-building-related training they received and the need for additional training. Descriptive statistics and basic inferential statistical tests, such as T-tests, one-way ANOVAs, and Chi-squares, were used to describe and analyze the data for this study.

To assess the financial literacy of respondents, a 41-item quiz comprising subscales on credit, saving, investments, mortgages, predatory services, public benefits, and a broad category of other financial management topics, was administered. The items tested respondents' financial knowledge at a rudimentary level, with true-false questions such as "If you use your home as collateral for a loan, there is no chance of losing your home"; and "Payday loans usually have low interest rates." The subscales on predatory services and public benefits were constructed using items from the Financial Links for Low-Income People (FLLIP) Program in Illinois (Anderson et al., 2004), while the other subscales use the financial knowledge instrument developed for the University of Michigan's monthly Surveys of Consumers conducted in November and December 2001 (Hilgert, Hogarth, & Beverly, 2003). In addition, respondents' debt literacy levels were assessed through a three-item instrument used by Lusardi and Tufano (2009) in their nationally representative study on debt literacy measuring the understanding of credit card repayment, compound interest, and the time-value of money. Specifically, respondents' understanding of compound interest and its impact on repayment, knowledge of credit card repayment, and understanding of the time value of money was assessed. Appendix 12.1 lists the items in the financial and debt literacy measures and provides a comparison with the results from the respective studies that surveyed nationally representative samples of Americans.

To look at the financial practices of respondents, respondents were asked about their own financial behaviors, as well as their use of various financial products ranging from savings and checking accounts to products from the alternative financial market, such as payday loans. The 38-item financial practices measure was comprised of subscales on cash-flow management, credit management, saving, investment, fringe services, and other. Examples of items include "Do you have a checking account?"; "Do you review your credit reports?"; and "In the past 12 months, how often have you used a check cashing service?" The fringe services subscale was constructed using items from the Survey of Financial Literacy in Washington State (Moore, 2003) that surveyed a representative sample from the State of Washington, and from the nationally representative National Financial Capability Study (Applied Research & Consulting LLC, 2009). The remaining subscales were constructed using items from the Surveys of Consumers (Hilgert et al., 2003). Appendix 12.2 lists the behaviors or products used to analyze each type of practice and provides a comparison with the results from surveys of other nationally representative samples.

With the approval of the Institutional Review Board (IRB), the online survey was fielded from April 2010 to July 2010. After the initial invitation in April 2010, e-mailed reminders were sent at 3- to 4-week intervals thereafter to those who did not respond. In addition, reminders via voicemail were sent to all nonresponders toward the end of May, and to those who partially completed the survey in late July. As an incentive, a $20 gift card was offered to every respondent who completed the survey.

FINDINGS

Respondent Profiles

As seen in Table 12.1, the final analysis sample consists of 125 respondents, of whom 50 classified themselves as members of middle-management, and the remaining 75 as case managers or other equivalent frontline positions. A further 30 respondents did not respond to any of the financial items and were therefore excluded from the analysis. Of these, 9 were from the middle-management level, and 21 were from the frontline. Chi-square tests of independence indicated that those who were excluded from the analysis were not statistically different from those who responded to the financial items with respect to their designations at their respective agencies.

In terms of gender, slightly over 74% of the respondents were female, and 20% reported being male, reflecting the gender imbalance of the social service field. Almost all of the respondents had at least some college education. The majority of the respondents (52%) had bachelor's degrees, and 18.4% had graduate degrees. Another 22.4% had some college or associate's degrees, while only 0.8% of the respondents had a high school diploma or equivalent.

With respect to age, about 3 in 4 respondents were more than 30 years of age at the time of the survey. More than half of the respondents also had less than 3 years of service in the asset-building field, while 25.6% had been in asset building for 5 years or more.

As for service providers' perceptions of the asset-building training they received, only 43.2% reported that they somewhat or strongly agreed with the statement "I received adequate training to deliver asset-building services." On the other hand, 68.8% of respondents reported that they somewhat or strongly agreed with the statement, "I need more training to effectively deliver asset-building services."

Self-Assessment of Financial Knowledge and Abilities

Existing research on financial capabilities of individuals frequently finds that respondents have favorable self-assessments of their own abilities, regardless of where they may objectively stand (e.g., Applied Research & Consulting LLC, 2009; Lusardi & Tufano, 2009). Consistent with this research, the results of this survey found respondents to have a positive assessment of their own financial capabilities, as measured by self-assessments of financial literacy and financial management.

In terms of financial literacy and abilities, the data in Table 12.2 suggest that respondents had very positive self-assessments. Over 9 in 10 respondents agreed

Table 12.1. Respondent Profiles (N = 125)

Designation	Percent (%)
Middle management	40
Frontline	60
Gender	
Female	74
Male	20
Missing	6
Highest Education	
High School Diploma or equivalent	1
Some college	11
Associate's degree	11
Bachelor's degree	52
Graduate degree	18
Other professional qualifications	1
Missing	6
Age	
25 years and younger	9
26 to 30 years	17
31 to 40 years	25
41 to 50	16
Older than 50 years	27
Missing	6
Years of Experience in Asset-Building Field	
Less than 1 year	18
1 to 2 years	11
2 to 3 years	18
3 to 5 years	14
More than 5 years	26
Missing	13
Perceived Adequate Training Received	
Strongly or somewhat disagree	32
Neither agree nor disagree	23
Somewhat or strongly agree	43
Missing	2
Perceived Additional Training Needed	
Strongly or somewhat disagree	8
Neither agree nor disagree	18
Somewhat or strongly agree	69
Missing	5

with the statement "I am financially literate," and a similarly high proportion of respondents agreed with the statement, "I am able to manage my finances well."

In general, more frontline staff had a higher self-assessment of their financial knowledge (50% strongly agreed), and of their financial ability (57% strongly agreed), compared to their counterparts from the middle-management level (46% & 44% respectively). In addition, service providers who had been in the asset-building field longer tended to have higher self-assessments of their financial literacy and abilities compared to those who had been in the field for less than 2 years.

Financial and Debt Literacy

On the overall 41-item financial literacy measure, service providers were able to correctly answer, on average, 66% of the items. With regard to the subscales that are common to both the Surveys of Consumers and this study, respondents correctly answered 64% of the items on average (see Figure 12.1). On the other hand, Hilgert and her colleagues (2003) found that the average American was able to answer 67% of the items correctly. A one-sample t-test analysis found that service providers were statistically similar to the general population with respect to their level of financial literacy.

Service providers in the asset-building field were also similar to low-income individuals who completed a financial education program with respect to their knowledge of predatory services and public benefits. On average, respondents correctly answered 77% of the items pertaining to predatory services, and 59% of the items pertaining to public benefits, compared to 79% and 67% respectively among low-income individuals in the FLLIP project (Anderson et al., 2004).

The level of financial literacy was found to be independent of the respondent's designation at the agency on all financial knowledge subscales. In addition, no significant differences were observed when comparing those who perceived that they received adequate training to deliver asset-building services and those who did not, and between those who perceived a need for additional training against those who did not.

However, the length of service in the asset-building field was found to be significantly associated with the financial knowledge levels of respondents. Respondents with fewer than 2 years of service had significantly lower levels of knowledge compared to those with 5 or more years of service on the subscales that pertain to credit ($F = 3.73$, $p < .05$; mean difference = 14%), saving ($F = 5.36$, $p < .01$; mean difference = 20%), and investment ($F = 4.66$, $p < .05$; mean difference = 20%), and on the overall scale ($F = 3.31$, $p < .05$; mean difference = 12%). Respondents with between 2 and 5 years of service were statistically similar to those with 5 or more years of service in their level of financial knowledge.

Table 12.2. SELF-ASSESSED FINANCIAL LITERACY AND ABILITY BY DESIGNATION AND LENGTH OF SERVICE.

		Designation (%)		Length of service (%)			Overall (%)
		MIDDLE MGT (N = 50)	FRONTLINE (N = 74)	LESS THAN 2 YEARS (N = 37)	2–5 YEARS (N = 40)	5 OR MORE YEARS (N = 31)	(N = 125)
I am financially literate	Strongly disagree	0	1	3	0	0	1
	Somewhat disagree	2	0	0	0	3	1
	Neutral	0	3	5	0	0	2
	Somewhat agree	52	46	54	50	29	48
	Strongly agree	46	50	38	20	68	48
I am able to manage my finances well	Strongly disagree	0	0	0	0	0	0
	Somewhat disagree	0	1	3	0	0	1
	Neutral	6	1	3	3	3	3
	Somewhat agree	50	41	41	50	36	44
	Strongly agree	44	57	54	48	61	51

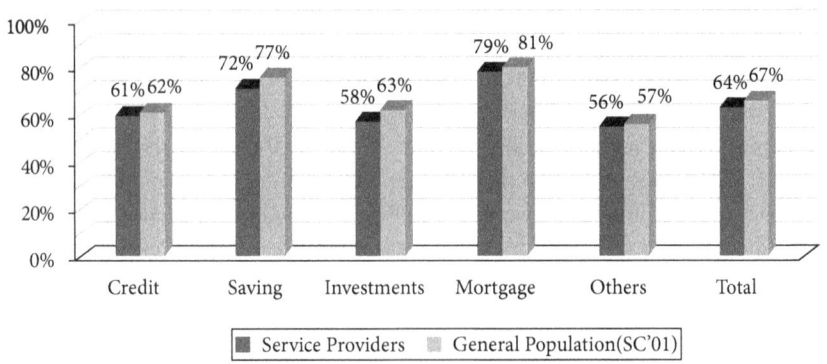

Figure 12.1 Mean Percent Correctly Answered by Domain

Debt Literacy

In terms of the level of debt literacy of respondents, the data indicate that 45% of respondents correctly answered the question assessing the understanding of compound interest and its impact on repayment, 41% correctly answered the question assessing knowledge of credit card repayment, while only 6% of respondents were able to correctly answer the item assessing the understanding of the time value of money. This compares to 36%, 35%, and 7% from a nationally representative sample who were able to correctly answer the same questions respectively, as found in the TNS Global study conducted in collaboration with Lusardi and Tufano (2009). Results of the Chi-square goodness-of-fit analyses indicate that the respondents in this study were statistically similar to the general population on each of the three items in the debt literacy measure.

Financial Management Practices and Experiences

In this survey, respondents were asked about their own financial behaviors, as well as their use of various financial products ranging from savings and checking accounts to products from alternative financial markets such as payday loans. To look at the financial practices of respondents, measures of financial management behaviors and financial product ownership were combined into different subscales (Hilgert et al., 2003). The financial practices were categorized as cash-flow management, credit management, saving, investment, fringe services, and other. In addition, the extent to which service providers were applying the various financial practices in their own financial lives was explored by creating indices that classified their practices as low, medium, or high (Hilgert et al., 2003; Sherraden et al., 2007). If respondents reported having fewer than 25% of the practices in each index, they were classified as low; respondents reporting between 25% and 70% of the practices were classified as medium; and those reporting more than 70% of the practices were classified as high. To be consistent with the Surveys of Consumers study, respondents who reported not paying bills on time were classified as having a low level of practice in the cash-flow management index, regardless of the respondent's experience with the other measures within that index.

Overall, service providers in the asset-building field exhibited desirable financial practices, often with higher frequencies than found in the general population as reported in the Surveys of Consumers 2001 study (Hilgert et al., 2003). Chi-square goodness-of-fit tests further indicate that the respondents were statistically different (at the .01 alpha level) from the general population as described in the Surveys of Consumers study (Hilgert et al., 2003) with regard to their financial practices. As can be seen in Figure 12.2, more respondents were classified as high in the various financial practice categories compared to the general population, while at the same time, far fewer respondents were classified as scoring low on the various financial practice indices. This finding suggests that service providers in the asset-building field had significantly more positive financial practices than the general population.

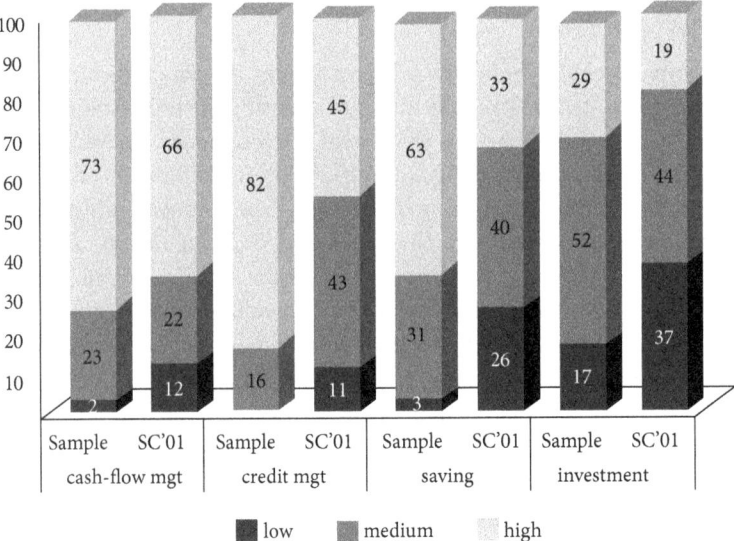

Figure 12.2 Distribution of Levels of Index Scores (%), by Type of Financial Practice

Regarding the various financial practices, the data indicate that respondents were strongest in cash-flow and credit management, with respondents, on average, self-reporting engagement in about 81% of the financial behaviors in each practice category. Examples of items in these categories include paying bills on time, having a checking account, paying credit card balances in full, and reviewing credit reports. This is followed by financial practices related to saving with respondents practicing, on average, 72% of the behaviors measured in the index. Having a savings account and saving for long-term goals are examples of items in this financial practice domain.

Respondents are however, weakest in practices related to investment, with respondents engaged in, on average, only 48% of the behaviors. For example, just a third of service providers reported having some kind of an investment account, an IRA/Keogh, or mutual fund account respectively, and slightly over half spread their money over different types of investments. In terms of engagement with the fringe financial services market, the results indicate that the majority of respondents had no engagement with the fringe market in the past twelve months, while 14% of respondents had low levels of engagement, 6% had a medium level of engagement, and 1% had a high level of engagement.

The data further indicate that the financial practices of respondents, with the exception of practices pertaining to investments ($t = 3.86$, $p < .001$), were statistically similar across designations (see Figure 12.3). Similarly, no statistical differences were found in financial practices between respondents across the different lengths of service in the asset-building field, with the exception of investment practices ($F = 7.97$, $p < .01$). Not surprisingly, those with less than two years of service (mean = 35%) had significantly lower levels of practice compared to

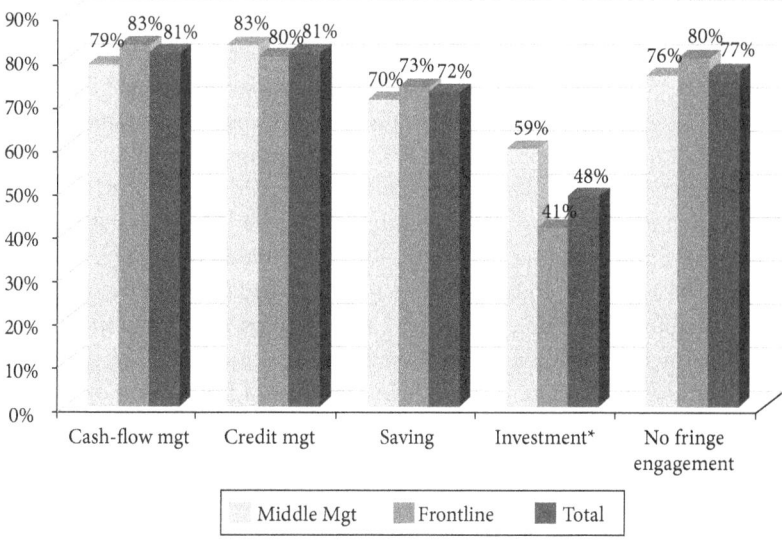

* Middle-management and frontline staff have significantly different means at the p < .001 level

Figure 12.3 Mean Practices by Financial Practice Categories and Designation

respondents with 2 to 5 years of practice experience (mean = 54%), and to those with more than 5 years of experience (mean = 58%). Respondents with more than 2 years of service were similar with respect to their investment practices.

Perceived Comfort and Preparedness Levels in Working with Clients

A series of questions were asked of respondents to assess their perceived level of comfort and preparedness to work on the financial matters of their clients' lives. When asked to what extent they agreed with the statement "I feel prepared to work on the economic aspects of my clients' lives," about 31% of respondents disagreed. In addition, another 24% of respondents disagreed with the statement "I feel comfortable working with clients on their financial matters." Over 36% of respondents also disagreed with the statement "I know where to refer clients for asset-building services that are not available at my agency," while another 41% of respondents disagreed with the statement "I am able to provide effective financial counseling to my clients." Together, these findings suggest that between 25% and 40% of service providers do not feel sufficiently equipped to work in the main areas of asset building—that of working on the financial lives of their clients either directly through financial counseling or by referring clients to external resources.

DISCUSSION

For service providers in the asset-building field to be effective in increasing the financial capabilities of their low-to-moderate income clients, they need to be equipped with at least a rudimentary level of financial knowledge, and the skills and ability to apply this knowledge to actual financial decision-making situations (FINRA, 2009; Sherraden, 2010). The data from this study indicate that respondents from the asset-building field generally had very positive assessments of their own financial knowledge and abilities. While this finding may reflect service providers' confidence in their ability to deliver asset-building services, it may also mask underlying gaps if objective measures of knowledge and behaviors do not align with these positive self-assessments. Results of the analyses suggest that there may, in fact, be such a gap between self-perceptions and the objective measures of financial capabilities of service providers. On the subscales pertaining to credit, saving, investments, mortgages, and other financial matters, the data indicate that service providers had similar or slightly lower levels of financial knowledge than the general population. They also had similar levels of debt literacy compared to the general population. In addition, respondents were similar to low-income individuals who completed a financial education program with respect to their knowledge of predatory services and public benefits.

Overall, respondents appear to be most knowledgeable on matters pertaining to mortgages, followed by knowledge of predatory services, saving, and credit. Respondents are least knowledgeable about public benefits, investment, and other financial management issues. It is plausible that the uneven level of financial knowledge observed could be a factor of the types of populations that respondents work with, or the range of asset-building services provided. However, the nature of the financial literacy items asked in this study is very rudimentary, where no specialized training or knowledge was required. Hence the impact of this plausible factor is likely to be small.

With regard to the proportion of respondents who were able to correctly answer all the items on the different subscales, the data indicate that, with the exception of the mortgage subscale, fewer than a third of respondents were able to answer all the items correctly for each subscale. In fact, for the credit subscale, only 4% of respondents were able to correctly answer all of the items, as seen in Figure 12.4. The proportion of respondents who had difficulty answering at least half of the items on each subscale correctly also points to definite gaps in the respondents' financial knowledgebase. In this regard, the data indicate between 15% and 48% of respondents had difficulties across the various subscales. In other words, there is a real possibility that low-income clients are getting incorrect and inaccurate information from service providers. This is an area that needs to be addressed and improved on.

During the current mortgage crisis when many service providers are actively providing assistance to clients on mortgage-related matters, it is not surprising that respondents were most knowledgeable on matters pertaining to mortgages. However, 10% of respondents were not able to answer any of the questions correctly, and another 11% were only able to correctly answer one or two of the questions related to mortgages. Given the magnitude of mortgage problems in the current economic environment, and the attention they have received in the media, one would expect service providers to be more knowledgeable about mortgage-related

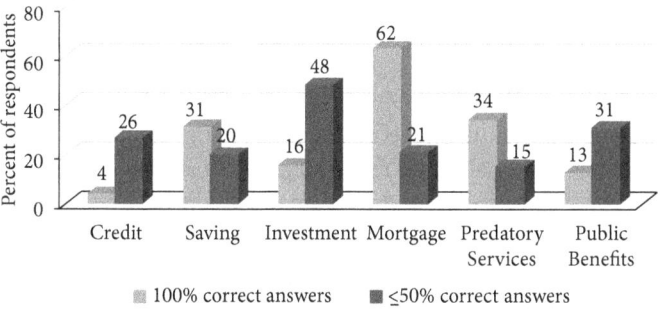

Figure 12.4 Respondents' Performance on each Subscale

matters. If low-to-moderate income clients are going to asset-building service providers for assistance with their mortgage issues, it is imperative that service providers be better equipped to help them.

Knowledge about public benefits is another area that needs to be improved. In the current difficult economic environment, more families are in need of assistance, both public and private. If service providers are themselves ignorant about the public benefits that are available, or about how the various policies interact with one another, they will not be able to effectively connect their clients to these resources. Yet the data indicate that 31% of respondents were not able to answer half or more of the items on the public benefits subscale correctly.

There is also a wide range in the knowledge of respondents regarding investments. Respondents in this study tended to be less knowledgeable than the general population, and some 48% of respondents were not able to answer half or more of the items correctly. One of the key objectives of the asset-building field is the creation of wealth for lower-income families, and a principal vehicle for wealth creation is investment. Knowledge of how to navigate the various investment tools and products available in the marketplace is therefore crucial if service providers are to be effective in achieving the goal of helping their clients create long-term wealth. Findings from this study suggest that service providers may require additional knowledge in the area of investments to better serve their clients. It is plausible that lower knowledge levels may be a reflection of service providers' own economic situations, where few have the means to interact with investment products. However, as alluded to earlier, the nature of the questions asked in this study are very rudimentary, and independent of one's experience with investing. Hence the effects of one's economic background are likely minimal as well.

When respondents were classified based on the number of items correctly answered, the data indicate that almost half the respondents answered between 60% and 80% of the questions correctly, while slightly less than a quarter of the respondents answered less than 60% of the items correctly. Only three in ten correctly answered 80% or more of the items. These findings suggest that, while service providers had a reasonable level of financial literacy that is comparable to the general population, this level of literacy may be less than ideal for the asset-building field. Furthermore, between 21% and 44% of respondents did not know how to answer any of the questions across the various financial domains, and up to 42% of respondents may actually have known less than the general population. Much remains to be done to increase the financial literacy of service providers.

With regard to the level of debt literacy, while respondents in the asset-building field had a statistically similar level of literacy as the general population, it has to be noted that less than half of all respondents were able to correctly answer the questions pertaining to compound interest and credit card repayment, and only a small handful were able to understand the time value of money. In addition, 37% of the respondents (44% if missing responses are included) failed to answer a single question correctly, while close to a quarter of respondents answered only one out of the three items correctly. Only 3% of respondents were able to answer all three items correctly. The data clearly indicate that the debt literacy levels of service providers were rather low, and that more attention to increasing knowledge in this area is needed.

Unlike for financial literacy where a gap between the self-reported knowledge and actual literacy levels was observed among service providers, the data suggest that the high levels of self-reported financial abilities by respondents are reflective of the highly positive financial practices observed among service providers. The majority of respondents exhibited the various desired financial behaviors and engagement with key financial products such as saving and checking accounts, and most were classified as having high levels of functioning in the various financial practice domains. However, there remains much room for improvement. For instance, 30% of respondents did not use a budget or track their expenses, while around 25% did not have any emergency funds, did not save or invest regularly, and did not have long-term saving goals (see Appendix 12.2). In addition, respondents' engagement in various investment practices could be further strengthened, as fewer than half of respondents had investments outside of their employment-related retirement plans.

Engagement with the alternative or fringe financial services market could also be further reduced from the present levels where potentially close to a quarter of respondents had interacted with fringe financial products in the past year. While it is reassuring to note that engagement with the fringe market by service providers was rather limited, it nonetheless raises the question as to why these fringe activities were used at all in the first place, especially check-cashing services. Engagement in the fringe financial services market is generally considered as a negative or nonprotective financial practice (Moore, 2003). This is because fringe financial products frequently have higher costs associated with their use, and coupled with a higher risk of financial loss, result in a greater likelihood of wealth reduction. Service providers in the asset-building field typically steer their clients away from fringe financial products. It is, therefore, surprising to find that potentially up to a quarter of respondents engaged in fringe services.

The level of comfort and preparedness to deliver asset-building services should also be strengthened. While the majority of respondents reported that they feel sufficiently comfortable and prepared to work on the financial aspects of their clients' lives, a sizable proportion felt otherwise. In addition, close to 4 in 10 respondents felt that they were not able to provide effective financial counseling, nor did they know where to refer clients for additional services outside their respective agencies. This finding is similar to the results of a national study on teachers' capacity to teach personal finance, which found that 63.8% of respondents felt unqualified to teach financial literacy, and less than 20% felt very competent to teach financial literacy (Way & Holden, 2010).

Several structural factors may influence why asset-building service providers do not possess an ideal level of financial capability and why many do not feel equipped to deliver financial related services to clients. For example, it is possible that frontline service providers reflect the demographic trend of their clients in relation to income. A survey of nonprofit wages and benefits in the King, Pierce, and Snohomish Counties (Washington's largest greater metropolitan area) indicates that frontline staff, similar to those surveyed, are earning salaries between $35,000 and $42,000 annually (United Way of King County, 2011). This reflects between 55% and 75% of Area Median Income for this three-county region. It is also possible that service providers merely reflect the demographic trend that low- and moderate-income populations tend to have lower levels of financial capability (Bernheim, 1998; Jacob et al., 2000; Zhan et al., 2006). In other words, service providers may be roughly in the same "economic boat" as their clients.

Whether or not the service providers reflect this demographic trend, however does not explain why they do not have adequate training to provide asset-building services effectively. One plausible reason may be that there is currently no agreement on training curriculum for service providers engaged in asset building with their clients. While many of these programs have been evaluated for their immediate effectiveness in increasing a person's financial literacy, few, if any, have been evaluated for their effectiveness in building a person's financial capabilities or changing one's long-term financial practices. In other words, while service providers may have received financial training, it is not clear if the trainings they have received are sufficient for building their own financial capabilities or preparing them to engage in relationships that most effectively help their clients make long-term changes. Another factor may be related to the educational backgrounds of service providers. Service providers in the asset-building field in Washington State come from a wide range of educational backgrounds, and do not necessarily have a higher education degree in social work or a related field. This is largely due to the fact that most social service agencies engaged in asset building in Washington State do not have sufficient funding to pay at a level that attracts candidates with degrees in social work. This may affect the level of confidence that service providers feel in providing asset-building services to clients.

To address the gap between service providers' self-assessments of their financial capabilities and what they actually know and practice, periodic objective assessments of the strengths and gaps in knowledge, skills, and practices are recommended. Several respondents indicated anecdotally that their financial capabilities had been assessed for the very first time as a result of this study. With periodic objective assessments, service providers will be able to pin-point the areas that need to be addressed in their own personal lives, as well as identify areas of success that could be further strengthened. The results from such periodic assessments could also be used to customize trainings for service providers.

There is also a need to establish a training curriculum that systematically addresses the various aspects of service delivery in the asset-building field, from enhancing service providers' financial knowledge and practices, to equipping them with the skills to work effectively with clients to create changes in their financial lives. At a minimum, there should be a mandate for service providers to attend various trainings that are currently available. Such training programs should have the dual focus of enhancing the financial capabilities of service providers themselves, and equipping them with the skills and knowledge to work with clients to increase their financial capabilities and build long-term wealth.

Finally, there is a need to establish a set of core competencies and standards with respect to service providers' financial capabilities. While it is not adequate that service providers have the same level of financial knowledge as the general population, how much more would service providers need to know before being "certified" as being sufficiently prepared for the field? In addition, what are the core practices that all service providers are expected to have? Given that it is unlikely that the financial constraints on social service agencies will improve in the near future, how should training programs be structured to ensure that providers have the skills and knowledge they need to engage in strengths-based, empowerment-based practice with their clients? On the part of the lower-income clients, are there certain core competencies, knowledge, and behaviors that they should have as a result of receiving asset-building services? Discussions on these questions need to begin for service providers to be more effective, and for the asset-building field to advance further.

LIMITATIONS

There are several limitations in this study. First, due to the nonprobabilistic sampling method adopted for this study, and the narrow focus on only the state of Washington, any generalization of the findings to the broader asset-building field needs to be approached with caution. Regional differences in service providers' sociodemographic characteristics, different emphases and availability of training for service providers, and different asset-building services provided may lead to findings that are dissimilar to the current study. Nevertheless, this exploratory study represents the first steps in establishing and documenting the financial capabilities of service providers in the asset-building field.

Second, respondents' scope of work and the range of asset-building services provided at the agencies may influence the results but are not controlled for in this study. For example, it would be reasonable for a respondent providing housing services to be familiar with mortgage issues and be less conversant in investment-related issues. Future researchers may wish to control for the effects of the different agency types or services on service providers' level of financial capabilities.

Third, the self-assessments of financial knowledge, abilities, and comfort level in working with clients were based on single-item measures. Such global measures may not be sensitive enough to capture the various nuances involved. Multi-item scales or indexes could be developed to better capture and assess service providers' self-perceptions in future studies.

Lastly, there may be ambiguity in some of the terms used in the study. For example, when asked to self-assess whether they are financially literate, respondents may have perceived the question to ask about their financial practices rather than about their financial knowledge. This may explain some of the gap seen between the self-assessments and the objective measures. In addition, the term "financial counseling" may have meant different things to different respondents. Future studies may benefit from adding greater specificity to these terms.

CONCLUSION

In conclusion, this study has found that respondents in the asset-building field had very positive self-assessments of their financial capabilities. For many respondents, this positive self-assessment was justified, with the vast majority reporting high levels of functioning across the different financial practice domains, and with some 30% of respondents being able to answer more than 80% of the financial literacy questions correctly. In fact, on the whole, respondents had reasonable levels of financial literacy that are similar to those found in the general population. That said, there is still much that could be done to improve the financial capabilities of service providers. It would be reasonable to expect and require all service providers to have a higher level of competence and expertise when compared to the general population. If service providers are to be effective in assisting clients with their financial issues, it is imperative that they be well trained. This study has established the need for additional training, and has identified possible areas of focus for the training. With periodic and objective assessments of financial capabilities, as well as a comprehensive training plan, service providers' own financial capabilities could be strengthened. They can then be even more effective in helping low-to-modest income families break out of the cycle of poverty and get onto the path of wealth creation.

APPENDIX 12.1

Results of the Financial Literacy Items

	Percent of respondents reporting	Percent of general population reporting[1]
Credit		
Creditors are required to tell you the APR that you will pay when you get a loan.	77.6	92
If you expect to carry a balance on your credit card, the APR is the most important thing to look at when comparing credit card offers.	72.0	84
Your credit report includes employment data, your payment history, any inquiries made by creditors, and any public record information.	75.2	81
The finance charge on your credit card statement is what you pay to use credit.	68.8	69
Using extra money in a bank savings account to pay off high interest rate credit card debt is a good idea.	71.2	68
Your credit rating is not affected by how much you charge on your credit cards.	80.8	60
If your credit card is stolen and someone uses it before you report it missing, you are only responsible for $50, no matter how much they charge on it.	22.4	50
If you have any negative information on your credit report, a credit repair agency can help you remove that information.	48.0	30
If you are behind on debt payments and go to a credit counseling service, they can get the federal government to apply your income tax refund to pay off your debts.	31.2	22
Saving		
You should have an emergency fund that covers two to six months of your expenses.	92.8	94
If you have a savings account at a bank, you may have to pay taxes on the interest you earn.	80.0	86
If you buy certificates of deposit, savings bonds, or Treasury bills, you can earn higher returns than on a savings account, with little or no added risk.	73.6	74

(continued)

CONTINUED

With compound interest, you earn interest on your interest, as well as on your principal.	69.6	72
Whole life insurance has a savings feature while term life insurance does not.	45.6	60
Investment		
The earlier you start saving for retirement, the more money you will have because the effects of compounding interest increase over time.	85.6	92
A stock mutual fund combines the money of many investors to buy a variety of stocks.	64.8	75
Employers are responsible for providing the majority of funds that you will need for retirement.	81.6	72
Over the long term, stocks have the highest rate of return on money invested.	36.0	56
Mutual funds pay a guaranteed rate of return.	42.4	52
All investment products bought at your bank are covered by FDIC insurance.	39.2	33
Mortgage		
If you use your home as collateral for a loan, there is no chance of losing your home.	84.0	91
You could save thousands of dollars in interest costs by choosing a 15-year rather than a 30-year mortgage.	84.0	84
If the interest rate on an adjustable-rate mortgage loan goes up, your monthly mortgage payments will also go up.	77.6	77
Repeatedly refinancing your home mortgage over a short period of time results in added fees and points that further increase your debt.	72.0	72
Other		
Making payments late on your bills can make it more difficult to take out a loan.	84.8	94
Your bank will usually call to warn you if you write a check that would overdraw your account.	84.0	62

(continued)

CONTINUED

The cash value of a life insurance policy is the amount available if you surrender your life insurance policy while you're still alive.	36.8	56
After signing a contract to buy a new car, you have three days to change your mind.	17.6	18
Predatory Services		
Rapid refund services usually charge a higher fee.	76.0	Not available
Nonbank currency exchanges usually charge less than banks for cashing checking and other financial services.	55.2	Not available
Rapid refund services usually charge a higher fee for preparing your tax returns than government and community programs do.	80.0	Not available
Buying an item through rent-to-own plans usually costs less overall than buying the same item with a bank loan.	76.0	Not available
Predatory lending means taking unfair advantage of consumers who need to borrow money.	84.8	Not available
Payday loans usually have low interest rates.	88.0	Not available
Door-to-door salesmen have the best deals on insurance.	76.8	Not available
Loans that allow no interest for a certain period often have very high interest rates later.	75.2	Not available
Public Benefits		
The Child Tax Credit is a government benefit you can receive if you have a child under 13.	27.2	Not available
The Earned Income Tax Credit (EITC) is a government payment that rewards people for working.	70.4	Not available
You must owe income taxes in order to receive the Earned Income Tax Credit (EITC).	68.8	Not available
You can lose TANF (Temporary Assistance for Needy Families) benefits if you receive the Earned Income Tax Credit (EITC).	64.0	Not available
You only can receive Medicaid if you also receive Temporary Assistance for Needy Families (TANF) benefits.	65.6	Not available

(continued)

Continued

Debt Literacy[2]		
Suppose you owe $1,000 on your credit card and the interest rate you are charged is 20% per year compounded annually. If you didn't pay anything off, at this interest rate, how many years would it take for the amount you owe to double?	45	36
You owe $3,000 on your credit card. You pay a minimum payment of $30 each month. At an Annual Percentage Rate of 12% (or 1% per month), how many years would it take to eliminate your credit card debt if you made no additional new charges?	41	35
You purchase an appliance which costs $1,000. To pay for this appliance, you are given the following two options: (a) pay 12 monthly installments of $100 each; (b) borrow at a 20% annual interest rate and pay back $1,200 a year from now. Which is the more advantageous offer?	6	7

APPENDIX 12.2.

Financial Practices and Financial Product Ownership

	Percent of respondents reporting	Percent of general population reporting[3]
Cash-flow management		
Have checking account	97.6	89
Pay bills on time	96	88
Track expenses	82.4	79
Reconcile checkbook at the end of the month	48.8	75
Use a spending plan or budget	69.6	46
Credit management		
Have a credit card	85.6	79
Pay credit card balances in full	54.4	61
Review credit reports	85.6	58
Compare offers before applying for a credit card	84	35
Saving		
Have a savings account	96.8	80
Have an emergency fund	75.5	63

(continued)

CONTINUED

Save or invest money out of each paycheck	72.8	49
Save for long-term goals such as education, car, or home	75.2	39
Have certificates of deposit	25.6	30
Investment		
Have money spread over different types of investments	56.0	74
Have any retirement plans/accounts	75.2	63
Have any investment account	37.6	52
Have mutual funds	33.6	46
Have 401(k) plan or company pension plan	69.6	45
Have IRA/Keogh	31.2	43
Calculated net worth in past two years	45.6	40
Participated in employer's 401(k) retirement plan	74.4	37
Have public stock	20.0	24
Put money into other retirement plans such as an IRA	43.2	22
Have savings bonds	19.2	6
Other financial experience		
Own home	59.2	75
Bought a house	66.4	72
Do owe taxes each year	11.2	40
Often or always plan and set goals for financial future	70.4	36
Refinanced mortgage or loan for home improvements	29.6	35
Read about money management	86.6	20
Fringe services engagement in past 12 months		
Taken a pay day loan	4.0	5[4]
Taken a car title loan where the lender holds the title to your car until the loan is repaid	12.8	7[4]
Taken a cash advance on any credit cards	3.2	34[5]
Used a rent-to-own transaction as a way to buy an appliance or furniture	1.6	5[4]
Used a check cashing service	4.8	12[5]
Used a pawn shop for a small loan while the shop holds items of yours as collateral until the loan is repaid	3.2	8[4]
Cashed a blank check from a credit card company or a printed check from a finance company offering credit if the check is completed	3.2	5[5]

NOTES

1. Comparative figures are based on the findings from the Surveys of Consumers conducted in November and December, 2001 (Hilgert et al., 2003).
2. Comparative figures are based on the study by Lusardi and Tufano (2009) on debt literacy.
3. Unless otherwise indicated, the comparative figures are based on the findings from the Surveys of Consumers conducted in November and December, 2001 (Hilgert et al., 2003).
4. Comparative data from the National Financial Capability Study (Applied Research & Consulting LLC, 2009).
5. Comparative data from the Survey of Financial Literacy in Washington State (Moore, 2003)

REFERENCES

Anderson, S., Scott, J., & Zhan, M. (2004). *Financial Links for Low-Income People (FLLIP): Final evaluation report.* Urbana-Champaign: University of Illinois at Urbana-Champaign.

Applied Research & Consulting LLC. (2009). *Financial capability in the United States—Initial report of research findings from the 2009 national survey—A component of the National Financial Capability Study.* New York: FINRA Investor Education Foundation.

Barr, M. (2004). Banking the poor. *Yale Journal on Regulation, 21*(1), 121–237.

Bernheim, B. D. (1998). Financial literacy, education, and retirement saving. In O. S. Mitchell & S. J. Schieber (Eds.), *Living with defined contribution pensions* (pp. 380–68). Philadelphia: University of Pennsylvania.

Birkenmaier, J., & Curley, J. (2009). Financial credit: Social work's role in empowering low-income families. *Journal of Community Practice, 17,* 251–268.

Brobeck, S. (2008a). *The essential role of banks and credit unions in facilitating lower income household savings for emergencies.* Washington, DC: Consumer Federation of America.

Brobeck, S. (2008b). *Understanding the emergency savings needs of low and moderate income households: A survey-based analysis of impacts, causes, and remedies.* Washington, DC: Consumer Federation of America.

Bucks, B. K., Kennickell, A. B., Mach, T. L., & Moore, K. B. (2009). Changes in U.S. family finances from 2004 to 2007: Evidence from the survey of consumer finances. *Federal Reserve Bulletin, 95,* A1-A55.

Burst for Prosperity. (2011). *Prosperity blueprint: Building, leveraging and protecting Washington State's future.* Seattle, WA: Burst of Prosperity & Washington Asset Building Coalition.

Caputo, R. K. (2006). The earned income tax credit: A study of eligible participants vs. non-participants. *Journal of Sociology and Social Welfare, 33*(1), 9–29.

Caputo, R. K. (2009). EITC & TANF participation among young adult low-income families. *Northwestern Journal of Law and Social Policy, 4*(Winter), 136–149.

Caskey, J. P. (2006). *Can personal financial management education promote asset accumulation by the poor?* Terre Haute: Networks Financial Institute, Indiana State University.

Center for Social Development. (n.d.). *Individual development accounts*. Retrieved September 20, 2011, from http://csd.wustl.edu/AssetBuilding/Pages/IndividualDevelopmentAccounts.aspx

Clancy, M., Grinstein-Weiss, M., & Schreiner, M. (2001). *Financial education and savings outcomes in individual development accounts*. St. Louis, MO: Washington University, Center for Social Development.

Denavas-Walt, C., Proctor, B. D., & Smith, J. C. (2010). Income, poverty, and health insurance coverage in the United States: 2009. *Current Population Reports, P60–238*. Washington, DC: US Census Bureau.

Fellowes, M., & Mabanta, M. (2008). Banking on wealth: America's new retail banking infrastructure and its wealth-building potential. Washington, DC: Metropolitan Policy Program, Brookings Institution.

FINRA . (2009). *Financial capability in the United States: National survey—executive summary*. Washington, DC: FINRA Investor Education Foundation.

FINRA . (n.d.). States ranked most and least likely to engage in five key measures of financial capability. Retrieved June 15, 2011, from http://www.usfinancialcapability.org/download/State_rankings_rev_101103v2.pdf

Hilgert, M. A., Hogarth, J. M., & Beverly, S. G. (2003, July). Household financial management: The connection between knowledge and behavior. *Federal Reserve Bulletin, 89*, 309–322.

Jacob, K., Hudson, S., & Bush, M. (2000). *Tools for survival: An analysis of financial literacy programs for lower-income families*. Chicago, IL: Woodstock Institute.

Johnson, E., & Sherraden, M. (2007). From financial literacy to financial capability among youth. *Journal of Sociology and Social Welfare, 34*(3), 119–146.

LIMRA. (2010). *Ownership of individual life insurance falls to 50-year low*. LIMRA reports. Retrieved June 15, 2011, from http://www.limra.com/newscenter/newsarchive/archivedetails.aspx?prid=145

Lusardi, A., & Tufano, P. (2009). *Debt literacy, financial experiences, and overindebtedness*. NBER Working Paper Series. Cambridge, MA: National Bureau of Economic Research.

Moore, D. (2003). *Survey of financial literacy in Washington State: Knowledge, behavior, attitudes, and experiences*. Pullman: Social and Economic Sciences Research Center, Washington State University.

Rand, D. (2004, May–June). Financial education and asset-building programs for welfare recipients and low-income workers: The Illinois experience. *Clearinghouse Review Journal of Poverty Law and Policy*, 49–64.

Schreiner, M., Clancy, M., & Sherraden, M. (2002). *Saving performance in the American Dream Demonstration—A national demonstration of individual development accounts*. St. Louis, MO: Washington University, Center for Social Development.

Sherraden, M. S. (2010). *Financial capability: What is it, and how it can be created?* St. Louis, MO: Washington University, Center for Social Development.

Sherraden, M. S., Laux, S., & Kaufman, C. (2007). Financial education for social workers. *Journal of Community Practice, 15*(3), 9–36.

Sledge, J., Tescher, J., & Gordon, S. (2010). *From financial education to financial capability: Opportunities for innovation*. Chicago, IL: Center for Financial Services Innovation.

United Way of King County. (2011). *2011–2012 wage and benefit survey of King, Pierce and Snohomish County nonprofit organizations*. Seattle, WA: United Way of King County.

Washington State Department of Commerce. (2008). *Expanding asset building in Washington.* Olympia, Washington: Washington State Department of Commerce.

Way, W. L., & Holden, K. (2010). *Teachers' background and capacity to teach personal finance: Results of a national study.* Denver, CO: National Endowment for Financial Education.

Zhan, M., Anderson, S., & Scott, J. (2006). Financial knowledge of the low-income population: Effects of a financial education program. *Journal of Sociology and Social Welfare, 33*(1), 53–74.

13

The Role of Social Work in Financial Capability

Shaping Curricular Approaches

JULIE BIRKENMAIER, TERI KENNEDY, JAMES KUNZ,
REBECCA SANDER AND SHELLEY HORWITZ

Social workers engage in financial capability in a wide variety of settings, yet often receive little preparation during their professional education. Several pioneering efforts are underway in social work to provide knowledge and skills for financial capability practice. Building on the work of previous chapters, this chapter offers approaches for social work educators interested in expanding financial capability curricular offerings, including new coursework, content for infusion in existing courses, or other options, such as continuing education and field education. Social workers should have financial literacy knowledge and skills, understanding of appropriate financial products and services for vulnerable families, and involvement in policy and program efforts to define and expand access to financial capability (US Department of the Treasury, 2010)

This chapter will: (1) discuss the role of social work in financial capability work and the overall aim of financial capability education within social work education; (2) explore the financial literacy knowledge needed for financial capability practice; (3) discuss several initial efforts by social work programs to increase the financial education, literacy, and capability among social work students at both the BSW and MSW levels, as well as with social work practitioners; (4) propose considerations for social work educators interested in exploring the possibilities for expanding the opportunities for students and practitioners to increase their financial capability to be prepared for practice; and (5) discuss the implications for financial capability education in the context of recent policy changes that impact financial capability.

THE ROLE OF SOCIAL WORK IN FINANCIAL CAPABILITY PRACTICE

Social workers are currently engaged in financial capability practice through a wide range of settings and activities, with a diversity of populations. Social workers teach basic financial education to individuals, families, and groups, in a wide variety of settings, including food pantries, neighborhood-based service centers, homeless shelters, mental health agencies (Barczyk & Lincove, 2010; Marson, Savage, & Phillips, 2006), substance abuse treatment settings, health and hospice settings (Barnett & Pearce, 2010; Davis, 1983), refugee resettlement agencies, workforce development sites (Anuszkiewicz, 2007), with older adults (Allen, 2000), and in domestic violence and other community-based agencies (Sanders, Weaver, & Schnabel, 2007; VonDeLinde & Correia, 2005). Financial capability practice is often less formal and is woven into other work, such as provision of basic needs, case management, clinical services, resettlement activities, and employment support services. Social workers assist clients by helping them set financial goals, develop and maintain budgets, manage financial resources, build and maintain good credit, and understand mainstream financial institutions (e.g., banks and credit unions), and financial products (e.g., checking and savings accounts and debit and credit cards) (Naleppa, 2006; Sanders & Schnabel, 2007). Social workers also teach clients about accumulating points needed for eligibility for social security retirement.

Social workers build financial capability among clients by assisting them to access mainstream financial services, such as opening a checking account or savings account, or borrowing money from a bank or credit union. Social workers also refer clients to resources for financial planning, such as credit counseling agencies, financial advisers, and attorneys. Social workers work with many client populations, such as older adults and their families (Naleppa, 2006), clients struggling with poverty (Zhan, Anderson, & Scott, 2006), clients who have experienced intimate partner violence (Sanders & Schnabel, 2007), and clients living with disabilities (Putnam et al., 2005). Social workers assist clients to increase their financial capability through saving in individual development account (IDA) programs (Schreiner, Tin Ng, & Sherraden, 2006), in microenterprise programs (Sherraden, Sanders, & Sherraden, 2004), and homeownership programs and credit building work (DiGiulo & Janosik, 1982), tax preparation and earned income tax credit (EITC) services (Lim & Lemieux, 2008), and financial policy advocacy work (Missouri Budget Project, 2009). Social workers also work with other organizations and their volunteers, such as AARP for tax preparation for older adults. The goal of these activities is financial inclusion, or "to provide increased opportunity to act through access to beneficial financial products and institutions" (Sherraden, chapter 1, this volume), and allow people to utilize their financial literacy toward their financial best interest. Social workers, therefore, play an important, if often unrecognized, role in assisting many populations, including low-income and vulnerable populations, to become financially literate, expand their opportunities, and to access mainstream financial institutions.

Practice Challenges

The first challenge for the social work profession is to define an appropriate role for financial capability work within broad areas of social work competence, and provide practitioners with appropriate knowledge and guidance. The most familiar area of financial capability practice for social workers is helping clients obtain social benefits. Moreover, social workers have expertise and experience in working with low-income and vulnerable families. They also should know when to collaborate with and refer clients to personal finance professionals—such as certified financial planners, consumer and family economists, housing counselors, credit counselors, peer counselors, and attorneys—who have specialized knowledge to assist with some kinds of financial challenges. Social workers benefit from working and collaborating with these professionals (Sherraden, chapter 1, this volume).

The second challenge for social work is developing appropriate knowledge and skills for financial capability work. Social workers typically learn knowledge and skills for this role *while in the field* (Huisamen & Weyers, 2009), or through packaged curriculum, observation, continuing education, or mentoring from others. Too often, social work students lack the personal finance knowledge to cope with their own financial challenges (National Student Loan Program, 2010), much less deal with the financial problems of others (Sherraden et al., 2007). There is no research on the degree to which on-the-job training prepares social workers for financial capability practice. Vernon Loke (chapter 12, this volume) concludes that service providers of asset-building services need additional training and preparation. Given the financial challenges of social work clients, it is reasonable to assume that, for effective practice, social workers should possess at least basic financial literacy knowledge. Following is a discussion of the core areas of financial knowledge for financial literacy and other knowledge that may be required for work with specific populations and settings.

FINANCIAL KNOWLEDGE AND SKILLS FOR SOCIAL WORKERS

Some combination of knowledge, skills, confidence, and motivation is needed for financial literacy, yet there is little general agreement about the specific areas of knowledge needed for financial literacy (Huston, 2010; US Department of the Treasury, 2010). Huston (2010) reviewed over 71 studies drawn from 52 different data sets, and found no consistency in the definition and measurement of financial literacy in practice and research. Remund (2010) reviewed more than 100 resources, including academic and professional journal articles, and proposed that the four most common operational definitions of financial literacy include the following:

- budgeting (i.e., creating financial goals and spending and savings plans);
- credit (i.e., learning to read and correct credit reports, accessing reports, reading credit card statements, and building credit);
- banking (i.e., accessing financial institutions and their products); and

- investing (i.e., investment products, such as stocks, bonds, mutual funds, and a diversification strategy) (OECD, 2005; Sanders & Schnabel, 2007; Sherraden, Laux, & Kaufman, 2007).

While these four topics can provide the core of knowledge, a wider range of topics may be needed for social workers to fully engage in financial capability with their clients. Areas of knowledge and skills that are often taught—in various combinations and with varying emphasis depending on the needs of particular populations—are displayed in Table 13.1. Which topics are covered depend on considerations such as time allocated for financial education, number of sessions, purpose, specific knowledge needed by clients, language and cultural issues, and client general literacy level (Anderson, Zhan, & Scott, 2007).

Tailoring financial knowledge and skills to meet the needs of specific populations is imperative. For example, it may be important to examine the curriculum through the lens of personal safety when working with victims of intimate partner violence (Sanders, Weaver, & Schnabel, 2007). The interaction of mental health, individual and family well-being and satisfaction, and financial strain is well known (Britt, Grable, Nelson Goff, & White, 2008; Jenkins et al., 2008), and could be a valuable addition to knowledge for social workers. Social workers can utilize this knowledge in direct practice in mental health and family service agencies (Britt et al., 2008). Lastly, social work educators can discuss the ways in which financial capability can be integrated into different types of settings, so students can apply knowledge in various employment settings. Social workers may want to include carefully chosen questions about financial circumstances and assets on family assessment forms in order to institutionalize financial capability as a part of direct practice. Another possibility is to assist clients in defining relevant financial issues and concerns, exploring options, and planning for action to address their financial circumstances. In other cases, social workers may assist clients to locate financial education and counseling services. At a minimum, basic financial literacy is needed in order to be able to assist vulnerable and low-income families.

FINANCIAL CAPABILITY IN THE CURRICULUM

Currently, many social work programs integrate aspects of financial capability in various courses, including: (1) economics, public benefits, and alternative financial institutions in social welfare policy, policy practice, and direct practice courses; (2) retirement planning, power of attorney, estate planning, and taxes in courses related to older adults; (3) discrimination and oppression, which impact financial services, in diversity courses; and (4) asset development in community practice and policy courses. Stand-alone courses on economics and community economic and social development complement the infusion of financial topics across curricula (Hooyman, 2006). These efforts provide a starting point for addressing financial capability in a holistic manner.

Table 13.1. FINANCIAL LITERACY KNOWLEDGE AND SKILLS

Alternative financial institutions and products *Skills*:	Earnings-related concepts *Skills*:	Retirement planning *Skills*:
Analyze the risks and benefits of utilizing alternative financial institutions and products, such as payday loans and car title loans.	Demonstrate knowledge of earnings-related concepts, such as gross and net pay, benefits, and taxes. Analyze the mandatory and voluntary paycheck deductions.	Calculate estimated retirement savings needs in today's dollars. Explain various types of retirement savings vehicles. Explain social security (retirement).
Asset-development opportunities *Skills*:	**Estate Planning** *Skills*:	**Risk management** *Skills*:
Identify, describe, and distinguish between various types of asset-building opportunities, such as individual development accounts, microenterprise, homeownership, and college savings program. Demonstrate understanding of risks and benefits of various assets.	Demonstrate understanding of the elements of an estate and planning tools, such as wills, trusts, and contracts.	Planning for crises through use of various types of insurance.
Bankruptcy *Skills*:	**Financial education curricular offerings and financial counseling for low-income and vulnerable populations** *Skills*:	**Saving and investing** *Skills*:
Demonstrate understanding of types of bankruptcy and the associated requirements.	Demonstrate knowledge of financial education curricular offerings for vulnerable and low-income populations.	Demonstrate understanding between saving and investing. Appropriately utilize investment opportunities (stocks, bonds, mutual funds, real estate, collectibles) for income and/or long-term goals.

(continued)

Table 13.1. Continued

Budgeting Skills:	Financial records Skills:	Taxes, tax deductions and credits Skills:
Create all components of a budget. Analyze a budget.	Assemble, create, and maintain the important financial records, such as a checkbook, tax records, bills, and legal documents related to purchases, insurance, and investments.	Demonstrate understanding of marginal tax rate. Analyze strategies to avoid overpayment of income taxes. Demonstrate understanding of earned income tax credit.
Cash management Skills:	**Identity theft** Skills:	**Time value of money and inflation** Skills:
Develop a spending plan.	Take needed precautions to avoid identity theft. Take appropriate steps if become victim to identity theft.	Demonstrate understanding of time value of money. Demonstrate understanding of inflation.
Consumer protection Skills:	**Policy impacting financial literacy and capability** Skills:	**Traditional financial institutions, services, and products** Skills:
Analyze subscription contracts and demonstrate understanding of rights and responsibilities.	Demonstrate understanding of major policies that impact financial literacy and capability, such as those pertaining to financial education requirements, and those related to access, such as the Community Reinvestment Act.	Compare the advantages and disadvantages of services and products, including banks, savings and loans, credit unions, saving accounts, checking accounts, and saving tools.

(continued)

Table 13.1. CONTINUED

Credit (i.e., cost, types, best uses, reports, building, counseling) Skills:	Public benefits Skills:	Values, financial goals, and decisions Skills:
Calculate the cost of credit, comparison shop, and analyze the risks and benefits of credit options. Plan and meet payment obligations. Track borrowing habits. Demonstrate understanding of credit report and credit card statements. Demonstrate understanding of ways to build credit.	Demonstrate understanding of major public benefits programs, such as TANF, WIC, Food Stamps, Social Security, and unemployment.	Demonstrate understanding about role of values and financial goals in financial decisions. Analyze trade-offs in spending decisions. Make financial decisions.
Culture, language, discrimination Skills:	**Purchase of durable goods** Skills:	
Demonstrate understanding of historical and current impact of culture, language, and discrimination on financial capability.	Analyze the risks and benefits of purchasing major assets, such as a home or vehicle.	

SOURCES: Anderson, Zhan, and Scott (2007); Bostic and Lee (2009); Garman and Forgue (2008); Sherraden, Laux, and Kaufman (2007).

In recent years, there have been several endeavors within social work education programs to increase the financial capability of social work students at the BSW and MSW levels. Social work programs have begun to introduce financial capability in several ways: (1) small units within existing courses (face-to-face and online); (2) continuing education courses for alumni; (3) nontraditional, short courses; (4) traditional courses including social issues and household finances approaches to economics, family asset and community capacity building, and financial literacy and capability for social workers; (5) out-of-classroom educational opportunities; and (6) field education placements in agencies that provide free tax preparation, credit counseling, financial education, financial counseling, asset development, and predatory lending prevention programs. Social work schools collaborate to develop curricular resources on financial capability. These efforts ultimately are geared toward developing financial capability knowledge and skills among social work practitioners who work at the individual, family, group, organizational, and community levels in direct and indirect practice, research, advocacy, and policy.

Three Curricular Models for Financial Capability

This section introduces pioneering efforts by three schools of social work—Arizona State University, University of Maryland, and a collaborative among several schools of social work in New York City—to build financial capability. While not exhaustive of all curricular efforts related to financial capability in social work education, the case examples represent a range of approaches to financial capability education. Each case is described with four elements in mind. First, **partnerships** with other units within the university and/or external entities provide resources, legitimacy, and support. These partnerships assist in curriculum development and/or implementation. Second, each of the programs responds to each school of social work **interests and resources**. Third, each program was developed in a way that was **flexible** for maximum student and stakeholder support and usage. Programs experimented with various curricular offerings, and made changes according to the interests of intended audiences. Fourth, each program **measured outcomes**. While some programs have only begun to develop tools for assessment, each recognizes the key role of evidence-based program development.

ARIZONA STATE UNIVERSITY

In 2004, an effort to address the needs of BSW students at Arizona State University began the development of financial capability curriculum with the development of three new courses. With administrative support to develop instructor capacity, the social work program **partnered** with a university-wide borderlands (i.e., land near the US-Mexico border) initiative to hire a new faculty member with expertise in economics, assets, and borderlands challenges. This partnership benefited the social work program and the borderlands initiatives by facilitating interdisciplinary knowledge and offering specialized expertise in social and economic justice with populations of the Southwest.

The initiative responded to program **interests and resources** by including (1) field education faculty, who expressed a need for social work students to have financial capability knowledge; (2) BSW students, who were struggling to integrate required macroeconomic content with social work; and (3) other faculty and administrators, who were eager to develop new courses. Anecdotally, students expressed an interest in alternative economic content that would offer clear linkages to direct social work practice. The first course, Economics: A Social Issues Perspective, is an introduction to economic principles through "the lens of contemporary social issues for social work, journalism, communication, justice studies, and related professions" (Kennedy, 2008, p. 1). The connection between economics and social work is made through contemporary social issues, and the course examines the way in which economic policy affects specific populations and examines the relationship between economics and relevant social policy issues (Steiner & Kennedy, 2004).

In 2005, a second course was developed entitled Latinos: Financial Services and Community Asset Building, and later renamed Border Families and Community Asset Building Policies. The course is about financial services and community asset development along the US-Mexico border. The course is divided into three topics: (1) socioeconomic status of border families; (2) wealth and asset-building policies that address the rise of predatory financial products and practices that strip wealth and assets from border families; and (3) advocacy for sustainable community economic development on the border (Robles, 2008, p. 1).

The third course, Financial Literacy for Social Workers, introduces students to "financial literacy and empowerment-practice with individuals and families across the life cycle" and is geared "for social work, justice studies, and related disciplines" (Kennedy, 2009, p. 1). The course is built on the premise that financial empowerment practice fills a critical gap in social work practice by providing content in financial education, consumer credit counseling, asset building, and financial planning at each stage of the life cycle (Kennedy, 2009, p. 1). Course objectives include increasing student ability to explain the role of financial capability and financial literacy in social work practice; discussing social work value and ethical considerations as they relate to the relationship between financial literacy and economic justice; identifying the economic needs of individuals and families across the life cycle; and describing the difference between economic stress that arises as a product of conditions in the general economy, normative events in the family life cycle, or as an unexpected stressor. Also discussed are key economic terms, concepts, and resources related to financial literacy, and the role of the social work profession in engaging in financial empowerment practice (Kennedy, 2009, pp. 1–2).

Over time, the delivery format and structure of courses has evolved to be appealing to students. In this way, *flexible* development has been an important aspect of curriculum development, both in terms of delivery format and integration into different aspects of school and university curricular offerings. For example, the economics course was first offered in a face-to-face format, and is now offered in an online format throughout the year. As a result, the course has proven a popular alternative to the traditional required economics course. The course on financial services and community asset building in the Latino community gained greater student interest and higher enrollments when it was renamed, offered online, cross-listed for both undergraduate and graduate students, and became part of a Graduate Latino Cultural Competency Certificate and an Undergraduate Certificate in Economic Justice (Office of Latino Projects, n.d.). The BSW elective for the school's social welfare concentration and minor is a cross-listed elective for the MSW foundation year, and is also part of the course offerings for an undergraduate university certificate in economic justice.

Considered together, these three courses are intended to impact the financial capability of students in social work and related degree programs. All of the courses are taught by social work faculty, which reinforces the idea that financial capability is a social work topic. While the courses are not structured as a unit, they collectively address areas of knowledge for integration of financial capability into practice, policy, and program design and implementation. To increase student enrollment, the courses are cross-listed.

Measuring outcomes for this initiative is in the developmental stage; all courses are individually evaluated by the students using a standard course evaluation form, and the courses are not currently evaluated together as an initiative. However, faculty who teach the courses are engaged in a planning process for evaluation of the financial capability initiative.

UNIVERSITY OF MARYLAND SCHOOL OF SOCIAL WORK

The Financial Social Work Initiative (FSWI) at the University of Maryland School of Social Work (UMSSW) is a platform enabling the school to play a leadership role in building economic strength in communities. Organized in the fall of 2008, the FSWI utilizes extensive *partnerships* to accelerate the integration of the evolving field of financial capability into social work practice and theory by capitalizing on both the academic infrastructure and its community outreach services. The FSWI is led by a steering committee of internal administrators, faculty and staff, and external partners. Internal staff includes the Office of the Dean, the Social Work Community Outreach Service (SWCOS), the Office of Continuing Education, the Office of Alumni and Development, the Director of Communications, the Office of Financial Education and Wellness, and the Office of External Affairs. External partners include the Maryland CASH Campaign (a network of free tax preparation sites and financial education and counseling programs from across the state), Baltimore CASH Campaign, and various corporate, community, and private foundations. The initiative actively builds and supports a professional network in this area by marshaling the wider institution's resources, providing regular communication among partners, and involving key administrators and faculty.

The FSWI responds to program *interests and resources* in a variety of ways by providing academic training, field placement experiences, research, and continuing education in financial social work. The FSWI was inspired by local social work practitioners who recognized the need for education and skills in financial stability, asset-building, and policy issues, and offered adjunct instructor capacity to the school. Demand from employers for social work graduates with knowledge and experience in financial capability had outpaced supply. Alumni with an interest in financial social work challenged the school to take a leadership role. Funders were willing investors in building training and community-based program capacity. Finally, field placements, supported by stipends, had been created by SWCOS that provided social work students with experience in supporting financial stability at the individual and community levels.

The initiative has developed *flexible* and diverse offerings rather than standard courses, such as:

- a day-long continuing professional education course entitled, Introduction to Financial Stability for Clients, offered throughout the State of Maryland;
- a three-credit, advanced year master's level elective course;
- out-of-classroom educational offerings for master's students, including Credit Cafes, a booth where students can review their credit report and learn about building credit) and informal "Lunch & Learn" brown bag sessions for students focused on financial capability;
- a "mini-mester" course offering minimal academic credit;
- a public webpage (www.ssw.umaryland.edu/fsw) that has links to educational offerings, policy and practice resources, a research scholar network and a LinkedIn networking site; and
- paid master's level field placements, including some new ones, that address financial issues at the individual and community level.

Partnerships have been created to offer field placements related to financial capability. SWCOS enables MSW students to be placed in community-based settings that ordinarily would not be able to support a social work intern.[1] External funds from partners pay for the costs of administration of the field placements, the salaries of faculty-based field instructors, and, where possible, stipends for students to attract and support students to these nontraditional placements.

Three recent initiatives involve financial capacity and asset building: Neighborhood Fellows, Maryland Community Fellows (MCF), and the Financial Literacy Volunteer Initiative (FLVI). The *Neighborhood Fellows* program is a neighborhood revitalization partnership that places 10 social work interns each year with organizations engaged in community economic development. Funded by small grants from local foundations and banks, interns engage in prevention and intervention activities including foreclosure prevention, earned income tax credit outreach, awareness campaigns about predatory lending, homeownership counseling, and locality development efforts to stabilize and market targeted Baltimore neighborhoods.

The *Maryland Community Fellows* program provides approximately eight social work students per year in financial social work knowledge and skills. Funded by the Maryland Department of Housing and Community Development, this program places students in Community Action Agencies around the state. Objectives include outreach, education, and free tax preparation aimed at building economic self-sufficiency. The Fellows work on a variety of asset-building strategies to alleviate poverty. For example, they have developed an "economic success" curriculum to use with clients and small groups. At their placement sites, all interns are trained and certified and serve as volunteer tax preparers at the basic level. During their internship, some interns have advanced to be certified at the intermediate and site manager level for tax preparation.

Finally, the *Financial Literacy Volunteer Initiative* (FLVI) teaches low-income middle-school youth in Baltimore City to earn, keep, and spend money wisely through delivery of a four-session financial literacy curriculum. The curriculum was designed to meet new state standards for financial education that will be required in the fall 2011 for students in grades 3 through 12. A stipend is provided for 14 second-year social work interns to coordinate 10 social work student volunteers who receive a smaller stipend for classroom facilitation. The initiative is funded by Citi Foundation and draws on the resources of its partners—Maryland CASH Campaign, Operation Hope, and Take Charge America—for curriculum content, training, and access to middle schools.

The FSWI is engaged in the development of *measuring outcomes* of all of its efforts. A research committee, supported by a research assistant, conducted an environmental scan of peer-reviewed journals and social work curricula, and designed a research project to examine the effects of the new continuing professional education course. The research committee also tracks field placement contributions, including the number of tax returns filed and the amount of money returned through the EITC. In academic year 2009–2010, social work students in the Community Fellows program assisted 335 individuals with tax returns that returned a total of $370,842 to those low-income families. Outcome measures have been developed for the FLVI in the Baltimore City public schools, including pre/post knowledge quizzes, and youth financial behavior indicators, such as their ability to create a budget, track spending, make financial decisions based on needs as opposed to wants, and save.

A system to measure impact of prevention efforts implemented by Neighborhood Fellows is in development. While data are collected on number of foreclosures averted and number of accounts opened at banks or credit unions, more challenging is capturing longer-term outcomes related to community economic stability and growth. Faculty are developing a system to collect both individual and community-level data to measure the effects of prevention efforts.

New York City Collaborative

With the support of deans and directors and supported by a grant from the New York Community Trust, seven New York City social work schools—Silberman School of Social Work at Hunter College, Fordham University, Lehman College, Long Island University, New York University, Touro College, and Yeshiva University—have created a collaborative *partnership* to deliver financial capability education to social work students. An interuniversity committee, the Economic Literacy Curriculum Committee (ELCC), coordinates the development, testing, and implementation of an innovative curriculum to advance economic literacy as a component in social work education. The goal of the curriculum is to identify and teach the competencies for social workers to assist families in economic distress to learn about financial management, get financial help, and gain access to asset-building resources. In keeping with the Council on Social Work Education's (CSWE) Educational Policy and Accreditation Standards (EPAS) (2008), the following economic competencies have been established. These include the ability to: (1) identify and discuss financial issues; (2) assist clients to obtain and retain appropriate benefits; (3) help clients understand asset-building options; and (4) describe a basic understanding of the market economy and how it contributes to economic well-being or economic stress experienced by individuals, families, and communities.[2]

The curricular offerings are structured for continual and *flexible* development. Drawing on the instructor capacity of the collaborating programs, the curriculum is an online course comprising stand-alone modules that can be integrated into the classroom courses that range from practice labs and casework to social welfare and social policy. The modular format offers a number of advantages. The curriculum is available to instructors at all universities participating in the ELCC. Faculty may choose to integrate one or more modules into their courses. Alternatively, social work programs may offer all of the modules combined into a single required or elective course. Interactive technology is a cost-effective and flexible method that allows curriculum content to be updated continuously and disseminated widely throughout the ELCC collaborative. Each university can choose the module(s) that cover the competency(ies) that match their program's *interests and resources*.

The curriculum includes cross-method practice skills and tools for clinical and community practitioners that target micro to macro client systems. A self-reflection section of exercises, vignettes, and case studies helps students increase self-awareness and personal understanding of how beliefs, culture, and class may influence financial capability topics in professional practice. Core social work values and ethics are interwoven throughout courses by using implicit and explicit case examples.

Another section of the curriculum provides an overview of the structure of the economy. The goal is to develop a context for understanding the relationship between the economy and a family's personal finances. This section includes learning how the economy functions, economic terminology and concepts, relevant economic policy debates, how public policy addresses fluctuations in the economy, and poverty measurements. The presentation is lively, with illustrative cartoons, charts, and sample discussion questions.

During the pilot phase, aspects of the curriculum were tested in student focus groups, workshops, and large group presentations. Students participated in self-reflective exercises designed to increase awareness of values about money, and to assess and rate their personal comfort in discussing financial issues with clients. Students were queried about the types of issues that clients commonly present in practice, and information they think would be most useful. Students mentioned that clients have trouble budgeting, managing debt, and understanding credit reports, and many identified their own struggles in these areas. Students also expressed interest in the relationship between social and economic justice and issues involving race, class, and gender.

Also during the pilot phase, a short survey prior to curriculum exposure assessed student knowledge of public benefits, asset-building options for low-income clients, and the market economy. Survey results indicated strong interest in asset-building. The majority of students were unfamiliar with the concept of asset building for lower income people, and few have had knowledge of the EITC. Survey results also indicate interest in the topic and a perception that the topic is relevant to their practice. Surveys do not indicate much difference across methods in terms of comfort and familiarity of content areas. This survey is also given in the current implementation phase, with similar results thus far. To date, several hundred students have been exposed to segments of the curriculum.

Measuring Outcomes

The curriculum is being measured in the implementation phase through pre- and posttest. A brief pretest assesses students' awareness and knowledge about financial literacy. A posttest provides feedback on the knowledge gained from the content, and asks students about its usefulness and applicability in their practice, as well as the clarity of the content and accessibility of the online delivery system. The posttest data will include the numbers of students who make use of this knowledge in their field placements. In the near future, an online posttest will be embedded in the curriculum.

During the first six months after the launch, the curriculum had 4,450 hits, averaging 800 per month. The data has not been yet been fully analyzed to determine to what extent there have been multiple hits by the same user. The evaluation results will inform future curriculum modifications.

Thus far, six schools have integrated course material into practice labs, five have incorporated information into the orientation for incoming students and utilized the curriculum in entitlement workshops, and four are using the material in policy classes. Several schools are providing training on the curriculum for field instructors to reinforce course content with students and provide a feedback loop.

Program Elements Emphasized

These three efforts illuminate the innovation occurring in social work programs across the country to teach financial capability to students and practitioners. Efforts vary in the degree to which they emphasize particular elements. For example, the Arizona State University initiative focuses heavily on the program *interests and resources*. The location of their program and resources available to them has led to a population-specific curricular model organized into discrete courses. The University of Maryland initiative, with extensive **partnerships**, is an example of a comprehensive initiative, designed to reach students within and outside of credit-bearing courses and field education, as well as alumni and other practitioners with financial education. The New York City Collaborative, a module-based approach that can be used as a stand-alone course or as modules in existing courses, is focused on *flexible* development and **partnerships**. Each effort emphasizes elements tailored to their program.

Viewed as a group, these efforts provide a breadth of curricular offerings, including stand-alone courses, modules integrated into existing courses, dedicated, varied field education experiences, extracurricular opportunities, and continuing education opportunities. In each case, the need for financial capability education was made known by a constituent group—students, field instructors, alumni, and/or the community—and administrators supported curriculum development.

Curriculum has been tailored to meet their curricular and community interests, and influenced by the faculty, administrative, and financial resources offered.

While these case studies are informative, there are other possibilities for curricular innovation. For example, programs could develop a minor or certificate in financial management or capability, or make a course offered in another unit available to social work students. Curriculum may be provided in face-to-face, online, or hybrid formats. Another option is to partner with university extension faculty, who already provide a wide range of financial education topics geared for the public, and could be an invaluable resource in developing continuing education courses for alumni and other practitioners (Sherraden et al., 2007). As social work faculty and administrators consider integrating financial capability topics into the curriculum, administrators and faculty may wish to consider tailoring program elements (i.e., partnerships, program interests and resources, flexible development, and measuring outcomes) to meet the school's mission and goals most effectively.

CONSIDERATIONS FOR BUILDING FINANCIAL CAPABILITY EDUCATIONAL OFFERINGS

Social work programs new to financial capability and financial education are in a position to build on the efforts of the three programs discussed above. In addition to the possibility of learning from future papers and reports on their efforts, their current collective experience of introducing financial capability and integrating it into course work, field education, and continuing education for undergraduate and graduate social work students and practicing professionals raises considerations when trying to develop partnerships, build on program interests and resources, create offerings that are flexible, and measure outcomes.

Development of Partnerships

As highlighted in the case examples, development of partnerships can be helpful for generating support and resources for developing financial capability curriculum. Three areas are particularly important: knowledge and skills, instructor capacity, and administrative, faculty, and community support.

NEEDED KNOWLEDGE AND SKILLS

Social work has a long, and largely overlooked, history with financial capability practice (Stuart, chapter 2, this volume). Faculty in social work and other disciplines, as well as alumni and students can provide guidance in identifying the knowledge and skills regarding financial capability that are important to develop in the curriculum. Partnerships in the form of a curricular offering planning committee or an advisory committee, for example, provide a forum through which decisions about knowledge, skills, delivery formats, and how these relate to EPAS competencies and practice behaviors can be made with input from others.

INSTRUCTOR CAPACITY

In the early stages of offering integration or distinct curricular offerings, social work programs may be challenged to identify instructor capacity to teach financial capability. The capacity needed will depend on the knowledge and skills chosen for the curricular offering, and the competencies and practice behaviors (discussed below) developed for the program related to financial capability. In addition, different types of instructor capacity will be required depending on how the material is integrated into the curriculum. Will the school integrate material into current courses, or develop new ones? What audience will be served?

Significant instructor capacity is required for stand-alone courses on topics such as economics, personal finance, or asset development. To find such faculty, programs may hire adjunct instructors from the field, partner with faculty from other campus units including university extension and business, grant leave to existing faculty to develop capacity, or seek expertise with new faculty hires. In contrast, when schools choose to integrate financial capability content into existing courses, less intense instructor capacity building is required. Financial capability concepts can be integrated into Human Behavior in the Social Environment (HBSE), policy, practice, research, field education, and other elective courses. Faculty may need to learn only particular aspects of financial capability that relate to their areas of expertise. For example, instructors of HBSE courses could learn more about economic needs and stresses that occur over the life span, and integrate that content into their existing courses. Policy instructors could learn more about alternative financial institutions and efforts to regulate predatory financial services and products, and integrate this content into their courses.

ADMINISTRATIVE, FACULTY, AND COMMUNITY SUPPORT

Administrative, faculty, and community support is vital to the success of curricular innovations (Hooyman, 2006). First, support may be gained from community organizations through alumni and other practitioners who provide financial capability services in a variety of practice settings. Gaining faculty and administrative support may involve education and advocacy efforts for faculty and administrators who are unfamiliar with the concept of financial capability. Other like-minded faculty, alumni, and potential funders, in addition to those faculty members who may champion such curricular change, may be helpful allies in the process. Demonstrating the ways in which financial capability can be integrated into existing courses in a way that benefits students in field education may also be helpful (Hooyman, 2006). Faculty interested in including financial capability efforts may find that supporting and publicizing faculty teaching, research, and publishing interests that relate to financial capability, such as financial exploitation, asset development, and other areas, is helpful in gaining administrative and faculty support. Additionally, developing a set of practice behaviors that correspond to the appropriate CSWE EPAS competencies will also provide guidance to the curricular change effort (Hooyman, 2006).

Building on Program Interests and Resources

Faculty and administrators interested in financial capability curricular offerings will want to examine their program interests and resources. A possible first step is a review of current curriculum to determine the extent to which elements of financial capability are currently included, the results of which can provide a basis for expansion. Review of the mission and goals, and faculty scholarship and interest in related areas can provide information and direction for a financial capability initiative. In addition, faculty may also be able to gain support if they can clearly demonstrate a connection between financial capability and the CSWE's 2008 EPAS. If little content is infused in the curriculum, social work faculty may need to articulate the link between the social work mission and their program to justify inclusion of financial capability content. Sherraden (chapter 1, this volume) provides conceptual background that may be helpful in articulating the role of financial capability practice in social work.

Measurement of Outcomes

Social work programs that embrace financial capability as an important element of their curricular offerings also should measure outcomes. There are several ways to do this, including measuring outcomes of specific courses, measuring overall financial capability knowledge among students, and measuring outcomes as related to competencies and practice behaviors of the CSWE's 2008 EPAS. Work to conceptually link financial capability educational approaches to the EPAS has begun in programs that offer integrated and infused curricular offerings. While this discussion is meant to be illustrative only, the topics covered provide a starting point for dialogue and consideration.

In competency-based education, the focus of educational design is on outcomes, rather than inputs (Voorhees, 2002). In the 2008 EPAS, social work identified 10 core competencies, defined as "combination[s] of skills, abilities, and knowledge needed to perform a specific task" (US Department of Education, 2002, p. vii), that are necessary for their field and comprise the domain of social work practice. Each competency is operationalized by a set of generalist practice behaviors (or knowledge, values, and skills). Assessment is focused on whether these competencies have been achieved by graduates of the program. For example, the competency "identifying as a professional social worker" is comprised of the following generalist practice behaviors: advocate for client access to social work services; practice personal reflection and self-correction to assure continual professional development; attend to professional roles and boundaries; demonstrate professional demeanor in behavior, appearance, and communication; engage in career-long learning; and use supervision and consultation. Thus, social work graduates of both BSW and MSW programs are expected to master these generalist practice behaviors. Programs must structure curriculum so that knowledge, values, and skills associated with these practice behaviors are taught. Programs must further develop a plan to assess whether mastery has been achieved, including the specification of assignments that address the practice behaviors within each competency. Programs may also incorporate financial capability practice behaviors into practicum via learning agreements and field instructor training.

The same competencies are applicable for advanced practice; however, MSW programs develop additional practice behaviors associated with each competency germane to a particular concentration. For example, an MSW program that has a gerontology practice concentration would specify additional practice behaviors associated with each of the core competencies that comprise the domain of competent advanced social work practice with older adults (CSWE, 2009). They would also structure their advanced practice curriculum to impart the appropriate knowledge, values, and skills for these practice behaviors, and specific assignments that can be used to assess student mastery.

As illustrated by the examples in this chapter, social work programs have incorporated financial capability education at both the BSW and MSW level, as well as for alumni and practitioners, in various programmatic formats. For programs that incorporate financial capability content as a vital component of generalist social work practice, crucial linkages can be made between financial capability education and one or more of the core competencies to justify the educational effort. That linkage could describe the generalist financial capability practice behaviors that students must demonstrate within each identified competency.

The linkage could be made in a number of ways for foundation and advanced practice. Table 13.2 demonstrates how programs can articulate practice behaviors associated with financial capability specifically linked to the competencies.

For example, a BSW program might determine that generalist social work practice should include knowledge of financial education services available to clients, so that they can advocate for client access (one of the practice behaviors that comprise EPAS 2.1.1: Identifying as a Professional Social Worker). For advanced social work practice, programs augment the generalist practice behaviors with advanced knowledge and skills. For example, an MSW program that offers financial capability practice within a concentration in Advanced Macro Social Work Practice could specify advanced financial capability practice behaviors required for competency EPAS 2.1.10 (related to practice with all client system levels). One practice behavior at the community level could be to conduct a community-level needs assessment to determine whether financial services meet basic community needs.

Once linkages between financial capability and EPAS are identified, programs can "map out" the locations where content is found and practice behaviors are measured in the curriculum. Content could be found in "stand-alone" financial capability courses or in courses that infuse financial capability content.

A final step in linking financial capability education to the EPAS is identifying measures that can quantify whether students have gained mastery over the practice behaviors and can demonstrate their competency, such as assignments. For example, students could be given an assignment to identify and analyze a federal or state law that relates to financial institutions and services within low-income communities, and formulate ideas about and advocate for policy change to increase access to financial services in low-income communities. This could be

Table 13.2. EXAMPLE FINANCIAL CAPABILITY PRACTICE BEHAVIORS AND THEIR ASSESSMENT FOR SELECTED EPAS COMPETENCIES

EDUCATIONAL POLICY 2.1.1—IDENTIFY AS A PROFESSIONAL SOCIAL WORKER AND CONDUCT ONESELF ACCORDINGLY.
Foundation—Demonstrate beginning knowledge of the array of financial education and literacy services that are available to clients, so that they can advocate for client access.
Assessment—Successfully demonstrate knowledge on a quiz or exam.
Advanced—Utilizing an in-depth knowledge of the array of financial education and literacy services available to clients, advocate for client access.
Assessment—Write a letter to an important decision-maker about the array of financial education and literacy services, and advocate for expanded access.
Educational Policy 2.1.5—Advance human rights and social and economic justice.
Foundation—Demonstrate knowledge about the high rate at which minorities and oppressed populations are un- or underbanked (FDIC, 2009), and the causes for this situation of oppression and discrimination.
Assessment—Successfully demonstrate knowledge on an exam.
Advanced—Demonstrate advanced knowledge about efforts to address the root causes for oppression and discrimination in accessing the services of mainstream financial institutions.
Assessment—Successfully demonstrate advanced knowledge through an essay question on a final.
EDUCATIONAL POLICY 2.1.8—ENGAGE IN POLICY PRACTICE TO ADVANCE SOCIAL AND ECONOMIC WELL-BEING AND TO DELIVER EFFECTIVE SOCIAL WORK SERVICES.
Foundation—Demonstrate knowledge about the impact of discriminatory financial policies by engaging in policy practice to influence relevant policy.
Assessment—Identify discriminatory financial policies related to consumer credit, and write a letter to a relevant policy decision-maker/decision-making body to advocate for change.
Advanced—Demonstrate in-depth knowledge of various forms of financial institutions and services, particularly those utilized by and available to low-income communities and populations in order to analyze, formulate, and advocate for improvements in policies that would create local financial institutions and services that serve the needs of the populations and communities.
Assessment—Identify and analyze a federal or state law that relates to financial institutions and services within low-income communities, and formulate ideas about and advocate for policy change to increase access to financial services in low-income communities.
EDUCATIONAL POLICY 2.1.9—RESPOND TO CONTEXTS THAT SHAPE PRACTICE.
Foundation—Identify community leadership that promotes sustainable change in the delivery of financial capability services for low-income populations.

(continued)

Table 13.2. CONTINUED

Assessment—Successfully demonstrate knowledge of institutions, efforts, and leaders in the local community who/that are engaged in promoting sustainable change through a writing assignment.
Advanced—Engage in community leadership to promote sustainable change in the delivery system of financial capability services.
Assessment—Students complete a service-learning component of a course in which they partner with local leadership efforts to combat predatory lending.
Educational Policy 2.1.10(a)–(d)—**Engage, assess, intervene, and evaluate with individuals, families, groups, organizations, and communities.**
Foundation—Collect, organize, and interpret client data regarding financial capability during the assessment phase.
Assessment—Ask questions about financial capability on an assessment form in a mock client interview.
Advanced—Demonstrate in-depth knowledge about available financial services within a community.
Assessment—Conduct a community-level needs assessment to determine the extent to which the financial services within a community meet community needs.

used to measure EPAS 2.1.8. While these assessments would be only a part of a program's overall assessment, they would help determine whether students have mastered the knowledge, skills, and values relating to financial capability.

Flexible Development

To ensure long-term viability, new curricula in financial capability also must garner attention of the intended audience. The case examples offered here suggest that programs may need to remain flexible during start-up and experiment with course titles, delivery format, and course credit. In this way, programs will learn more about the best fit for their context. In the process, programs can also seek opportunities to reach a wider student audience and develop partnerships with related degree and certificate programs across the university. Strategies may include cross-listing courses at both the BSW and MSW foundation levels; incorporating courses into existing related major, minor, and certificate courses; offering honors credit; offering online courses; and cross-listing courses with other departments, such as business schools and justice studies programs. Regular courses, workshops, and seminars can also be offered for continuing education credit for practicing professionals. Additionally, short, nontraditional courses, continuing education, out-of-classroom opportunities, and online modules may also generate student interest that results in their taking traditional credit courses. Lastly, programs may also develop specialized practicum opportunities that generate student interest in practicing financial capability. Following the example of the University of Maryland initiative, programs may seek external funding for stipends to attract students to such placements.

RESEARCH IMPLICATIONS

While a body of research addresses effectiveness of financial education (see Sherraden, chapter 1, this volume), including with college students (Borden, Lee Serido, & Collins, 2008), little is known at this point about effective education models for financial capability in social work (Despard & Chowa, 2010; Sherraden, Laux, & Kaufman, 2007). While research is currently underway, more research on outcomes and impacts is needed. Student learning can be evaluated using traditional course evaluation tools and other methods of curriculum evaluation, such as student exit interviews and alumni and employer surveys (Hooyman, 2006). Student learning outcomes can be related to the core competencies of CSWE's 2008 EPAS through the development of practice behaviors, as well as competencies that are developed by the program for advanced practice.

IMPACT OF POLICY DEVELOPMENTS

National policy developments related to the recent US and global economic crisis have important implications for financial capability curricular development. Social workers must be prepared to participate in related policy development. For example, changes to practices of credit card companies resulting from the Credit Card Accountability, Responsibility, and Disclosure Act of 2009 have important implications for the financial well-being of students, their families, and their future clients. This Act requires more clear and additional consumer notification of changes to credit terms, a grace period on interest rate increases, limits on issuing credit cards to people under the age of 21, and other consumer-friendly provisions (Schultz, 2010). New financial regulations on financial institutions are being closely watched in anticipation of the financial institutions passing additional costs onto customers (Hauser, 2010). Also noteworthy is the creation of the new US Bureau of Consumer Financial Protection in 2010. This bureau, part of the Federal Reserve Bank, has the authority to write and enforce new standards for mortgages, credit cards, payday loans, and other financial products (*New York Times*, 2010). These and other policy developments have significant implications for the financial matters of all consumers, but especially low-income populations. In the future, financial capability education must include a strong educational component on consumer policy development. Such policy content must include at least a basic understanding of consumer law and the institutions and interests that shape it. Social workers must have the education to join with other advocates to participate in policy development concerning all consumers, with a special focus on the resulting impacts on the working poor and those in poverty.

CONCLUSION

Social workers play an important role in the delivery of financial education to low-income populations and assist in developing client financial capability. In response to both internal and external forces, the area of financial capability is a developing curricular area within social work education. Through the development of partnerships, building on program needs and resources, measuring outcomes for assessment purposes, and developing programs in a flexible manner, several pioneering curricular efforts provide models for efforts to include this content into social work education. Future work in this area includes the development of financial capability practice behaviors and the linking of these to CSWE EPAS competencies, strong evaluation efforts of student learning, publication and distribution of evaluation efforts, and the development of curricular materials for social work that include a strong component of consumer policy development. Ultimately, the social work practitioner role within financial capability work must be supported by strong curricular offerings within social work. Students must be better prepared for the financial capability challenges that await them in the field.

NOTES

1. Dr. Jodi Jacobson is the Chair of the FSWI. Readers are encouraged to check the FSWI website for more information about FSWI as well as current SWOCS placements.
2. Dr. Mimi Abromovitz from the Hunter College School of Social Work and Dr. Jessica Rosenberg from Long Island University are responsible for the drafting and editing of the financial capability curriculum for the New York City Collaborative Effort.

REFERENCES

Allen, J. V. (2000). Financial abuse of elders and dependent adults: The FAST (Financial Abuse Specialist Team) approach. *Journal of Elder Abuse and Neglect, 12*(2), 85–91.

Anderson, S. G., Zhan, M., & Scott, J. (2007). Improving the knowledge and attitudes of low-income families about banking and predatory financial practices. *Families in Society, 88*(3), 443–452.

Anuszkiewicz, B. (2007). *Financing workforce development programs for youth transitioning out of foster care*. Washington DC: The Finance Project. Retrieved from www.financeproject.org

Barczyk, A. N., & Lincove, J. A. (2010). Cash and counseling: A model for self-directed care programs to empower individuals with serious mental illnesses. *Social Work in Mental Health, 8*, 209–224.

Barnett, H., & Pearce, P. F. (2010). Battling the uncompensated care spiral: Outcomes from a single institution assisting uninsured hospitalized patients to obtain health insurance. *Professional Case Management, 15*(5), 280–289.

Bostic, R. W., & Lee, K. O. (2009). Homeownership: America's dream? In R. M. Blank & M. S. Barr (Eds.), *Insufficient funds: Savings, assets, credit, and banking among low-income households* (pp. 218–256). New York: Russell Sage Foundation.

Borden, L. M., Lee, S.-A., Serido, K., & Collins, D. (2008). Changing college students financial knowledge, attitudes, and behavior through seminar participation. *Journal of Family and Economic Issues, 29*(1), 23–40.

Britt, S., Grable, J. E., Nelson Goff, B. S., & White, M. (2008). The influence of perceived spending behaviors on relationship satisfaction. *Financial Counseling and Planning, 19*(1), 31–43.

Council on Social Work Education. (2008). *Educational policy and accreditation standards.* Alexandria, VA: Author.

Council on Social Work Education. (2009). *Advanced gero social work practice.* Alexandria, VA: Author.

Davis, M. A. (1983). *Social services in hospices: An analysis* (Doctoral dissertation). University of Illinois at Chicago. Retrieved from Dissertation Abstracts. (#8307).

Despard, M., & Chowa, G. (2010). Social work interest in building individual's financial capabilities. *Journal of Financial Therapy, 1*(1), 23–41.

DiGiulo, J., & Janosik, G. (1982) Successful partners: Credit counseling and family services. *Social Casework, 63,* 482–488.

Garman, E. T., & Forgue, R. E. (2008). *Personal finance.* New York: Houghton Mifflin Company.

Hauser, C. (2010, June 25). Banks likely to offset impact of new law, analysts say. *New York Times.* Retrieved from http://www.nytimes.com/2010/06/26/business/26reax.html

Hooyman, N. (2006). *Achieving curricular and organizational change: Impact of the CSWE geriatric enrichment in social work education project.* Washington DC: Council on Social Work Education.

Huisamen, A., & Weyers, M. (2009). Teaching employees money management skills and showing a profit in the process. *Maatskaplike Werk/Social Work, 45*(4), 443–460.

Huston, S. (2010). Measuring financial literacy. *Journal of Consumer Affairs, 44*(2), 296–316.

Jenkins, R., Bhugra, D., Bebbington, P., Brugha, T., Farrell, M., Coid, J., ... Meltzer, H. (2008). Debt, income, and mental disorder in the general population. *Psychological Medicine, 38*(10). Retrieved from http://journals.cambridge.org/action/displayAbstract?fromPage=online&aid=2178012.

Kennedy, T. (2008). *Economics: A social issues perspective.* Phoenix: Arizona State University, School of Social Work.

Kennedy, T. (2009). *Financial literacy for social workers.* Phoenix: Arizona State University, School of Social Work.

Lim, Y., & Lemieux, C. (2008). Potential impact of EITC adjustments on financial self-sufficiency among low-income families: A simulation model. *Journal of Sociology and Social Welfare, 35*(2), 49–65.

Marson, D. C., Savage, R., & Phillips, J. (2006). Financial capability in persons with schizophrenia and serious mental illness: Clinical and research ethics aspects. *Schizophrenia Bulletin, 32*(1), 81–91.

Missouri Budget Project. (2009). *Creating a state earned income tax credit for Missouri.* Retrieved from http://www.mobudget.org/archived_press_room.html

Naleppa, M. J. (2006). Case management. In B. Berkman (Ed.), *Handbook of social work in health and aging* (pp. 521–528). New York: Oxford University Press.

National Student Loan Program. (2010). *Financial literacy now: Why college students can't wait*. Retrieved from www.nslp.org/pages/pdf/NSLP_WhitePaper_4.8.10.pdf

New York Times. (2010, September 14). *Bureau of consumer financial protection*. Retrieved from http://topics.nytimes.com/top/reference/timestopics/organizations/c/consumer_financial_protection_bureau/index.html

Office of Latino Projects. (n.d.). *Latino cultural competency certificate—Overview*. Phoenix, AZ: Author. Retrieved from http://olp.asu.edu/latinocertificate/lclc_overview/

Organisation for Economic Co-operation and Development (OECD). (2005). *Improving financial literacy: Analysis of issues and policies*. Paris, France: OECD Publishing.

Putnam, M., Sherraden, M., Edwards, K., Porterfield, S., Wittenberg, D., & Welch, P. (2005). Building financial bridges to economic development and community integration: Recommendations for a research agenda on asset development for people with disabilities. *Journal of Social Work in Disability and Rehabilitation*, 4(3), 61–86.

Remund, D. (2010). Financial literacy explicated: The case for a clearer definition in an increasingly complex economy. *Journal of Consumer Affairs*, 44(2), 276–295.

Robles, B. (2008). *Border family and community asset building*. Phoenix: Arizona State University, School of Social Work.

Sanders, C., & Schnabel, M. (2007). Organizing for economic empowerment for battered women. *Journal of Community Practice*, 14(3), 47–68.

Sanders, C., Weaver, T. L., & Schnabel, M. (2007). Economic education for battered women: An evaluation of outcomes. *Affilia*, 22(3), 240–254.

Schreiner, M., Tin Ng, G., & Sherraden, M. (2006). Cost-effectiveness in individual development accounts. *Research on Social Work Practice*, 16(1), 28–37.

Schultz, J. (2010, February 22). What the Credit Card Act means for you. *New York Times*. Retrieved from http://bucks.blogs.nytimes.com/2010/02/22/what-the-credit-card-act-means-for-you/

Sherraden, M., Laux, S., & Kaufman, C. (2007). Financial education for social workers. *Journal of Community Practice*, 75(3), 45–49.

Sherraden, M. S., Sanders, C. K., & Sherraden, M. (2004). *Kitchen capitalism: Microenterprise in poor households*. Buffalo: State University of New York Press.

Steiner, S., & Kennedy, T. (2004). *Economics: A social issues perspective*. Tempe, AZ: Arizona State University, School of Social Work.

US Department of Education, National Center for Education Statistics . (2002). *Defining and assessing learning: Exploring competency-based initiatives* (NCES 2002-159). Washington, DC: US Department of Education.

US Department of the Treasury. (2010, August 26). Financial education core competencies; Comment request. *Federal Register*, 75(165), 52596–52597.

VonDeLinde, K. C., & Correia, A. (2005). *Economic education programs for battered women: Lessons learned from two settings* (Publication number 18). Harrisburg, PA: The National Resource Center on Domestic Violence. Retrieved from: http://new.vawnet.org/category/index_pages.php?category_id=10

Voorhees, P. (2002). Creating and implementing competency-based learning models. *New Directions for Institutional Research*, 110, 83–96.

Zhan, M., Anderson, S. G., & Scott, J. (2006). Financial knowledge of the low-income population: Effects of a financial education program. *Journal of Sociology and Social Welfare*, 33(1), 53–74.

14

Building the Capacity of Social Workers to Enhance Financial Capability and Asset Development

J. MICHAEL COLLINS AND JULIE BIRKENMAIER

Personal financial management has many direct and indirect links to family and individual well-being (Gjesfjeld, Greeno, Kim, & Anderson, 2010; Gupta & Huston, 2009; Hallero & Gustafsson, 2011). Personal finance can be complex and typically requires focused effort to gain skills and knowledge. Social work students report that they understand the relevance of personal finance to social work practice, as well as their own need to gain knowledge and skills in this area (Kindle, 2010), but most have not been formally trained in finance as part of their social work education (Sherraden, Laux, & Kaufman, 2007). As discussed in Birkenmaier, Kennedy, Kunz, Sander, and Horwitz (chapter 13, this volume), financial education curricula are beginning to be offered through social work programs designed specifically for students and professionals working with low-income and marginalized populations. Other curricula offered through different venues are designed for helping professionals working with a diversity of populations.

On one hand, this array of options is a positive development. On the other hand, the increasing abundance of options presents challenges for practitioners. Practitioners may struggle to understand what knowledge and skills are needed for enhancing their practice to include more financial capability work with targeted populations. Therefore, while professionals in a variety of direct practice settings would likely benefit from acquiring certain skills and knowledge, especially those in settings that offer economic development opportunities (e.g., employment services, income tax assistance centers, and asset development programs), there is little formal guidance regarding opportunities for education and training.

This chapter provides an overview of the rationale for social workers to enhance their capacity to help clients with personal financial issues. We review the types of resources, education, and certifications available, and discuss current and future needs of social workers regarding core competencies for practice that promote financial capability. In general, financial capability training programs and certifications for personal finance are early in development, but there is a range of ways current and newly developing professionals can take advantage of existing resources. The chapter ends with a call for leadership to develop certificate offerings of financial capability education and training to best meet the needs of social workers and their clients.

CONNECTING FINANCIAL CAPABILITY TO SOCIAL WORK PRACTICE

Social workers have always been involved with clients' personal financial management issues with clients (Stuart, chapter 2, this volume). Social work education, however, rarely prepares them for this work (Sherraden, Laux, & Kaufman, 2007). Over 25 years ago, Blostein (1985) found that social work training programs generally neglected personal financial management topics. After more than two decades, little has changed in this regard (Sherraden, Laux, & Kaufman, 2007). Neither the National Association of Social Worker's Standards of Practice (NASW, 2011) nor the Council on Social Work Education's Educational Policy and Accreditation Standards (EPAS) (Council on Social Work Education, 2008) mentions anything specific about personal finance, even though both make reference to the importance of economic development and justice. However, social work and related professions continue to face demands to support clients in managing household financial issues and the emotional stress related to financial insecurity (Kindle, 2010). Although more research is needed to determine the effectiveness of specific interventions to relieve financial stress and improve financial security, students and professionals seeking skills in this area cannot effectively respond to current client needs if they themselves lack an understanding of core concepts in financial management. Practitioners are left to identify their own strategies for education and training plumbed from a highly heterogeneous set of options.

While a small number of social workers already deliver financial capability services (e.g., providing financial education and promoting access to formal financial institutions and resources) in settings such as tax assistance centers, asset development programs, and employment and career services, few social workers work in settings where financial capability is a central function. Nonetheless, social workers may be well suited to promote financial capability to a much wider population of low-income clients through the integration of financial education, financial advice and counseling, and financial coaching with other agency services (Engelbrecht, 2008). Social workers have the perspective, skills, and commitment to work with a variety of low-income populations (Council on Social Work Education, 2008). Social workers routinely work with both low-income clients who are future-oriented and able to engage in financial capability efforts, as well as clients who are more present-oriented and less able to engage in such efforts. Importantly, access to low-income present-oriented clients who are not able to readily engage in financial capability efforts offers the prospect of reaching new audiences with financial capability promotional efforts through integration with other social services. Targeted populations may not be accessible through other social or programmatic channels, yet improving financial capability could prove to be vitally important for clients, their families, and their communities.

In addition to reaching an important population that can benefit directly from efforts to build financial capability, social work researchers can learn more about working with underresearched populations, including clients who are not able to readily engage in financial capability efforts. For example, there have been a number of studies evaluating the effects of stand-alone programs intended to improve the financial literacy or capability of low-income populations. Collins and O'Rourke (2010) reviewed 41 different financial education and counseling research studies and found that most studies suggest positive effects on financial knowledge, attitudes, or behavior. However, these studies suffer from a variety of methodological problems. First, few of these studies use random assignment. Second, because many of the programs are voluntary, we can assume that participants are highly motivated, and motivation is a powerful predicator of positive outcomes. Thus, the positive outcomes found in these programs may not be representative of outcomes for less motivated participants. In addition, motivation cannot be measured in these studies, which may bias the results. This bias is most clearly highlighted in a study by Meier and Sprenger (2008), which shows that people who opt to take a short credit management course offered at a low-income tax preparation site are, in fact, the most motivated, future-oriented people, while those declining the course are more present-oriented. Thus, financial education classes are likely to attract clients who are already motivated and thus fail to reach the less motivated, who are, perhaps, those most in need of financial capacity building.

While social workers have some advantages in terms of proximity to people in need, the potential value of integrating financial capability efforts extends beyond the context of service delivery, to include integrating their services with those of other helping professionals. Social workers typically work across a broad set of behavioral and cognitive issues (including physical health and safety, mental health, relationships, and family functioning); they work with people across the life course; and they provide access to services for education, information, support, guidance, and increased economic security (NASW, 2011). Within diverse settings, social workers increasingly engage in financial capability initiatives by partnering with other professionals, such as financial institution leaders, consumer and family economists, credit counselors, accountants, lawyers, financial planners, policy makers, policy advocates, educators, and researchers (Abt Associates, 2006; Rupured, Most, & Sherraden, 2000). Through such diverse partnerships social workers can contribute to efforts to develop and utilize curricular materials; teach, advise, and coach about financial capability; assess the effectiveness of financial capability efforts; work on policy initiatives related to financial capability; and contribute to other related efforts (Maton, Maton, & Martin, 2011; Taylor, Bernes, Gunn, & Nixon, 2007).

However, integrating financial capability efforts into the delivery of social services may offer the best mechanism for building financial capability, especially with low-income clients. Social workers provide individualized services to clients by helping clients set goals and determine priorities without prescribing specific courses of action. This flexible and adaptable approach is used in all types of settings, and may be employed as an alternative to using a standardized financial education curriculum. Social workers offer a unique perspective even to families who can afford the services of trained financial advisors, consultants, and planners. Social workers can integrate financial capability issues into other services, such as mental health, health, housing, and nutrition, without the self-interested influence of fees associated with the sale of financial products. While financial advisors have a great deal of training and expertise in their subject matter, their focus tends to be on the sale or trade of financial products instead of overall client well-being (Collins, 2010; Garman & Forgue, 2011).

THE FIELD OF FINANCIAL CAPABILITY EDUCATION AND TRAINING

Many different types of professionals provide financial information, advice, guidance, and support, including accountants, lawyers, bankers, financial planners, persons working in nonprofits, and insurance agents. As seen in Table 14.1, these professionals take on a wide variety of roles.

For example, "counselor" is a common term, and much like social workers, financial counselors help clients work through specific problems. Financial counselors might specialize in a specific area, such as housing, general budgeting, or

Table 14.1. FINANCIAL SUPPORT PROVIDER ROLES

Title	Description
Advisor	Provides financial advice to clients, and can include oversight and fiduciary duties. Often associated with private firms or financial institutions, and paid on commission based on financial products sold.
Coach	Uses a strengths-based approach, and supports clients in their quest to achieve specific objectives. Similar to a financial counselor.
Counselor	Assists client to overcome a specific problem, such as credit management.
Educator	Teaches class-based delivery of financial education curriculum.
Mentor	Provides one-on-one support, financial advice, and technical expertise.
Planner	Assists with creating a long-term financial plan. A form of financial advisor.

SOURCES: Collins, Baker, and Gorey (2007); Garman and Forgue (2011)

credit management. Counselors may be paid a fee by creditors or consumers, or their services may be offered as part of charitable programs. Advisors are often associated with private firms or financial institutions. As suggested by the name, advisors give advice, which can also trigger additional levels of oversight and fiduciary duties (Collins, 2010). A few financial advisors are fee-only, meaning compensation is based on a flat fee. More commonly, advisors are paid by commission based on the sale of financial products. Financial planners are advisors who focus on developing long-range financial plans (College for Financial Planning, 2009). Financial coaches are like counselors, but use a strengths-based approach (Collins, Baker, & Gorey, 2007). Often focused on goal formation and attainment, coaches do not offer advice or specific financial problem-solving services, but rather support client-driven objectives over a period of time. Financial mentors also offer one-on-one support, but may provide additional financial advice and technical expertise. Both mentoring and coaching are newer subfields evolving from counseling and planning. Financial educators often operate in a traditional classroom setting, and deliver a standardized curriculum. Educators focus mostly on conveying information rather than on one-on-one counseling or advice (Collins, 2011; Collins, Baker, & Gorey, 2007; Garman & Forgue, 2011). As will be discussed in detail later, widely recognized certifications are available for financial planning and financial counseling; yet only credentials with far less recognition are available for financial educators and financial coaches.

CONTENT AREAS RELEVANT FOR HELPING PROFESSIONALS

As an area of research and practice, financial capability is an emerging field. The first surveys of financial education emerged in the mid-2000s (Vitt, Reichbach, Kent, & Siegenthaler, 2005). Research in this field crosses several disciplines and is not grounded in any particular theoretical framework (Lyons & Neelakantan, 2008), although theoretical work is underway by scholars (see Sherraden, chapter 1, this volume). Research and practice in the financial education and counseling field draw on a wide variety of approaches and formats. A discussion of the skills and knowledge needed for social workers requires a prevailing model or framework, as well as a body of causal evidence in terms of program impacts; however, these are yet to emerge in the field.

Given the concern about financial literacy among the US public (Lusardi, 2008), the federal government has recently attempted to lead efforts to coordinate financial literacy and capability programs. One project led by the U.S. Department of the Treasury resulted in the development of a set of five core financial capability competencies for adults: earning, spending, saving, borrowing, and protecting (US Treasury Department, 2010). Each core concept is associated with with multiple areas of knowledge and behavior, as shown in Table 14.2, and was developed with guidance from experts in the financial education field.

The core concepts, topics, and behaviors discussed in this framework can provide guidance to social workers regarding needed content and skills. However, helping professionals need much more specific guidance about focused topical

Table 14.2. FINANCIAL CAPABILITY CORE COMPETENCIES FOR ADULTS

Core Concept	Knowledge	Action/Behavior
Earning	Gross versus net pay Benefits and taxes Importance of education	Understand your paycheck Learn about potential benefits/taxes Invest in your future
Spending	The difference between needs and wants	Develop a spending plan Track spending habits Live within your means Understand the social and environmental impacts of your spending decisions
Saving	Saved money grows	Start saving early Pay yourself first
	Know about transactional accounts	Understand and establish a relationship with the financial system
	Know about financial assets (savings accounts, bonds, stocks, mutual funds)	Comparison shop Balance risk and return
	How to meet long-term goals and grow your wealth	Save for retirement, child's education, and other needs Plan for long-term goals Track savings and monitor what you own
Borrowing	If you borrow now, you will pay back more later. The cost of borrowing is based on how risky the lender thinks you are (credit score)	Avoid high cost borrowing, plan, understand, and shop around Understand how information in your credit score affects borrowing Plan and meet your payment obligations Track borrowing habits Analyze renting versus owning a home
Protect	Act now to protect yourself from potential catastrophe	Choose appropriate insurance Build up an emergency fund Shop around
	Identity theft/fraud/scams	Protect your identity Avoid fraud and scams Review your credit report

SOURCE: US Treasury (2010)

areas when working with specific clients. While a more complete list of financial capability practice topics is listed in Birkenmaier et al. (chapter 13, this volume), here we address some of the needs related to financial capability of targeted populations and how the US Treasury core competencies might be applied. We have selected an illustrative set of populations that at least anecdotally represent a range of social work clientele. These examples may provide some guidance as to the variations that might exist across various forms of practice. Researchers have considered the diversity of economic needs by categorizing families along a continuum of in-crisis, at risk, safe, and thriving, and have suggested that social services will have different impacts depending on a family's position along that continuum (Bauer, Braun, & Olson, 2000). For our purposes, the focus is on families in crisis and at risk, and we also consider financial needs within family services contexts. These examples illustrate client needs across different types of social work settings (e.g., clients served by community-based, family, and health/mental health settings, as well as in community settings), and with a diversity of populations (i.e., families, youth, and older adults).

Clients in Financial Crisis

One type of client that seems to be relatively common is someone with an income near or below the poverty line with low or no savings or assets, high debt levels and impending legal issues related to unpaid bills or collections on defaulted credit (Aratani & Chau, 2010). These Clients may include both those in chronic poverty as well as those experiencing downward economic mobility as a result of circumstances such as job loss, a family health crisis, divorce, or foreclosure. Clients may also experience severe material hardship due to a chronic disability or health crisis. These factors result in a number of economic and social stressors (O'Neill, Sorhaindo, Xiao, & Garman, 2005). These clients may be under- or unbanked (Maryland Cash, 2008; Project Match, 2010). This group likely includes clients who are eligible for public benefits or those trying to enroll in public benefits such as food assistance, job training, public housing, or foster care. A related group of clients are those exiting from these programs who are coping with the implications of the loss of financial support (Blank, 2002). In some cases, loss of electronic benefits may result in the loss of a debit card or related transaction account, which may lead to reliance on high-cost transaction services (Maryland Cash, 2008; Project Match, 2010).

US Treasury core competencies for this group of clients include earning and spending. There are several pertinent issues for low-income families in financial crisis. First are tax-related questions, such as utilizing tax credits such as the earned income tax credit, maximizing deductions, and adjusting tax withholding on a paycheck. Second, education about public benefits could bring in additional cash or in-kind resources. Even clients who are already receiving public benefits may not be aware of all programs for which they may qualify. Examples include public health insurance (i.e., Medicaid, SCHIP, or, in the future through the new federal health care law, state health insurance exchanges), home heating/energy assistance or discounts, housing subsidies, or supplemental food supports. Third is education in using spending plans, tracking spending, and managing bills to assess available income and ongoing expenses or financial obligations.

Other US Treasury core competencies may be relevant to low-income families in financial crisis as well. These include opening a bank account or starting a small emergency savings fund. Learning about borrowing is also important, especially ways to pay high cost debt and restructure outstanding loans to balance income and liabilities. This may also include debt collection and legal remedies, such as garnishment and judgments (Maryland Cash, 2008; Project Match, 2010). Protecting against financial risk is also an important area to apply to this population. Social workers would find it helpful to understand legal issues related to identity theft and fraud. The threat of wage or bank account garnishment might present a strong deterrent against using a bank account or reporting income. Knowing how and when to refer clients to legal advice, housing or mortgage counseling, bankruptcy counseling, debt restructuring, or other services is vital for social workers working with these families.

Asset Poor and Financially At-Risk Clients

Clients who are employed and able to meet most income needs from earnings may be challenged to make ends meet and set money aside for emergencies and investments. Often these clients have few or no financial assets and no clear mechanisms to build assets. With earned income, they may benefit from being connected to asset-building programs in the community, such as programs that offer assistance to purchase a used car, start or expand a small business, purchase a home, build credit, locate financing for secondary education, or maintain a home (Rothwell & Han, 2010).

The US Treasury core competencies also have relevance for this group. Not being in ongoing crisis, this group can take more proactive steps toward investing in the future; therefore, core competencies that can especially be emphasized with this group include spending, saving, borrowing, and protecting. For example, regarding spending, more discussions about goals and priorities may take place, including understanding the social impacts of spending decisions. Saving actions that are relevant for this group include "pay yourself first" (saving from gross income using automatic deposit) and financial planning. For this group, choices about saving for retirement, child's education, and other needs may take a back seat to spending in the present, but by focusing on long-term goals clients may begin to take steps in the direction of more savings. However, long-term savings may not be the first course of action for these clients. Building up liquid savings as an emergency fund to pay for unpredictable expenses or future potential shortfalls may be a common first step for these clients, complemented or followed by longer savings plans (Chase et al., 2011). As these clients begin to accrue assets, they may need support in behaviors related to managing assets, including tracking and monitoring accounts. Finally, risk management—including not only the need for precautionary savings but also life, health, and property insurance—is another important topic in order to foster financial security. These clients may be interested in discussing retirement, insurance needs, investment, and education planning topics (Maryland Cash, 2008; Project Match, 2010). Social workers may handle these topics in a variety of ways: discussing some information directly with clients; partnering with other financial professionals to develop curricular materials for clients; and referring clients to other professionals (Collins, Baker, & Gorey, 2007).

Family Services Clients

Clients in this group may fall into the first or second category, yet are also seeking family services. Families need a range of supports in handling major life transitions, including career changes or shifts in family size due to marriage, separation, divorce, birth, or death. Major events can have profound financial implications, especially situations that require income adjustments or deplete savings (Poduska & Hugh, 1990; Schmeiser, 2010). In recent years, therapeutic programs addressing financial issues in interpersonal relationships have emerged. Financial planners in some cases partner with marriage and family therapists, social workers, and other helping professionals to deal with these issues (Maton, Maton, & Martin, 2011; Taylor, Bernes, Gunn, & Nixon, 2007). Partnerships can take the form of referrals, sharing office space, creating an alliance where services are cobranded for marketing, integrating and coordinating services, and one professional working for the other to create a tightly integrated service delivery system (Maton et al., 2011). Clients in these programs work on mental health and/or family topics and financial challenges at the same time. For example, clients may reflect on their values and goals and ways in which money contributes to their quality of life and relationships, while also developing spending plans or budgets and working on rebuilding credit and managing debt (see Maton et al., 2011 for further information about partnership models). Legal issues such as estate and family law are also common topics (National Public Radio—Marketplace, 2009).

These clients may have a special focus on core competencies useful for dealing with radically revised spending plans, including living on less money, understanding public benefits, and using income tax deductions. Saving may be part of the strategy—especially for an expected future expenses related to children. However, for many clients facing a negative event, a main task is managing the liquidation of assets such as the sale of a home, borrowing against retirement funds, or spending down financial investments to match expected future needs for funds. Clients may require legal advice about issues such as family and tax laws as well as financial advice on investment choices, trusts, and estates. Social workers need to understand these issues sufficiently in order to make appropriate referrals and partner with local professionals.

People with disabilities and parents of children with disabilities, often experience severe material hardship even when their income is above the federal poverty level (Parish, Rose, Grinstein-Weiss, Richman, & Andrews, 2008). These families struggle to create a lifetime of resources for their children while also trying to qualify for available benefits that may be means-tested. This requires careful financial planning and in some cases legal advice (Kuhlthau, Smith Hull, Yucel, & Perrin, 2005).

Another important group is people—often but not exclusively women—dealing with domestic violence. Control over finances can itself be a form of abuse, and knowing how to open and manage a bank account might be critical for a victim trying to break free of an abuser. Likewise, issues of protecting personal financial information and establishing or improving credit histories while ensuring safety might be needed to help overcome the financial consequences of abuse (Sanders, chapter 4, this volume; Sanders, Weaver, & Schnabel, 2007).

Older adult clients face the prospect of paying for basic expenses and medical care on a fixed income. They must plan carefully for spending down available assets, and especially consider the impact of housing choices. Many seniors may have illiquid assets such as a home, and some may consider using reverse mortgages as a way to tap home equity (Leviton, 2001). There are growing concerns about reduced ability to make financial choices as cognition levels decline with age (Herd & Holden, 2010: Mazzonna & Peracchi, 2009). Older adults also may face issues of credit mismanagement, identification theft, financial exploitation, and outright fraud, as well as financial abuse by caregivers and relatives (AARP, 2003; McCallion, Ferretti, & Park, chapter 6, this volume). In addition to access to public benefits, this population may need help understanding complex programs, such as Medicare, Medicaid, and long-term care coverage, as well as with issues related to estate planning and of being a surviving spouse (Choi, Kulick, & Mayer, 1999; Lusardi & Mitchell, 2007).

EDUCATION, RESOURCES, CURRICULA, AND CERTIFICATIONS

Social workers and other helping professionals seeking financial education and training find a myriad of education, resources, curricula, and certifications. Understanding the options, including those designed for financial professionals, can help social workers develop a training plan that matches their needs. There are currently no standard accreditation or evaluation standards that are widely accepted by providers or consumers. Therefore, professionals interested in strengthening their knowledge and skills have the challenge of screening program offerings and determining the models that offer the most value for their investment of time and other resources, and that are a match with their profession, again without significant guidance from providers or consumers.

Table 14.3 describes 18 training and/or accreditation programs or types of programs that address one or more of the desired personal finance competencies for helping professionals. We include only programs or types of programs recognized by professionals as offering a legitimate certification. They were located through searches of relevant articles and trade publications, Internet searches, and discussions with leading practitioners. The list includes entities and programs we identified in mid-2011. The length, intensity, focus and cost of programs vary significantly, as do the approach and philosophy. Programs range from those

Table 14.3. FINANCIAL CERTIFICATION/TRAINING PROGRAMS

#	Type	Training Program	Description
1	FCoun	Center for Financial Social Work (NC) http://www.financialsocialwork.com/ (For-profit)	Certified Financial Social Work Educator. Four self-study workbooks; consumer credit counseling, collections, bankruptcy, banking, investing, and other related financial topics.
2	FCoun	Financial Social Work Initiative (FSWI) https://lists.umaryland.edu (Nonprofit, Education)	University of Maryland, Baltimore, School of Social Work. Continuing education workshops titled "Introduction to Financial Stability for Clients" throughout the state. The cost is $125, and social workers can receive 6 CEUs for attending.
3	FCoun	The School of Social Work at the University of Missouri http://ssw.missouri.edu/minor_financial.shtml (Nonprofit, Education)	Certificate in Financial Literacy for Helping Professionals. Minor in undergraduate BSW program. Coursework includes personal and family finance, financial counseling, community agencies, and exploration in social and economic justice.
4	FE	Redevelopment Opportunities for Women/AllState Foundation (Nonprofit)	REAP Curriculum/Domestic Violence Program. Financial education tailored to meet the needs of advocates for women experiencing domestic violence.
5	FCoun	Various States: Cooperative Extension (Nonprofit, Education)	Certificate of Completion in Personal Finance.
6	FCoun	Association for Financial Counseling and Planning Education (AFCPE) www.afcpe.org (Nonprofit)	Accredited Financial Counselor™ (AFC)—a financial counselor who has certified skills to assist individuals and families in the process of financial decision making. Two self-study college-level courses.
7	FCoach	Dan Clark Associates http://www.danclark.com (For-profit)	Financial Coach. 3-day course using the Solution Focused Financial Coaching Manual.
8	FCoach	Financial Independence Foundation http://fifblog.wordpress.com (Nonprofit)	Certified Financial Coach (CFC™) 5 days on-site training and 20 hours via telephone and online.

(continued)

Table 14.3. CONTINUED

#	Type	Training Program	Description
9	FCoun	Institute for Financial Literacy: Center˚ for Financial Certifications http://www.financiallit.org (Nonprofit)	Certified Personal Finance Counselor (CPFC™). Three-part self-study curriculum.
10	FCoun	Institute of Consumer Financial Education (ICFE) http://www.financial-education-icfe.org/ (Nonprofit)	Certified Credit Report Reviewer™ or Certified Identity Theft Risk Management Specialist Program. Self-study guides.
11	FCoun	National Association of Certified Credit Counselors (NACCC) http://www.naccc.us/ (For-profit)	Senior Credit Counselor Certification, Financial Health Certification and Debt Settlement Specialist Certification, Credit Counselor Certification. Self-study curriculum with manual and CD.
12	FCoun	National Foundation for Credit Counseling (NFCC) www.nfcc.org/ (Nonprofit)	Certified Consumer Credit Counselor Self-study curriculum of six books; Certification is only available to NFCC member agencies.
13	FCoun	NeighborWorks NTI www.nw.org (Nonprofit)	Certificate of Completion for Financial Fitness 3-day course
14	FCoun	The Lampo Group www.daveramsey.com/ (For-profit)	Dave Ramsey's Certified Counselor 5-day course.
15	FPlan	American Bankers Association® Institute of Certified Bankers (ICB) www.aba.com (For-profit)	Certified Trust and Financial Advisor (CTFA)—a financial services professional who has completed a professional certification program on the provision of fiduciary services related to trusts, estates, guardianships, and individual asset management accounts.

(continued)

Table 14.3. CONTINUED

#	Type	Training Program	Description
16	FP	American College in Bryn Mawr www.theamericancollege.edu (Nonprofit, Education)	Chartered Financial Consultant (ChFC)—a professional with a designation in financial planning that enables him/her to apply a comprehensive financial planning process to clients' needs; eight-course program of study, primarily self-study.
17	FP	Certified Financial Planner (CFP®) Board of Standards www.cfp.net (For-profit)	Certified Financial Planner™—a financial professional who has met the CFP® Board's education, examination, experience, and ethics requirements.
18	FP	National Association of Personal Financial Advisors (NAPFA) www.napfa.org (Nonprofit)	NAPFA-Registered Financial Advisor—a registered fee-only financial professional.

offered through college or universities, to targeted programs on a specific topic, like credit reports, via self-study. Only a few (Center for Financial Social Work and the Financial Social Work Initiative) are solely focused on working with low-income families, although many programs have been used by social workers serving low-income and other vulnerable populations.

While not promoting any of the programs, the following section will discuss the programs relative to the potential "fit" with social work professionals, given their professional commitment to serving low-income and vulnerable populations. The first five are broadly defined as financial counseling, coaching, or education, and consider the social work role or emerge from higher education or higher education-related settings. The Center for Financial Social Work is one of the few programs to specifically target social workers. This certification is provided by a private firm and includes web-based content and support. The Financial Social Work Initiative (FSWI) is one of the newer efforts to integrate financial topics into social work and includes both practitioner and undergraduate education. The School of Social Work at the University of Missouri presents another emerging effort to link social work education to financial education by offering an undergraduate certificate and continuing education. There are at least two sources of financial education for those working to financially empower women experiencing intimate partner violence. Redevelopment Opportunities for Women has created the REAP curriculum (Sanders, chapter 3, this volume), and the AllState Foundation has also created a curriculum tailored to the needs of this population. Programs from state Cooperative Extension, including Maryland and Ohio among others, offer community-based training supported by an academic specialist at a land-grant university. Additionally, although not listed in Table 14–3, a few social work programs have developed stand-alone financial capability courses to better integrate content into social work theory and practice, such as Saint Louis University, Arizona State University, and a consortium of social work programs in New York City (see Birkenmaier et al., chapter 13, this volume) These programs may be accessible training options for social work professionals.

The next nine programs are also broadly defined as financial counseling, coaching, or education, and may offer relevant content for social workers, although they are not designed for the needs of social workers or from an educational setting. The Association for Financial Counseling and Planning Education (AFCPE) is a nonprofit professional organization that provides training and certification, mostly for nonprofit and public sector financial counselors. The AFCPE is one of the larger, more established providers and also offers content around working with lower-income client populations. Dan Clark Associates offers a financial coaching curriculum based on a standard service delivery guide. The Financial Independence Foundation also offers a coaching training, using a more intensive instruction method. The Institute for Financial Literacy offers one of several financial counselor designations, and follows a self-study design. The Institute of Consumer Financial Education (ICFE) offers a similar model, but each certification is narrowly designed as a specific task such as credit review. The narrow focus of these last two programs may be useful for some in social work and allied professions, especially if gaining skills is accomplished incrementally over time. Another self-study model is offered by the National Association of Certified Credit Counselors (NACCC), which also offers an array of certifications. The National Foundation for Credit Counseling (NFCC) is a leading provider of credit counseling training, but the training is only offered to NFCC certified agencies. The NeighborWorks Training Institute (NTI) offers week-long place-based courses on counseling topics, including a number of courses specific to housing, foreclosure, and community development; however, not all of these courses offer accreditation. The Lampo Group was started by Dave Ramsey, a popular writer and radio show host. This program is often used through churches and community groups.

The last four programs listed are designed for professional financial planners or advisors and are probably the least suitable for the typical social worker or related helping professional. The Certified Trust and Financial Advisor (CTFA) is a useful program, especially for people dealing with seniors and estates, but likely too detailed and technical for most social workers. Like the CTFA, the Chartered Financial Consultant (ChFC) program are more comprehensive and technical than needed for most helping professionals. The Certified Financial Planner (CFP) is a widely known designation, and CFP Board–registered educational programs are intensive. Finally, the National Association of Personal Financial Advisors (NAPFA) is notable in that it is designed for fee-only financial professionals—that is, NAPFA advisors are only paid for giving advice and do not sell financial products or collect any commissions on referrals for investment sales.

Given this broad set of opportunities, it is clear that with no standard for training or certification, professionals interested in advancing their knowledge and skills in this area must make a series of choices without much guidance. This can be a challenging task, especially given that different training models sometimes use the same terms but with different meanings. The programs described above differ in their content, delivery format (including self-study and/or place-based), rigor, methods, and whether they offer a credential. The financial planning and advising credentials are among the more rigorous and well accepted, coming closest to a standard for the financial marketplace; however, it is not clear that these models are appropriate for a social worker who primarily engages with low-income families and/or in nonfinancial forms of service delivery. Regarding delivery methods, place-based models often offer more rigor and opportunity for learning, but self-study is more feasible to pursue during the course of other duties. In practice, self-study may serve as a complement to place-based courses, where place-based courses provide the foundation for learning core concepts and self-study is used to develop more precise expertise on salient topics. Self-study can often be accomplished more flexibly and at a lower cost, but may lessen access to colleagues and expert trainers. Like delivery methods, social workers might benefit from aspects of more than one model. Social workers may enhance understanding of content from one model and techniques from another. For example, social workers may use a delivery model for financial capability for homeless clients, and also use techniques learned from models tailored for populations experiencing intimate partner violence. In another example, social workers may use a model tailored toward single, low-income parents in an asset development program, yet use interactive financial education techniques designed for teaching at-risk teens within the program. It is also apparent that this field is developing new approaches, including some more targeted to people in helping professions. However, knowing better the distinctions among models might help social workers navigate and choose among the available credentials. A future area of inquiry is a rigorous evaluation of the fit between these options and social work practice.

MATCHING RESOURCES WITH THE NEEDS OF SOCIAL WORKERS

Social work professionals who attempt to obtain relevant education and training to promote financial capability must consider several factors: the relevance of the content in general and for specific low-income populations specifically, the coverage of access to formal financial services, and the integration of the content into the delivery of social services. The following section highlights these considerations in creating a social work workforce prepared to engage in facilitating financial capability.

A Financial Capability Approach

Certification programs for social workers organized around financial capability would include financial education and access content relevant for the populations and subpopulations served by social workers (Sherraden, 2010), and provide guidance for the integration of such material into social services. First, the content must be relevant for low-income and underserved minority populations, and be structured to include a life-span perspective, so that it recognizes that people's financial needs and goals will vary at different points in their lives. Many of the most recognized programs offered are designed for middle- and upper-income clients, and are not tailored for low-income populations or for helping professionals. Curricula geared toward low-income populations should include material related to public benefits, basic banking, and credit (Zhan, Anderson, & Scott, chapter 7, this volume), and assume a low level of preparation regarding finances for the helping professional. Additionally, these populations are targeted by financial scams, and may be financially exploited (AARP, 2003; Karger, 2005). Information about protecting against fraud and identity theft and exploitive providers should also be included (Anderson, Zhan, & Scott, 2004).

Second, curricula tailored to specific subpopulations would be helpful for financial capability efforts. For example, educational offerings that highlight the topic of remittances for Latina populations, safety for women experiencing intimate partner violence, and/or financial exploitation of older and adults with disabilities would be helpful for social workers who are working with those populations. Tailoring must be responsive to the needs of subpopulations, and be based on research findings about financial capability efforts with the targeted population (Bachman & Comeau, 2010; Putnam & Tang, 2006).

Third, educational offerings for financial capability must include information about both personal financial literacy as well as access to appropriate financial products and services. The expansion of focus to include access, types of financial institutions, and the ways in which access and knowledge intersect is critical content for populations that may have had limited or difficult experiences with formal financial services in the past. For example, the curricula could include discussions of the efforts to connect unbanked populations to transaction accounts through the various "Bank On" initiatives that are occurring in many areas of the United States (Lawton, 2011). Curricula could also include a discussion of various financial services that are especially well suited for low-income populations due to lower cost products and more flexible guidelines, such as credit unions and Community Development Financial Institutions (CDFIs) (Birkenmaier & Curley, 2009). A financial capability approach requires inclusion of such items as accessibility of mainstream financial institutions to low-income areas, and the availability of low-cost financial products and services at regulated financial institutions.

Fourth, educational offerings must also include content about the integration of such topics into other types of social services. If social workers are able to seize the opportunity to integrate financial capability topics into other social services, such as discharge planning from physical and/or mental health facilities, case management with children in foster care, and within-couples counseling, educational offerings must offer guidance on ways in which to integrate these topics while also meeting other service goals. The educational offering must include guidance about the inclusion of appropriate questions during assessment, handling of such topics during the intervention and termination, and the inclusion of such topics in evaluation efforts of service delivery. For example, assessments could include a question about connection to the formal financial services industry (i.e., whether the client has an account at a formal financial institution), questions about the use of the earned income tax credit, and/or questions about issues with bill payment and debt collection. Client goals could include one or more of these topics, and support could be offered toward goal achievement.

Finally, it is always important to include some training on how to measure client progress, financial behavior, and related outcomes. The financial capability field lacks a finite set of well-defined measures but metrics like savings, debt, credit behavior, attitudes, confidence, basic knowledge, and progress toward achieving goals all have potential to be tracked and reported as part of ongoing case management.

Certification

In addition to the issues of the relevancy and comprehensiveness of financial capability curriculum, the diversity of meaning around the concept of certification also challenges the forward movement of financial capability education efforts. While heterogeneity of the field provides avenues for new, creative initiatives, the lack of standardization of available certifications also hampers recognition and development of the financial capability field. The advantage of standardization of certification in financial capability would be broader recognition of this field of practice (whether stand-alone or integrated into other practice areas), and the potential to move forward in policy development and research. There is some evidence, at least from the medical field, that certification standards can elevate the quality of practice (Brennan et al., 2004; Cassel & Holmboe, 2006).

Within social work, a standardization of the requirements of certification in financial capability would facilitate a coordinated approach in social work education and continuing education efforts. One way to progress toward standardization is an interprofessional commission that could study the financial capability field and research, make recommendations to the relevant professions about standardization and certifications, and consider next steps. A commission would need to consider, for example, required core content for one or more certifications, general agreement on definitions of terms, the development of specialized curricula for specific populations, benchmarks for earning the certification(s), related certifications that may be transferable, and recognition of the certification by the professions.

Financial Capability Leadership

To promote financial capability, the field of social work, perhaps in concert with other helping professions, needs leadership on this topic to assist in decision making regarding practice and policy. In much the same way as the John A. Hartford Foundation's work has led to advances in service delivery for older adults

(Hooyman, 2009) and the Center for Social Development's research on assets has spurred the development of a new field (Center for Social Development, 2008), leadership in financial capability could assist the field in broader recognition of the topic. Moreover, greater leadership would allow the field to move forward with general agreement about core issues, including such issues as definitions, core competencies, educational curricula, and certification. Leadership by professional associations, educational institutions, professional organizations, and funders could facilitate the development of a commission, and/or provide educational curriculum, as well as financial, marketing, outreach, evaluation, and other types of support for the development of the area of financial capability certification. Additionally, leadership could advance the field through policy initiatives and advocacy, as well as research.

The social work professional associations could embrace the social work imperative to promote economic justice by exercising leadership to ensure that the field of financial capability develops with a specific focus on low-income populations. For example, in addition to taking leadership on the challenge of developing interprofessional dialogue on certification, the professional associations could promote research and practice in this area by social work academics (e.g., Despard & Chowa, 2010; Kindle 2010; Loke, Watts, & Kakoki, chapter 12, this volume; Sherraden, Laux, & Kaufman, 2007) at professional gatherings and within professional publications, as an emerging priority for the profession.

CONCLUSION

While still in its infancy, certification provides opportunities for social work students and practitioners to gain knowledge and skills about financial capability. Social workers are encouraged to examine current options in light of their practice needs, and take advantage of the program that best fits their content and curriculum delivery needs. There is no well-defined path of professional development in this area, and it would be reasonable to pursue multiple avenues for gaining skills and knowledge over time. Clearly the best fit for any particular professional will depend on the needs of his or her clients and the social worker's skills, background, and learning style.

Future efforts in this area include a role for leadership—from professional associations, social work educators, funders, and other actors—to shape certification options that best match social work's mission, including delivery methods, so that the field is better prepared to address client financial needs. Leadership is also needed to create methods to assess the degree to which certification offerings are meeting the needs of both clients and social work professionals. The effective integration of financial capability and social work offers the opportunity and potential to substantially improve the delivery of social services and the lives of low-income and vulnerable clients.

REFERENCES

AARP. (2003) *Off the hook: Reducing participation in telemarketing fraud.* Conducted for the United States Department of Justice, Office of Justice Programs. Washington

DC: Author. Retrieved September 30, 2011, from *assets.aarp.org/rgcenter/consume/d17812_fraud.pdf*

Abt Associates. (2006). *Evaluation of First Accounts Demonstration: Providing financial services to unbanked individuals.* Retrieved September 30, 2011, from http://www.abtassociates.com/page.cfm?PageID=1800&FamilyID=1800&PBL=1

Anderson, S., Zhan, M., & Scott, J. (2004). Targeting financial management training at low-income audiences. *Journal of Consumer Affairs, 38*(1), 167–178.

Aratani, Y., & Chau, M. (2010, February). *Asset poverty and debt among families with children* (Working Paper). New York: Columbia University National Center for Children in Poverty (NCCP).

Bachman, S. S., & Comeau, M. (2010). A call to action for social work: Minimizing financial hardship for families of children with special health care needs. *Health Social Work, 35*(3), 233–237.

Bauer, J. W., Braun, B., & Olson, P. D. (2000). Welfare to well-being framework for research, education, and outreach. *Journal of Consumer Affairs, 34*(1), 62–81.

Birkenmaier, J., & Curley, J. (2009). Financial credit: Social work's role in empowering low-income families. *Journal of Community Practice, 17*(3), 251–268.

Blank, R. M. (2002). Evaluating welfare reform in the United States. *Journal of Economic Literature, 40*(4), 1105–1166

Blostein, S. (1985). A day late and a dollar short: A national survey of the teaching of financial management in school of social work. *Journal of Social Work Education, 21,* 34–42.

Brennan, T. A., Horwitz, R. I., Duffy, F. D., Cassel, C. K., Goode, L. D., & Lipner, R. S. (2004). The role of physician specialty board certification status in the quality movement. *JAMA, 292,* 1038–1043.

Cassel, C. K., & Holmboe, E. S. (2006). Credentialing and public accountability: A central role for board certification. *JAMA, 295,* 939–944.

Center for Social Development, Washington University . (2008). *Overview.* Retrieved September 30, 2011, from http://csd.wustl.edu/AssetBuilding/overview/Pages/default.aspx

Chase, S., Gjerston, L., & Collins, J. M. (2011). *Coming up with cash in a pinch: Emergency savings and its alternatives* (Center for Financial Security Working Paper 11-3). Madison: University of Wisconsin-Madison.

Choi, N. G., Kulick, D. B., & Mayer, J. (1999). Financial exploitation of elders: Analysis of risk factors based on county adult protective services data. *Journal of Elder Abuse and Neglect, 10*(3/4), 39–62.

College for Financial Planning (2009). *2009 Survey of trends in the financial planning industry.* Retrieved September 30, 2011, from http://www.cffpinfo.com/pdfs/2009SOT.pdf.

Collins, J. M. (2010). *A review of financial advice models and the take-up of financial advice* (Center for Financial Security Working Paper FLRC 10–5). Madison: University of Wisconsin-Madison.

Collins, J. M. (2011). Improving financial literacy: The role of nonprofit providers. In O. S. Mitchell and A. Lusardi (Eds.), *Financial literacy implications for retirement security and the financial marketplace* (pp. 290–310). Oxford, England: Pensions Research Council, Oxford University Press.

Collins, J. M., Baker, D., & Gorey, R. (2007). *Financial coaching: A new approach for asset building.* Washington, DC: The Annie E. Casey Foundation. Retrieved September 30, 2011, from: http://www.aecf.org/

Collins, J. M., & O'Rourke, C. M. (2010). Financial education and counseling: Still holding promise. *Journal of Consumer Affairs, 44*(3), 483–498.

Council on Social Work Education. (2008). *Education policy and accreditation standards.* Washington, DC: Author.

Despard, M. R., & Chowa, G. A. N. (2010). Social workers' interest in building individuals' financial capabilities. *Journal of Financial Therapy, 1,* 23–41.

Engelbrecht, L. (2008). The scope of financial literacy education: A poverty alleviation tool in social work? *Maatskaplike Werk/Social Work, 44*(3), 252–262.

Garman, E. T., & Forgue, R. (2011). *Personal finance.* Mason, OH: Centgage Learning.

Gjesfjeld, C. D., Greeno, C. G., Kim, H., & Anderson, C. M. (2010). Economic stress, social support, and maternal depression: Is social support deterioration occurring? *Social Work Research, 34*(3), 135–143.

Gupta, A. E., & Huston, A. C. (2009). Depressive symptoms and economic outcomes of low-income women: A review of the social causation, social selection, and interactionist hypotheses. *Social Issues and Policy Review, 3*(1), 103–140.

Hallero, B., & Gustafsson, J.-E. (2011). A longitudinal analysis of the relationship between changes in socio-economic status and changes in health. *Social Science and Medicine, 72*(1), 116–123.

Herd, P., & Holden, K. (2010) *Early-life schooling and cognition and late-life financial literacy* (Center for Financial Security WP 10). Madison: University of Wisconsin Madison.

Hooyman, N. (2009). *The first decade of the Hartford Geriatric Social Work initiative.* Washington, DC: Council on Social Work Education.

Karger, H. (2005). *Shortchanged: Life and debt in the fringe economy.* San Francisco, CA: Berrett-Koehler.

Kindle, P. A. (2010). Student perceptions of financial literacy: Relevance to practice. *Journal of Social Service Research, 36*(5), 470–481.

Kuhlthau, K., Smith Hull, K., Yucel, R., & Perrin, J. M. (2005). Financial burden for families of children with special health care needs. *Maternal and Child Health Journal, 9*(2), 207–218.

Lawton, K. (2011, April 21). *New American Foundation webinar on city financial empowerment initiatives.* Retrieved September 30, 2011, from http://cfed.org/blog/inclusiveeconomy/local_innovation_national_impact_webinar/

Leviton, R. (2001). Reverse mortgage decision-making. *Journal of Aging and Social Policy, 13*(4), 1–16.

Lusardi, A. (2008). *Financial literacy: An essential tool for informed consumer choice?* (NBER Working Paper No. 14084). Cambridge, MA: The National Bureau of Economic Research. Retrieved September 30, 2011, from http://www.nber.org/papers/w14084

Lusardi, A., & Mitchell, O. (2007). Financial literacy and retirement preparedness: Evidence and implications for financial education. *Business Economics, 42*(1), 35–44.

Lyons, A. C., & Neelakantan, U. (2008). Potential and pitfalls of applying theory to the practice of financial education. *Journal of Consumer Affairs, 42*(1), 106–112.

Maryland CASH. (2008). *Asset-building continuum.* Baltimore, MD: Author. Retrieved September 30, 2011, from http://www.mdcash.org

Maton, C. C., Maton, M., & Martin, W. (2011, August). Collaborating with a financial therapy: The why, who, what and how. *Journal of Financial Planning.* Retrieved September 30, 2011, from http://www.fpanet.org/

Mazzonna, F., & Peracchi, F. (2009). *Aging, cognitive abilities and retirement in Europe* (CEIS Research Paper 152). Rome: Tor Vergata University, CEIS.

Meier, S., & Sprenger, C. (2008). *Discounting financial literacy: Time preferences and participation in financial education programs.* Bonn, Germany: Institute for the Study of Labor (IZA). Retrieved September 30, 2011, from tp.iza.org/dp3507.pdf

National Association of Social Workers. (2011). *Practice.* Retrieved September 30, 2011, from http://www.socialworkers.org/practice/

National Public Radio, Marketplace. (2009, January 12). *Financial social work.* Retrieved September 30, 2011, from http://marketplace.publicradio.org/display/web/2009/01/12/pm_financial_social_work/

O'Neill, B., Sorhaindo, B., Xiao, J. J., & Garman, E. T. (2005). Financially distressed consumers: Their financial practices, financial well-being, and health. *Financial Counseling and Planning, 16*(1), 73–87.

Parish, S. L., Rose, R. A., Grinstein-Weiss, M., Richman, E., & Andrews, M. E. (2008). Material hardship in U.S. families raising children with disabilities. *Exceptional Children, 75*(1), 71–92.

Poduska, B. E., & Hugh, G. (1990). Family finances: The missing link in MFT training. *American Journal of Family Therapy, 18*(2), 161–168.

Project Match. (2010). *Surprising diversity in financial stability: A cluster analysis of Center for Working Family clients in 12 low-income Chicago communities.* Chicago: Author.

Putnam, M., & Tang, F. (2006). Future planning and financial education needs for asset building among persons with multiple sclerosis in rural areas. *Journal of Social Work in Disability Rehabilitation, 5*(2), 69–93.

Rothwell, D. W., & Han, C.-K. (2010). Second thoughts: Who almost participates in an IDA program? *Journal of Social Service Research, 36*(2), 107–117

Rupured, M., Most, B. W., & Sherraden, M. (2000). Improving family financial security: A family economics-social work dialogue. *Family Counseling and Planning, 11*(2), 1–8.

Sanders, C. K., Weaver, T. L., & Schnabel, M. (2007). Economic education for battered women. *Affilia, 22*(3), 240–254.

Schmeiser, M. D. (2010). *Trigger events and financial outcomes over the lifespan.* Washington, DC: Social Security Administration.

Sherraden, M., Laux, S., & Kaufman, C. (2007). Financial education for social workers. *Journal of Community Practice, 15*(3), 9.

Sherraden, M. S. (2010). *Financial capability: What is it, and how it can be created?* (CSD Working Paper 10–17). St. Louis, MO: Washington University, Center for Social Development.

Taylor, T. D., Bernes, K. B., Gunn, T., & Nixon, G. (2007). How financial planners can collaborate with professional counselors. *Journal of Financial Planning, Between the Issues*, 2.

US Treasury Department. (2010). *Financial education core competencies.* Retrieved October 10, 2011, from http://www.treasury.gov/resource-center/financial-education/Pages/commission-index.aspx.

Vitt, L. A., Reichbach, G., Kent, J., & Siegenthaler, J. (2005). *Goodbye to complacency: Financial literacy education in the US 2000–2005.* Middleburg, VA: Institute for Socio Financial Studies.

15

Conclusion

Building Financial Capability and Assets of Financially Vulnerable Families

MARGARET S. SHERRADEN

What have we learned about financial capability? What is it? How is it created? What difference does it makes in people's lives?

What should we do? How can social work and other human service professionals contribute to financial capability and help families build assets? How can we plan and implement this work so it improves the lives of low-income families?

This book sheds light on these large questions. Let us consider some of the key themes and lessons.

INNOVATIONS IN FINANCIAL CAPABILITY AND ASSET BUILDING: IMPLICATIONS FOR POLICY AND PRACTICE

To begin, the authors in this volume provide evidence that low income and vulnerable populations benefit from interventions that include financial education and guidance and well-designed financial products and services. In fact, examples in this book suggest that it may be unrealistic to expect that one is possible without the other. As Cynthia Sanders (chapter 4, this volume) points out, victims of domestic violence must have confidence and trust that their participation in a financial capability initiative is safe and will not jeopardize their well-being and the well-being of their children. Offered simultaneously, financial education and access to savings begin to pave the road to financial security for victims of domestic violence. Jonas Parker (chapter 8, this volume) emphasizes the emotional aspects of money management that may interfere with financial learning and positive action. He notes that poor women in a savings program that includes financial education feel more in control when they discuss their financial situation without feeling the shame so often associated with money troubles.

Second, people are never too young or too old to develop financial capability. Therefore, it makes sense, from a policy and practice perspective, to adopt a developmental approach that is responsive to events and transitions in people's lives (Midgley, 1995). Financial education in childhood and adolescence, perhaps especially in school, can lay a foundation of financial knowledge and skills (Beverly & Burkhalter, 2005). Simultaneously, financial products and services and asset-building opportunities can engage children and youth in increasingly sophisticated ways in developing financial capability (Johnson & Sherraden, 2007; Sherraden et al., 2010). As Adams and Beverly (chapter 5, this volume) suggest, education savings accounts can introduce young children and their parents to the benefits of saving for college and at the same time a path to future education (Elliott, 2009). Different decisions confront people during other phases of life. For example, a steady job offers the opportunity for adults to begin planning for retirement years, and older age is a time when people often make provisions for the next generation. In other words, people are likely to be receptive to targeted financial education, products, and services at times during important life milestones, including birth of a baby, a first job, college matriculation, tax time, job benefit enrollment, and retirement (McCarthy & McWhirter, 2000).

Third, certain demographic groups and age cohorts require specialized financial capability interventions. In chapter 7, Min Zhan, Steven Anderson, and Jeff Scott report that financial capability among lower-income immigrants is quite low compared to low-income nonimmigrants, but a financial education program has greater positive effects on immigrants' financial knowledge than other participants' knowledge. Kristen Wagner's research (chapter 10, this volume) depicts the difficult financial situation in many Native American families, especially those living on reservations. She cautions, however, that financial capability initiatives should be informed by cultural priorities of responsibility toward family and community, and should develop institutions that address distrust of mainstream financial institutions that are the result of a long history of economic and political exploitation.

In another example, Cynthia Sanders (chapter 4, this volume) points out that with the addition of safety measures, financial education and asset-building programs can benefit survivors of domestic violence. Among groups who may require specialized approaches are minority populations, people with disabilities, the homeless, the very poorest, ex-offenders, people with addictions, and children in foster care or youth transitioning from foster care, and older adults (McCallion, Ferretti, & Park, chapter 6, this volume; Peters, Sherraden, & Kuchinski, 2012).

In addition, the economic crisis has made very clear that certain age cohorts may also need specially designed interventions (Elder & Giele, 2009). As David Stoesz (chapter 3, this volume) points out, a large segment of society, especially poor and minority youth are suffering a cohort effect, exacerbated by the current economic downturn, of increasing income and asset inequality. Trends such as this require focused financial capability and asset-building initiatives aimed at particular cohorts.

Reaching target populations, however, can be costly. It makes sense to build custom education, guidance, products, and services on a foundation of universal policies. In this way, the extra costs of customization would apply only to measures that meet special needs of certain populations. In other words, if everyone has access to financial education in schools as well as a simple transaction and savings account (possibly through mobile phone technology, electronic cards, or "electronic wallets"), these would build a firm foundation for additional outreach, information, and incentives aimed at target groups. Once accounts are in place (Goldberg, 2005), policy and local initiatives can provide incentives and subsidies to target groups. For example, as Wagner (chapter 10, this volume) notes, the EITC is a promising platform for building financial capability, but the uses of tax credits and the financial education and planning that may accompany the EITC, should sometimes be tailored to the group.

Fourth, several authors, including David Stoesz (chapter 3, this volume), Philip McCallion et al. (chapter 6, this volume), Kristen Wagner (chapter 10, this volume), Bárbara Robles (chapter 11, this volume), and Jennifer Romich, Nicole Keenan, Jody Miesel, and Crystal Hall (chapter 9, this volume) describe how older adults, ethnic minorities, and the poor often fall prey to risky financial products and services. These chapters discuss ways that low quality financial products may deplete household and community financial resources. Greater financial knowledge on the part of consumers, along with well-designed and regulated products, services, and programs can help protect financially vulnerable families and communities from unscrupulous and predatory practices. Both mainstream and alternative financial sectors should be targeted because they each offer high cost and insecure financial products (Sherraden, chapter 1, this volume). For example, low-income families often face high fees associated with checking and savings accounts at banks. At the same time, they also accumulate high interest payments, fees, and debt from using alternative financial products, such as payday and car title loans, and rent-to-own deals. Financial innovations aimed at reaching low-income households, such as prepaid cards and mobile phone banking that offer the potential for lower fees and flexible services, should also be subject to regulation and consumer disclosures (Newville & Koide, 2011).

Fifth, several chapters suggest a vital role for communities in building financial capability and assets in financially vulnerable households (Williams, Boddie, & Rice, 2010). They also raise the possibility that a capabilities approach may give "voice" to socially, economically, and geographically isolated communities, providing guidance for greater social and cultural relevance, and contributing to collective capability (Ballet, Dubois & Mahieu, 2007). Bárbara Robles (chapter 11, this volume) highlights the importance of the whole community in ensuring that financial capability and asset building efforts are appropriate and culturally relevant for residents. Her research, based on data gathered at free tax preparation sites in the US-Mexico border region, underscores community involvement in program design and "action research" that provides crucial information and understanding of financial issues, decisions, knowledge, and use of financial services among border families. Understanding of community financial traditions and practices—such as saving in rotating savings and credit associations (ROSCAs)—can help inform appropriate designs for financial capability in border communities.

Similarly, Kristen Wagner (chapter 10, this volume) underscores the critical role of financial institutions that are inclusive and reflect preferences of and unique issues facing Native American communities.

In a different context, Jonas Parker (chapter 8, this volume) writes about organizations that employ saving clubs to support financial capability and asset building in working poor households, mostly headed by women. He finds that group dynamics in saving clubs can build trust among participating members, which encourages active participation and facilitates learning about personal finances and economic issues. Like Robles, Parker concludes that community participation increases the cultural and local relevance of larger policies and programs. Further, he states that "democratizing" saving clubs would not only cut costs of professional coordination, but also empower communities to engage in meaningful participation. The respective roles of individuals and communities in building financial capability are important areas for future innovation and research.

Finally, research findings in this book suggest that lessons about financial capability should be integrated into coherent and coordinated policies that address the array of financial and economic challenges encountered by vulnerable families. As David Stoesz (chapter 3, this volume) points out, important policy developments have built on New Deal income support policies, including tax credits and asset accumulation policies. Unfortunately, Stoesz writes, they tend not to reach the poorest, and in the case of asset building, are of limited scale. As a whole, they fall short of assuring "upward mobility." Stoesz provides stimulating ideas for building financial capability through policies that are universal, integrated, reliable, and respectful.

A UNIQUE OPPORTUNITY FOR SOCIAL WORK

The idea of financial capability dovetails with the person-in-environment perspective in social work (Kondrat, 2002). Social workers view human conditions and well-being as the result of individual action in interaction with social and economic institutions. Similarly, in the capability approach, people have capabilities when they have access to "real opportunities" regarding the lives they value and want to lead (Sen, 1987, p. 36). Following this, people have financial capability when they have knowledge and skills along with genuine opportunities to act on their economic and financial goals in ways that contribute to their financial well-being. In this way, financial capability is not an individual construct; it exists as an attribute of the relationship between individuals and social institutions.

As Paul Stuart chronicles (chapter 2, this volume), social workers historically engaged in financial capability practice, including financial education, financial counseling, and financial services. One hundred years ago, social workers, community organizers, and family economists—with a clear focus on poverty—assisted families in managing their household income and expenses, in saving, and in financial education of the next generation. Studying the causes of poverty led them to ideas for preventing and addressing financial hardship. These were the focus of professional discussions. Pioneering the idea of the "family budget," social work with families and communities in the industrializing US cities led to groundbreaking financial capability reforms such as creation of credit unions, loan associations, the minimum wage, and family assistance.

However, increasing specialization and professionalization in social work and resulting fragmentation in reform efforts led social work away from this work during the second half of the 20th century. Social workers started paying more attention to psychological interpretations than to practical problem solving (Specht & Courtney, 1995). By the turn of the century, amidst growing debt in poor and middle class households and the mortgage meltdown of 2008, Stuart observes a renewed interest in the profession back toward financial capability practice. As evidence of this shift, many chapters in this book are written by social workers and analyze the experiences of social work practitioners involved in this resurgence.

What is the potential? How prepared are social workers for financial capability work? Unfortunately, social workers may themselves lack financial knowledge and skills and feel unqualified to help clients become financially capable (Despard & Chowa, 2010; Kindle, 2010; Sherraden, Laux, & Kaufman, 2007). Vernon Loke, Julie L. Watts, and Sally A. Kakoti (chapter 12, this volume) examine knowledge and skills of frontline practitioners in the asset-building field. Although practitioners report high financial literacy and financial management skills, their knowledge is similar to that of the population as a whole, and in some areas, no better than that of the low-income clients they serve. Of course, financial knowledge is not the only factor in practitioner ability; nonetheless, it is essential. These results suggest a need for more focused education and training in this area of practice. The profession should rebuild its historical role in financial capability—and this will require a focus on curriculum design and training.

J. Michael Collins and Julie Birkenmaier (chapter 14, this volume) address the challenges of professionals who seek to build their knowledge and skills for financial capability practice. They take on the tough issues of professional boundaries and areas of work. Today, social workers along with other professionals, including financial counselors, financial planners, credit counselors, accountants, lawyers, consumer and family economists, and bankers, work in the area of financial capability (Rupured, Most, & Sherraden, 2000; Tufano, 2009). They note that social workers' likely niche in financial capability is in their focus on clients in financial crisis, the asset poor and financially at-risk, and clients in family services. Collins and Birkenmaier suggest that education, training, and certification should include content on low-income and vulnerable populations, especially those who face special financial challenges. Especially, professional education should focus on how to integrate financial capability principles into broader social services, and how to measure changes in financial capability. Of special note, social workers should be financially capable themselves, and empowered to act on behalf of themselves and others (Loke et al., chapter 12, this volume).

Citing growing interest, Julie Birkenmaier, Teri Kennedy, James Kunz, Rebecca Sander, and Shelley Horwitz (chapter 13, this volume) document a shift in schools of social work toward financial capability curricula. Most schools of social work have courses that cover income support policies and retirement pensions. Some teach economics for social workers and community economic development. Today, however, there are growing numbers of schools adding content and courses on financial education, asset building, and economic advocacy (Sherraden, Laux, & Kaufman, 2007). The idea of financial capability offers an opportunity for colleges and universities to renew social work's focus on household financial functioning. Birkenmaier and colleagues provide a snapshot of innovative approaches in three US universities, and how key partnerships and stakeholder participation have supported curricular developments. Although social workers have begun to articulate how financial capability fits into the social work tradition, professional values, and accreditation standards, these issues require far more attention.

Financial capability practice represents an extraordinary opportunity for social work to reach low-income and vulnerable populations in ways that can help them gain a secure economic foothold. No other profession is as well-positioned to assume leadership in developing approaches and delivering services aimed at these populations. For over a hundred years, social work has had a unique focus on the poor and marginalized. It is in an optimal position to take up the challenge. It should renew its historical commitment to the financial stability and development of families through practice, policy, and research in financial capability and asset building.

RESEARCH ON FINANCIAL CAPABILITY AND ASSET BUILDING

Each of the chapters informs future research, raising conceptual, substantive, and methodological questions. Findings suggest a range of variables for measuring financial capability in individuals and families as well as potential indicators of financial capability, permitting more precise measurement. However, at this point, we do not know the relative importance of the elements of financial capability and the extent to which effects are direct or a result of interactions. What types and how much financial education, guidance, and financial products and services are most important, for whom, and during which life phases? How can specialized interventions help targeted groups? How do these interventions weather good and bad economic times?

More research is required to specify, operationalize, and test the effects of financial capability and financial well-being (Sherraden, chapter 1, this volume). A series of well-designed experiments are needed to sort out effects, specify theory, and inform more appropriate design of financial capability policies and programs. Qualitative and quantitative methods will permit greater insight and understanding, and permit generalizability of research findings. In this way, research can help to generate understanding and guide financial capability interventions. Such an ambitious research agenda requires both leadership and resources.

PROGRESS AND DIRECTION

The authors in this book contribute to understanding the precarious financial situations of large numbers of US households, and the ways that policies and programs can contribute to financial capability. Readers learn about the financial challenges faced by diverse groups of low-income families, including single parents, rural ethnic minority families, immigrant families, victims of domestic violence, and the families of young children and older adults. Authors examine a number of policies and programs that aim to generate financial capability in these families. Some chapters examine existing policy, such as EITC, which provides a unique and ongoing opportunity to engage families and communities in resource development and financial planning. Other chapters examine financial services innovations, such as Individual Development Accounts and Children's Development Accounts, which build household assets and provide a platform for teaching financial management skills. Some chapters highlight work with individuals, while others use group and community approaches. Some chapters focus on financial education programs, encouraging optimal financial decision making and use of safe financial services, while others focus more on building a foundation of assets. Some chapters focus on training, education, and certification of financial capability professionals including their knowledge and skills, approaches to professional preparation, and professional accountability. Together, they underscore the central role of building financial capability and assets to improve the life chances of the financially vulnerable in society.

Much remains to be done. Although this book sheds light on financial capability innovations for several target population groups, many more areas of work deserve attention. Among topics missing from these pages are financial counseling programs, changes in financial regulations, and financial services innovations, such as mobile banking. Future research should focus on policy development and revenues for financial capability programming. In research, there is a pressing need for development of indicators to measure the financial capability construct. In the education and training arena, more attention should focus on social workers collaboration with other human service and financial professionals in serving financially vulnerable households and communities.

The overriding challenge raised by this book is how to bring low-income and financially vulnerable people into the financial mainstream in ways that enable them to survive financially and with dignity, and in ways that provide opportunities for a more secure and hopeful future. As Paul Stuart (chapter 2, this volume) recounts, more than half a century ago Harold Wilensky and Charles N. Lebeaux called attention to the dangers of growing household debt that threatened household stability and economic opportunity. They asked for action by family services. As Stuart points out, little was done. Fifty years later, this agenda has far greater urgency as people's financial lives have become considerably more complex and income and wealth gaps widen (Congressional Budget Office, 2011; Taylor, Fry, & Kochhar, 2011).

For good and bad, the world has become more financialized (Martin, 2002). It is no longer possible for a family to lead a stable, middle-class life that is separate from complex financial arrangements in payments, credit, and managing resources. To take only one indicator of this complexity, in the absence of an acceptable credit score, any household will be highly constrained not only in borrowing for a home or car, but in very ordinary transactions, such as renting an apartment, obtaining a job or insurance, or booking an airline ticket. Any family that is not "in the game" successfully will pay more or do without. As David Caplovitz (1967) observed decades ago, "the poor pay more," but now the mechanisms are even more complex. For families who are more vulnerable, not having a good credit score can mean no mainstream credit at all and the need to operate in a financial world of check cashers and payday lenders—a world of entrapment, designed for predation—leading all too often to a downhill spiral. This is the reality of the US economy and financial services in the 21st century.

The imperative for financial capability has never been stronger, and professional capacity has never been more urgent. It is in everyone's interest that it be developed. Households comprise 70% of US economic activity. If large numbers of households are financially inefficient, this has deep implications for fairness, inclusion, and social justice, but also has deep implications for the functioning of the economy as a whole. In the Great Recession that began in 2008, we have seen the financial risks and the costs that fall to families and the effects on the entire economy.

Financial capability and asset building today can take a place beside shelter, food, and physical security as a basic necessity of modern life. In this regard, a wide chasm separates reality from basic necessity. Knowledge of financial capability and asset building and professional capacity must be developed as never before. We hope that this book is a meaningful step in this direction.

REFERENCES

Ballet, J., Dubois, J. L., & Mahieu, F. R. (2007). Responsibility for each other's freedom: Agency as the source of collective capability. *Journal of Human Development*, 8(2), 185–201.

Beverly, S. G., & Burkhalter, E. (2005). Improving the financial literacy and practices of youth. *Children and Schools*, 27(2), 121–124.

Caplovitz, D. (1967). *The poor pay more: The consumer practices of low-income families.* New York: The Free Press.

Congressional Budget Office. (2011, October). *Trends in the distribution of household income between 1979 and 2007.* CBO Summary. Retrieved from http://www.cbo.gov/ftpdocs/124xx/doc12485/WebSummary.pdf

Despard, M. R., & Chowa, G. A. N. (2010). Social workers' interest in building individuals' financial capabilities. *Journal of Financial Therapy*, 1(1), 23–41.

Elder, G. H., Jr., & Giele, J. Z. (Eds.) (2009). *The craft of life course research.* New York & London: Guilford.

Elliott, W. (2009). Children's college aspirations and expectations: The potential role of children's development accounts. *Children and Youth Services*, 31, 274–283.

Goldberg, F. (2005). The universal piggybank: Designing and implementing a system of savings accounts for children. In M. Sherraden (Ed.), *Inclusion in the American Dream: Assets, poverty and public policy* (pp. 303–322). New York: Oxford University Press.

Johnson, E., & Sherraden, M. S. (2007). From financial literacy to financial capability among youth. *Journal of Sociology and Social Welfare*, 34(3), 119–145.

Kindle, P. A. (2010). Student perceptions of financial literacy: Relevance to practice. *Journal of Social Service Research, 36*(5), 470–481

Kondrat, M. E. (2002). Actor-centered social work re-visioning "person-in-environment" through a critical theory lens. *Social Work, 47*(4), 435–448.

Martin, R. (2002). *Financialization of daily life*. Philadelpia, PA: Temple University Press.

McCarthy, M., & McWhirter. E. (2000). Are employees missing the big picture?: Study shows need for ongoing financial education. *Benefits Quarterly, 16,* 25–31.

Midgley, J. (1995). *Social development: The developmental perspective in social welfare.* London and Thousand Oaks, CA: Sage.

Newville, D., & Koide, M. (2011). *Prepaid cards and consumer protection.* Washington, DC: Center for Financial Services innovation. Retrieved from http://cfsinnovation.com/system/files/CFSI_PrepaidPolicy_July2011.pdf

Peters, C., Sherraden, M. S., & Kuchinski, A. M. (2012, September). *Enduring assets: Findings from a study on the financial lives of young people transitioning from foster care.* Report to Jim Casey Youth Opportunities Program, St. Louis Retrieved from http://www.jimcaseyyouth.org/enduring-assets-findings-study-financial-lives-young-people-transitioning-foster-care.

Rupured, M., Most, B., & Sherraden, M. (2000). Improving family financial security: A family economics-social work dialogue [Electronic version]. *Financial Counseling and Planning, 11*(2), 1–7.

Shanks, T. R. W., Boddie, S. C., & Rice, S. (2010). Family-centered, community-based asset building: A strategic use of Individual Development Accounts. *Journal of Community Practice, 18,* 94–117.

Sherraden, M. S., Johnson, L., Guo, B., & Elliott, W. (2010). Financial capability in children: Effects of participation in a school-based financial education and savings program. *Journal of Family and Economic Issues, 32,* 1577–1584.

Sherraden, M. S., Laux, S., & Kaufman, C. (2007). Financial education for social workers. *Journal of Community Practice, 15*(3), 9–36.

Sherraden, M. S., & McBride, A. M., with Beverly S. G. (2010). *Striving to save: Creating policies for financial security of low-income families.* Ann Arbor: University of Michigan Press.

Specht, H., & Courtney M. (1994). *Unfaithful angels: How social work has abandoned its mission.* New York: The Free Press.

Taylor, P., Fry, R., & Kochhar, R. (2011, July 26). *Wealth gaps rise to record highs between Whites, Blacks, Hispanics: Twenty to one.* Washington, DC: Pew Research Center. Retrieved from http://www.pewsocialtrends.org/files/2011/07/SDT-Wealth-Report_7-26-11_FINAL.pdf

Tufano, P. (2009). Consumer finance. *Annual Review of Financial Economics, 1,* 227–247.

INDEX

Index entries followed by *t* indicate a table; by *f* indicate a figure.

AARP, 141
ability to act, 20, 29n44, 75
abuse, survivors of domestic violence enduring, 85–87
account managers, 76–77
Account monitoring research at Michigan SEED (Loke et al.), 119–20, 125n7
accounts
   families opening, 119–20, 125n7
   families owning, 116–18, 117*t*, 212
   families' positive outcomes linked with, 212
   financial education's relationship with, 178
   low-income parents owning, 116–19, 117*t*, 118*t*
   ownership, 212
   safety, 90
action research
   from learning and listening to, 231–32
   mixed methodological approaches in framework of, 246n8
action without individual behavior, 21
ADD. *See* American Dream Demonstration
Addams, Jane, 46, 51
Adult Protective Services (APS), 139
adult protective workers, 151–52
adults. *See also* older adults; young adults
   education, 176–78
   financial knowledge of, 7
   in financial socialization studies, 9
"Advocacy and protection of older adults" (Kosberg, Rothman, and Dunlop), 151–52

AFDC. *See* Aid to Families with Dependent Children
AFIA. *See* Assets for Independence Act
AFS. *See* alternative financial services
Aid to Families with Dependent Children (AFDC), 64, 65
alternative financial services (AFS), 72–73
   costs of, 12–13
   Native Americans using, 212, 216
   service provider financial capability information on, 267
American Dream Demonstration (ADD), 175
American Home Economics Association, 53
American Indians. *See* Native Americans
American Mobility Program (AMP), 75
America Saves, 176
AMP. *See* American Mobility Program
Analyzing the relationship between account ownership and financial education (Baker and Dylla), 178
Annie E. Casey Foundation, 230
anti-poverty paradigms, 62, 74, 77, 78. *See also specific anti-poverty paradigms*
antipoverty policy, xiv
   capability increasing from changes in, 75–77
   failure of, 78
Appelbaum, Diana Karter, 51
APS. *See* Adult Protective Services
Arizona State University, 285–87, 291
aspirations, expectations distinguished from, 26n6

asset building
  of border families, 233
  EITC used for, 219
  financial capability enhanced by, 254
  innovations in financial capability and, 323–26
  programs and services, 253–54
  research, 328
asset-building field, beginning of, 252–53
Asset-Building Paradigm, 68–71
asset creation
  description of, 253
  in Washington State, programs, 253
asset management
  description of, 253–54
  in Washington State, 254
asset poverty, 110
asset protection and preservation, description of, 254
assets
  building financial capability and, xii–xiv
  clients poor in, 309–10
  families becoming prosperous due to, 69, 71
  families owning, 116–17, 117*t*
  families poor in, xi
  low-income families' liquid, 72
  low-income parents owning, 116–19, 117*t*, 118*t*
  in safety, role of, 98
  women's purchases of, 100–101
Assets and the poor: A new American welfare policy (Sherraden, Michael), 69, 178
Assets for Independence Act (AFIA), 90
ATM withdrawal protection, 29n48
Austin, M. J., 150

Baby Boomers, 130, 132–33
Bailly, R. M., 151
Baker, C., 178
Baltimore Charity Organization Society, 47
banked
  definition of, 223n4
  Native American households, 216
"Banking on wealth: America's new retail banking infrastructure and its wealth-building potential" (Fellowes and Mabanta), 28n23

Bank On, 18, 24
Barr, Michael, 13
Barriers to asset accumulation for families in the SEED Pre-School Demonstration and Impact Assessment (Beverly and Barton), 119, 123
Barton, J., 119, 123
basic needs. *See* needs
behavior. *See also* financial behavior
  action without individual, 21
  budgeting, 181*t*
  context influencing, 4–5
  cultural, 231
  expectations as predictor of, 26n6
  financial capability practice, 296*t*–297*t*
  financial products taking into account, 5
  REAP's economic education changing, 94
  women's IDAs causing changes in, 96
behavioral economics, 5
  on financial decisions, 16
  savings innovations built upon, 16–17
Benoit, L., 140*t*
Bernanke, Ben, 6
Beverly, S. G., 119, 123, 178, 259
Blostein, S., 303
BLS. *See* Bureau of Labor Statistics
border communities, financial capabilities of, 232
border families, xvi
  asset building of, 233
  financial services used by, 233
  savings behaviors of, 233
  tax preparation services influencing, 230
border family survey
  CBOs and, 235, 246n11, 246n12
  conclusions and research issues, 243–45
  data and methodology in, 232–34
  demographics of respondents to, 235–36, 236*t*
  empirical analysis and findings of, 234–43, 234*t*, 235*t*, 236*t*, 238*t*, 239*t*, 240*t*, 242*t*
  filing status of respondents to, 235–36, 236*t*
  financial behaviors, 235*t*
  financial behaviors reported in, 237, 238*t*–239*t*
  financial products and, 241, 242*t*

financial services and, 241, 242*t*
IDA program information in, 241–43
income of respondents to, 235–36, 236*t*
questions, 232–34, 243, 246n12
RAL usage reported in, 239, 240*t*
response rates, 235, 246n10
savings reported in, 237, 238*t*–239*t*, 239
survey methodology and data in, 232–34
tax refund information in, 239–41, 240*t*
borderlands. *See* Southwest border region
Border Portfolio, 230
Boyatzis, R., 177
branchless banking, 18–19, 28n37
Breckinridge, Sophonisba, 53–54
Broken trust (Metlife), 139
Brown, D., 134, 135–38, 136*f*, 137*f*, 139, 140–41, 142*t*–149*t*, 150–53
Brown, Mary Willcox, 47
budget
behavior regarding, 181*t*
conversations, 182–85
family, 50–53, 56
iterative cycles, 184*f*, 185
in social work educational programs, 52–53
Budget Planning in Social Case Work (Winslow), 53
Building assets: An impact evaluation of the MI SEED Children's Savings Program (Marks et al.), 125n7
Bureau of Consumer Financial Protection, US, 18, 298
Bureau of Labor Statistics (BLS), 56

CAA. *See* Community Action Agency
capability. *See also* financial capability
antipoverty policy changes increasing, 75–77
definition of, 4, 74
description of, 74–75
Capability Paradigm, 74–77
capitalism, welfare, 66
Caplovitz, David, 28n26, 56, 330
cash management, low-income households using, 14
Cash & Save, 15

Castleton Charity Organization Society, 47–48
CBOs. *See* community-based organizations
CBPR project. *See* community-based participatory research project
CCUs. *See* community credit unions
CDAs. *See* Child Development Accounts
CDFI Loan Fund. *See* Community Development Financial Institutions Loan Fund
Center for Social Development, 252–53
Chambers, R., 26n1
"Changes in the philosophy of social work" (Towle), 45
Chapin, Robert C., 51
charity organization societies (COS), 46
Charity Organization Society of the City of New York (NYCOS)
on family budget, 52
Provident Loan Society organized by, 49
savings fund established by, 48
The charity visitor: A handbook for beginners (Sears), 52–53
The Chattel Loan Business (Ham), 49
chattel loans, 49
ChexSystems, 10, 28n24
The Chicago Standard Budget (Nesbitt), 53
Child Development Accounts (CDAs), xv, 23, 29n46. *See also* Saving for Education, Entrepreneurship, and Downpayment study
description of, 109
history of, 69–70
Child Tax Credit, 194
choice architecture, 5
Cities for Financial Empowerment, 18
Clancy, M., 175
clients
asset poor and financially at-risk, 309–10
family services, 310–11
in financial crisis, 308–9
Clinton, Bill, 65
collaborative inquiry, 245n6
Collins, J. M., 304
colonias (neighborhood or community), 229–30, 245n3
combined capabilities, 4

Committee on Standards of Living and Labor, 51–52
community
  cultural traditions treasured by, 244
  financial capability curriculum supported by, 293
  stress metrics identified by, 231, 245n7
Community Action Agency (CAA), 180
community-based organizations (CBOs), border family survey and, 235, 246n11, 246n12
community-based participatory research (CBPR) project
  focus group and interview findings, 182–88
  methods, 178–79, 188n2, 188n3
  survey findings, 180–81, 181*t*
community college
  knowledge of, 121–22
  SEED study question about, 113–14, 121, 125n3
community credit unions (CCUs), 76–77
Community Development and Regulatory Improvement Act of 1994, 70
Community Development Financial Institutions (CDFI) Loan Fund, 70
community development organizations, 70
community development projects, CCUs capitalizing, 77
"A conceptual framework of financial exploitation of older persons" (Rabiner, O'Keeffe, and Brown, D.), 134, 135–38, 136*f*, 137*f*, 139, 140–41, 142*t*–149*t*, 150–53
conservatism
  poverty addressed by concept of, 79n3
  welfare criticized due to, 65
Consumer Price Index (CPI)
  income gap, 71–72, 79n2
  low-income families influenced by, 72
consumer protection regarding taxes, 204
consumers, financial guidance sought by, 11
consumer skills, money management and, 141, 150
context, behavior influenced by, 4–5
COS. *See* charity organization societies

cost of living as minimum wage basis, 51–52
costs of alternative financial services, 12–13
CPI. *See* Consumer Price Index
Creating an opportunity society (Haskins and Sawhill), 75
Credit Card Accountability Responsibility and Disclosure Act of 2009, 18, 298
credit cards
  credit rating influenced by, 7
  New York City, used in, 27n19
  regulatory changes regarding, 26n8
  unbanked turning to, 27n19
credit counseling, financial education and, 88–89
credit rating, credit cards influencing, 7
culture
  behaviors, 231
  communities treasuring traditions of, 244
  data collection including, 231–32
Curley, J., 175

data collection, culturally inclusive, 231–32
"A day late and a dollar short: A national survey of the teaching of financial management in school of social work" (Blostein), 303
debt. *See also* problem debt
  distress caused by, xii
  families distressed by, xii
  families incurring, 44
  levels of understanding about, 7
debt literacy, 7, 261, 266
Debt literacy, financial experiences, and overindebtedness (Lusardi and Tufano), 256, 261
"The determinants of being unbanked for U.S. immigrants" (Rhine and Greene), 158
Development as Freedom (Sen), 5–6, 74
direct deposit, 29n47, 116, 125n4
disabilities, 310–11
Discounting financial literacy: Time preferences and participation in financial education programs (Meier and Sprenger), 304

Index

distress, debt causing, xii
Dodd-Frank Wall Street Reform and
  Consumer Protection Act of 2010, 18,
  28n32
domestic violence. *See also* survivors of
  domestic violence
  causes of, 85–86
  economic abuse intersecting, 86–87
  economic factors intersecting, 86–87
  economic status decreasing, 87
  economic well-being's intersection with,
    85–87
  financial capability's intersection with,
    103–4
  financial issues intersecting, 86–87
  REAP influencing, 103–4
  research on financial capability and,
    103–4
Do Not Call Registry, 150
Dunlop, B., 151–52
Dylla, D., 178

EAP. *See* economic action plan
Earned Income Tax Credit (EITC), xv–xvi
  asset building and saving with, 218–19
  creation of, 66–67
  description of, 194, 209
  families using, 209, 213
  financial behavior influenced by, 210
  financial security, used for, 217–18, 218*f*
  financial utilization of, 212–13
  households using, 212–13
  Native American families
    receiving, 209
  Native American families using, 217–19,
    217*t*, 218*f*
  Native American households assisted by,
    207, 209–13, 223
  Native Americans' views on, 222
  NC-EITC and access to, 215
  needs, used for, 217, 218*f*
  RAL fees and, 13
  saving and asset building with, 218–19
  as savings, 212–13, 218–19
  study on Native American households'
    utilization of, 213–19, 214*t*, 215*t*,
    216*f*, 217*t*, 218*f*

The earned income tax credit (Hotz and
  Scholz), 212–13
EBT. *See* electronic benefit transfer
economic abuse
  description of, 85–87
  domestic violence intersecting, 86–87
  economic factors intersecting, 86–87
  financial issues intersecting, 86–87
  interventions and, 102
economic action plan (EAP), 88–89
economic advocacy and support
  services, 90
"Economic context and multiple
  abuse techniques" (Lambert and
  Firestone), 87
economic dependence, women
  influenced by, 86
economic education
  behavioral changes created by REAP's, 94
  cognitive and affective impacts of
    REAP's, 91, 93–94
  learning caused by REAP's, 94–95
  in REAP program, 91, 93–95
economic factors, 86–87
economic status, domestic violence
  decreased by, 87
economic well-being
  domestic violence's intersection with,
    85–87
  in Native American households, 207–8
economists, 56
"Editorial introduction: Vulnerability,
  coping and policy" (Chambers), 26n1
education. *See also* economic education;
  financial education
  adult, 176–78
  experiential, 176–78
  financial capability training and, 305–6
  social work, xvi–xvii, 102–3, 151–52,
    221–22, 278, 281, 284–99, 296*t*–297*t*,
    311, 312*t*–314*t*, 314–19
EITC. *See* Earned Income Tax Credit
electronic benefit transfer (EBT), 28n38
environmental modification, 45
expectations
  aspirations distinguished from, 26n6
  as behavior predictor, 26n6

experiential education, 176–78
experiential learning, 177–78, 177f, 184–85, 184f
Experiential learning: Experience as the source of learning and development (Kolb), 177
"Experiential learning theory: Previous research and new directions" (Kolb, Boyatzis, and Mainemelis), 177
external conditions, 4, 22, 23

FABN. *See* Frontera Asset Building Network
Facing the challenges: Addressing financial literacy and exploitation issues for PSA workers (McCallion, Ferretti, and Benoit), 140t
families. *See also* border families
   account and asset ownership of, 116–19, 117t, 118t, 212
   accounts opened by, 119–20, 125n7
   agencies, 55
   anti-poverty paradigms as useless to, 74
   asset and account ownership of, 116–19, 117t, 118t
   asset poor, xi
   assets causing prosperity of, 69, 71
   assets owned by, 116–17, 117t
   Barton on SEED, 119
   Beverly on SEED, 119
   budget, 50–53, 56
   case work, 55
   CPI influencing low-income, 72
   debt distressing, xii
   debt incurred by, 44
   EITC contributions to Native, 209
   EITC used by, 209, 213
   financial decisions faced by, ix–x, xi
   financial inclusion of, 123
   financial problems causing ills for, xi–xii
   financial products geared to poor, 76
   financial products needed by, xiii
   financial services needed by, xiii
   financial survival of, xi
   Great Recession of 2008 influencing, 73–74
   income, median, x
   knowledge needed by, xii–xiii
   liquid assets of low-income, 72
   Negro, 65
   policy influencing, ix–x
   savings of, 118–19, 118t, 125n5, 125n6
   services influencing, ix–x
   skills needed by, xii–xiii
   social workers working with, xvi
   society's view of, ix
   tax credits assisting, 192
   taxes and, 193–97, 195t
Family Assistance Plan (FAP), 66–67
Family Independence Initiative, 76–77, 79n3
family services clients, 310–11
FAP. *See* Family Assistance Plan
Federal Deposit Insurance Corporation (FDIC). *See also* Small Dollar Loan program
   creation of, 50
   Money Smart program of, 141
federalism, 64
Federal Reserve Act of 1913, 50
Fellowes, M., 28n23
Ferretti, L. A., 140t
financial abilities, service provider financial capability study information on, 259, 260t, 266
financial abuse. *See also* economic abuse
   consequences of, 134
   definition of, 133
   health concerns caused by, 134
   interventions, 138–53, 140t, 142t–149t
   legal remedies for, 151
   of older adults, 129, 133–53, 136f, 137f, 140t, 142t–149t
   perpetrators of, 134
   professionals involved in, 139
   risk assessment of, 139, 140t
   risks for, 134–35
   signs of, 140t
   victim profile, 134–35
   of women, 134–35
Financial access for immigrants: Lessons from diverse perspectives (Paulson et al.), 158
financial advice

Index

description of, 10–11
financial guidance and, 10–11
results of, 11
studies on, 11
in UK, 27n15
financial attitudes of low-income parents, 114–15, 115*t*
financial behavior
  border family survey, 235*t*
  border family survey reporting, 237, 238*t*–239*t*
  confidence and, 141
  EITC influencing, 210
  of immigrants, 166, 167*t*, 168–69
  of low-income parents, 116, 116*t*
  parents modeling, 8, 22, 27n11, 96, 111
financial capability. *See also* Capability Paradigm
  administrative support for curriculum for, 293
  asset building enhancing, 254
  of border communities, 232
  building assets and, xii–xiv
  building blocks of, 6–25
  challenges to building, 19–20, 29n43
  community support for curriculum for, 293
  components of, 208
  core competencies, 306, 307*t*, 308–10
  curricular models for, 285–92
  definition of, 3, 4, 26n5, 129, 243, 251, 254
  description of, xiii, 3–6, 26n4, 251, 254
  development of curricula for, 297–98
  domestic violence's intersection with, 103–4
  education and training, 305–6
  empirical evidence on, 23–25
  faculty support for curriculum for, 293
  financial education challenged by, 188
  financial education necessary with, 111
  financial inclusion as building block of, 12–20
  financial literacy as building block of, 6–11
  financial literacy differentiated from, 3
  flexible development of curricula for, 297–98

households, built in, xviii
innovations in asset building and, 323–26
innovations in policy and practice of, xiv–xvi
institutions influencing, 5
instructor capacity in curriculum for, 293
interests in curriculum for, 294
knowledge and skills in curriculum for, 292
leadership, 318–19
in low-income households, promotion of, 23
Native American households and, 208–9, 222
outcomes measured in curriculum for, 294–97, 296*t*–297*t*
policy influencing curricular development for, 298
policy support for building, 103
professional roles in building, xvi–xviii
progress and direction, 328–30
research, 103–4, 222, 304, 306, 328
research on social work education including, 298
resources available to practitioners, xvii–xviii
resources in curriculum for, 294
risks to older adults', 129–30, 132–33
schematic depiction of, 21*f*
service provider financial capability study information on, 259, 267–68
of service providers, xvii, 251–52
settlement houses improving, 48
skills and knowledge in curriculum for, 292
in social work education curriculum, 281, 284–98, 296*t*–297*t*
social workers delivering services of, 303–4, 305
social workers interested in, 45, 55–57, 302
social work practice connected to, 303–5
social work practice incorporating building of, 44–45
steps in building, 25–26

financial capability (*Cont.*)
    taxes and, 197–98, 209–11
    voice in, 6
Financial capability: What is it, and how it can be created? (Sherraden, Margaret), 111
financial capability practice, xiii
    behaviors, 296t–297t
    social workers engaging in, 279–80
    social work's role in, 279–80
    universities preparing social workers for, xvii
financial certification programs, 311, 312t–314t, 314–18
financial coaching, 11, 27n14
Financial Coaching Corps, 27n14
financial competencies, 26n7
financial counseling, 11
financial crisis, clients in, 308–9
financial decisions
    behavioral economics on, 16
    families facing, ix–x, xi
    financial literacy improving, 6
    long-term wealth influenced by, 251
financial deregulation, 72
financial education
    credit counseling and, 88–89
    description of, 8, 9–10
    effectiveness of, 174
    effects of, 110–11, 160
    financial capability challenging, 188
    financial capability necessary with, 111
    financial inclusion *vs.*, 12
    financial knowledge influenced by, 9–10
    financial products included with, 25
    financial products including, 24
    financial services included with, 25
    in IDA programs, 179, 188n4
    of immigrants, 160
    influence of, 9–10
    leading with, 25
    movement, 174
    of Native Americans, 216–17, 217t
    in NC-EITC, 216–17
    need for, xv, 110
    programs, 9
    research, 306
    results of, 9–10
    savings accounts, relationship with, 178
    studies on, 9–10
"Financial education and counseling: Still holding promise" (Collins and O'Rourke), 304
Financial education and savings outcomes in Individual Development Accounts (Clancy et al.), 175
financial exploitation
    consequences of, 134
    definition of, 133
    health concerns caused by, 134
    interventions, 138–53, 140t, 142t–149t
    legal remedies for, 151
    of older adults, 129
    revised conceptual model of, 136f, 137f
    risk assessment of, 139, 140t
    signs of, 140t
    of women, 134–35
Financial exploitation of the elderly (Bailly et al.), 151
financial guidance, 27n13
    consumers seeking, 11
    description of, 8, 10–11
    financial advice and, 10–11
    results of, 11
    studies on, 11
financial illiteracy, 11
financial inclusion
    argument for, 20
    challenges to building financial capability through, 19–20, 29n43
    definition of, 12
    description of, 12–20
    of families, 123
    as financial capability building block, 12–20
    financial education *vs.*, 12
    financial literacy linked with, 20–25
    of immigrants, 156, 157–60
    innovations, 18–19, 28n33, 28n39
    of Native American households, 220
    of Native Americans, 211–12
    schematic depiction of, 20f
financial information, description of, 8
financial institutions. *See* institutions

Index 341

financial issues, 86–87, 221–22
financial knowledge
 of adults, 7
 financial education influencing, 9–10
 of immigrants, 156–57, 159–60, 164–66, 164*t*, 165*t*, 167–68
 low-income households influenced by, 7
 of low-income parents, 113–14, 114*t*
 need for, 3
 pretraining, 164–65, 164*t*
 for social workers, 280–81, 282*t*–284*t*
 of survivors of domestic violence, 85
 young adults gaining, 8, 21
Financial Links for Low-Income People (FLLIP) program, 161–70, 163*t*, 164*t*, 165*t*, 167*t*
financial literacy. *See also* financial illiteracy
 argument for, 20
 definitions of, 280–81
 description of, 138–39
 as financial capability building block, 6–11
 financial capability differentiated from, 3
 financial decisions improved by, 6
 financial inclusion linked with, 20–25
 financial vulnerability reduced by, 138–39
 of immigrants, 159
 of older adults, 132–33
 person with, 6
 programs, 140–41, 142*t*–149*t*, 150
 of retirees, 130
 schematic depiction of, 20*f*
 service provider financial capability study information on, 259, 260*f*, 260*t*, 261, 264–66, 265*f*, 270–73
 of service providers, xvii
 for social workers, 282*t*–284*t*
 studies on, 6–7
 support services increasing, 253–54
Financial literacy: An essential tool for informed consumer choice? (Lusardi), 150
Financial Literacy and Ignorance (Lusardi), 11

"Financial literacy and retirement preparedness: Evidence and implications for financial education" (Lusardi and Mitchell), 132–33
"Financial literacy explicated: The case for a clearer definition in an increasingly complex economy" (Remund), 280–81
"Financial literacy in high school" (Mandell), 9–10
Financial Literacy Volunteer Initiative (FLVI), 288–89
financial mentoring, 11
financial planning, 11
financial practices, service provider financial capability study measure of, 256–57, 261–63, 262*f*, 273–74
financial problems
 families suffering ills from, xi–xii
 health and, xii
 ill effects caused by, xi–xii
financial products
 accessibility of, 14–15
 affordability of, 15, 28n25
 behavior taken into account by, 5
 border family survey and, 241, 242*t*
 families, geared to poor, 76
 families needing, xiii
 financial attractiveness and, 15
 financial education included with, 24
 financial education including, 25
 flexibility of, 17
 fringe, 72–73
 for immigrants, 170
 inclusive, features of, 14–18, 27n22
 leading with, 24
 low-income households' needs met by, 13
 of low-income parents, 123
 needs for, 19, 29n41
 regulation of, 18, 28n32
 reliability of, 17–18
 security of, 17–18
 service provider financial capability study information on, 273–74
 tax preparation options and, 195–97
 unbanked turning to, 12–13
 usage ease of, 16–17

financial resources of survivors of
    domestic violence, 85
financial security, EITC used for,
    217–18, 218f
financial services. *See also* alternative
    financial services
  access to, 3
  affordability of, 15, 28n25
  appropriate, 14
  border families using, 233
  border family survey and, 241, 242t
  families needing, xiii
  financial education including, 25
  financially attractive, 15, 28n26
  flexibility of, 17
  fringe, 13
  immigrants using, 157–59, 170
  inclusive, features of, 14–18, 27n22
  low-income households' needs
    met by, 13
  Native American communities' access
    to, 211–12
  Native American households' access to,
    216, 220
  needs for, 19, 29n41
  predatory, 159
  regulation of, 18, 28n32
  reliability of, 17–18
  security of, 17–18
  unbanked turning to, 12–13
  usage ease of, 16–17
financial skills
  low-income households influenced by, 7
  need for, 3
  for social workers, 280–81, 282t–284t
financial socialization
  adults in studies of, 9
  agents of, 9
  description of, 7–9
  across life course, 8–9
  parents influencing, 8
Financial Social Work Initiative (FSWI),
    287–89, 291
financial support provider roles, 305–6,
    305t
financial therapy, 11
financial training programs, 311,
    312t–314t, 314–18

financial vulnerability
  definition of, 26n1
  financial literacy reducing, 138–39
  of households, x–xi
  model for understanding, 135–38,
    136f, 137f
financial well-being. *See also* economic
    well-being
  of older adults, xv, 311
  self-control influencing, 8
FINRA Investor Education Foundation, 129
Firestone, J. M., 87
First Accounts, 24
First Nations Development Institute, 13
Fisher, Gordon M., 51, 56
FLLIP program. *See* Financial Links for
    Low-Income People program
FLVI. *See* Financial Literacy Volunteer
    Initiative
fringe economy, 71–73
fringe services. *See* alternative financial
    services (AFS)
*From financial literacy to financial
    capability among youth* (Johnson and
    Sherraden, Margaret), 176
Frontera Asset Building Network (FABN),
    234t, 245n2. *See also* border family
    survey
  description of, 230–31
  tax preparation services offered by, 232
frontline workers. *See* service providers
FSWI. *See* Financial Social Work Initiative

G2P programs. *See* government-to-people
    programs
gender, wealth differences of, xi
Get Checking, 10
Giddens, Anthony, 78
Gilded Age, 45
Glass-Steagall Act of 1933, 50
Goodyear, Caroline, 52
government-to-people (G2P) programs,
    28n37
Great Recession of 2008, 71, 73–74
Great Society program, 44–45
Greene, W. H., 158
Greenwich House, 48
Grinnell, Richard M., Jr., 45

Index

Hall, Helen, 55–56
Ham, Arthur H., 49–50
Haskins, Ron, 75
Head Start, xv. *See also* Saving for Education, Entrepreneurship, and Downpayment study
health
    financial abuse causing concerns of, 134
    financial exploitation causing concerns of, 134
    financial problems and, xii
    older adults' concerns regarding, 133
health care plans, of retirees, 133
Hilgert, M. A., 178, 259
Hispanic population, 228, 245n1
Hogarth, J. M., 178, 259
home economics, social work and, 53–54
homemaker services, 54
home ownership, of immigrants, 158
Hopkins, Harry, 63
Hotz, V. J., 212–13
Houghteling, Leila, 50–51
"Household financial management: The connection between knowledge and behavior" (Hilgert, Hogarth, and Beverly), 178, 259
Household management (Nesbitt), 53
households. *See also* low-income households; Native American households
    economic activity of, 330
    EITC used by, 212–13
    financial capability built in, xviii
    financial vulnerability of, x–xi
    income, 223n1
    underserved, 12–14
Housekeeping Aides Program, 54
Hull House, 46
Huston, S., 280

IDAs. *See* Individual Development Accounts
The idea of justice (Sen), 74
immigrants, xv
    description of, 157
    financial behavior of, 166, 167t, 168–69
    financial education of, 160
    financial inclusion of, 156, 157–60

    financial knowledge of, 156–57, 159–60, 164–66, 164t, 165t, 167–68
    financial literacy of, 159
    financial management programs for, 156–57, 170
    financial products for, 170
    financial services used by, 157–59, 170
    FLLIP program influencing, 165–67t, 165t
    home ownership of, 158
    IDAs targeting, 160
    institutions reaching, 170
    multigenerational households, 237, 246n13
    remittances sent by, 158–59
    social work and, 169, 170
    social workers and, 169, 170
    unbanked, 13, 158
immigrant study
    conclusion and implications, 169–70
    data analysis, 162
    data collection, 161–62
    discussion, 167–69
    limitations and research, 169
    methods of, 161–62
    purpose of, 160
    sample, 162–64, 163t, 169
income
    of border family survey respondents, 235–36, 236t
    CPI gap in, 71–72, 79n2
    family, median, x
    household, 223n1
    inequality, x
    in Seattle tax study, 199–200
    tax refunds influencing, 200
income tax. *See* taxes
Independent Order of St. Luke, 48
Individual Development Accounts (IDAs), 23, 29n41
    border family survey information on, 241–43
    challenges facing program of women's, 101
    coordinator, 180, 185–86
    description of, 89, 174, 252–53
    financial education in programs of, 179, 188n4

Individual Development Accounts (*Cont.*)
  immigrants targeted by, 160
  incentives of, 69
  psychological and cognitive effects of women's, 96–97
  REAP, 89–90, 91, 92–93
  research, 178–79, 180–88, 181*t*, 184*f*, 188n2, 188n3
  savings clubs, components of, 179–80
  savings clubs, conversations in, 182–85, 187–88
  savings clubs offered by programs of, 174, 188n1
  savings outcomes of women's, 98–101, 99*t*, 100*t*
  strategic partnerships enhancing, 180
  studies on, 24
  withdrawals from REAP, 99–100, 100*t*, 104n3
  women in REAP's program of, 91, 92–93
  women's, 89–90, 95–97
Industrial Society and Social Welfare (Wilensky and Lebeaux), 44, 45, 63
inequality, 78
  income, x
  wealth, x–xi
informal savings circles. *See* rotating savings and credit associations
institutions
  accessibility of, 14–15, 28n23
  change of, 5–6
  constructs, 5
  financial capability influenced by, 5
  immigrants reached by, 170
  Native American tribes choosing, 220
  saving shaped by constructs of, 5
insufficient funds, 28n24
internal capabilities, 4, 22, 23
"The inter-relation of social movements: Report of the Committee on Families and Neighborhoods" (Richmond), 54–55
interventions
  economic abuse and, 102
  financial abuse, 138–53, 140*t*, 142*t*–149*t*
  financial exploitation, 138–53, 140*t*, 142*t*–149*t*

intimate partner violence (IPV). *See* domestic violence

Jargowsky, Paul, 70
Johnson, E., 176
Jump$tart Coalition for Personal Financial Literacy, 7, 9–10

Keep the Change, 16–17, 28n27
Kelley, Florence, 51–52
Kelso, Robert W., 55
Kemp, S. P., 45
Kenya, mobile banking in, 29n42
knowledge. *See also* financial knowledge
  of community college, 121–22
  families needing, xii–xiii
  in financial capability curriculum, 292
  social workers reporting need of, 302
Kolb, D. A., 177
Kosberg, J., 151–52

Lambert, L. C., 87
Learn$ave, 24
learning
  action research arrived at from listening and, 231–32
  dialogues, 230
  experiential, 177–78, 177*f*, 184–85, 184*f*
  REAP's economic education causing, 94–95
  of women, 94–95
"Learning together: Collaborative inquiry among grant makers and grantees" (McGarvey), 245n6
Lebeaux, Charles, 4, 45, 63, 329
Lee, Joseph, 49
legislation
  adult protective, 152
  minimum wage, 51, 52
Lessons from SEED: A national demonstration of Child Development Accounts (Sherraden, Michael, and Stevens), 246n14
"The living wage" (Lowell), 46
loans
  chattel, 49

small, 48–50
social work providing, 48–50
Locke, Gary, 253
Loke, V., 119–20, 125n7
Long, Russell, 66–67
lotteries, 17, 28n28
Lowell, Josephine Shaw, 46, 47
low-income families. *See* families
low-income households
   access barriers of, 14–15, 28n23
   cash management used by, 14
   financial capability in, promotion of, 23
   financial knowledge influencing, 7
   financial products meeting needs of, 13
   financial services meeting needs of, 13
   financial skills influencing, 7
   opportunity structure rebuilt for, 78
   savings in, 14
   taxes paid by, 194
   tax refunds spent by, 67–68
   welfare impeding capability of, 65–66
low-income immigrants. *See* immigrants
low-income parents
   account and asset ownership of, 116–19, 117*t*, 118*t*
   direct deposit used by, 116, 125n4
   financial attitudes of, 114–15, 115*t*
   financial behaviors of, 116, 116*t*
   financial knowledge of, 113–14, 114*t*
   financial products of, 123
   saving-related attitudes of, 114, 115*t*, 122, 125n8
   savings of, 118–19, 118*t*, 122–23, 125n5, 125n6
Lusardi, Annamaria, 11, 132–33, 150, 256, 261

Mabanta, M., 28n23
Mainemelis, C., 177
Malks, B., 150
Mandell, Lewis, 9–10, 25
Marks, E. L., 125n7
Marlatt, K. W., 150
Maryland Community Fellows program, 288
McCallion, P., 140*t*
McGarvey, C., 245n6

"Measuring financial literacy" (Huston), 280
mediating structures, 79n3
Medicare, older adults' concerns regarding, 130, 133
Meier, S., 304
Metlife, 139
microfinance, 176
Midgley, James, 63
minimum wage
   cost of living as basis for, 51–52
   legislation, 51, 52
Mitchell, O. S., 132–33
mobile banking, 18–19, 29n42
money management, consumer skills and, 141, 150
Money Smart program, 141
mothers
   pensions, 52
   welfare, 65
Moynihan, Daniel Patrick, 65, 66–67
Muste, A. J., 55

National Conference of Social Work, 53
National Conferences of Charities and Correction, 50, 51–52
National Consumers League, 47, 139
National Crime Victimization Survey, 86
National Federation of Remedial Loan Associations, 49
National Strategy for Financial Literacy, 6
Native American households
   banked, 216
   economic and social well-being in, 207–8
   EITC assisting, 207, 209–13, 223
   financial capability and, 208–9, 222
   financial inclusion of, 220
   financial services access of, 216, 220
   poverty in, 208
   social work education including financial issues of, 221–22
   social workers assessing, 220–21, 223
   study on EITC utilization of, 213–19, 214*t*, 215*t*, 216*f*, 217*t*, 218*f*
   tax information access of, 219
   tax preparation services access of, 219

Native American households (*Cont.*)
  unbanked, 216, 216*f*
  VITA services used by, 215, 219–20, 222
Native Americans, xvi
  alternative financial services used by, 212, 216
  EITC contributions to families of, 209
  EITC used by families of, 217–19, 217*t*, 218*f*
  EITC viewed by, 222
  financial education of, 216–17, 217*t*
  financial inclusion of, 211–12
  financial service access in communities of, 211–12
  institutions chosen by tribes of, 220
  population of, 208
  RALs used by, 13, 211
  TANF received by tribes of, 221–22, 223n5
  tax, exempt from, 210
  unbanked, 212, 223n4
  underbanked, 212
  VITA sites assisting, 211
Native Community EITC Survey (NC-EITC)
  description of, 213–14
  discussion and implications, 219–22
  EITC access and, 215
  financial education in, 216–17
  participants, 214–15
  results, 214–19, 214*t*, 215*t*, 216*f*, 217*t*, 218*f*
  sample, 213, 214–15, 214*t*
  states included in, 223n3
  survey items, 214
  tax services and, 215, 215*t*
  unbanked in, 223n4
NC-EITC. *See* Native Community EITC Survey
needs, EITC used for, 217, 218*f*
Negro family, 65
Neighborhood Fellows program, 288
Nesbitt, Florence, 53
net savings, 99, 104n2
net worth
  age disparities in, xi
  median, x–xi

Newberger, R. G., 140
New Frontier program, 44–45
New York City, New York
  credit cards used in, 27n19
  unbanked reduction measure in, 23
New York City Collaborative, 289–91
New York Consumers' League, 47
New York Provident Loan Society. *See* Provident Loan Society of New York
1988 Family Support Act, 65
Nixon, Richard, 45, 66–67
Nudge (Thaler and Sunstein), 5
Nussbaum, Martha, 4, 22, 74
NYCOS. *See* Charity Organization Society of the City of New York

"The objective value of a social settlement" (Addams), 46
Office of Refugee Resettlement, 160
Off the hook: Reducing participation in telemarketing fraud (AARP), 141
O'Keeffe, J., 134, 135–38, 136*f*, 137*f*, 139, 140–41, 142*t*–149*t*, 150–53
older adults. *See also* retirees
  financial abuse of, 129, 133–53, 136*f*, 137*f*, 140*t*, 142*t*–149*t*
  financial exploitation of, 129
  financial literacy of, 132–33
  financial stability of, programs key to, 131*t*–132*t*
  financial well-being of, xv, 311
  health concerns of, 133
  Medicare concerns of, 130, 133
  risks to financial capability of, 129–30, 132–33
  Social Security concerns of, 130
  telemarketing fraud resisted by, 141
Opportunity Finance Network, 77
opportunity to act, 20, 29n44, 75
opt-out savings plan, 16
organic philanthropy, 245n6
O'Rourke, C. M., 304
Otero, Maria, 19
Otto, J., 150

Paine, Robert Treat, 48
parents. *See also* low-income parents

Index

financial behavior modeled by, 8, 22, 27n11, 96, 111
financial socialization influenced by, 8
partnerships, development of, 292–93, 304
Paulson, A. L., 140, 158
payday lending, proliferation of, 72–73
payment cards, 19
Penny Provident Fund, 48
pensions
  mothers', 52
  private plans for, 66
Personal Responsibility and Work Opportunity Reconciliation Act (PRWORA), 65, 253
Person-environment practice: The social ecology of interpersonal helping (Kemp, Whittaker, and Tracy), 45
person-in-environment principle, 26n3
Peterson, Esther, 56
policy. *See also* antipoverty policy
  American public, 62
  families influenced by, ix–x
  financial capability building support of, 103
  financial capability curricular development influenced by, 298
  innovations in financial capability practice and, xiv–xvi
  public influencing, 5–6
  support for survivors of domestic violence, 103
  tax, 69
The poor pay more: The consumer practices of low-income families (Caplovitz), 28n26, 56, 330
Porter, Michael, 70
post–World War II era, 44, 56, 63
poverty, 78. *See also* asset poverty
  conservative concept addressing, 79n3
  fringe economy exacerbating, 73
  in Native American households, 208
  rates, x
  social work and, 45–47
  social workers' work on lines of, 51
Poverty and famines: An essay on entitlement and deprivation (Sen), 6
poverty lines, 51

practitioners, financial capability resources available to, xvii–xviii
prepaid cards, 29n40
President's Advisory Council on Financial Capability, 26n5
problem debt, xii
professionals
  content areas relevant for helping, 306–8, 307t
  financial abuse, involved in, 139
  financial capability building roles of, xvi–xviii
  social workers working with helping, 304
Progressive Era, 45, 48
Progressive Party, 51
provident loan associations, 48–50
Provident Loan Society of New York, 49, 50
Provident Savings Bank, 48
PRWORA. *See* Personal Responsibility and Work Opportunity Reconciliation Act
psychology, social workers' interest in, 55
public
  American policy, 62
  policy influenced by, 5–6
Public relief and private charity (Lowell), 47

Rabiner, D. J., 134, 135–38, 136f, 137f, 139, 140–41, 142t–149t, 150–53
RALs. *See* refund anticipation loans
randomized control trials (RCTs), 77
Reagan, Ronald, 65
"Realizing Your Economic Action Plan," 88–89
realm of possibility, 4–5
real opportunities, 4–5
Redevelopment Opportunities for Women's Economic Action (REAP) Program
  curriculum, 88–89
  description of, 87–90
  discussion and implications, 101–4
  domestic violence influenced by, 103–4
  economic advocacy and support services in, 90
  economic education in, 91, 93–95
  IDAs, 89–90, 91, 92–93

Redevelopment (*Cont.*)
  outcomes, 90–101, 92*t*–93*t*
  perceived effects of, 91
  safety and, 97–98
  social work practice influenced by studies of, 102
  withdrawals from IDAs of, 99–100, 100*t*, 104n3
  women in IDA program of, 91, 92–93
reform campaigns, 55
refund anticipation loans (RALs), 67
  border family survey reporting, 239, 240*t*
  criticism of, 196
  description of, 196, 223n2
  EITC and fees of, 13
  Native Americans using, 13, 211
regulation
  credit cards, changes regarding, 26n8
  of financial products, 18, 28n32
  of financial services, 18, 28n32
  of small lenders, 50
  small loan, 49–50
remedial loan associations, 48–50
remittances, immigrants sending, 158–59
Remund, D., 280–81
Report on state adult protective services response to financial exploitation of vulnerable adults (Otto, Stanis, and Marlatt), 150
research. *See also* action research
  asset building, 328
  border family survey conclusions and issues with, 243–45
  on domestic violence and financial capability, 103–4
  financial capability, 103–4, 222, 304, 306, 328
  on financial capability included in social work education, 298
  on financial capability of Native American households, 222
  financial education, 306
  on IDAs, 178–79, 180–88, 181*t*, 184*f*, 188n2, 188n3
  immigrant study limitations and, 169
  on Native American households' financial capability, 222
  on savings clubs, 175–76
  in social work, 50–51
  on social work education including financial capability, 298
retirees
  financial literacy of, 130
  health care plans, 133
retirement
  of Baby Boomers, 130, 132–33
  extended years in, 130
  unbanked suggesting challenges for saving for, 27n18
retirement savings plan, 21, 29n44
revolving credit plans, 44
Rhine, S. L. W., 158
Richmond, Mary, 47, 54, 55
The role of institutions in the saving participation and performance of low-income households in individual development accounts (Curley), 175
Roosevelt, Theodore, 51
rotating savings and credit associations (ROSCAs), 175–76
  names for, 246n9
  survey question about, 233
Rothman, M., 151–52
Russell Sage Foundation (RSF), 49, 50

SafeStart Bank Accounts, 23
safety
  accounts, 90
  assets' role in, 98
  REAP and, 97–98
  savings influencing, 97
  of women, considerations, 88–89, 90
The Salary Loan Business in New York City (Wassam), 49
Save More Tomorrow, 16
SaveNYC, 23
Save to Win, 17
SaveUSA, 23
Saving for Education, Entrepreneurship, and Downpayment (SEED) study
  background, 109
  Barton on families in, 119
  Beverly on families in, 119
  community college question in, 113–14, 121, 125n3

Index 349

conclusions, 120–24
demographic and economic
 characteristics of sample in, 112, 113*t*,
 125n2
description of, 108–9
discussion, 119–20
methods in, 112, 124n1
results of, 112–19, 113*t*, 114*t*, 115*t*, 116*t*,
 117*t*, 118*t*
sample in, 112, 113*t*, 125n2
Saving Gateway, 24
savings. *See also* accounts; retirement
 savings plan
 automatic, 16
 border families engaging in behaviors
  of, 233
 border family survey reporting,
  237, 238*t*–239*t*, 239
 EITC as, 212–13, 218–19
 of families, 118–19, 118*t*, 125n5, 125n6
 innovations, 16–17, 23
 institutional constructs shaping, 5
 in low-income households, 14
 of low-income parents, 118–19, 118*t*,
  122–23, 125n5, 125n6
 low-income parents' attitudes toward,
  114, 115*t*, 122, 125n8
 matched program for, 110
 net, 99, 104n2
 NYCOS establishing fund for, 48
 plan, opt-out, 16
 safety influenced by, 97
 thrift and, 47–48
 women's IDA program outcomes
  regarding, 98–101, 99*t*, 100*t*
savings banks, history of, 47
savings clubs
 CAAs and, 180
 community-based participatory
  research in, 187–88
 components of IDA, 179–80
 conversations in IDA, 182–85, 187–88
 democratizing, 186–87
 IDA programs offering, 174, 188n1
 meetings, 179, 182–88
 peer support in, 185–86
 research on, 175–76
 social capital and, 187

veteran participants in, 187
women using, xv
savings society, 47–48
Sawhill, Isabel, 75
scam
 awareness, 139
 description of, 133–34
Schmidt, C., 150
Scholz, J., 212–13
Schreiner, M., 187
Scribner, Anne Townsend, 47
Sears, A., 52–53
Seattle tax study
 background, 198–99
 data collection and analysis, 205
 findings, 199–202
 income in, 199–200
 refund predictions in, 199–201
 respondents, 199–201, 205
 social contract referenced in, 201
 sources of information of respondents
  in, 201–2
 summary and limitations of, 202–3
self-control, financial well-being
 influenced by, 8
Sen, Amartya, 4, 5–6, 23, 74
service provider financial capability study
 AFS information in, 267
 comfort and preparedness levels
  information in, 263–64, 263*f*, 267
 conclusion, 269
 debt literacy information in, 261, 266
 discussion, 264–68, 265*f*
 financial abilities information in,
  259, 260*t*, 266
 financial capabilities information in,
  259, 267–68
 financial literacy information in, 259,
  260*f*, 260*t*, 261, 264–66, 265*f*, 270–73
 financial management information in,
  261–63, 262*f*
 financial practices measure in, 256–57,
  261–63, 262*f*, 273–74
 financial product ownership
  information in, 273–74
 findings, 257–64, 258*t*–259*t*, 260*f*, 260*t*,
  262*f*, 263*f*
 limitations, 268–69

service provider (*Cont.*)
    methodology, 255–57
    participants, 255–56
    procedures, 256–57
    purpose of, 254–55
    respondent profiles, 257, 258*t*–259*t*
service providers
    financial capabilities of, xvii, 251–52
    financial literacy of, xvii
services
    asset building programs and, 253–54
    families influenced by, ix–x
settlement houses
    description of, 46
    financial capability improved by, 48
    specialization of, 55
Sherraden, Margaret, 111, 176
Sherraden, Michael, 69, 78n1, 178, 246n14
SIPP. *See* Survey of Program Participation
skills. *See also* consumer skills; financial skills
    families needing, xii–xiii
    in financial capability curriculum, 292
    social workers reporting need of, xvii, 302
Small Dollar Loan program, 24
small lenders
    regulation of, 50
    social responsibility of, 55
small loans, 48–50
social brokers, 221
social capital, 187
social contract, 201
social desirability bias, 120–21
social movements, social work profession building and, 54–56
Social Security, older adults' concerns regarding, 130
Social Security Act of 1935, 63–64
social service agencies in Washington State, 252
social well-being in Native American households, 207–8
social work. *See also* social work practice
    budgets in educational programs for, 52–53
    building profession of, social movements and, 54–56

    description of, xiii–xiv
    education, xvi–xvii, 102–3, 151–52, 221–22, 278, 281, 284–99, 296*t*–297*t*, 311, 312*t*–314*t*, 314–19
    expansion period of, 54
    financial capability practice role of, 279–80
    home economics and, 53–54
    immigrants and, 169, 170
    loans provided through, 48–50
    opportunity, 326–28
    person-in-environment principle in, 26n3
    poverty and, 45–47
    research in, 50–51
    specialization in, 54–55
Social Work Community Outreach Service (SWCOS), 287, 288
social workers, xiv
    advocacy and investigative roles for, 151–52
    families worked with by, xvi
    financial capability interest of, 45, 55–57, 302
    financial capability practice engaged in by, 279–80
    financial capability services delivered by, 303–4, 305
    financial knowledge and skills for, 280–81, 282*t*–284*t*
    financial literacy for, 282*t*–284*t*
    helping professionals worked with by, 304
    immigrants and, 169, 170
    knowledge need reported by, 302
    Native American households assessed by, 220–21, 223
    poverty lines work of, 51
    psychological interest of, 55
    psychosocial responses by, 152–53
    resources matched with needs of, 316–19
    skills need reported by, xvii, 302
    as social brokers, 221
    taxes discussed by, 203–4
    universities preparing, xvii
social work practice
    challenges, 280

financial capability building
  incorporated into, 44–45
financial capability connected to, 303–5
REAP studies influencing, 102
society, families viewed by, ix
Southwest border region, xvi
  description of, 229–30
  population, 229
  socioeconomic snapshot of, 229–30
Sprenger, C., 304
Standards of public aid to children in their own homes (Nesbitt), 53
Stanis, P. I., 150
state college savings (529) plan, 119–20, 125n7
Stevens, J., 246n14
stickk.com, 176
"Strategies of success in financial education" (Newberger and Paulson), 140
subprime loans, 22
success metrics, community-identified, 231, 245n7
Sunstein, Cass, 5
Survey of Consumer Finances, 12, 130
Survey of Program Participation (SIPP), 110
survivors of domestic violence, xiv–xv
  abuse endured by, 85–87
  as economically dependent, 85
  financial independence of, 87, 311
  financial knowledge of, 85
  financial resources of, 85
  policy support for building financial capability of, 103
SWCOS. *See* Social Work Community Outreach Service
symbolic markers, 199–200

Talbot, Marion, 54
TANF. *See* Temporary Assistance for Needy Families
Tax Credit Paradigm, 66–68
tax credits. *See also* Earned Income Tax Credit
  advantages of, 67
  case study, 192–93, 194–95, 195t, 203, 204
  description of, 194

disadvantages of, 68
  examples of, 67
  families assisted by, 192
taxes. *See also* Seattle tax study
  basics, 193–94
  border families influenced by preparation services for, 230
  case study, 192–93, 194–95, 195t, 203, 204
  consumer protection regarding, 204
  description of, 193–94
  FABN offering services to prepare, 232
  families and, 193–97, 195t
  features of system of, 200–201
  financial capability and, 197–98, 209–11
  financial products and preparation options for, 195–97
  formal providers of services related to, 202
  information, 210
  liabilities as expected, 198
  low-income households paying, 194
  Native American households' access to information about, 219
  Native American households' access to preparation services for, 219
  Native Americans exempt from, 210
  NC-EITC and services of, 215, 215t
  nonprofit community programs for, 196–97
  policy, 69
  preparation options, 195–97, 198, 210–11, 215t, 239, 240t
  services, 195–96, 215, 215t
  social workers discussing, 203–4
tax preparation sites, xv, xvi
tax refunds, xv–xvi. *See also* Seattle tax study; tax credits
  border family survey information on, 239–41, 240t
  case study, 192–93, 194–95, 195t, 203, 204
  expected, 198, 200, 202, 204
  income influencing, 200
  low-income households spending, 67–68
  Seattle tax study predictions of, 199–201

telemarketing fraud
    older adults resisting, 141
    prevention, 141
Temporary Assistance for Needy Families (TANF), 65–66, 78
    Native American tribes receiving, 221–22, 223n5
Thaler, Richard, 5
The third way (Giddens), 78
thrift, savings and, 47–48
Titmuss, Richard, 63
Top 10 scams of 2009 (National Consumers League), 139
Towle, Charlotte, 45
Tracy, E. M., 45
Treasury, US, 28n33, 211, 306, 308–10
Tufano, P., 256, 261

UK. *See* United Kingdom
UMSSW. *See* University of Maryland School of Social Work
unbanked, 12–14, 27n17. *See also specific unbanked reduction efforts*
    credit cards turned to by, 27n19
    financial deregulation increasing number of, 72
    financial products turned to by, 12–13
    financial services turned to by, 12–13
    immigrants, 13, 158
    Native American households, 216, 216f
    Native Americans, 212, 223n4
    in NC-EITC, 223n4
    New York City's measure to reduce, 23
    retirement, suggesting challenges for saving for, 27n18
    in 2008, 72
    in 2009, 72
    VITA sites reducing, 211
underbanked, 13, 27n20
    financial deregulation increasing number of, 72
    Native Americans, 212
    in 2008, 72
    in 2009, 72
underserved households, 12–14
unemployment
    Great Recession of 2008 influencing, 73
    statistics, x

unfreedom, 23
Uniform Small Loan Law, 50
Union Bank, 15
United Kingdom (UK), 27n15
United Way of Greater St. Louis Great Rivers Community Reinvestment Corporation, 90
universities, social workers prepared by, xvii
University of Maryland School of Social Work (UMSSW), 287–89, 291

Vaile, Gertrude, 52
Violence Against Women Act (VAWA), 103
virtuous circle, 78n1
VITA sites. *See* Volunteer Income Tax Assistance sites
voice, 6
Volunteer Income Tax Assistance (VITA) sites, xvi, 196, 197t
    Native American households using, 215, 219–20, 222
    Native Americans assisted by, 211
    unbanked reduced by, 211
Vonderlack, R., 187

Walker, Maggie Lena, 48
War on Poverty, 64
Washington State
    asset creation programs in, 253
    asset management in, 254
    social service agencies in, 252
Wassam, Clarence W., 49
wealth
    disparities in, 69
    financial decisions influencing long-term, 251
    gender differences of, xi
    inequality, x–xi
    women earning, xi
welfare
    capitalism, 66
    conservatism causing criticism of, 65
    low-income households' capability impeded by, 65–66
    mothers, 65
    reform, 65–66
Welfare Entitlement Paradigm, 63–66
Whittaker, J. K., 45

Wilensky, Harold, 44, 45, 63, 329
Winslow, Emma, 53
women
  asset purchases of, 100–101
  challenges facing IDA program for, 101
  domestic violence survivors, xiv–xv
  economic dependence influencing, 86
  financial abuse of, 134–35
  financial exploitation of, 134–35
  IDAs of, 89–90, 95–97
  learning of, 94–95
  psychological and cognitive effects of IDAs of, 96–97
  in REAP's IDA program, 91, 92–93
  safety considerations of, 88–89, 90
  savings clubs used by, xv
  savings outcomes of IDA participation of, 98–101, 99t, 100t
  wealth earned by, xi
Women, microfinance, and savings: Lessons and proposals (Vonderlack and Schreiner), 187
Women and human development: The capabilities approach (Nussbaum), 74
Women's Trade Union League, 46
WorkFirst, 253
World War II, 66

young adults, financial knowledge gained by, 8, 21
youth, matched savings program reports of, 110